# The Linguistic Legacy of Spanish and Portuguese

The historical spread of Spanish and Portuguese throughout the world provides a rich source of data for linguists studying how languages evolve. This volume analyses the development of Portuguese and Spanish from Latin and their subsequent transformation into several non-standard varieties. These include Portuguese- and Spanish-based creoles, bozal Spanish and Chinese Coolie Spanish in Cuba, Chinese Immigrant Spanish, Andean Spanish, and Barranquenho, a Portuguese dialect on the Portugal–Spain border. J. Clancy Clements demonstrates that grammar formation takes place not only in parent-to-child communication, but also, importantly, in adult-to-adult communication. He argues that cultural identity is also an important factor in language formation and maintenance, especially in the cases of Portuguese, Castilian, and Barranquenho. More generally, the contact varieties of Portuguese and Spanish have been shaped by demographics, by prestige, by linguistic input, and by general cognitive abilities and limitations, as well as by the dynamics of speech community.

J. CLANCY CLEMENTS is Professor of Linguistics and Spanish and Portuguese at Indiana University.

*Cambridge Approaches to Language Contact*

*General Editor*
Salikoko S. Mufwene, *University of Chicago*

*Editorial Board*
Robert Chaudenson, *Université d'Aix-en-Provence*
Braj Kachru, *University of Illinois at Urbana*
Raj Mesthrie, *University of Cape Town*
Lesley Milroy, *University of Michigan*
Shana Poplack, *University of Ottawa*
Michael Silverstein, *University of Chicago*

Cambridge Approaches to Language Contact is an interdisciplinary series bringing together work on language contact from a diverse range of research areas. The series focuses on key topics in the study of contact between languages or dialects, including the development of pidgins and creoles, language evolution and change, world Englishes, code-switching and code-mixing, bilingualism and second language acquisition, borrowing, interference, and convergence phenomena.

*Published titles*

Salikoko Mufwene, *The Ecology of Language Evolution*
Michael Clyne, *Dynamics of Language Contact*
Bernd Heine and Tania Kuteva, *Language Contact and Grammatical Change*
Edgar W. Schneider, *Postcolonial English*
Virginia Yip and Stephen Matthews, *The Bilingual Child*
Bernd Heine and Derek Nurse (eds), *A Linguistic Geography of Africa*
J. Clancy Clements, *The Linguistic Legacy of Spanish and Portuguese*

*Further titles planned for the series*

Guy Bailey and Patricia Cukor-Avila, *African-American English*
Maarten Mous, *Controlling Language*
Umberto Ansaldo, *Contact Languages*
Jan Blommaert, *The Sociolinguistics of Globalization*
Bridget Drinka, *Language Contact in Dsachranse Perspective*

# The Linguistic Legacy
# of Spanish and Portuguese

## Colonial Expansion and Language Change

J. Clancy Clements

*Indiana University*

CAMBRIDGE
UNIVERSITY PRESS

CAMBRIDGE UNIVERSITY PRESS
Cambridge, New York, Melbourne, Madrid, Cape Town, Singapore,
São Paulo, Delhi

Cambridge University Press
The Edinburgh Building, Cambridge CB2 8RU, UK

Published in the United States of America by Cambridge University Press, New York

www.cambridge.org
Information on this title: www.cambridge.org/9780521539449

First published 2009

Printed in the United Kingdom at the University Press, Cambridge

*A catalogue record for this publication is available from the British Library*

*Library of Congress Cataloguing in Publication data*
Clements, J. Clancy.
  The linguistic legacy of Spanish and Portuguese : colonial expansion and language
  change / J. Clancy Clements.
    p.   cm. – (Cambridge approaches to language contact)
  Includes bibliographical references and index.
  ISBN 978-0-521-83175-8 (hardback) – ISBN 978-0-521-53944-9 (pbk.)
  1. Spanish language–Variation–History.   2. Portuguese language–Variation–
  History.   3. Creole dialects, Spanish–Social aspects–History.   4. Creole dialects,
  Portuguese–Social aspects–History.   I. Title.   II. Series.
  PC4074.7.C54 2009
  467.009–dc22        2009000064

ISBN 978-0-521-83175-8 hardback
ISBN 978-0-521-53944-9 paperback

For Richa, and Barack

In memory of my teacher, Antonio Tovar Llorente

# Contents

| | | page |
|---|---|---|
| *List of figures* | | viii |
| *List of maps* | | ix |
| *List of tables* | | x |
| *Series editor's foreword* | | xiii |
| *Acknowledgements* | | xv |
| *List of abbreviations and acronyms* | | xvii |
| 1 | Language contact, language learning, and language change | 1 |
| 2 | The general socio-historical context of Portuguese and Castilian | 28 |
| 3 | Portuguese- and Spanish-lexified creole languages | 42 |
| 4 | Bozal Spanish of Cuba | 68 |
| 5 | Chinese Coolie Spanish in nineteenth-century Cuba | 102 |
| 6 | Chinese Immigrant Spanish | 124 |
| 7 | Andean Spanish | 158 |
| 8 | Barranquenho | 190 |
| 9 | Contact, cognition, and speech community | 210 |
| | *Appendix A* | 218 |
| | *Appendix B* | 224 |
| | *Bibliography* | 239 |
| | *Author index* | 252 |
| | *General index* | 254 |

# Figures

1.1 Language vs dialect involving political boundaries     *page* 7
1.2 Language varieties in the Dutch–German border area     7
3.1 Distribution of thematic roles in the causal chain     56

# Maps

2.1 Distribution of peoples in the pre-Roman Iberian peninsula   *page* 29
2.2 General areas of the Roman Iberian peninsula                        31
3.1 The Malaysia–Indonesia area                                          64
8.1 The area of *A Raia* on the southern Portugal–Spain border          191

# Tables

1.1 Properties of pre-grammatical and grammatical
communication                                              *page* 2
1.2 Concepts involving selection in biology and language,
and the generalized theory of selection                        9
1.3 The Primacy of Aspect Hypothesis                          15
1.4 Raw frequency counts of eleven forms of eight Spanish verbs  16
1.5 Cross-categorization of forms by verb class and (im)perfectivity
of finite forms, in percentages and raw numbers               17
1.6 Lexical strength vs lexical connections: Spanish *contar*
'tell, count'                                                 20
1.7 Lexical strength vs lexical connections of present-tense
forms of *be*                                                 22
1.8 Lexical strength (*e[s]*, *é*) vs lexical connections in the
Portuguese and Spanish copula *ser* 'be'                      23
3.1 Number of slaves brought to Portugal from sub-Saharan
Africa (1441–1505)                                            44
3.2 Suffixes in the Portuguese-based creoles                  51
3.3 Number of suffixes relative to the homogeneity of the
contact situation and the strength and duration of
Portuguese presence                                           53
3.4 Oblique case markers in Portuguese- and Spanish-based creoles  58
3.5 Subsequent and antecedent roles in African Portuguese creoles  59
3.6 Subsequent and antecedent roles in Asian Portuguese creoles  59
3.7 Subsequent and antecedent roles in Malayalam             61
3.8 Forms used to mark the oblique in various Philippine languages  66
3.9 Subsequent and antecedent roles in Philippine Creole Spanish  66
4.1 Distribution of the estimated 1,331,000 slaves in the
Spanish-speaking Caribbean Islands and in South America
(excluding Brazil)                                            70
4.2 Population of blacks and whites in raw numbers and
percentages in Cuba 1774–1899                                 76
4.3 Population of Cuba in percentages from 1532 to 1811       77

4.4 Population distribution between whites, free coloureds,
    and slaves in Havana 1774–1899                                          78
5.1 Number of coolies arriving in Cuba from 1847 to 1859                    105
5.2 Distribution of correctly and incorrectly used verb tokens
    in Chinese Coolie Speech                                                112
5.3 Predicate forms in Chinese Coolie Spanish                              113
5.4 Distribution of stative, durative atelic, durative telic, and
    punctual predicates in Chinese Coolie Spanish and
    Chinese Immigrant Spanish                                               114
5.5 Phonological traits of Chinese Coolie Spanish                          116
5.6 Morphosyntactic traits of Chinese Coolie Spanish                       118
6.1 Distribution of correctly and incorrectly used finite
    and non-finite verb tokens in Jenny's speech                           133
6.2 Distribution of correctly and incorrectly used finite
    and non-finite verb tokens in Luis' speech                             133
6.3 Verb forms in Jenny's speech                                           135
6.4 Verb forms in Luis' speech                                             136
6.5 Comparison of the distributions of verb forms (raw numbers
    and percentages) according to imperfective (present, imperfect)
    and perfective (preterit) verb forms in spoken language in Spain,
    Jenny's speech, and Luis' speech                                       139
6.6 Form–function correspondences between Jenny's and Luis'
    speech and Spanish- and Portuguese-based creoles                       140
6.7 Phonological traits of Chinese Immigrant Spanish                       142
6.8 Morphosyntactic traits of Chinese Immigrant Spanish                   142
7.1 Census data from Peru, 1878, by ethnic group                          166
7.2 Comparison of the population distribution in Peru and
    Junín in 1878                                                          166
7.3 Speakers five years and older in Junín department, and in
    Huancayo, Concepción, and Jauja provinces (located in
    Junín department), according to their mother language or dialect       167
7.4 Relative percentages of the Quechua–Spanish-speaking
    population and the monolingual Quechua-speaking
    population from 1940 to 1989 in Peru                                   167
7.5 Distribution of speakers five years and older in urban and
    rural areas of Junín department in the 1972 and 1993
    censuses, according to their mother language or dialect                168
7.6 Speakers five years and older in Huancayo, Concepción,
    and Jauja provinces (in Junín department) in 1993,
    according to their mother language or dialect                          169
7.7 Population distribution of whites, indigenous people, and
    blacks in 1778 in Salta province                                       170

7.8  The reconstructed consonant inventory of proto-Quechua       172
7.9  The consonant inventory of Cuzco Quechua                     172
7.10 The frequency of present-tense forms of the transitive
     verbs *hacer* 'do, make', *ver* 'see', and *querer* 'want,
     love' from the CREA data base (spoken language only)         180
8.1  The instances of enclisis and proclisis in the speech
     of four male Barranquenho speakers                           205

# Series editor's foreword

The series *Cambridge Approaches to Language Contact* was set up to publish outstanding monographs on language contact, especially by authors who approach their specific subject matter from a diachronic or developmental perspective. Our goal is to integrate the ever-growing scholarship on language diversification (including the development of creoles, pidgins, and indigenized varieties of colonial European languages), bilingual language development, code-switching, and language endangerment. We hope to provide a select forum to scholars who contribute insightfully to understanding language evolution from an interdisciplinary perspective. We favour approaches that highlight the role of ecology and draw inspiration both from the authors' own fields of specialization and from related research areas in linguistics or other disciplines. Eclecticism is one of our mottoes, as we endeavour to comprehend the complexity of evolutionary processes associated with contact.

We are very proud to add to our list J. Clancy Clements' *The linguistic legacy of Spanish and Portuguese*, a very informative account of, first, the evolution of Portuguese and Spanish from Latin and, then, their subsequent transformation into several non-European varieties. The general perspective throughout the book is that of colonial expansion, language spread, language contact, and language shift. Without explicitly espousing uniformitarianism, Clements highlights the role of substrate influence through naturalistic second language acquisition, as well as the particular ways in which the external ecologies of language contact variably constrain the significance of this particular factor, against inheritance from the lexifier, in the relevant evolutionary processes. He also addresses the question of why there are no Spanish creoles, which must prompt in the more informed reader that of why no Portuguese creole emerged in Brazil despite the colony's early and continuous engagement in sugarcane cultivation and mining, using extensive African slave labour, throughout the colonial period.

Clements invokes mechanisms of naturalistic second language acquisition to account for similarities between Chinese Coolie Spanish in nineteenth-century Cuba and the xenolectal speech of recent Chinese immigrants to

Spain. He highlights the role that lack of integration within the local population – in these cases largely a consequence of the behaviour and social
attitudes of the immigrants themselves – plays in determining which particular substrate features the immigrants as individuals or as a population tend
to incorporate in their idio- and ethnolects of the host language. The author
also shows in the case of Andean Spanish how homogeneity of a common
substrate, Quechua, a major regional lingua franca, influenced the colonial
Spanish variety that evolved in western and southern parts of South America,
making it distinct from the Central American and Caribbean varieties. He
uses this contrast to explain the role that African substrate influence must
have played in making Cuban Spanish equally distinct in its divergence from
metropolitan Spanish varieties.

Also significant in this book is the way Clements invokes cultural identity
to account for the mixed Portuguese–Spanish varieties spoken by border
populations in both Europe and South America. These evolutions are largely
the consequences of histories in which the relevant populations have felt
tributaries of both Portuguese and Spanish heritages and find it natural to
integrate into their speech elements from both languages. They are happy to
distinguish themselves from their compatriots who speak Portuguese or
Spanish varieties more typically associated with their respective nationalities.
This is the case of both Fronterizo on the Uruguay–Brazil border (only
mentioned in this book) and Barranquenho on the Portugal–Spain border, to
which a whole chapter is devoted.

Overall, *The linguistic legacy of Spanish and Portuguese* is a rich, though
not comprehensive, history of language diversification, focusing on the
Iberian branch of imperial Latin in South-western Europe, the geographical
expansion of Portuguese and Spanish since the fifteenth century with the
European 'great explorations' and subsequent colonization of Africa, the
Americas, and Asia, and on the concurrent evolution of the metropolitan
varieties brought to the colonies into new ones. It is an excellent starting point
for anybody interested in understanding how the local external and internal
ecologies of a language interact to determine its differential evolution in
various parts of the world and at different times in its history. It will certainly
inspire similar studies seeking to account for the uniqueness of some other
Portuguese and Spanish varieties that Clements does not discuss, as well as
for the evolution of other languages. I am proud of this addition to CALC.

*University of Chicago*                                    SALIKOKO S. MUFWENE

# Acknowledgements

This project began as a graduate seminar and through many circuitous routes culminated in the present volume. Thanks to all my students in those courses who discussed the material with me and provided invaluable feedback. Thanks also to John Holm and the students in the mini-course at the University of Coimbra for their helpful feedback, and to the editors Andrew Winnard, Helen Barton, and Sarah Green for their patience and encouragement, and especially to copy-editor Karen Anderson Howes for her help in the preparation of the typescript. I extend special thanks to the series editor Salikoko Mufwene, first, for encouraging me to develop the idea into the present volume and, subsequently, for all his advice, his thoughtful and extensive feedback, and his active engagement in the project at every stage of its development.

I owe a great debt of gratitude to Jenny and Luis, who were kind enough and patient enough to be interviewed and recorded, to Shu-Yuan Chen and Jesús Martin Carabuig for all their support in contacting members of the Chinese community in Madrid, to Andrew Koontz-Garboden for his part in the development of parts of chapter 3, to Stuart Davis for introducing me to the Francis Lieber–José de la Luz correspondence, to Mauro Fernández and Ian Smith for their insights into the development of case-marking in the Asian Portuguese creoles, to Scott Paauw for his input on the language situation in fifteenth- to seventeenth-century Indonesia, to Ana Luis and Patricia Amaral for discussions on Barranquenho and especially to Augusto Gerardo Lorenzino for suggesting Barranquenho as a research project and for all his support in the data collection, to Maria Celeste Vidinha de Sousa and Maria da Purificação Fialho de Almeida who were instrumental in interviewing and recording the informants, and finally to the Barrancos Municipality for the support and hospitality showed Gerardo Lorenzino and myself during our stay in Barrancos. I would also like to thank Neddy Vigil and Derek Roff for all their help with the maps.

Part of this book was written while I was a resident scholar at the Zentrum für Allgemeine Sprachwissenschaft, Typologie und Universalienforschung in the summer of 2006. Thanks to Patrick Steinkrüger for making my stay there possible and for his hospitality. I am grateful to the Office of the Vice President for Research at Indiana University for financial support in finishing the typescript for this book.

Finally, my deepest gratitude goes to my wife, Richa Clements, for all her support and for helping me in all aspects of preparing the typescript.

# Abbreviations and acronyms

| | |
|---|---|
| 1 | first person |
| 2 | second person |
| 3 | third person |
| ACC | accusative |
| AUX | auxiliary |
| BEN | benefactive |
| BP | Brazilian Portuguese |
| C | consonant |
| Cast. | Castilian |
| CAUS | causative |
| CCS | Chinese Coolie Spanish |
| CIS | Chinese Immigrant Spanish |
| CL | clitic |
| COH | Causal Order Hypothesis |
| COMIT | comitative |
| COMP | complementizer |
| COND | conditional marker |
| CONT | continuous marker |
| CP | Continental Portuguese |
| CREA | Corpus de Referencia del Español Actual |
| DAT | dative |
| DBH | Distribution Bias Hypothesis |
| DIM | diminutive |
| DIR | directional |
| DO | direct object |
| EMPH | emphatic marker |
| EVID.1st.HAND | first-hand evidential marker |
| EVID.2nd.HAND | second-hand evidential marker |
| EVID.CONJ | evidential marking expressing conjecture |
| FAM | familiar pronominal form |
| FEM | feminine |

| FORMAL | formal pronominal form |
|---|---|
| Fr. | French |
| FUT | future marker |
| G | glide |
| GEN | genitive |
| GOAL | goal marker |
| IMP | imperative |
| IMPER | imperfective |
| INDIC | indicative mood |
| INF | infinitival form |
| INSTR | instrumental |
| IO | indirect object |
| IP | Indo-Portuguese |
| KCP | Korlai Creole Portuguese |
| L2 | second language |
| LIM | limiting particle |
| LINK | adposition that links phrases |
| LOC | locative |
| MASC | masculine |
| MC | main clause |
| N | noun |
| NEG | negation |
| NEUT | neuter |
| NP | noun phrase |
| OBJ | object marker |
| OBL | oblique |
| PASSIVE | passive marker |
| PAST | past tense |
| PL | plural |
| POA | Primacy of Aspect Hypothesis |
| POSS | possessive determiner |
| PPART | past participle |
| PREP | preposition |
| PRES | present tense |
| PRET | preterit |
| Ptg. | Portuguese |
| Q | Quechua |
| REC | recipient |
| REFL | reflexive marker |
| SA.SUB | same-subject subordinator |
| SC | subordinate clause |
| SG | singular |

| | |
|---|---|
| SOV | subject-object-verb |
| Sp. | Spanish |
| SUB | subjunctive mood marker |
| SUBJ | subject |
| SUBORD | subordination marker |
| TMA | tense-aspect-mood marker |
| V | vowel |
| VM | Vehicular Malay |
| VP | verb phrase |

and cognitive processing, shown in Table 1.1, which I have adopted slightly

# 1 Language contact, language learning, and language change

## 1.1 Introduction

Any account of human language must address a host of facts and observations about the structure and use of language varieties of the world, including non-standard varieties such as immigrant speech, pidgins, creoles, and mixed languages. Most linguists, as well as scholars who study different languages from other perspectives (e.g., psychologists, sociologists, etc.), would likely agree with Givón (1998:41) that human language combines two major 'mega-functions' of *representation of knowledge* and *communication of represented knowledge*. As the point of departure for a functional approach to human language, Givón (ibid.:42) proposes the evolutionary-adaptive approach in biology, in which structure (anatomy) and function (physiology) are studied not as separate from, but rather as complements to, one another. Rather than positing a single mutation in human kind that triggers the change from a protolanguage into a full human language (that is, a 'catastrophic' event which was the cause for the emergence of basic phrasal–clausal structure (Bickerton 2000:281)), functionalists such as Givón assume a gradual process whereby the link between proto- and full human language is gradual and incremental. Givón frames the distinction not in terms of language, but rather in terms of communication systems, differentiating between pre-grammatical and grammatical communication. He notes that 'humans can – under a variety of developmental or neurological conditions – communicate readily without grammar, using a well-coded lexicon with some rudimentary combinatorial rules' (1998:49). The differences between pre-grammatical and grammatical communication are expressed by Givón in terms of the structural, functional, and cognitive properties, shown in Table 1.1, which I have adapted slightly to express the differences as being a matter of degree rather than being dichotomous.

Naturally, there are counterexamples to the generalizations expressed in Table 1.1. For instance, there are languages that belong in the 'grammatical' category, such as Chinese, that have no morphology and are topic-prominent. Such cases notwithstanding, the lists of characteristics for pre-grammatical

Table 1.1. *Properties of pre-grammatical and grammatical communication*

| Properties | Grammatical code | Pre-grammatical code |
|---|---|---|
| *Structural* | | |
| a. Grammatical morphology | more abundant | less abundant |
| b. Syntactic constructions | more complex/embedded | less complex/conjoined |
| c. Use of word order | tendency towards grammatical (SUBJ/OBJ) | tendency towards pragmatic (topic/comment) |
| d. Pauses | more fluent | less fluent, more halting |
| *Functional* | | |
| e. Processing speed | faster | slower |
| f. Mental effort | less effort | more effort |
| g. Error rate | lower | higher |
| h. Context dependence | lower | higher |
| *Cognitive* | | |
| i. Processing mode | more automated | less automated |
| j. Acquisition | later | earlier |
| k. Evolution | later | earlier |

and grammatical communication in Table 1.1 capture important tendencies, especially for immigrant language varieties, pidgins, and creoles.

In the creation of pidgins, the pre-grammatical code has been characterized as the incipient or unstable pidgin phase or the phase of interlanguage (Mufwene 1997:43–44) and grammatical code as the stabilized and expanded stages, two phases along a continuum of grammatical development.[1] The incipient phase is characterized by one- or two-word utterances (holophrastic language) and pragmatic structuring (e.g., topic-comment) (Mühlhäusler 1986:135–147), whereas in the stabilized and expanded phases of development tense-aspect-mood markers, as well as other grammatical devices, develop (ibid.:147–205).

Both pre-grammatical and grammatical codes develop through communication in discourse. In both codes, frequency of use of certain items is crucial to the development of codes. That is, frequent repetition of certain patterns in discourse (i.e., in language use) is the basis of the sound–meaning mappings, pre-grammatical structures, and ultimately the development of a grammar code. In this sense, we can say that language develops structure through repetition in discourse. And although it is useful for the purpose of

---

[1] I define a *pidgin* as a contact language variety that emerges in a situation in which speakers of two or more speech communities not sharing a common language need to speak with one another. A pidgin can be unstable or stable, typically has a lexicon from predominantly one language, and is characterized by having a morphological system that is reduced relative to its lexifier language.

understanding language to distinguish between levels, such as the lexical, the propositional, and the discursive levels (see Givón 1984), it is important to remember that children learn meaning in context (holophrastic language) and only later are able to map meaning on to sound chains independently of context (see, for example, Dromi 1987). That is, acquisition is largely a top-down process, at least initially, whereby humans make use of hippocampus-based episodic memory to learn the lexicon and pre-grammatical communication (Squire 1987; Squire and Zola-Morgan 1991; Petri and Mishkin 1994 cited in Givón 1998:45).

From the foregoing discussion, the picture that emerges is that the basis of the development of pre-grammatical as well as grammatical code is repetition in discourse. This view is consistent with Hopper's (1987, 1988, 1998) view that discourse is the *sine qua non* for the understanding of grammar. Hopper (1998:155–156) describes the basis of his Emergent Grammar model as follows:

Emergent Grammar is a conception of linguistic structure that proposes to bypass the problem of a fixed, prediscourse adult grammar, with its attendant problems of necessarily 'degenerate' input for both child acquisition and adult maintenance of language, by relocating structure, that is, 'grammar', from the center to the periphery of linguistic communication. Grammar, in this view, is not the source of understanding and communication but a by-product of it. Grammar is, in other words, epiphenomenal . . .

The notion of Emergent Grammar is meant to suggest that structure, or regularity, comes out of discourse and is shaped by discourse in an ongoing process. Grammar is, in this view, simply the name for certain categories of observed repetitions in discourse. It is hence not to be understood as a prerequisite for discourse, a prior possession attributable in identical form to both speaker and hearer.[2]

One crucial aspect of this approach is that frequency underlies the formation of structure, or templates. However, it also has to be acknowledged that frequency would not be as important as it is if the human mind did not function as it does. Among myriad other complex things, the human mind functions as a highly sophisticated pattern recognizer. Assuming that, in dealing with linguistic and other input, our minds work to create processing short cuts, these can be regarded in language learning as pattern generalizations over

---

[2] Hopper (1998:156) goes on to state that '[i]ts forms are not fixed templates but emerge out of face-to-face interaction in ways that reflect the individual speakers' past experience of these forms, and their assessment of the present context, including especially their interlocutors, whose experiences and assessments may be quite different.' I conceive of Emergent Grammar more along the lines of Goldberg (1999:200), who sees grammar as emerging primarily during initial acquisition, from a combination of linguistic input, the functional demands of communication, and general cognitive abilities and constraints. See section 1.3 for more discussion of Emergent Grammar.

linguistic elements, extracted out of the input received by speakers in discourse. If the nature of the input changes, so too may the frequency of use of a given item and, in turn, the corresponding patterns. The essential point is that language is a dynamic, ever-changing system that represents knowledge for the purpose of communication and that in such a system a varying amount of structure (i.e., templates, fixed to a greater or lesser degree) exists at any given time. In the following chapters, I explore how such an approach accounts for the formation of speech varieties such as immigrant speech, pidgins, and creoles.

Pattern recognition and its role in language form, function, and change involve the notion of prototype because with it we can understand the role of frequency of occurrence in language use and how structures and classes emerge. Givón follows the notion of Roschen prototypes: membership in a natural category is defined by a set of features, some more critical than others for category membership. Thus, there can be a gradient of membership, whereby critical features are strongly associated with membership and may imply having other, less critical features. Moreover, the vast majority of token-members of such a natural category tend to cluster around a categorial mean, i.e., around the prototype. An example of a prototype is the notion of topic (defined here as the clause-initial element) being definite in discourse. For Spanish, López Meirama (1997) reports on statistical data she collected on one-argument Spanish clauses, where roughly 85 percent of the clause-initial subjects were high on the definiteness hierarchy (noun phrases realized as proper nouns, personal pronouns, or nouns with a deictic determiner) and around 90 percent of clause-noninitial subjects were relatively low on the hierarchy (noun phrases without determiner). For Spanish, then, a prototypical topic is high in definiteness. In other words, definiteness is a critical feature for the prototype of a topic in Spanish. However, in one-argument Spanish clauses definiteness is not necessarily a feature of subjects since many indefinite noun phrases can be subjects.

It is important to note that the notion of prototypes is not categorical. There is gradient membership, which implies that there is variation. A prototype assumes at least some variation within degrees of membership in a certain category or class. Such variation is indicative of dynamicity of a linguistic system, and not surprisingly this is also the case in fields such as biology, in which variation is basic:

Variation is the heart of the scientific study of the living world. As long as essentialism, the outlook that ignored variation in its focus on fixed essences, held sway, the possibility of evolutionary change could hardly be conceived, for variation is both the product and the foundation of evolution. Few other sciences make variation as a primary focus of study as does evolutionary biology. (Futuyma 1986:82 cited in Givón 1999:92–93)

In linguistics, variation has been taken most seriously in socio-linguistics and in functionalist-oriented approaches to language. Drawing on insights from these traditions, as well as on those from evolutionary biology, Croft (2000) and Mufwene (2001) construct the notion of language as a species, defined not by one 'essentialist' trait, but rather by a behavioural property, in much the same way as a species is defined in biology. This idea is taken up in the next section.

## 1.2 Language as species

Both Croft (2000) and Mufwene (2001) approach language change from a population-genetics perspective, viewing the process within real-time situations in which socio-historical aspects of change are considered the ecology of a language. Croft (2000:13–15) explains the differences between the population-theoretical and the above-mentioned essentialist perspective: 'In the *essentialist* view of a species, each species has immutable essential structural properties that identify it . . . That is, the essentialist view is that a species instantiates an abstract type.' One major problem with this view, Croft notes, is that there are reproductively isolated populations (known as sibling species) that cannot be distinguished structurally according to the essentialist definition, as well as populations (known as polytypic species) that are structurally very different among themselves as per the essentialist definition, yet reproduce among themselves. In the population theory of species, '[a] species consists of a population of interbreeding individuals who are *reproductively isolated* from other populations' (ibid.:13). In this view, there is no species type, defined by an abstract structure trait, but rather a fundamental property that the individuals of a given population share, namely, that they are reproductively isolated.

Corresponding to the essentialist view of a species is taxonomic classification, based on similarities and/or differences with regard to structural traits. Phylogenetic classification, on the other hand, corresponds to the population-theoretical view of a species. This type of classification is historical: '[A] proper phylogeny requires the differentiation of traits based on their history. If two taxa share a trait, it could be a retained trait from the parent population (a *symplesiomorphy*), or it could be a shared innovation of the two taxa (a *synapomorphy*). Only a shared, innovated trait can justify grouping the two taxa together phylogenetically' (Croft 2000:15).

Assuming a population-theoretic definition, languages are related phylo-genetically, i.e., in terms of their historical classification. To illustrate this point, Croft points out linguistic analogues to sibling and polytypic species in biology. Two languages such as Hindi and Urdu, for example, would be sibling languages (analogous to a sibling species) in that they are phylogenetically related to the point that many consider them dialects of the same language; yet they are perceived by at least one major group of speakers to be distinct, due most ostensibly to religious differences: Urdu speakers are Muslims, Hindi speakers are Hindus. Moreover, Urdu uses Persian and Arabic as its source for neologisms, whereas Hindi draws on Sanskrit for this. Thus, their definition of language in this case depends on cultural and lexical, as well as other, differences.

One instance of a polytypic language is Chinese, whose dialects, though often mutually unintelligible, share the same writing system and political unity, factors which suggest identification as a single language. In this respect Wardhaugh (2002:31) comments that speakers of Cantonese and Mandarin will say that they speak different dialects of the same language. However, if one speaker knows only Cantonese and the other only Mandarin, they will not be able to talk to one another, but if they both are literate they will be able to communicate with one another through their shared writing system. The insistence by speakers of these two varieties that they are dialects of Chinese is grounded not only in the shared writing system, but just as importantly in the strong shared tradition of cultural, social, and political unity. Concepts involving culture, society, and politics, then, turn out to be essential parts of their definition of language.

A possible example of a polytypic language within the Iberian Romance family may be Portuguese, whose major varieties (Brazilian and Continental Portuguese, BP and CP) are quite different from one another on various levels. Here reference is made to the oral varieties rather than the written ones. In phonology, unstressed syllables are reduced further in BP than in CP (McCune 2005), unstressed /e/ in BP raises to /i/ but not in all varieties of CP, and /t/ and /d/ are palatalized preceding front vowels in BP but not in CP (*te dou o dente* or *dou-te o dente* 'I give you the tooth' [či-dóu-džén-či] in BP vs [dóu-təu-dén-tə] in CP). In morphosyntax, in BP there is variable agreement of gender and number in the noun phrase, the same pronouns are used for subjects and objects in some cases (*ele matô ele mesmo* [lit. he killed he self] 'he killed himself'), the conjugation system is reduced such that 2SG, 1PL, and 3PL forms are often reduced to the 3SG form (the default), and there is a greater presence of overt subject pronouns, among numerous other traits (Mello, *et al.* 1998; see also Guy 1989 and Naro and Scherre 1993). Moreover, the order of clitic BP pronouns is always pre-verbal with finite verbs, whereas in CP they are immediately post-verbal in declarative main clauses.[3] BP also allows null objects more commonly than does CP (Schwenter and Silva 2002, 2003; and Schwenter 2006). Lastly, there are various differences on the lexical level and in orthographic conventions. All these differences notwithstanding, the two varieties are still seen as forming part of a single

---

[3] See chapter 8 for a more detailed account of clitic placement in Continental Portuguese.

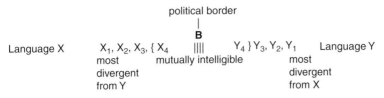

Figure 1.1. Language vs dialect involving political boundaries.

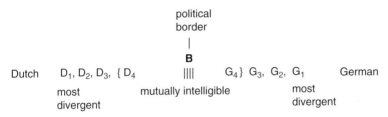

Figure 1.2. Language varieties in the Dutch–German border area.

language, due arguably to the close cultural and social ties between Brazil and Portugal.

In the case of the two Lusophone countries of Brazil and Portugal, the political differences have not led to the creation of two separate speech communities. However, the sentiment of national identity can play a role in the definition of a speech community, affecting how two similar speech varieties are defined. For instance, even though speech varieties on either side of a national border may be mutually intelligible and even belong to the same dialect, they may officially be considered different languages. That is, assuming two languages, language X and language Y, where each corresponds to a different country (see Figure 1.1), if the standard variety for X and Y is $X_1$ and $Y_1$, respectively, and if X and Y each have various varieties, and one of each is $X_4$ and $Y_4$, respectively, each of which is geographically the closest to the political border B, it may well be that, although the varieties $X_4$ and $Y_4$ are mutually intelligible, they are considered different languages due to the political boundary. There are various situations that correspond to the scenario just described. One is on the Dutch–German border, where the language varieties immediately on either side of the border are mutually intelligible, although Standard German and Standard Dutch are not. Nevertheless, the variety spoken just inside the Dutch side of the border is considered a dialect of Dutch, just as the variety spoken on the German side of the border is considered a dialect of German (see Figure 1.2). The obvious key factor in these cases is national and political identity (see Wardhaugh 2002:30–31).

Thus, a speech community is often defined not necessarily by linguistic factors, but rather by cultural, social, or political ones (see ibid.:27–32).

Given the importance of social, cultural, and political considerations in the definition of a language, and following the population-theoretic definition of a species, Croft follows Chambers and Trudgill (1980) in suggesting a social, rather than a linguistic, definition of a language. The population-theoretic definition of a language implies that 'every speaker perceived every other speaker as someone he or she should be able to communicate with by using what they perceive as the same language' (Croft 2000:18). An important part of this definition is the interaction between individuals in the community of speakers. Croft states that '[c]ommunicative interaction depends not only on the degree of structural similarity of the varieties spoken, but also on the social behavior of the speakers. Serbian and Croatian are mutually intelligible to a high degree, but many speakers do not communicate with the opposite community due to the recent political changes in former Yugoslavia' (ibid.:19). Thus, the analogue of reproductive isolation is, in the case of language, *communicative isolation*, and interbreeding in a biological population would equate to *conversational intercourse* in a speech community.

If a biological species is defined as a set of reproductively isolated individuals and a linguistic species as a set of communicatively isolated individuals, then in Croft's view the notions of geographical race and deme in biology correspond to a social network in a given communicatively isolated group. A geographical race is a subpopulation of a species defined geographically, and typically has diverged structurally to some extent, though not enough to impede interbreeding. A deme, less inclusive than a geographical race, is a subpopulation within a species which, as with a geographical race, has a high likelihood of interbreeding and a lower likelihood of breeding with members belonging to adjacent demes (Croft 2000:19). Analogously, a social network is 'a group of people who are most likely to communicate with each other, and not so much with those outside the network' (ibid.:20).

Drawing on Hull's (1988) general model of selection, developed to shed light on the evolution of concepts in science, Croft (2000:38) proposes the linguistic analogues to those of biology and science, shown in Table 1.2. The left-hand column contains the terms of Hull's generalized theory of selection, with an analogue of each from biology in the centre column, and from language in the right-hand column. I include Mufwene's concepts where they correspond to and/or extend those proposed by Croft.

There are some differences between Mufwene's and Croft's terminology and conceptualizations. Mufwene (2001:151–152) sees a language as akin to a parasitic, symbiotic kind of species: 'Parasitic species are a fairly adequate

Table 1.2. *Concepts involving selection in biology and language, and the generalized theory of selection*

| Generalized theory of selection | Paradigm instantiation of selection in biology | Paradigm instantiation of selection in language |
|---|---|---|
| *replicator* (spatiotemporally bound individual, i.e., a token; it has structure) | gene | lingueme (Mufwene's feature) |
| *replicators in a population* | gene pool | lingueme pool (Mufwene's feature pool) |
| *structured set of replicators* | string of DNA | utterance |
| *normal replication* | reproduction by interbreeding | utterance production in communication, i.e., communicative intercourse (see also Mufwene 2001:150) |
| *altered replication* | recombination, mutation of genes | mechanisms for innovation, causally motivated by functional factors (e.g., phonetic or conceptual factors) (Mufwene's (2001:12) restructuring) |
| *alternative replicators* | alleles | variants |
| *locus for alternative replication* | gene locus | linguistic variable |
| *interactor* | organism (Croft envisages a plantish organism here, Mufwene a parasitic organism) | speaker (including grammar) (Mufwene's individual speaker) |
| *hybrid interactor* | hybrid organism | bilingual speaker (including grammars) (Croft 2000:201) |
| *environment* | ecological environment | social-communicative context (Mufwene also includes here the intra-linguistic, the inter-linguistic, and the socio-historical contexts) |
| *selection* | survival and reproduction of organisms | entrenchment of convention by speakers and its propagation in communication (Mufwene's (2001:147) group selection) |

analog chiefly because a language does not exist without speakers, just like parasites do not exist without hosts. The life of a language is, to borrow from Brown (1995:191), "closely tied to the distribution of [its] hosts, which provide many of the essential environmental conditions necessary to [its] survival and reproduction." ' In addition, Mufwene views language transmission as taking place not necessarily vertically on the parent-to-offspring model, but rather primarily in a horizontal fashion. Moreover, language transmission according to Mufwene can be variably polyploidic. Polyploidy is form of rapid speciation, most commonly found among flowering plants, which creates the incipient stages of a new species in two or three generations. The analogue for polyploidy in language change is, at the most basic level, the creation of idiolects in individual speakers, and on a higher level the creation of pidgin or creole languages within just one or two generations.

Croft agrees that the parent-to-offspring model does not capture language transmission or language change, but uses a different analogy. He suggests that languages can have multiple parents in language transmission, a process he likens to the phenomenon of introgression, whereby if two plant species hybridize, and if one hybrid organism then backcrosses with one of its parent species, it thereby introduces genes from the other species into the gene pool of the first species (Croft 2000:198, 238). Although there are differences in their respective views, both authors agree that the parent-to-offspring model falls short of capturing language transmission accurately, and that for language evolution there are more appropriate models from biology, namely plant reproduction and parasite behaviour.

An illustrative example in which the parent-to-offspring model does not adequately account for the facts is the emergence of pidgin Portuguese, to be discussed in chapter 3 below. In the latter part of the fifteenth and the first part of the sixteenth century, Africans came to make up 10–15 per cent of the population in southern Portugal (Ramos Tinhorão 1997:92, 102–103), and it is reasonable to assume that the portrayals of their speech found in popular plays of the era reflect roughly the manner in which Africans were then speaking Portuguese. The Portuguese used by the vast majority of first-generation Africans at that time was learned naturalistically in communication with native Portuguese speakers, most of whom we can assume to have been adults. As I will discuss, some of the key structures in the untutored L2 Portuguese are found in portrayals of African Portuguese in plays of some fifteenth- and sixteenth-century playwrights. We can reasonably assume that the varieties of Portuguese spoken by Africans in Portugal were conventionalized in adult-to-adult communication and that these served as the basis for pidgin Portuguese, which in turn became the basis for the Portuguese-based creoles. The conventionalized features of these varieties were the result of 'negotiated' solutions among African and Portuguese adults.[4] Revealingly, immigrant language varieties involving Chinese and Spanish also exhibit features similar to those found in African L2 Portuguese, and generally it turns out that immigrant languages display surprisingly similar characteristics, which taken together have been argued to comprise what Klein and Perdue (1992) call the 'basic variety'. Such common solutions to communication also reflect adult-to-adult language transmission. (See chapter 6 below.)

Several factors underlie Klein and Perdue's (1992) 'basic variety' of immigrant speech. I believe that at least some of these factors are processing-related phenomena, observed in L2 acquisition (see Zobl 1982) and in L1 acquisition (see Bates and Goodman 1999), that involve different types of bootstrapping. I review these in the next section and then come back to address the effect of input in language acquisition.

## 1.3    Bootstrapping in L1/L2 acquisition and the linguistic structure of contact varieties

Croft (2000:42–63) argues that innovations of the sorts introduced by children into language are in general neither maintained by speakers until adulthood nor of the same type as found in language change. Thus, children most often are not the source of innovations that are propagated and end in language change.

In this section, I discuss certain learning strategies in L1 and L2 acquisition that involve bootstrapping. In general, the term refers to processes whereby a complex system emerges by starting simply and, bit by bit, developing more complex capabilities on top of the simpler ones. I discuss various kinds of bootstrapping, following work done by Bates and Goodman (1999), and drawing on examples from language contact phenomena to be examined in detail in this volume.

The general issue at hand is that portions of language are acquired initially in the acquisition process and that they help learners in the further acquisition of a language. One example of this is: meaning is used as a basis on which to build syntactic structure. Increasingly, researchers recognize the strong relation between meaning on the one hand, and argument structure of verbs and syntactic structure on the other (Bresnan 1982, 2001; Goldberg 1995, 1999; Langacker 1987). Levin and Rappaport Hovav (1995:1), for example, suggest a causal relation between the regularities linking arguments bearing certain semantic roles and particular syntactic expressions: the extent that the

---

[4] On the concept of 'negotiation', see Thomason 2001:142–146. As I understand Thomason's notion of 'negotiation', it refers to what she also called 'mutual linguistic accommodation' in Thomason and Kaufman 1988.

semantic role of an argument is determined by the meaning of the verb selecting it, the existence of linking regularities supports the idea that verb meaning is a factor in determining the syntactic structure of sentences. The striking similarities in the linking regularities across languages strongly suggest that they are part of the architecture of language. If this is true of language in general, it is also true of language acquisition. In this respect, Bates and Goodman (1999) comment on a large number of studies that show the correlation between not only verb acquisition and syntax but also, more generally, between vocabulary acquisition and grammar acquisition. They state that 'the dependence of early grammar on vocabulary size is so strong and the nonlinear shape of this function is so regular that it approaches the status of a psychological law' (ibid.:51). To explain why the relation between grammar and the lexicon is so strong, they propose that it has to do with different types of bootstrapping, of which they distinguish five, none of which excludes any of the others (ibid.:51–53) and four of which will be discussed here.[5]

The first is perceptual bootstrapping. Bates and Goodman cite studies in which it is argued that for efficient word perception to happen a certain amount of top-down processing is necessary. It permits the listener to separate out the inappropriate possibilities from all the items that overlap (at least partially) with the blurred word tokens encountered in fluent speech. Assuming this to be accurate, Bates and Goodman suggest that it is even more accurate in reference to the perception of grammatical function words and bound inflections. These are hard to perceive because they usually consist of at most a few sounds and are unstressed, even in deliberate and slow speech. In informal and rapid speech, speakers tend to shorten them further,

deforming their phonetic structure and blurring the boundaries between these morphemes and the words that surround them. In fact, when grammatical function words are clipped out of connected speech and presented in isolation, adult native speakers can recognize them no more than 40 per cent to 50 per cent of the time (Herron and Bates, 1997). This is true of speech directed to children as well as speech directed to adults (Goodman, et al. 1990). (Bates and Goodman 1999:52)

They note that it is not surprising that young children are not able to acquire grammatical forms before they have learned a certain quantity of lexical items. The bootstrapping aspect of this is that the critical mass of content words allows the learner enough top-down structure to perceive and then learn the closed-class elements that turn up between the actual lexical items.

---

[5] The type I will not discuss is the apparent relation between the non-linear shape of vocabulary acquisition and grammar development on the one hand, and non-linear dynamics of learning in neural network simulations on the other. Bates and Goodman note that 'multilayered neural networks produce an array of nonlinear growth functions, reflecting the nonlinear dynamics of learning and change in these systems' (1999:53), and that this avenue of research would be fruitful.

One can appeal to perceptual bootstrapping to account for the same phenomenon found in L2 acquisition. Zobl (1982) reports on findings suggesting that a critical degree of lexical learning must take place before functional elements are acquired. I argue that it also accounts for the under-acquisition of functional elements in naturalistically learned L2 speech (see chapters 3, 4, 5, and 6 in this volume). In general, Klein and Perdue (1992) find that in immigrant language the functional elements as a group are not acquired in the same way as lexical items.

This phenomenon in L1 and L2 acquisition can also be accounted for by the second type of bootstrapping discussed by Bates and Goodman (1999), namely logical bootstrapping. They report on studies targeting several different languages that show that, with the exception of a few items like *up* and *no*, function words tend to appear after the first verbs and adjectives, and well after the first nouns. Interestingly many early prepositions are also not used by children in the same ways as adults use them. For example, Dromi (1987) describes how a word such as *up* is used at first by a child in a specific context (e.g., while bathing) and only later context-independently. It is revealing that in pidgin development an all-purpose preposition is common; moreover, in immigrant languages of different sorts we also find an all-purpose preposition. Bates and Goodman mention the suggestion that the development from names to predication to grammar is logically necessary because '[c]hildren cannot understand relational terms until they understand the things that these words relate. One can argue about the extent to which this assumption holds for individual structures, but it may provide a partial explanation for the dependence of grammar on lexical growth' (1999:52).

While perceptual and logical bootstrapping address the link between lexical growth and subsequent grammar development, syntactic bootstrapping uses different aspects of a sentence frame to be able to interpret utterances, aspects such as sentence-level semantics, morphological cues, word order, and prosody. It is, however, not unreasonable to assume that syntactic structure such as word order is used in the interpretation of utterances in children. In her view of Emergent Grammar, Goldberg states that:

grammar emerges primarily during initial acquisition, from a combination of linguistic input, the functional demands of communication, and general cognitive abilities and constraints. Once grammar is acquired, it is assumed that it has a highly conventionalized status, and that although minute changes in the system constantly occur, the system as a whole is fairly stable. (1999:200)

From this definition, it follows that structural information in a sentence can be used to learn about a novel word. In fact, Goldberg (ibid.:201) remarks that two- to three-year-old children learn word-specific word orders even though they are also somewhat sensitive to word order independently of a specific verb. Four-year-olds, however, rely substantially more on the generalization of word order independently of specific verbs. The basis of this is not only development of the lexicon, but also the factor of frequency of use of the most commonly used verbs, which serve as exemplars for certain constructions. I use this term to refer to the set of instances of use of the most frequently occurring verbs (e.g., the verb *do* in English for a transitive construction) that serve as the first model for the set of transitive verbs in a language. Goldberg (ibid.:208) suggests that 'the semantics that comes to be associated with a syntactic pattern emerges from early uses of a pattern with particular verbs'.

More generally, this idea can be linked to the aforementioned one advanced by Levin and Rappaport Hovav that the semantics of the verb plays a role in determining the syntactic structure of sentences. So far, the types of bootstrapping discussed involve language acquisition more directly. However, the notion of a lexically based grammar, that is, a grammar in which the lexicon is responsible for more of the syntactic structure in language, is seen by Bates and Goodman as a stronger claim because it extends to the lexicon–grammar relation in adults. The observation that the lexicon and grammar belong to two different modules may be, they point out, a subsequent development, following the processes of modularization described by Karmiloff-Smith (1992), Bates, Bretherton, and Snyder (1988) and Friederici (1990).[6]

So far, I have talked about the role different types of bootstrapping play in the acquisition of language, both L1 and L2. For L2 acquisition in particular, issues of language input have also been discussed in the literature. In this volume, I attempt to show that input is important for understanding more fully how immigrant varieties, pidgins, and creoles form and develop. Above, I stated that language learners acquire words first, before grammar. Andersen and Shirai (1996) and Andersen (1993) argue that the process of acquiring grammatical morphemes is constrained by inherent lexical aspect, which in turn may be influenced by the nature and extent of the input. Regarding the role of inherent aspect on the acquisition of grammar, Andersen and Shirai (1996:529) note that '[i]t has been consistently observed that L1 and L2 learners, in the early stages of acquiring verbal morphology, use tense–aspect selectively according to the inherent lexical aspect of the verb to which the tense–aspect marker is attached or with which it is associated.' To account for these facts, they propose the Primacy of Aspect (POA) Hypothesis, given in Table 1.3.

---

[6] Bates and Goodman (1999:53) comment that the question of modularity in the adult steady-state is referred to in the literature on language disorders in adults and children, where strong claims about the modularity of grammar and the lexicon can be found.

Table 1.3. *The Primacy of Aspect Hypothesis*

---

a. Learners will initially restrict past or perfective marking to telic verbs (achievements and accomplishments) and later gradually extend the marking to atelic predicates (activity and then stative predicates), with states being the last category to be marked consistently.
b. In languages with an imperfective marker, imperfective past appears much later than perfective past and then is initially restricted to atelic predicates (stative and activity verbs), then extended to telic predicates (accomplishments and then achievements).
c. Progressive marking is initially restricted to dynamic atelic predicates (activity verbs), then extended to telic predicates (accomplishments and then achievements).
d. Progressive marking is not incorrectly overextended to states.

---

*Source:* Andersen and Shirai 1996:559.

In untutored (that is, naturalistic) as well as tutored L2 acquisition, the POA hypothesis predicts that learners will display sensitivity to the link between the lexical aspect of the predicate and the forms most semantically congenial to them. That is, telic predicates will appear first in perfective forms and atelic predicates will appear first in imperfective forms, although states will not appear in the progressive. It is important to note that this hypothesis refers to what learners produce, not to what they have as input or what they take in from the input.

The Distribution Bias Hypothesis (DBH), by contrast, addresses the issue of what learners receive as input. It projects that the distribution of forms to predicate classes (i.e., stative, atelic, and telic predicates) is such that speakers of any given language will produce in normal discourse more imperfective forms with states and activities and more perfective forms with accomplishments and achievements. Andersen (1993:320) describes it in the following way: 'Native speakers will tend to use past or perfective inflections more with telic and punctual events than with states or activities, progressive inflections primarily with activities, and imperfective inflections more with states and activities than with telic and punctual events.' To my knowledge, this hypothesis has never been tested against a data base. To test it, I undertook a frequency count of imperfective and perfective forms of eight verbs in an oral corpus of Spanish from Spain, shown in Table 1.4.[7]

Three predicates (*saber* 'know', *poder* 'be able', *querer* 'want, love') are stative, two are atelic (*trabajar* 'work' and *buscar* 'look for'), and three are

---

[7] The data were taken from the Corpus de Referencia del Español Actual (CREA) available at the website of the Real Academia Española (www.rae.es). Some of the forms, such as *trabajo* 'I work' and 'work' and *busca* 's/he looks for' and 'search', are homophonic. In these cases, the noun uses were excluded from the count. However, although all infinitives in Spanish can be used as nouns, as in *el saber que* 'knowing that', such uses represent a small percentage of the frequency of use of the infinitives and therefore were included for all verbs.

Table 1.4. *Raw frequency counts of eleven forms of eight Spanish verbs*

| | Static situations | | | Dynamic situations | | | | |
| | Stative predicates | | | Atelic predicates | | Punctual predicates | | |
| | saber | poder | querer | trabajar | buscar | morir | nacer | romper |
|---|---|---|---|---|---|---|---|---|
| *Present* | | | | | | | | |
| 1SG | 5288 | 1275 | 1618 | 46 | 24 | 15 | 1 | 7 |
| 2SG | 1308 | 814 | 635 | 61 | 16 | 14 | 1 | 5 |
| 3SG | 1130 | 4550 | 1392 | 222 | 103 | 88 | 56 | 42 |
| 1PL | 444 | 861 | 338 | 40 | 29 | 3 | 10 | 2 |
| 3PL | 512 | 1129 | 495 | 84 | 38 | 42 | 29 | 19 |
| *Present subtotal* | *8682* | *8629* | *4478* | *453* | *210* | *162* | *97* | *75* |
| *Past* | | | | | | | | |
| 1/3SG-PRET | 12/38 | 73/157 | 41/67 | 31/25 | 5/13 | 5/159 | 48/148 | 5/36 |
| 2SG-1MP/PRET | 43/4 | 76/2 | 49/1 | 9/1 | 2/1 | 2/2 | 1/10 | 0/0 |
| 1/3SG-1MP | 394 | 667 | 875 | 86 | 17 | 17 | 9 | 13 |
| 1PL-1MP/PRET | 53/10 | 104/38 | 59/7 | 145/1 | 4/0 | 2/0 | 0/4 | 1/1 |
| 3PL-1MP/PRET | 52/14 | 137/40 | 111/21 | 20/8 | 5/5 | 10/30 | 1/16 | 4/9 |
| *Past subtotal* | *620* | *1294* | *1231* | *326* | *52* | *227* | *237* | *69* |
| *Non-finite* | | | | | | | | |
| gerund | 51 | 19 | 25 | 449 | 211 | 29 | 4 | 10 |
| infinitive | 813 | 439 | 109 | 620 | 349 | 186 | 58 | 87 |
| *Non-finite subtotal* | *864* | *458* | *134* | *1069* | *560* | *215* | *62* | *97* |
| Total | 10,166 | 10,381 | 5843 | 1848 | 822 | 604 | 396 | 241 |

*Note:* Total number of tokens is 27,441.

Table 1.5. *Cross-categorization of forms by verb class and (im)perfectivity of finite forms, in percentages and raw numbers*

| | Static situations | | | Dynamic situations | | | | |
|---|---|---|---|---|---|---|---|---|
| | States | | | Atelic situations | | Punctual situations | | |
| | saber | poder | querer | trabajar | buscar | morir | nacer | romper |
| Imperfective | 99.3 | 96.8 | 97.6 | 91.5 | 90.8 | 49.6 | 30.5 | 64.6 |
| forms | (9224) | (9513) | (5572) | (713) | (236) | (193) | (99) | (93) |
| Perfective | 0.7 | 3.2 | 2.4 | 8.5 | 9.2 | 50.4 | 69.5 | 35.4 |
| forms | (68) | (310) | (137) | (66) | (24) | (196) | (226) | (51) |

*Notes:* Imperfective forms = 1SG, 2SG, 3SG, 1PL, 3PL of the present tense and 1SG, 2SG, 3SG, 1PL and 3PL of past imperfect. Perfective forms = 1SG, 2SG, 3SG, 1PL, and 3PL of the preterit.

punctual (*morir* 'die', *nacer* 'to be born', *romper* 'break').[8] The verb forms included are five simple present-tense forms, eight past-tense forms (the 1SG and 3SG imperfect forms are homophonous and not distinguished for this count), and two non-finite forms (the gerund and the infinitive). Table 1.5 shows the distribution of forms by verb class and grammatical aspect of the form (i.e., (im)perfectivity).

In this sampling of representative stative, atelic, and punctual predicates in Spanish, the distribution of the finite verb forms (26,842 tokens) strongly supports the DBH. As hypothesized, stative and atelic predicates appear overwhelmingly (over 90 per cent of the time) in imperfective forms and two punctual predicates (telic) (*morir* 'die' and *nacer* 'be born') appear in perfective forms much more frequently than stative and atelic predicates (over 50 per cent of the time). Although punctual *romper* 'break' appears only 35.4 per cent of the time in perfective forms, the overall tendency is, nevertheless, unambiguous: in an oral corpus of native-speaker Spanish from Spain, there is a clear bias in the distribution between verb form and verb class. Andersen and Shirai (1996:553) state that in native speaker-to-non-native speaker discourse, the distribution bias may be even more pronounced.[9]

---

[8] Durative telic predicates were excluded in this count because in terms of form they are not comparable to the other three in that they often correspond not to verb-only predicates as in the case of the other three classes, but rather to complex predicates, such as *build a house* or *run a kilometre*.

[9] Andersen and Shirai (1996) also caution that it is not clear whether the conversation topic or the simplified nature of learner-directed speech may influence the distributional form–function bias. This consideration notwithstanding, it is clear from the information in Tables 1.4 and 1.5 that in native speaker-to-native speaker speech there is a distributional form–function bias. Andersen and Shirai suggest that it would not be surprising if the distribution bias became more pronounced in learner-directed speech of native speakers. I assume that such learner-directed speech would include, as well, foreigner-directed speech.

The foregoing discussion strengthens the view that language change can and does take place as part of acquisition (e.g., naturalistic L2 acquisition) in adult-to-adult communication. However, it does not negate the importance of parent-to-offspring language transmission, though in language change it may not always play as big a role as has been attributed to it, for example, in the process of creolization.

## 1.4    Borrowing vs shift situations and language processing in the feature pool

Thomason and Kaufman (1988) identify two general tendencies in contact-induced language phenomena: borrowing and shift. The extent of borrowing or shift depends on factors prevalent in the contact situation in question. For borrowing, Thomason and Kaufman (ibid.:73–75) propose a scale, whereby the more intense the contact situation, the more lexical and structural features tend to be borrowed. That is, the borrowing-community speakers borrow words from one or more of the source languages and, if the contact intensity is stronger, they begin to borrow linguistic structure as well. In such a situation, bilingualism is a prerequisite for borrowing.

In the case of shift, however, there need be no bilingualism involved prior to the shift, but it would develop as shifting speakers learn the target-language vocabulary. As they learn the target language, they typically carry their native-language structures into the language to which they are shifting.

The general developmental paths borrowing and shift, as I understand them, are shown in (1.1) and (1.2), based on Croft (2000:213–221).

(1.1) **Borrowing → extensive borrowing → death by borrowing**
    (primary parent language is typically the language of the borrowing community)
(1.2) **Naturalistic second language acquisition → semi-shift → total shift**
    (primary parent language is typically the language targeted by the new language learners)

In both borrowing and shift situations, three key factors to be considered are: *contact intensity*, *markedness* of a linguistic feature to be borrowed or to be learned in language shift, and *typological fit* between the languages involved in the contact situation. Contact intensity is often (though need not be)

---

Another consideration is that Andersen and Shirai's study of form–function bias may be language-specific. For example, Paz González (2003) found that the POA Hypothesis did not predict L2 Spanish learner data if they had Dutch as an L1. However, it seems that the L2 Spanish results are more accurately predictable from the nature of the Dutch verb-marking input (see especially P. González 2003:105). Thus, the DBH may predict the distribution found by González where the POA Hypothesis does not.

interpreted from the perspective of (a) non-dominant language(s) in a contact situation; it impacts the lexical and structural make-up of the feature pool. Non-dominance itself can be understood in at least two different ways. For example, overall, Spanish in the Andean region of South America is more prestigious for a wider range of uses than Quechua. In some rural communities of the region, however, more people speak Quechua than Spanish and many of those who speak Spanish speak Quechua more fluently. Thus, whereas Spanish may be the dominant language in term of general prestige in the speech communities of the region, Quechua in some areas is dominant in terms of the number of speakers and their degree of fluency relative to the number of Spanish speakers and their respective degree of fluency. These two different types of dominance in the region affect the feature pool differently in each community. Many Spanish-related lexical and structural features may be socio-linguistic markers of prestige. However, for this to be the case, they must be significantly represented in the feature pool such that they constitute a presence. In a speech community with strong Quechua dominance, its lexical and structural features would be substantially better represented in the corresponding feature pool. Thus, in a situation of Spanish acquisition by Quechua speakers, the Quechua features would be highly dominant and would consequently find their way into the variety of Spanish learned by these speakers. We also need to keep in mind that the input received by such Spanish learners already contains features from Quechua.

Whereas contact intensity impacts the lexical and structural make-up of the feature pool, markedness of features and typological fit in borrowing and shift situations involve ease-of-processing concerns for L2 learners. As it is used here, the term *markedness* refers to the degree of representation (in terms of frequency of occurrence) a given lexical (including function words) or structural feature has within the feature pool of a given contact situation. Regarding overall (un)markedness of a feature in the world's languages, it is always expressed in a specific language or language contact situation. The less a feature is found in the world's languages, the less likely it would be for us to find it represented in the feature pool of a language or language contact situation and the less likely it would be for the feature to be borrowed or learned in L2 acquisition. Such a feature would be, for instance, inflectional infixation, which is exploited much less than inflectional suffixation or pre-fixation in the world's languages because, arguably, edges of words are more easily accessible in production and processing than the interior part of words. However, if two languages in contact share the feature of inflectional infix-ation, it would not be surprising for a contact language emerging from such a situation to display infixation. Thus, the specific prediction would be that unless infixes are shared by the languages in a contact situation, they would be seldom if ever borrowed and would also be difficult to learn in a

Table 1.6. *Lexical strength vs lexical connections: Spanish* contar *'tell, count'*

| | |
|---|---|
| c u é n t o <br> \| \| \| \| \| | 'I tell, count' |
| c u é n t a s <br> \| \| \| \| \| \| | 'you tell, count' |
| **c u é n t a** <br> \| \| \| \| \| \| | 's/he tells, counts' |
| c u é n t a n <br> \|    \| \| | 'they tell, count' |
| c  o   n t á m o s | 'we tell, count' |

*Note:* Bold marks the most frequently used form.

naturalistic L2 acquisition or shift situation. Thus, one would not expect to find them forming part of a contact language variety such as immigrant speech, a pidgin, or a creole unless, of course, they had an overwhelming presence in the feature pool of the contact situation in question.

If a feature is highly unmarked in the world's languages, it is assumed not only that it is found in all known languages, but also that it is easy to produce and process in language use. For example, the syllable structure CV is considered the most unmarked as compared to other syllable structures (e.g., V or VC structures). Thus, the prediction would be that in a given emerging contact language, if there are two candidates for a given function in a given slot, the candidate with the CV structure would have an advantage over the others. But in some cases, the universally unmarked CV structure competes with frequency of occurrence. Above, I noted that frequency plays an important part in determining the form of a language. However, if a frequently used form is not perceptually salient, it might not be as easily processed (or produced) as other perceptually more salient forms. A case in point is the syllable structure of the copulas found in Portuguese- and Spanish-based creoles, to be discussed in chapter 3. Bybee (1985) calls frequency of occurrence of an item its *lexical strength*, and refers to its phonological similarity to the other members of its paradigm as its *lexical connections*. In some cases, the lexical strength of a form and its lexical connections overlap. For example, in the present-tense paradigm of the Spanish stem-changing verb *contar* 'tell, count', the most frequent form (3SG-PRES) is also the one with more lexical connections, as shown in Table 1.6.

In this paradigm, the form *cuenta* is the most unmarked paradigmatically in that its content /kuenta/ is contained in three of the five forms. The most marked form of the paradigm is *contamos*. In terms of frequency, in a data-base search of oral Mexican Spanish, the form *cuenta* is found 639 times, overwhelmingly in the idiomatic expressions *tomar en cuenta* 'take into account' and *dar cuenta de* 'account for'. As a verb, it is found 48 times, mostly in the expression *contar con* 'count on, depend on'. The form *cuento* is found 7 times, two of which are verb forms; *cuentan* is found 30 times and *contamos* 45 times, in both cases only as verb forms; and *cuentas* is not found at all.[10] Thus, in terms of raw tokens and as a member of a paradigm, the lexical strength and the lexical connections of *cuenta* conspire to make it the default form. In any situation of paradigm levelling, the prediction would be that *contamos* would either be replaced by another construction, such as *la gente cuenta*,[11] or that *contamos* would be adapted to fit the paradigm, as with *cuéntamos* or *cuentámos*. In fact, in some contact varieties we find *cuentamos* as a form in formal speech.[12]

In paradigms with syncretisms, such as copulative verb paradigms, the most frequent verb forms are often not the ones that have most lexical connections in the paradigm. In English, for instance, we assume *is* [ɪz] to be the most frequently occurring of all the present-tense forms. However, *are* [ar] has the most lexical connections.[13] Neither form has the most unmarked syllable structure (i.e., CV). If we were to predict which of these forms were to be present in English-based creole languages, the prediction might be that [ɪz] is more likely because the consonant [z] is more frequent and also more consonantal than [r], and thus more perceptually salient. It turns out, however, that in the English-based creoles Jamaican, Guyanese, Gullah, Krio, and Sranan the initial equative copulative verb was not derived from any form shown in Table 1.7, but from form *da* (or *na*), both with CV structure. The source of these forms is debated, but it seems reasonably safe to say that the periphrastic *do* of seventeenth- and eighteenth-century English as well as forms from African substrate languages are the source of copula *da* and *na*. Pargman (2004:22) argues that the West African substrate languages provided a selective advantage for the CV form over the competing variants (see also Ihalainen 1976). For their part, Holm *et al.* (1999:100) state that 'the oldest form of the equative copula before NPs was apparently *na* (judging from the conservative nature of the creoles in which this form is found) . . . In the

---

[10] The database used is CREA (Corpus de Referencia de Español Actual) at www.rae.es.

[11] The corresponding sentence *a gente conta* 'the people say/tell' is used in Continental Portuguese to refer to the 1PL PRES.

[12] As an illustration, in a text found on the website Fundación por los Niños del Perú, where Quechua and Spanish are in contact (see chapter 7), we find the form *cuentamos* (También *cuentamos* con 05 Cunas Jardín (centros de cuidado infantil para niños . . .) 'We also boast five Garden Cradles (child-care centres . . .).'

[13] Frequency counts of *is* and *are* were taken from the Linguistic Data Consortium American English Spoken Lexicon at the University of Pennsylvania (https://online.ldc.upenn.edu/aesl/). The number of tokens for *are* is 5,242,695, that of *is* 10,669,918. That is, although the lexical connections of *are* are superior, the lexical strength of *is* turns out to be twice that of *are*. The token frequency of *am* in the corpus is 191,590, far below that of the other two forms.

Table 1.7. *Lexical strength vs lexical connections of present-tense forms of* be

| | | |
|---|---|---|
| I am [æm] | you are [a r] (SG) | s/he is [ɪz] |
| | \|  \| | |
| | we are  [a r] | |
| | \|  \| | |
| | you are  [a r] (PL) | |
| | \|  \| | |
| | they are  [a r] | |

English-based creoles of the Caribbean proper, basilectal *a* [*da* < *na* according to Holm *et al.*] became mesolectal *iz.*' Although Pargman and Holm *et al.* do not coincide on the actual source of *da* and *na* in the English-based creoles mentioned above, it is indisputable that a form containing CV structure was favoured, even though in some registers of these creoles the most frequently used copula form *iz* does prevail. I suggest that *na* or *da* emerged as the copula due to its CV structure and in the de-creolization process *iz* replaced it in some registers because of its lexical strength. Here, perceptual salience seems to have been more important than frequency.

As I will discuss in chapter 3, this also seems to be true for reflexes of the equative copula *ser* in the Spanish- and Portuguese-based creoles. Although the 3SG present-tense forms (Spanish *es*, with variants [es], [eh], and [e], and Portuguese *é*) occur roughly six times as frequently as all the other forms combined, the other forms have the advantage in terms of perceptual salience: they all contain a CV(C) structure, shown in Table 1.8.[14]

---

[14] As an example, the frequency counts in two contemporary databases (the CRPC and CETEMPúblico for Portugal and the PORCUFORT for Brazil (www.geocities.com/Paris/Cathedral/1036/)) are as follows:

| | Distribution | | |
|---|---|---|---|
| | Portugal | | Brazil |
| Form | CRPC | CETEMPúblico | PORCUFORT |
| sou | 22 (1.3%) | 62 (1.0%) | 271 (2.0%) |
| és | – | – | – |
| é | 1,581 (89.9%) | 5136 (81.1%) | 12,104 (88.3%) |
| somos | 9 (0.5%) | 32 (0.5%) | 81 (0.6%) |
| sois | – | – | – |
| são | 146 (8.3%) | 1101 (17.4%) | 1,245 (9.1%) |

Table 1.8. *Lexical strength (e[s], é) vs lexical connections in the Portuguese and Spanish copula* ser *'be'*

| Portuguese | | Spanish | |
|---|---|---|---|
| CV(G) | V(C) | CV(G/N) | V(CVC) |
| s o u 'I am' | é s 'you.SG are' | s o y 'I am' | e r e s 'you.SG are' |
| &#124; &#124; | &#124; | &#124; &#124; | &#124; |
| &#124; &#124; | é 's/he is' | &#124; &#124; | e (s) 's/he is' |
| s o m o s 'we are' | | s o m o s 'we are' | |
| &#124; | | &#124; &#124; | |
| s ã o 'they are' | | &#124; &#124; | |
| | | s o n 'they are' | |

We would expect, then, that if any of these forms came to be part of a creole lexified by Spanish or Portuguese or in rudimentary immigrant varieties, then perceptual salience would trump the lexical strength of the 2SG forms. Indeed, in immigrant Spanish and in Portuguese/Spanish-based creoles, although the 3SG present-tense copula form Spanish *es* ([es], [eh], or [e]) and Portuguese *é* are roughly six times more frequently used than the other present-tense forms combined, *é* is found only in Capeverdean Creole Portuguese, due most likely to the de-creolizing influence of Portuguese. If the other varieties display any reflex of *ser*, the form contains a CV structure. For example, in immigrant Spanish and Makista Creole Portuguese, we find *son* and *sã*, respectively. This suggests, then, that markedness involves frequency, as well as the most basic sorts of structures found in the world's languages, such as CV structure.

As for typological fit, the farther the languages in a contact situation are from one another typologically, the more difficult it is for speakers to borrow from one another's language, or to find common structures in a borrowing or

Analogously, the Spanish forms in a contemporary Spanish data base (CREA maintained by the Real Academia Española, www.rae.es) are comparable.

| Form | Distribution |
|---|---|
| soy | 23756 (1.9%) |
| ere(s) | 9767 (0.8%) |
| e(s) | 978813 (78.3%) |
| somos | 12563 (1.0%) |
| sois | 1085 (0.1%) |
| son | 223417 (17.9%) |

an L2 learning situation. Conversely, the closer two languages are to each other typologically, the easier the processing would be in a borrowing or an L2 learning situation. This could be understood as local markedness in that, if two or more languages in contact share a specific feature, it would be unmarked for the speakers of those languages. For example, an Italian speaker would find the acquisition of the preterit–imperfect distinction in Spanish relatively easy to learn because in this respect Italian and Spanish are typologically very similar and thus share the distinction. By contrast, a monolingual native English speaker would find it more challenging to master the preterit–imperfect distinction in Spanish because English and Spanish are typologically more distant from one another and thus do not share the feature.

The fact that much or all of what has just been discussed involves either bilingualism (borrowing-type phenomena) or L2 acquisition (shift-type phenomena) has significant ramifications for the structure of contact-induced language change, including immigrant speech and pidgin/creole formation. In a given speech community in which there is substantial language contact, the feature pool contains a host of features – both lexical and structural – from the languages involved. To the extent that the languages in contact are typologically similar (for example, if they share the features of inflectional verb morphology), their respective features may reinforce each other in the feature pool of the speech community, as in the case of the preterit–imperfect distinction in Spanish and Italian. Lack of a clean typological fit among languages in a contact situation – as is the case with Quechua and Spanish, which have been in contact around 500 years – can lead to the re-analysis of certain particles. A well-known example, discussed in chapter 7, involves possessor–possessum marking in Andean Spanish. In all varieties of Quechua, the possessor as well as the possessum is marked, with the suffixes *–pa* 'of' and *–n* 'his/her/their' respectively. An example of this is shown in (1.3), taken from Huanuco Quechua (Weber 1989:254), a dialect spoken in Peru.

(1.3)   Hwan-**pa**       wasi-**n**
        Hwan-GEN     house-3POSS
        'Hwan's house'

Of note here are the two obligatory markers of possession, in contrast to standard Spanish, which only has one, as in (1.4), where the possessive marker *de* precedes the possessor. Also, the possessum itself (*la casa*) precedes the possessor (*Juan*).

(1.4)   la     casa     **de**     Juan
        the    house    of       Juan
        'Juan's house'

In several varieties of Andean Spanish, a highly common structure in the possessive noun phrase is that shown in (1.5), where the possessor (*Juan*) does not follow but precedes the possessum, as in Quechua, and where this is double marking: *de* marks the possessor and the possessive determiner *su* marks the possessum.

(1.5)   **de** Juan    **su**       casa
        of Juan      3POSS     house
        'Juan's house'

The only structural difference between (1.3) and (1.5) is the placement of the functional elements: in Quechua they are suffixes, whereas in Andean Spanish they appear before their respective nouns. In chapter 7, I provide demographic and other evidence for two varieties of Andean Spanish in support of the claim that the feature pools in the geographical areas in question have been historically heavily weighted in favour of Quechua structures, to the extent that Spanish undergoes noticeable restructuring. What is intriguing about this particular case is that the Andean Spanish structure in (1.5) is found in several varieties of Andean Spanish, a re-analysis that has most likely taken place independently in each area. This observation brings up the question of how speakers, independently from one another, arrived at the same structure given similar Spanish input. Although the details are undoubtedly complex, the general answer is that Quechua speakers learning Spanish were/are sensitive to double possessive marking because of their native language and re-analysed the functional elements nearest to the lexical items denoting the possessor and possessum. They imposed a right-branching structure on the noun phrase and sought possible candidates in order to map the functions of –*pa* 'of' and –*n* 'his/her/their' on to them. Given that, arguably, the Spanish phrases *de N* 'of N' and *su N* 'his/her/their N' occur frequently as chunks in discourse, it is relatively straightforward to relate suffixes –*pa* 'of' and –*n* 'his/her/their' to *de* 'of' and *su* 'his/her/their', especially if the order of the possessor and possessum are altered to match the order in Quechua. Underlying this type of structural change of the Spanish possessive noun phrase would be a contact situation more like the one represented in (1.2) above, in which a predominantly Quechua-speaking community has learned Spanish to varying degrees, depending on the need to do so in each case. With Quechua predominance in many areas, at least historically, the presence of Quechua structural features must have been considerably stronger than the corresponding Spanish structural features. Finally, the mapping was probably aided by the fact that the elements *su* and *de* exhibit CV structure and are thus relatively easy to perceive. Thus, perceptual salience and frequency of occurrence seem to have played a role in the creation of a Spanish structure such as (1.5) in Andean Spanish.

## 1.5    Concluding remarks

In this chapter, I have sketched out a view of language consonant with a type of Emergent Grammar model in which linguistic structure is created through routinization; and routinization is made possible by frequency of use of certain elements or structures through communication in discourse. In constructing this view, the notion of speech community becomes important. Following Croft (2000) and Mufwene (2001), I consider a language to be analogous to a biological species and a speech community as a group of intercommunicating individuals, parallel to an interbreeding population in biology.

Regarding the actual formation and development of linguistic structure, I align myself with Goldberg's (1999) view in which grammar emerges primarily during acquisition, affected by a combination of linguistic input, functional demands of communication, and general cognitive abilities and constraints. In acquiring or building a grammar, both in L1 or L2 acquisition, I follow Bates and Goodman (1999) in assuming that we use several different types of bootstrapping, building more complex structures upon simpler, more basic ones. This happens, I argue, not only in parent-to-offspring language transmission, but – importantly – in adult-to-adult communication, as well.

In a language contact situation in which a new language variety emerges, such as immigrant varieties, pidgins, and creoles, these same principles apply: language structure emerges through language use in discourse and is shaped by functional demands of communication and cognitive abilities/constraints, including processing and production constraints. Moreover, I maintain that language use and processing constraints in contact situations interact with universal markedness constraints and the typological fit of the languages in contact to further shape the emerging linguistic system. The more universally unmarked a feature is, the more easily processable it is and thus the more likely it is to be found in an immigrant variety, a pidgin, or a creole (see Thomason and Kaufman 1988). I discussed the example of CV structure in the choice of the copula in some English-, Spanish- and Portuguese-based contact language varieties and found that CV – a universally unmarked structure – can play a major role in the emerging syllable structure of a language contact variety. Typological fit among languages in contact also has an impact on the make-up of an emerging language. It turns out that even relatively marked features such as inflectional morphology can find their way into language contact varieties if they are shared by the languages in contact.

In general, in order to understand how language contact varieties form, we will need to know at least the following:

(1) content and structural features of the languages involved in the contact situation;

(2) the number of languages and the number of speakers of each language;
(3) relative markedness of the competing features in the feature pool;
(4) dominance relations among the different language group speakers; and
(5) the access to the feature pool of the different speakers.

In chapter 2, I briefly discuss how Spanish and Portuguese came to be considered languages in their own right, which will then set the stage for the beginning of the colonization of Africa, the Americas, and Asia. In the subsequent chapters, I apply the model outlined here with the goal of arriving at a more in-depth understanding of some of the key structures in several Portuguese- and Spanish-based contact varieties that emerged in the process of language contact.

# 2 The general socio-historical context of Portuguese and Castilian

## 2.1 The Romanization of the Iberian peninsula

In contrast to Gaul, which Caesar conquered in just ten years, Iberia, defying the best Roman generals, succumbed to Rome only after a bitter struggle spanning more than two centuries. In fact, during most of the 202 years between 218 BCE and 16 BCE, it is not an overstatement to say that Iberia was a war zone (Curchin 1991:7).

Before the soldiers of Rome reached Iberia in 218 BCE, speaking colloquial varieties of Oscan, Umbrian, and Latin, the Iberian peninsula was inhabited by numerous tribes. In the west and north of the peninsula were the people the classical writers describe as Celtic, who had been in the region as early as the ninth century BCE, though they may have arrived in various waves (Tovar 1977:121–122). In the south-west lived the Lusitanians, and the Galicians inhabited the north-western corner of the peninsula. Whereas the language of the Lusitanians may have been pre-Celtic, or an early Celtic language, that of the Galicians (Callaeci) was definitely Celtic, possibly a more recent variety than that of the Lusitanians (ibid.:109–110). The differences between their languages notwithstanding, the Lusitanians and Galicians were quite similar to one another in the degree and form of their civilization (de Oliveira Marques 1972:17).

In the north-central part of the peninsula lived the Basques, who spoke a non-Indo-European language. The central region of Iberia was inhabited by various tribes collectively known as the Celtiberians, who spoke varieties of Celtic (Tovar 1977:105–106), and in the south-central area were the Tartesians. For their part, the Iberians inhabited the eastern coast, up to the current border with France. Both the Tartesians and Iberians spoke non-Indo-European languages, and the Iberians had developed a script.

The Romanization of the Iberian peninsula took place in stages. The initial reason for Rome's incursions into Iberia was to defeat the Carthaginians stationed on the eastern seaboard and in the valley of the River Baetis (Guadalquivir) (218–202 BCE), who were perceived by the Romans as wanting to monopolize trade in that area. After expelling the Carthaginians,

Map 2.1. Distribution of peoples in the pre-Roman Iberian peninsula.

the Romans maintained their continued presence on the peninsula, necessary in order to keep them from regaining a foothold in the area. The Tartesians and Iberians, accustomed to interacting with foreigners, not only adapted well to the presence of the Romans, but also readily assimilated to Roman culture, quickly abandoning their own languages and cultures, and shifting to the Latin variety spoken by the Romans stationed in Spain. Between 201 and 16 BCE, the other peoples on the Iberian peninsula fought Rome's domination bitterly. In 197 BCE, Rome divided the peninsula into Hispania Citerior, 'nearer Hispania' – comprising, roughly, the territory inhabited by the Iberians, Celtiberians, and Galicians – and Hispania Ulterior, 'farther Hispania', the territory inhabited by the Lusitanians and Tartesians. The war against Lusitania was waged from 155 to 138 BCE, the Celtiberian war was fought during the period 153–133 BCE, the north-west campaigns against the Galicians 138–136 BCE, and the final Cantabrian war took place between 26 and 16 BCE. It was probably after the Cantabrian mountains in north-central Iberia were taken by the Romans that the peninsula was divided into three provinces: Hispania Ulterior was subdivided into Baetica (capital in Corduba (Córdoba)) and Lusitania (capital in Emerita Augusta (Mérida)). Roughly speaking, Hispania Citerior was renamed as Tarraconensis (its capital in Tarraco (Tarragona)).

By the early first century CE there were nine Roman colonies in Baetica, eight in Tarraconensis, and four in Lusitania. An inscription from one of these colonies – the *colonia* Genetiva Iulia at Urso (Osuna), which contains material from the time of its foundation under Julius Caesar – shows a community of Roman citizens with their own magistrates and religious officials, a town council, and common land assigned to the town. We can assume that Roman colonies in the peninsula had this general structure and that at least some of the indigenous people assimilated to the new order, becoming Roman citizens. Evidence for this includes the facts that the philosopher Lucius Annaeus Seneca (c. 4 BCE–CE 65) was originally from Corduba, that the poet Martial (c. CE 38–c. 103) was born at Bilbilis (near Calatayud), and that senators Trajan and Hadrian were both from Italica colony near Seville. These last two later went on to become emperors (CE 98–117 and 117–138, respectively).

Even around 50 BCE, i.e., only 150 years after the arrival of the Romans in the peninsula, we find comments such as that of a Greek grammarian Artemidor from Ephesus, who had settled in Hispania to teach. He commented that the inhabitants of Baetica saw themselves as Romans in that they had given up their own customs and language to take on those of their Roman conquerors. Cicero (106–43 BCE) mentions that the poets from Corduba appreciated the Roman consul Metellus' poetry. These poets, it is stated, spoke Latin with a local accent (Tovar 1977:87–88).

While the assimilation of the Tartesian and Iberian populations took place relatively swiftly and completely, that of the rest of Hispania's people did not. In sharp contrast to the early use of Latin names among the indigenous population in inscriptions (also in Latin) from both Baetica and Tarraconensis, in Lusitania the use of indigenous languages for names and inscriptions was the norm. And even though the inscriptions throughout central and north-western Iberia were eventually written in Latin, pre-Roman words were used in them, words that found their way into Portuguese and Castilian. Some examples include: *paramus* 'desert highland', probably of Celtic origin (cf. Old Portuguese *parámio* (or *paranho*) 'house in ruins', Castilian *páramo* 'highland desert') found in toponyms and Latin inscriptions in the central and north-west regions of the peninsula; *lausa* 'slate', also of probable Celtic origin (cf. Portuguese *lousa* and Castilian *losa* 'stone slate'), which was found in a mining law text in southern Portugal; *cama* 'cot' (cf. Portuguese and Castilian *cama* 'bed'); *sarna* 'mange' (Portuguese and Castilian *sarna*

Map 2.2. General areas of the Roman Iberian peninsula.

'mange'). These last two words, of Celtic origin, were found in the Latin writings of highly educated people of that time, such as the philosopher Isidore of Seville (560(?)–636) (Tovar 1977:93–94). There are lexical items not found in such sources, but which nevertheless are pre-Roman, and possibly Celtic. Corominas (1954:433–435) comments on one such word, Portuguese *morcela* and Castilian *morcilla* 'blood sausage made with pig intestine', which very likely were once diminutive forms derived from Celtic *\*murca* 'animal intestine', which in turn seems to be related to Welsh *migwrn* 'knuckle, joint', Breton *migourn, -orn* 'cartilage', and Gaelic *mugairn* 'joint'.

Apart from the lexical evidence, there is interesting phonological evidence of the Celtic (i.e., Lusitanian, Galician, and/or Celtiberian) influence on Portuguese and Castilian. We know that mutations involving lenition are currently used extensively in Celtic languages to mark morphological distinctions (e.g., Irish *cù* /ku:/ 'dog' *-a chù* /ə xu:/ 'his dog'; or Welsh *ci* /ki:/ 'dog' *-ei gi* /i gi:/ 'his dog'). In the past, today's morphologized mutations in

Celtic languages were conceivably active phonological processes. We know that the sonorization of voiceless stops in central and north-western Iberia (e.g., *pratu* > *prado* 'meadow') had already begun to take place in 27 CE (Tovar, cited in Baldinger 1972:242), although Tovar (1977:93) places it somewhat later, around the second–third century CE. He attributes the western Romance sonorization to Celtic lenition in a situation of Latin–Celtic language bilingualism, presenting a large amount of evidence in favour of his argument (see also Tovar 1954, 1955, 1967). Tovar also suggests that the deletion of intervocalic -*n*- in Galician and Portuguese (CANE(M) > *cão* 'dog'), although it does not show up before the ninth century, may be linked to Celtic influence, as it appears initially only in the north-west of the peninsula, and in no other early Iberian Romance varieties, such as Mozarabic (Baldinger 1972:165–166).

Summarizing, we can conclude that, between roughly 100 BCE and 300 CE, the Celtiberians, Lusitanians, and Galicians began acquiring some variety of Latin and gradually became bilingual in their respective native Celtic varieties and Latin. It is important to note that the acquisition of Latin was a slow process with much resistance on the part of the indigenous people of central and north-west Iberia. For example, as late as the first century CE, there is attestation of Celtiberians still being competent in their native language. Tacitus (cited in Tovar 1977:124) writes about an indigenous person who cried out in his mother tongue while being tortured near the region of Guadalajara. 'It is therefore understandable', writes Tovar (ibid.), 'that during the centuries of bilingualism western [pre-Roman] traits found their way into the Romance varieties' (my translation).

The foregoing still does not tell the whole story. That is, although it addresses the question of substrate influence, it does not account for the relative uniformity evident in the Latin that evolved into Portuguese and Castilian. Tovar (1977:95) offers a reasonable explanation for this:

> The traits of those Romance dialects of the Iberian peninsula that would have survived, i.e., those found in Spanish, in Portuguese, and in Catalan, Valencian, and Balearic, would have been, as far as we are able to judge from the Mozarabic dialects, less western and would have shared more characteristics with Italian if the Arabic invasion had not taken place, which gave a different direction to the foreseeable development of Latin in Spain. It altered the cultural reference points in that the influential centres of Mérida, Toledo, Seville, Cartagena, Tarragona, Zaragoza, and Lisbon were replaced by Oviedo, León, Burgos, Compostela, Braga, and Old Catalonia with Barcelona. The dominance of the Moors gave the northern regions, with the push of the re-conquest, predominance in the creation of new languages (my translation).

The consequence of this historical development was that the centres of linguistic influence were all in the north of the peninsula and were relatively more closely grouped (with the exception of Old Catalonia) than the centres that could have been influential in the south. Tovar suggests that this accounts for the lexical material shared by Galician/Portuguese and Castilian, an illustrative list of which is given in (2.1).

(2.1) **Portuguese and Castilian**    **Catalan (with French)**

| Portuguese and Castilian | Catalan (with French) |
|---|---|
| comer 'eat' | menjar 'eat' (Fr. manger) |
| dar 'give' | donar 'give' (Fr. donner) |
| falar, hablar 'speak' | parlar 'speak' (Fr. parler) |
| ir 'go' | anar 'go' (Fr. aller) |
| madeira, madera 'wood' | fusta 'wood' (Fr. bois) |
| mesa 'table' | taula 'table' (Fr. table) |
| mulher, mujer 'woman, wife' | dona 'woman, wife' (Fr. femme) |
| ouvir, oír 'hear, listen' | sentir 'hear, listen' (Fr. entendre) |
| perguntar, preguntar 'ask' | demanar 'ask' (Fr. demander) |
| perna, pierna 'leg' | cama 'leg' (Fr. jambe) |
| querer 'want' | voler 'want' (Fr. vouloir) |

In each of these cases, the Latin reflexes of the Portuguese and Castilian are of an older variety than those found in Catalan and often also in French, the latter two reflecting a more recent variety of Latin. While this pattern is clear, there is evidence for another pattern as well, one that unites the peripheral languages (including Romanian) against those in the centre. For example, Portuguese, Spanish, Catalan, and Romanian share the lexical item 'more' (*mais, más, mes*, and *mai*, respectively) compared to French *plus* and Italian *più*. However, this does not diminish the fact that Portuguese and Castilian often share lexical items that Catalan does not have.

Given this brief synoptic view of the Romanization in Hispania, we know that the language varieties known as Iberian and Tartesian ceased to exist as their respective speakers shifted to Latin, a process completed by approximately 50 BCE (or in about six generations, where a generation is calculated as a unit of twenty-five years), and with no resistance on the part of the shifting speakers. We can infer from various sources that the Celtic varieties of Lusitanian, Galician, and Celtiberian, although they endured much longer due to the fierce resistance on the part of their speakers against the Roman conquerors/colonizers, ceased to be spoken for the most part between 200–300 CE.

Due to the defiant attitude of these speech communities and their numerical superiority vis-à-vis the Romans in Spain, we might expect to find the presence of pre-Roman lexical features in non-core vocabulary rather than in core vocabulary and more so in the lexical inventory than in derivational or inflectional material. That is, we would first expect to find non-core lexical items that reflect the Celtic, Lusitanian, and/or Celtiberian cultures or their surroundings prior to the arrival of the Romans. By non-core vocabulary, I mean those lexical items that do not form part of core vocabulary lists such as the one developed by Comrie and Smith (1977) or the Swadesh list.

Non-core lexical items are indeed present in Central and Western Iberian Romance. Above, I mentioned Old Portuguese *paranho*, 'house in ruins', Castilian *páramo* 'highland desert'; Portuguese *lousa*, Castilian *losa* 'stone slate'; Portuguese and Castilian *cama* 'bed'; Portuguese and Castilian *sarna* 'mange'; Portuguese *morcela*, Castilian *morcilla* 'blood sausage made with pig intestine'. Another is Portuguese *cerveja*, Castilian *cerveza* 'beer', related to Middle Irish *coirm* (Corominas 1954, and found in Latin since Pliny (23–79 CE)). Other examples are found in Lapesa (1981:46–52).

In a typical shift situation, which generally happens in three to six generations and in which the shifting population is a minority numerically and otherwise, we would expect to find no core vocabulary in the variety of speech of the shifting speakers once the shift is completed. However, the situation at hand was one of assumed extensive bilingualism over a period of time spanning centuries, ending in the eventual language shift in a community that was arguably numerically superior to the group whose language they were shifting to. In such a case, the 'lexical pool' (a subpart of the feature pool that existed during the extended period of bilingualism) would be weighted in favour of the varieties of the shifting speakers, and it should not be surprising also to find some core vocabulary in the lexicon of their variety of Romance, that is, some core vocabulary items in Spanish and Portuguese of pre-Roman origin.[1] Based on Comrie and Smith's (1977) core vocabulary list, we find two pre-Roman core vocabulary items in West and Central Iberian Romance (and thus in Portuguese and/or Spanish), namely Castilian *manteca*, Portuguese *manteiga* 'grease, fat' and Castilian *perro* 'dog'.

Another strong indication of extensive bilingualism, and thus a rich bi- or multi-lingual feature pool, is the presence of pre-Roman morphology in Central and Western Iberian Romance. In Iberian Celtic varieties, nouns with *-o* as their thematic vowel formed the nominative plural with *-os*. This entered into the feature pool with other suffixes from the pre-Roman and Latin nouns. The numerically best represented Latin nouns were arguably those from the second declension, with the thematic vowel in *-us* (*-us, -i, -o, -um, -o; -i, -orum, -is, -os, -is*). The result was that thematic nouns in *-o* in Portuguese and Castilian now form their plural in *-os* (analogous to the accusative plural suffix in Latin) instead of *-i* (the nominative plural suffix in Latin). The pejorative pre-Roman derivational suffixes *-orro, -urro* as in *machorro* 'macho man' and *baturro* 'oaf, redneck' must have been well represented to survive in Castilian (of Mediterranean origin, according to Lapesa (1981:44)). The same can be said for the pre-Celtic or Celtic suffixes *-aiko, -aecu*, which are well attested in Hispania's inscriptions and found in Castilian *-iego*, as in *mujeriego* 'womanizing (adj.), womanizer (n.)', *palaciego* 'palatial (adj.), courtier (n.)'.

---

[1] I am using the term 'feature pool' in Mufwene's (2001) sense. See Table 1.2.

Other features due to contact-induced language change may also be attributable to Celtic-language influence. Features attributed to one or more of the languages in Hispania Ulterior (e.g., Lusitanian, Galician, Celtiberian) are the change of word-initial PL-, CL-, FL- > [č] > [š] in Portuguese (PLOVERE > *chover*, CLAMARE > *chamar*, FLAMMA > *chama*), and > [λ] in Castilian (*llover, llamar, llama* respectively), and the loss of -*n*- in Galician and Portuguese (LUNA(M) > *lúa* 'moon', CANE(M) > *cão* 'dog'). Finding such phonetic particularities is not surprising given the nature of the shift situation described above.

By the fourth, or at the latest the fifth, century CE, the speakers of all pre-Roman languages on the Iberian peninsula, i.e., Iberian, Tartesian, Lusitanian, and Celtiberian, and the Celtic Galician varieties, had probably become extinct. There remained only speakers of Iberian Romance, which arguably had a wide range of heterogeneity across the peninsula, depending on the substrate language(s) involved in the shifting process of the different speech communities (Penny 2000).[2]

By the time the Roman Empire fell into decadence around the fourth century, all areas in Iberia except the mountainous regions of the Basque country were Romanized. It is conceivable that the early Iberian Romance spoken varieties were mutually intelligible to a large extent. That is, the dialectal differences around the fourth century were arguably not enough to have created language speciation of Iberian Romance. At this stage, one could say we are dealing with a series of linguistic demes or races rather than species. The boundaries of these races would be found primarily along geographical boundaries of the peninsula, and secondarily along Roman administrative boundaries. The subsequent Germanic invasions (415–711) into the peninsula undertaken by the Visigoths, Suebes, and Vandals added some administrative boundaries, which would become important later. Linguistically, however, the Germanic presence in the Iberian Romance languages is limited to lexical items such as war-related *esporas* 'spur' (Ptg.) *espuelas* 'spurs' (Cast.), *guerra* 'war' (Ptg. and Cast.), *yelmo* 'helmet' (Cast.), etc.

The Moorish invasion from northern Africa was, however, another matter, as Tovar points out in the quotation given above. After Muslim Moors conquered Iberia (711–719 CE), most Christians relocated to the northern part of the peninsula, where the enclaves they formed later turned into principalities or kingdoms that eventually undertook the centuries-long struggle of re-conquering the peninsula. It is during this process that speciation of the

---

[2] However, one must also keep in mind that the Celtic tribes were nomadic at least up until the first century BCE (Tovar 1977:109) and most likely later on as well. This might have created a certain koiné effect in the areas inhabited by Celtic-language speakers, similar to the one described by Mufwene (2001:28, 211) for dialects in the colonization of the United States. This will not be explored further here.

Iberian Romance varieties took place. The political developments of the re-conquest were instrumental in the speciation of Portuguese, Castilian, Catalan, etc. Recall that speciation, as understood here, does not depend on linguistic criteria but rather is defined in terms of population genetics. That is, in a population-genetic definition the important aspect is which people see themselves as being able to communicate with whom. That is, by this definition 'every speaker perceived every other speaker as someone he or she should be able to communicate with by using what they perceive as the same language' (Croft 2000:18). As long as this perception held among speakers, although they were of different clans, there would be no speciation by definition. I suggest that the conversational isolation that led to speciation on the Iberian peninsula was significantly helped along by, if not entirely a consequence of, the formation of counties, principalities, and kingdoms. The formation of these political entities led to a certain development of awareness on the part of the people, which in turn led them to recognize that what they spoke was different from the variety spoken by people in another kingdom, principality, or county (see also Posner 1993).

With specific regard to the speciation of Portuguese and Castilian, prior to the Moorish invasion, two general though diverse groups were distinguished in the far western part of the peninsula: the Lusitanians in the south-west and Galicians in the north-west (de Oliveira Marques 1972). At the time of the Moorish colonization, these two groups spoke two general varieties of what would become Portuguese. As a consequence of the Moorish presence, speakers of these two varieties were pushed together and the dialectal differences apparently levelled to a degree (de Oliveira Marques 1998:18; compare also Mufwene 2001:28, 211). It was due to issues of royal succession in the Christian enclave in Galicia that Portugal became a county in 1094 and a kingdom in 1179. The Portuguese language of today is considered by some to be Galician of the re-conquest (Eugenio Coseriu, personal communication, 17 October 1977).

The speciation of Portuguese and Castilian as separate languages, then, was a function not primarily of linguistic differentiation, but rather of socio-political differentiation, a process that led to relative isolation in communicative intercourse (analogous to reproductive isolation in biology), which in turn led to greater linguistic differentiation among the two communities of speakers. I will briefly sketch the main developments that led up to the socio-political divisions and the subsequent linguistic differentiation.

## 2.2    The formation of Portuguese and Castilian

In chapter 1, I spoke of language situations in which two distinct linguistic varieties are seen as one language, even though they belong to two different nations and display some significant differences in phonology, morphosyntax, and the lexicon. Such is the case, I suggested, with the oral varieties of Continental and Brazilian Portuguese, which although substantially different are considered to constitute one and the same language, arguably due to relatively strong cultural, social, and political ties between Brazil and Portugal. In population-theoretic terms, these varieties may be considered polytypic languages, because they are thought of as one language despite their considerable linguistic differences.

The differences between the current oral varieties of Portuguese spoken in Brazil and Portugal can be compared roughly to those differences that distinguished the varieties of Iberian Romance (eighth–eleventh centuries) that were spoken in the north of the Iberian peninsula from the far north-west to the north-central area. Leguay, de Oliveira Marques, and Beirante (1993:206) liken the differences among the various Iberian Romance dialects between the eighth and eleventh centuries to those that exist today among the Portuguese dialects from the Minho in the north of the country to the Algarve in the south, which are more alike than Continental and Brazilian Portuguese are today. The question then becomes: how did the original dialects that came to be spoken in Portugal and Castile evolve into distinct languages whereas other varieties, such as those spoken in León or Asturias, did not? A crucial part of the answer to this question has to do with the development of Portugal and Castile as powerful kingdoms. In other words, the answer has more to do with socio-politics than with linguistic differentiation. In fact, linguistic differentiation and language speciation most likely were a consequence of the political divisions.[3]

Starting with the first victory of the re-conquest found in the chronicles, Pelayo won in the Battle of Covadonga in 722, which resulted in the origin of the kingdom of Asturias. The reign of Alphonse I, Pelayo's son-in-law, began thereafter, during which he made incursions into Galicia and the Douro Valley. During the long reign of Alphonse II (791–842), the fourth successor after Alphonse I, the kingdom of Asturias took shape and simultaneously opened towards Europe. After the extraordinarily successful reign of Alphonse III (866–911), this monarch was forced to divide up his kingdom into three, thus creating the kingdoms of Galicia, León, and Asturias. At this

---

[3] Another question that must be addressed is: despite seven centuries of Arabization, Arabic never managed to be completely dominant, even in the southern part of the peninsula where between the eighth and eleventh centuries the Arabic language and culture were dominant in Al Andaluz, from the Mediterranean to the Atlantic. Why could Arabic not dominate entirely? The answer is that the Christians successfully resisted complete Arabization, maintaining their religious and cultural identity intact. In fact, the only clear vestige of Arabic in Portuguese and Spanish is the lexical items that we find in both languages (see Dozy and Engelman 1965; Maillo Salgado 1983).

point, there were two border regions, Portugal on the extreme west and Castile east of Asturias, between which were the territories of Galicia, León, and Asturias. As Leguay, de Oliveira Marques, and Beirante (1993:258) note, the city of Portucale (the Porto of today) was occupied by Christians, and by 938 CE the name gradually came to refer to the territory surrounding the city. At around the same time, in 943 CE, Fernán González became the count of Castile. Over roughly the following 100 years there were internal struggles among the Christian kingdoms and counties, as well as attacks from the Normans coming from the north and the Islamic northern Africans from the south. In 1035, Fernando Magno became the first king of Castile. Meanwhile, Portucale was lost and re-conquered again, becoming a political entity, a county in 1094 and a kingdom in 1179 (Leguay, de Oliveira Marques, and Beirante 1993:263 and de Oliveira Marques 1998:35–37).

In discussing the beginnings of the state of Portugal, de Oliveira Marques (1998:27) refers to 'Portucale', but he states that it was pronounced *Portugal* in the dialect spoken at that time (938 CE). At around 950 CE, when Portugal and Castile were taking shape as political entities, Sarton (1927, cited in Deutsch 1968:599) notes that there were in Europe at that time only six full-fledged languages, that is, languages with a written grammar, a literature, and some use in business and public administration. They were Latin, Greek, Hebrew, Arabic, Anglo-Saxon, and Church Slavonic. Three hundred years later (1250 CE), seventeen languages were flourishing in Europe: apart from Latin, Greek, Hebrew, Arabic, and Church Slavonic, there were High German, Low German, French, Icelandic, Russian, Castilian (Sarton uses 'Spanish'), Portuguese, Catalan, Italian, Norwegian, Danish, and Swedish. On the Iberian peninsula, all three Romance vernaculars mentioned in the list (Portuguese, Castilian, Catalan) were attached to a kingdom, Portugal, Castile, and Cata-lonia, respectively. By 1250 CE, the varieties that around 1000 CE were dialects spoken in Portucale and Castile had developed into languages. The reason Deutsch (1968:602–603) offers for the speciation of Dutch, Flemish, and German is also applicable to the speciation of Portuguese and Castilian: 'It was not at first these languages that made history; it was history that made these languages.' That is, the importance of social, political, and cultural considerations is such that they define a language, which follows from the population-theoretic definition of a species as advanced by Croft (2000) and Mufwene (2001). As pointed out in chapter 1, the population definition of a language implies that every speaker views other speakers as people s/he can communicate with in what everyone involved perceives as the same language (Croft 2000:18). Crucial in this definition is the interaction between indi-viduals in the community of speakers. Communicative intercourse in a population depends not only on the degree of structural similarity of the varieties spoken, but also on the communicative behaviour of the speakers.

In the case of the incipient political entities of Portugal and Castile, their becoming kingdoms created a consciousness of belonging among the speech communities as defined by the political borders of the kingdoms. Given that the kingdoms were often in conflict with one another, especially earlier on, identities of self and the other were forged in these politically defined speech communities. Over time, the politically defined territories came to shape the definition of the respective communities, not only politically but culturally and linguistically as well. But the process began with the political definition of territoriality. In this way, it can be said that history defined the language communities in question.

## 2.3 Developments leading up to the colonization of Africa and Asia

By the fourteenth century, both Portuguese and Castilian had become full-fledged languages. By this time, the kingdoms of Castile and Portugal had also been at battle both with one another and with the Moors. Out of these conflicts, numerous reasons emerged in both Portugal and Castile for carrying the fight beyond their respective southern borders into Africa. One was the wish on the part of the aristocrats in both kingdoms to extend the *Reconquista* to Morocco in order to acquire more land. Perhaps more important, however, was that both Portugal and Castile were in need of a steady source of North African grain because of a low supply on the peninsula. The most pressing motive, however, for aristocrats as well as the bourgeoisie, was a desperate need for gold 'to meet the overwhelming deficit which threatened to destroy the economy' (Chaunu 1979:104). During the final 250 years of the re-conquest, roughly 1250 to 1500 CE, both Portugal and Castile spent enormous sums of money to re-conquer and re-populate the southern half of the Iberian peninsula. Moreover, from 1350 to 1389, Castile – and to a lesser extent Portugal – were obliged to deal with the expenses of the Castilian phase of the Hundred Years War (MacKay 1977:121–125). Thus, the economic woes of these powers made expeditions to northern Africa not just attractive but necessary. The search for slaves, sugar, and spices also became important as time went on.

Even before 1350, the Portuguese and Castilians had begun to deploy their naval power to explore further out into the Atlantic. Although Genoese explorers are said to have arrived there first, a Spaniard made first claim to the Canary Islands in 1344, and en route to the Canaries in 1341 a Portuguese expedition happened upon the unoccupied Azores Islands for the first time (Chaunu 1979:105). But it was not until the 1440s that these islands were settled and exploited. Like the initial exploring impulse, the settlement of these islands and the subsequent construction of sugar plantations on them were spurred by 'unusual economic difficulty and stagnation' on the peninsula (ibid.:107).

At the beginning of the fifteenth century, the Castilians began to prepare for a long trade war with the Hanseatic League of north European towns, a war in which the Portuguese did not participate. Because of this, the Portuguese were in a better position than their Castilian counterparts to expand into Africa. In 1415, the Portuguese king Henry the Navigator crossed the straits of Gibraltar and took Ceuta in northern Africa, thereby launching the Portuguese colonization of the west coast of the African continent. And with each trip, Portugal's ships travelled a bit further south along the West African coast. Chaunu (1979:111–112) distinguishes four main stages in the Portuguese exploration and settlement of the West African coast. Stage one, 1415–1434, from the conquest of Ceuta up until the rounding of Cape Bojador, was marked by cautious progress. During stage two, 1434–1444, the Portuguese moved from Cape Bojador to the Cape Verde Islands. In stage three, 1444–1475, with a more refined knowledge of sailing on the open sea, the Portuguese were able to reach around the coast of Sierra Leone to the Congo. Finally, during stage four, 1475–1498, Bartholomew Diaz rounded the Cape of Good Hope and Vasco da Gama found his way up the eastern coast of Africa to Mombasa, and in 1498 ventured across the Arabian Sea to the tip of the Indian subcontinent, with the help of Ahmed-ben-Madjid, a well-known Arabian navigator who was purportedly an expert on the navigation of India (Serrão 1978:100, de Oliveira Marques 1998:207).

The settlement of a large part of the west coast of India (Cochin, Calicut, Goa, Chaul, Bassein, and Diu, among other areas), as well as Sri Lanka, was accomplished by 1550. Daman – which gave the most resistance – fell in 1559, and by 1581 it was recognized as a Portuguese city. The Portuguese moved quickly to the east, founding settlements in Malaysia (Malacca), Indonesia (Sumatra, Ternate, and Timor, among others), and China (Macau) well before the end of the sixteenth century.

In contrast to the Portuguese, after 1389 the Castilians were committed politically and commercially to two fronts: the Mediterranean and southwards on the one hand, and the Atlantic coast from the Bay of Biscay (in conjunction with the Basques) to Flanders and northwards on the other. In the southern waters, the Castilians and the Portuguese were already old rivals; they put their energies into maritime expansion at around the same time and, as alluded to above, for roughly the same reasons. Castile had earlier taken the Canary Islands (1341–1344), and by the beginning of the fifteenth century was already beginning to use Seville as a depot for trading in slaves from the Canaries (MacKay 1977:131). MacKay states:

Throughout the fifteenth century, the disputes over colonial possession affected all the diplomatic negotiations between the two powers and even spilled over into clashes in the general Council of the Church which sat intermittently at Basle [in Switzerland] from 1431 to 1449.

As the clashes between the two Iberian powers continued, Portuguese dip-
lomacy at the papal court led to the highly important papal bull *Romanus
Pontifex* in 1455, guaranteeing Portugal the Guinean coast and islands south
of Cape Bojador. Another papal bull in 1481 granted the Canaries to the
Castilians. When in 1493 Columbus returned triumphantly from his famous
voyage to the New World, the Catholic kings of Castile took advantage of
their influence with the new pope Alexander VI to have several new papal
bulls issued, granting Castile all territory west of the Cape Verde Islands.
King João of Portugal, however, promptly pointed out that no Castilian ship
could leave port with safe passage west because it would have to travel
through Portuguese waters. João thus forced the Treaty of Tordesillas in 1494,
whereby the Portuguese laid claim to all territory east of a line that was drawn
370 leagues west of the Cape Verde Islands. This allotted most of what would
later become Brazil to Portugal, and – together with a second treaty – it gave
to Castile what would be the Philippines (Willis 1993:24–26).

This global rush to empire on the part of the two Iberian powers set the
stage for the introduction of Spanish and Portuguese into Africa, Asia, and the
Americas. This book will examine some of the results of the introduction of
Spanish and Portuguese to these continents. One basic part of this linguistic
expansion involves the naturalistic learning of Spanish and Portuguese by
the colonized people. It is reasonable, then, that we begin our discussion of
contact-induced varieties of Spanish and Portuguese by examining immigrant
speech. In the next chapter, I look at some key aspects of Portuguese- and
Spanish-based creoles and how they relate to immigrant speech.

# 3    Portuguese- and Spanish-lexified creole languages

## 3.1    Introduction

Portugal's linguistic legacy in the world was essentially established by 1550, about 135 years after Portugal began its maritime expansion to Africa, Asia, and the Americas. Varieties of Portuguese or derived from Portuguese are not only spoken as official languages in a number of nations (Portugal, Brazil, Cape Verde, Angola, Mozambique), but also found in numerous communities from West Africa to India, to Malaysia, and Macau. Rather than attempting to survey all the Portuguese- and Spanish-lexified creole languages, I have chosen to examine two phenomena in this chapter: affixal tense–aspect markers (TMAs) and grammatical/semantic relation markers (G/SRMs). These two groups of markers were chosen in order to illustrate two fundamentally different outcomes in contact-induced language change, as well as to examine the extent to which universal processes were involved in the formation of these creoles.

To be able to talk about the emergence of the tense–aspect markers in the creole languages under consideration, I give in section 3.2 a brief overview of the external ecology of fifteenth- and sixteenth-century Portugal, the socio-historical background which led to the formation of restructured varieties of Portuguese that constituted one of the bases of pidgin Portuguese. In section 3.3, I focus on the presence of affixal tense–aspect markers, the presence of which in some of the creoles is most revealingly understood, I argue, within the backdrop of the demographic make-up of Portugal during that time. In section 3.4, I examine the anomalies in the case-marking systems of Portuguese- and Spanish-based creoles: as noted by Croft (1991) – who shows that natural languages avoid certain syncretisms – there are violations of a fairly strong typological tendency. For example, languages avoid marking identically the instrumental and benefactive relations, because in the causal chain of an event an instrument relation is antecedent to the event denoted by the verb of an utterance, whereas the benefactive relation is subsequent to the event. Croft accounts for this with the Causal Order Hypothesis (COH). We find no violations of the COH in the African creoles examined but various Asian creoles exhibit distinct violations of the COH. I show that these can be traced back to the violations in the substrate languages of the creoles.

## 3.2    External ecology of fifteenth- to sixteenth-century Portugal and Portuguese L2 varieties

Ramos Tinhorão (1997:45, 437 n. 90) notes that throughout medieval times slavery was known and used by the Portuguese not only in war, but also in commerce. He reports that from the middle of the fourteenth century there were slave-selling establishments in the Rua Nova of Lisbon where captured Moors and other Africans (some of whom were even brought from Seville, the entrepôt for Castile) were bought and sold.[1]

The first four slaves known to have been taken from sub-Saharan Africa were brought to Portugal in 1444 by Dinis Dias from his voyage to the Senegalese coast and the Cape Verde Islands. Such slaves became invaluable to Henry the Navigator, who used them as interpreters on voyages to Africa as well as to gather reconnaissance on places in Africa (Ramos Tinhorão 1997:47). From around the middle of the fifteenth century until 1505, as many as 150,000 sub-Saharan Africans were enslaved and taken to Portugal. The details regarding these slaves are shown in Table 3.1. Some of these slaves were taught Portuguese, educated, and instructed in Catholicism for use in the king's court. And through the ties cultivated in these positions some of the slaves were able to procure royal protection by the end of the fifteenth century (ibid.:93). However, the vast majority of African slaves were set to work in agriculture in the rural areas or in menial jobs in urban Portugal.

The reason for such an influx of African slaves in rural Portugal was twofold. First, the Portuguese population had not yet recovered from the bubonic plague (1348–1350) and various other epidemics that followed in the second half of the fourteenth and first half of the fifteenth centuries. This series of diseases decimated the population and weakened the resistance to disease of various generations. From north to south, there were during this time innumerable reports of a lack of able-bodied people (de Oliveira Marques 1998:100–101). The social ramifications of this crisis were deep, with the urban areas being affected most. In Lisbon itself, this was evident in the social upheavals that took place in 1371, in the revolution of 1383–1385, and in the rebellions of 1438–1441 and 1449. This social unease was partly due to the migration of many rural people, who thought to better their lot in

---

[1] He also mentions the record of a nun from the Chelas convent who bought a female Moor as a slave in 1368. Thus, the church also participated in the slave trade from early on.

Table 3.1. *Number of slaves brought to Portugal from sub-Saharan Africa (1441–1505)*

| Interval | Description | Number |
|---|---|---|
| 1441 to 1448 | From the predatory period in the region of Cabo Branco up until the establishment of Arguim | 1,000 to 2,000 |
| 1448 to 1450 | From the beginning of the use of slaves to buy back prisoners, in Arguim, to the issuing of licences to particular individuals for buying prisoners | 1,500 to 2,000 |
| 1450 to 1505 | From the period of issuing licences for buying prisoners, in Arguim, to the establishment of the monopoly of slave trade, extending the traffic of slaves to the interior territories (approximately 700 to 800 individuals annually) | 38,500 to 44,000 |
| 1450 to 1460 | Initial period of trade in the Senegal region, with an average of 400 to 500 individuals annually | 4,000 to 5,000 |
| 1460 to 1470 | Period of full operation of ransoming slaves for prisoners in the south of Senegal, with twice the volume annually, that is, 800 to 1,000 individuals per year | 8,000 to 10,000 |
| 1470 to 1475 | Period of Fernão Gomes' contract, with an average increase up to 1,000 to 1,200 individuals per year | 10,000 to 12,000 |
| 1475 to 1495 | Period of the heaviest slave trafficking along the whole coast, calculated by Duarte Pacheco to be 3,500 individuals per year (excluding the exportation of slaves by Arguim, which is calculated separately) | 54,000 to 56,000 |
| 1495 to 1505 | Period of the decline of slave trafficking after the death of Don João II (the yearly average was estimated at 2,500 individuals, excluding the exportation of slaves by Arguim, which is calculated separately) | 19,000 to 20,000 |
| | Total | 136,000 to 151,000 |

*Note:* Three of the calculations in Ramos Tinhorão's table are not clear. During the six-year period from 1470 to 1475, approximately 1,000 to 1,200 individuals per year were taken to Portugal, but the totals are not 6,000 to 7,200, but significantly higher, at 10,000 to 12,000. During the 21-year period of 1475 to 1495, 3,500 slaves per year were calculated, which would yield 73,500, but the actual range given is much lower, at 54,000–56,000. Similarly, during the eleven-year period of 1495–1505, a total of 19,000–20,000 individuals were calculated to have been taken to Portugal, based on the assumption of approximately 2,500 individuals yearly. However, such an annual amount would give a total of 27,500 individuals over this period of time. If the adjustment is made according to these corrections, the maximum number of Africans taken to Portugal between 1441 and 1505 is 165,200 instead of 151,000.
*Source:* Ramos Tinhorão 1997:86.

life by moving to the cities in search of jobs. The result of this migration was, of course, that rural areas were left without sufficient labour.

Second, the Portuguese maritime expansion, from 1417 onwards, became a new and highly attractive source of labour for the people migrating to the cities. Recently arrived migrants to Lisbon took advantage of the increasing demand for sailors and word spread to rural Portugal, from where the exploits of the crown prompted more rural inhabitants to migrate to the urban areas in search of new opportunities. This only exacerbated an already precarious situation in the rural areas and resulted in the partial abandonment of agricultural work (de Oliveira Marques 1998:102).

The lack of a rural and urban work force and the general decline in the population in Portugal due to the bubonic plague took its toll on society in several ways. The abandonment of lands led to low cereal production. The subsequent fear of many land-owners for their lives because of the plague led them to donate their property to the church in the hope of salvation, and, as mentioned, the migrations to the cities from the countryside led to social upheavals.

Over time, the abandonment of the rural areas and the flood of people flocking to urban areas led to the introduction of African slaves into rural, as well as urban, Portugal in order to meet the demand for labour. Indeed, Portugal was the first kingdom to incorporate slaves into its own domestic economy. In order to control the African slave trade during this time, King Alphonse V made it obligatory that the slaves be brought to Portugal before being sold on, in many cases, to the Americas or Asia. Thus, Lisbon became an entrepôt for African slaves, who were bought to be used in urban as well as in rural areas. Between 1450 and 1505, as many as 150,000+ African slaves were introduced into the work force. By the first part of the sixteenth century, black Africans came to make up more than 10 per cent of the rural population in Portugal south of the Douro (Ramos Tinhorão 1997:101). Moreover, by around 1533–1538, Lisbon had a population of around 100,000 inhabitants, Africans making up around 15 per cent (15,350) of that total (ibid.:113).

With the influx of so many African slaves into the domestic Portuguese work force, one wonders what the structure of the Portuguese spoken by the Africans looked like. I assume that the vast majority of these slaves learned Portuguese naturalistically. Thus, the speech of the first generation of Africans would be the fifteenth- to sixteenth-century equivalent of immigrant varieties of Spanish or Portuguese spoken today in Spanish- and Portuguese-speaking countries (see chapter 6). In the plays of the fifteenth (e.g., Enrique da Mota) and sixteenth centuries (e.g., Gil Vicente), we find approximations of African speech in the mouths of some of the characters of their plays. It is not unreasonable to assume that these approximations, variously called *guinéu* 'Guineanese', *lingua de guiné* 'language of Guinea', and *lingua de negro/preto* 'negro/black language', would reflect typically occurring traits in the speech of the Africans during that period. Examples (3.1)–(3.9) represent what could reasonably be considered portrayals of African speech that reflect naturalistically acquired L2 Portuguese. That is, given the demographic make-up of Lisbon and southern Portugal in the late fifteenth and early sixteenth centuries, it is very likely that these portrayals of *fala de guiné* reflect L2 varieties of Africans of the period and form part of the basis for a Portuguese-based pidgin developed by the Portuguese with indigenous people during their colonization of Africa and Asia. The text in (3.1)–(3.3) is taken from *A lamentação do clérigo* 'the lamentation of the priest', a poetic farce written in the last quarter of the fifteenth century by Enrique da Mota, in which a priest laments a cask of wine that had fallen on the ground and spilt. In the poem, the voice of a slave woman speaks the lines below (taken from Tarracha Ferreira 1994:282–283).

(3.1)   a mym nunca sar    ruim.
        to me  never  be      bad
        'I'm not [or never] bad.'

(3.2)   Vós   logo          todos chamar.
        you   right.away    all    call
        'You call everyone right away.'

(3.3a)  Aqui estar juiz  no    fora.
        here  be   judge in-the outside
        'The judge is outside here.'

(3.3b)  a mim logo          vai    'té   lá.
        to me right.away    goes   until there
        'I'm going to go there.'

(3.3c)  Mim também falar      mourinho.
        me   also    speak    moorish
        'I also speak Moorish.'

(3.3d)  mim não medo no toucinho.
        me   no  fear in lard
        'I have no fear of lard.'

Naro (1978) compiled numerous examples from plays which were spoken by black slaves. I cite six of his examples (ibid.:329–332), given in (3.4)–(3.9).

(3.4)   logo          a   mi   bae      trazee.
        right.away    to  me   go-3sG   bring
        'I'll go bring it right away.'

(3.5)   Quando já     paga a   rinheiro, deytá a mi  fero   na pé.
        when   already pay  the money    put  to me iron   on foot
        'When he paid the money, he put irons on my feet.'

(3.6)  bosso   barba   já          cajaro.
       your    beard   already     white
       'Your beard {has turned/is already} white.'

(3.7)  Ya              mim    disee   isso    ja.
       already         me     say     this    already
       'I already said that.'

(3.8)  Porque tu       nam    burguntando?
       why    you      NEG    asking
       'Why aren't you asking?'

(3.9)  . . . e    levare    elle   na      bico.
       and        carry     he     PREP    beak
       '. . . and carry it off on the sly.'

It is revealing that the *fala de guiné* portrayed in these examples shares several key traits with bozal Spanish, discussed in chapter 4, Chinese Coolie Spanish, in chapter 5, and Chinese Immigrant Spanish, in chapter 6. To illustrate certain similarities, the main tense–aspect-related traits common to both Chinese Immigrant Spanish and *fala de guiné* are:

- the use of adverbials such as *logo* 'right away' and *já* 'already' ((3.2), (3.3b), (3.4), (3.5), (3.6)) for tense/time markers with no corresponding verbal inflection;
- use of the gerund form, such as *burguntando* (< Ptg. *perguntando*) in (3.8), for dynamic, [+durative] predicates (in this case an accomplishment);
- use of 3SG-PRES or infinitive forms as default forms (*vai* or *bae* (< Ptg. *vai* 's/he goes') for *vou* 'I go', *sar* (< Ptg. *ser* 'be') for *sou* 'I am', *chamar* 'call' for *chamades* 'you.PL call', *estar* 'be (located)' for *está* 's/he is (located)', *paga* 'pays' for *pagou* 's/he paid', *deytá* 'put-INF' for *deytou* 's/he put', *disee* (< Ptg. *dizer* 'say-INF') for *disse* 's/he said'.

More general traits shared by such varieties are lack of copula (3.8) and the use of an all-purpose preposition. Based on findings by Klein and Perdue (1992) regarding what they call the 'basic variety' of immigrant speech, I suggest that the similarities between the traits of Portuguese attributed to the Africans in Portugal in the fifteenth and sixteenth centuries and the afore-mentioned varieties of immigrant Spanish are not coincidental. Rather, in large part they are the consequence of naturalistic L2 acquisition. Such varieties of Portuguese also emerged in interactions between the Portuguese sailors and African natives along the African coast, and these varieties would have similar features as well.

It is also quite probable that the Portuguese sailors, in their interactions with Africans in Portugal and Africa, developed restructured varieties of Portuguese which they used on their voyages. That is, drawing on the lin-guistic feature pool in these contact situations, the Portuguese sailors and

Africans constructed a system of communication based primarily on the Portuguese lexicon. The most commonly used lexical and structural features in the feature pool found their way into the emerging linguistic systems in each contact situation. It is out of these contact situations that I assume pidgin Portuguese likely developed, which was one of the sources (along with L2 varieties of Portuguese and substrate languages) for the Portuguese-based creoles, especially those creoles that formed after pidgin Portuguese was developed. If this is true, then the Portuguese creoles should display features found both in Immigrant Spanish and L2 African Portuguese. For example, we would expect to find stative verbs to be based on the most commonly used verb forms for stative predicates (see Tables 1.4 and 1.5). Revealingly, stative verbs in the Portuguese- and Spanish-based creoles are based on the 3sG present-tense form. More generally, Bybee and Pardo (1981) in a study on Spanish verbal forms show that the 3sG present verb form is one of the most frequently used forms not only for stative, but also for some non-stative verbs. It is not surprising, then, that the 3sG present forms of stative verbs are found in the creole languages just mentioned (see also Holm 1989:268).

Let us now turn to examine two phenomena of Portuguese- and Spanish-based creoles: affixal tense–aspect markers and grammatical/oblique semantic relation markers. While the first reveals that L2 varieties played a crucial role in the formation of creoles, an examination of the grammatical/semantic relation markers suggests that during and subsequent to the formation of the creoles it was also shaped by substrate structures and patterns.

## 3.3     Affixal tense–aspect markers in Portuguese- and Spanish-based creoles

Holm (1989:268) notes that all Portuguese-based creoles have reflexes of Portuguese *vai* 'goes'. Moreover, all share the all-purpose preposition *na*, attested in the examples (3.5) and (3.9) above. Given that the presence of these two features in all the varieties in question could not be entirely due only to Portuguese Foreigner Talk or to L2 African Portuguese, it constitutes an argument for the prior existence of a pidgin Portuguese variety, spoken from the west coast of Africa to as far east as Macau and Hong Kong. I argue that the reflexes of *vai* and *na* came about due to a number of factors. First, the default motion verb *vai* 'go' and location preposition *na* were frequently used. That is, in terms of frequency, they were well represented in feature pools of contact situations involving Portuguese and varieties of African or Asian languages. Second, they were easy to perceive and produce because of their CV(G) structure. Third, although African naturalistic learners of Portuguese may have acquired these items to denote, respectively, 'go' and various semantic roles (location, direction, etc.), the Portuguese interlocutors must have reinforced this by accommodating the speech of the Africans. I suggest that it is through this 'negotiation', as well as the other, afore-mentioned factors that these two forms became part of pidgin Portuguese (unstable as well as stable varieties) and subsequently part of all the creole languages derived from it (see Thomason and Kaufman 1988:172–181 and Thomason 2001:142–146).

With specific regard to Asian–Portuguese creoles, they had at one point or still have reflexes of the Portuguese *logo* 'right away' and *já* 'already' as tense–aspect markers.[2] Again, the presence of these items in the Asian creoles follows from the process of negotiation. That is, not only would the Portu-guese (and other Portuguese speakers in the colonization process) have isolated these markers in their pidgin as those for temporal reference, but the Asian naturalistic learners acquiring some form of Portuguese would also have targeted these frequently used temporal reference markers as a way of marking tense on the verb.[3]

I now turn to the discussion of affixal tense–aspect markers in the creoles in question. These elements are of particular interest because creole languages are known to reduce morphological material in the processes of pidginization and creolization. The linguistic factors involved in the retention or loss of morphology in these processes are whether or not there was a typological similarity in the content and structural features of the languages involved in the contact situations, and to what extent the competing features in the feature pool were marked relative to one another. As used here, the term *markedness* refers to the degree of representation (in terms of frequency of occurrence) a given lexical (including function words) or structural feature has within the feature pool of a given contact situation. In general, CV structure is con-sidered to be highly unmarked and inflectional infixation highly marked. However, the selection of (i.e. preference for) the (more common) infix over prefix/suffix could happen if two languages in contact shared the feature of inflectional infixation for a particular function. In this case, inflectional infixation would be considered unmarked, and it would not be surprising for a contact language emerging from such a situation to display this feature.

The key non-linguistic factors affecting pidginization and creolization in the contact situations in question are: the number of languages in a contact

---

[2] The exception is Daman Creole Portuguese, which marks the future with the particle *ad* (< Ptg. *ha de* 'ought', 'must') and does not use *ja* as a marker of the past. I consider this to be due to the constant influence of Portuguese in Daman, which still has a presence there in the church and in Portuguese cultural groups. Many Damanenses maintain their contact with Portugal; some have family members living there.

[3] The Spanish analogues *luego* and *ya* appear often in Immigrant Spanish. See chapter 6 for discussion of this.

situation and the number of speakers of each language (heterogeneity), the dominance relations among the speakers of different language groups, and finally the extent of access to the target-language features by the target-language learners.

In the Portuguese- and Spanish-based creoles under consideration, we find that the presence of affixal features in their respective tense–aspect systems depends on the linguistic and extra-linguistic factors just mentioned. Specifically, the more typologically similar the languages were in the contact situations involving Portuguese in Africa and Asia, the more likely it was for typologically similar features to become part of the subsequent creole language. As for markedness of features, the more marked a given feature was, the less likely it was for it to become part of the respective creoles *unless* the feature was shared by the languages in contact. By contrast, the more unmarked the features were in these contact situations, the more likely they were to become part of the respective creoles, especially if they were shared by the languages in contact (see Thomason and Kaufman 1988:72–74 and Thomason 2001:63–66). As for the extra-linguistic features, the more heterogeneous the contact situation was, the lower the likelihood was of having shared features among languages and the greater was the likelihood for unmarked features to become part of the respective creoles. For my purposes here I define *heterogeneity* in terms of the number of languages in the contact situation. That is, the more languages involved in a given contact situation, the more heterogeneous the situation is. Thus, a contact situation with two languages is relatively less heterogeneous (or more homogeneous) than one with four contact languages (see Clements 1992a).

In each individual contact situation, the nature of the dominance relation dictated the likelihood of there being a target language or not. In all the cases in question here, we can safely say that at least the Portuguese lexicon was a target of those communicating with the Portuguese in Africa and Asia. That is, in all these creoles, we have a high percentage of Portuguese lexicon, with the exception of Philippine Creole Spanish, in which the Portuguese was subsequently re-lexified by Spanish (Whinnom 1956). Lastly, assuming a target language, the factor of accessibility is important. That is, it is important to know whether those who targeted the language had greater or lesser access to it. Here I have quantified this in terms of the length of the Portuguese presence in each of the contact situations. For example, Cape Verdean, which has been in contact with Portuguese from its inception up to the present, has had greater access to Portuguese than Angolar, whose contact with Portuguese ended around 1520.

Taking these factors into consideration, I list in Table 3.2 the affixes present in the different creoles and their respective uses, and in Table 3.3 the approximations of the relative heterogeneity (left-hand column) and presence

Table 3.2. *Suffixes in the Portuguese-based creoles*

| | Deverbal -du/-ru | Pluperf/Past (stative verbs) -ba | Passive -du/-ru | Anterior Passive -da (< -duba) | Perfect -du/-ru | Simple Past -o | Gerund -n(do) | Plural -s |
|---|---|---|---|---|---|---|---|---|
| KV | + | + | + | + | – | – | – | – |
| KR | + | + | + | – | – | – | – | – |
| PR | + | – | + | – | + (Aux + V-du) | – | – | – |
| AN | + | – | – | – | – | – | – | – |
| ST | + | – | – | – | – | – | – | – |
| FA | + | – | – | – | – | – | – | – |
| KO | + | – | + | – | + | + | + | – |
| DN | + | – | + | – | + | + | + | – |
| BP | + | – | – | – | (+) | – | – | + |
| PK | + | – | – | – | – | – | – | + |
| PS | + | – | – | – | – | – | – | (+) |
| PP | – | – | – | – | – | – | + (recent) | – |
| PL | – | + | – | – | – | – | + | – |

*Sources and notes:* KV=Kabuverdianu (Quint 2000), KR=Kriyol (Kihm 1994), PR=Principense (Günther 1973), AN=Angolar (Maurer 1995 and Lorenzino 1998), ST=Sãotomense (Ferraz 1979), FA=Fa d'Ambu (Post 1995), KO=Korlai (Clements 1996), DN = Daman (Clements and Koontz-Garboden 2002), BP=Batticaloa (Smith 1977), PK = Papia Kristang (Baxter 1988), PS = Philippine Creole Spanish (Forman 1972), PP=Papiamentu (Maurer 1998), PL = Palenquero (Schwegler 1998).

of Portuguese (centre column) for the different creole languages. I suggest that there is a correlation between the degree of heterogeneity and the presence of Portuguese within a contact situation and the number of affixes retained in the corresponding creole. That is, the more homogeneous and the more constant the Portuguese presence (in relative terms) was in a given contact situation, the greater the number of affixes and affix functions found in the respective creoles. The two-language contact situations in Korlai and Daman (where a strong Portuguese presence was constant at least up to 1740 and 1961 respectively) have the highest rate of morphology retention.

Those situations with less than constant Portuguese presence and/or a greater heterogeneity have retained fewer affixes and/or fewer functions per affix. The main contact languages of the upper Guinea creoles (Kabuverdianu and Kriyol) were Mandinka and Wolof. However, I assume that there were several languages involved in their respective contact situations because of the many spoken in the area. The prediction here is that Kabuverdianu would possess more affixes than Kriyol, and this turns out to be the case, which I attribute to the greater presence of Portuguese in the case of Kabuverdianu (see Table 3.3). For their part, the Gulf of Guinea creoles (Principense, Sãotomense, Fa d'Ambu, and Angolar) had substantially less constant contact with Portuguese and they also involved contact situations with several languages, though the main ones were Kikongo and Kimbundu. With the exception of Principense which retains the suffix -du with three functions, all Gulf of Guinea creoles in question have only one suffix (also -du) with one function.

Papia Kristang emerged in a largely three-language contact situation, namely Hokkien Chinese, Malay (including Malay, Bazaar Malay, and Baba Malay), and Portuguese. It is important to note that Bazaar Malay, a restructured form of Malay, was the lingua franca used between the Hokkien and Malay speakers and that in the 1500s it became nativized, receiving the name Baba Malay. Bazaar Malay and Baba Malay are different from Vehicular Malay, known more recently, which is a restructured variety of Malay that has been used for centuries in Indonesia (personal communication, Scott Paauw, 15 January 2004). Comparing it to the other Asian creoles such as Korlai and Daman, it should possess fewer affixes due to the greater heterogeneity of the contact situation, and this is in fact true.

Philippine Creole Spanish, originally a Portuguese-based creole formed and spoken in Ternate, Indonesia, as early as the mid-1500s (Whinnom 1956), had as its original contact languages Vehicular Malay/Malay and Portuguese. Around 1665, a community of Portuguese creole speakers from Ternate was relocated by the Spanish to the Philippines, where the creole was re-lexified through intermarriage (Holm 1989:318). This situation is relatively

Table 3.3. *Number of suffixes relative to the homogeneity of the contact situation and the strength and duration of Portuguese presence*

| | Contact situation | Presence of Portuguese (Spanish) | Number of suffixes (with number of functions in square brackets) |
|---|---|---|---|
| DN | 2 langs. | Relatively constant up to 1961; presence has remained until today | 3 (-du [3], -o, -n(do)) |
| KO | 2 langs. | Relatively constant up to 1740; strongly diminished presence (parish priest) up to 1960s | 3 (-du [3], -o, -n(do)) |
| BP | 2 langs. | Relatively constant up to 1658 | 2 (-du [2], -s) |
| PS | 2=> 3 langs. | Constant up to around 1580, relatively constant Spanish presence, starting in 1665 | 2 (-du [1], -s) |
| PK | 3 langs. | Relatively constant up to 1640 | 2 (-du [1], -s) |
| KV | 5+ langs. (Mandinka and Fula the most widely spoken) | Relatively constant up to the present | 2 (-du [3], -ba [2]) |
| KR | 5+ langs. (Mandinka and Fula the most widely spoken) | Relatively constant but weaker than in KV | 2 (-du [2], -ba [1]) |
| ST | 5+ langs. (Kikongo and Kimbundu the most predominant) | Relatively less constant | 1 (-du [1]) |
| PR | 5+ langs. | Relatively less constant | 1 (-du [3]) |
| FA | 5+ langs. | Relatively less constant, with influence from Spanish from 1885 | 1 (-du [1]) |
| PP | 5+ langs. | Relatively less constant, heterogeneous Portuguese and Spanish influence | 1 (-ndo [1]) (recent development, due to Spanish influence) |
| PL | 5+ langs. | Relatively less constant | 2 (-ba [1], -ndo [1]) |
| AN | 5+ langs. (Kikongo and Kimbundu the most predominant) | Least constant, ended in 1520 | 1 suffix (-ru (< -du) [1]) |

*Note:* See Table 3.2 for abbreviations.
*Source:* See Clements and Mahboob 2000, and the references therein.

comparable to that of Papia Kristang. Revealingly, Philippine Creole Spanish has the same number of affixes as Papia Kristang, with the same number of functions.

The history of Papiamentu and Palenquero is more complex, as these creoles are thought to be largely exogenous; that is, they formed in an area in which the Africans who initially created them had been uprooted from their respective homelands and transported to the New World. The formative period of Papiamentu, now a largely Spanish-based creole spoken on the islands of Curaçao, Bonaire, and Aruba off the northern coast of Venezuela, was between 1650 and 1700, according to Bartens (1995:247). The first slaves arrived in Curaçao around 1650 from Africa. About ten years later, there was an influx of African slaves arriving from the north of Brazil, brought there by Sephardic plantation-owners, who themselves were speakers of Judeo-Portuguese and/or Judeo-Spanish, as well as pidgin Portuguese. From 1634, there was also a substantial Dutch presence, the bona fide colonial language of Curaçao still today, although only 9 per cent of the population speak Dutch, while 80 per cent speak Papiamentu. The Africans were arguably from many linguistic backgrounds, and belonging to at least two waves initially: those brought from Brazil and those transported to Curaçao directly from Africa. Thus, the European side, then – Portuguese, Judeo-Portuguese/Spanish, Dutch, and later Spanish – played a role, while from the African side we can only assume that numerous languages were represented. Given the complex history of Papiamentu, we would expect it to possess no affixes. Indeed, the one affix it does have is, according to Philippe Maurer (personal communication, 26 June 2003), a recent development.

Similarly, Palenquero, another Portuguese-based creole, formed in the early 1600s when around thirty African slaves escaped from Cartagena, Colombia, fled into the interior of the country, and there built El Palenque, a fortified village, which then became a refuge for fugitive slaves and a base from which to launch raids on Europeans (Holm 1989:310). The documentary evidence (e.g., certain magic rituals) suggests that the slaves who founded what is now the village of El Palenque de San Basilio were from Kikongo- and Kimbundu-speaking areas, which has led some researchers to posit a connection between Palenquero on the one hand and Sãotomense and Fa d'Ambu on the other (see Bartens 1995:268–269). Given that slaves arrived there from various language groups, I assume that on the African side there were numerous languages in the contact situation. On the European side, the initial influence seems to have been pidgin Portuguese and thereafter Spanish. Although the villagers isolated themselves strongly from the outside world for purposes of their own survival, if it had connections to Sãotomense or Fa d'Ambu, we would expect it to rank low on affix retention. However, it has two affixes, each with one function. Thus, the prediction based on length of contact with the lexifier language and heterogeneity of the contact situation does not hold with regard to Palenquero. Given that Armin Schwegler (personal communication, 16 April 2005) reports that *-ndo* is an integral part of the grammar of Palenquero and used by its oldest speakers, its presence cannot be attributed to the increased influence of Spanish in the twentieth century. Note that Palenquero (with *-du*) shares no suffixes with Sãotomense and Fa d'Ambu (with *-ba* and *-ndo*), but it does share *-ba* with Kabuverdianu and Kriyol. Thus, it could be that Palenquero is more closely related to the upper Guinea creoles and that *-ndo* became part of Palenquero after El Palenque had existed for a while. Be that as it may, the contact situation of Palenquero is complex and due to this cannot be easily accommodated into the analysis being presented here.

Thus, with the exception of Palenquero, the general prediction based on length of contact with the lexifier language and heterogeneity of the contact situation seems to hold: the longer the contact with the lexifier language and the more homogeneous the contact situation (i.e., the fewer languages involved in it), the greater the likelihood of affixes being incorporated into the creole languages. But why were the affixes maintained at all in these creoles? The answer seems to be that – given that all the major languages in the contact situations just alluded to have suffixes – the more homogeneous the contact situation and the stronger the presence of the target language, the more likely it is for suffixal morphology to become part of the grammar of an emerging creole language.

## 3.4    Case marking

In this section, I limit my discussion to oblique case marking,[4] with commentary on direct and indirect object case marking when relevant. Croft's (1991) research into how oblique relations are coded across languages led him to formulate the Causal Order Hypothesis. At the core of the COH is the distinction between antecedent and subsequent semantic roles (ibid.:185). As an illustration, Croft gives the two examples shown in (3.10).

(3.10a)    Sam baked a cake for Jan.

       Sam      cake     Jan

       •  ⟶  •  ⟶  •

       SUBJ    OBJ    OBL

       ###  *bake*  ###

---

[4] The analysis in this section is based largely on Koontz-Garboden and Clements 2002a and 2002b.

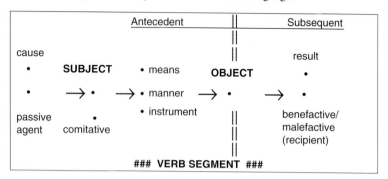

Figure 3.1. Distribution of thematic roles in the causal chain (from Croft 1991:185).

(3.10b)   Sam whipped the egg with a fork.
          Sam      fork      egg
           •  ⟶  •  ⟶   •
          SUBJ     OBL      OBJ
          ###      whip     ###

In (3.10a), the baking event involves the cake. The benefactive *for Jan* is, however, subsequent to the baking of the cake. By contrast, the whipping event in (3.10b) logically entails the use of the instrument, the fork, in order that the event can be carried out. Whereas in (3.10a) the benefactive can be said to follow the baking event, the picking up of the fork to use it in the whipping event in (3.10b) precedes the whipping event itself. Thus, a benefactive is subsequent to the event, whereas an instrumental is antecedent to the event. In Figure 3.1, I reproduce Croft's view of the distribution of thematic roles in the causal chain.

A prediction emerges from the distinction of oblique relations into antecedent and subsequent roles: in the coding of oblique relations, if there are syncretisms in the coding of these roles, they will be found within the group of antecedent roles or within the group of subsequent roles, but not across the groups. That is, one would not expect to find in the world's languages the same word, clitic, or affix coding an instrumental (antecedent role) and a benefactive (subsequent role). However, it would be predicted that there would be syncretisms *within* each of the two groups. Thus, one would expect to find examples of the same word, clitic, or affix coding instrumental and comitative relations, or result and benefactive relations.

In a survey of forty languages, Croft found only two syncretisms across antecedent and subsequent roles. By contrast, he found thirty-nine syncretisms within the antecedent role group, thirty within the subsequent role group, and five that showed no directionality because the languages in question only have one adposition (Croft 1991:188). In the Portuguese- and Spanish-based creoles, then, we expect the antecedent–subsequent distinction to be respected with regard to oblique case marking, especially since the creoles tend to contain many unmarked features. In this chapter, I examine the antecedent roles cause, instrumental, and comitative, and the subsequent roles benefactive and dative/recipient.

A summary of the data is given in Table 3.4. There are several points that merit comment. First, there is a small set of lexical items used to encode many different roles in most of the creoles, in particular items like *de* (< Ptg. *de* 'of, from'), *ku* (< Ptg. *com* 'with'), *pa* (< Ptg. *para* 'for'), and *na* (< Ptg. *na* 'in-the.FEM'). Second, the lexical item *ku/kon* is broadly used in many of the Asian creoles, but less so in the African creoles. In almost all of the creoles, *ku/kon* marks the antecedent roles instrumental and comitative. In some of the Asian creoles, however, it also marks the subsequent roles dative/recipient and benefactive, in violation of Croft's COH. In order to appreciate more clearly the distribution of the markers, I divide the data in Table 3.4 into African–Portuguese creole markers (Table 3.5) and Asian–Portuguese creole markers (Table 3.6).

While all syncretisms in the African creoles are found within the group of antecedent relation markers (i.e., *ku*, marked in grey), several of the Asian creoles (i.e., Korlai, Papia Kristang, and Philippine Creole Spanish) display syncretisms across the antecedent–subsequent divide, marking the antecedent roles instrumental/comitative as well as the subsequent roles dative/recipient, a clear violation of the COH. The question is: why do only the Asian creoles violate the COH, especially given that the COH appears likely to be a universal tendency? As Koontz-Garboden and Clements (2002a) note, the violation cannot be traced back to European Portuguese or to the substrate languages of some of the creoles (e.g., Korlai and Daman). It seems, however, that these syncretisms are found in various Asian languages in areas where the Asian creoles formed. I will discuss the relevant case marking features in Malayalam, Vehicular Malay, and the Philippine languages, the key languages in the formation of Indo-Portuguese, Malay Creole Portuguese, and Philippine Creole Spanish, respectively.

In the final stage of Portugal's exploration and settlement of the West African coast (see Chaunu 1979:111–112), Vasco da Gama rounded the Cape of Good Hope and found his way up the eastern coast of Africa to Mombasa (now in Kenya). With the help of Ahmed-ben-Madjid, an Arab purported to be the best navigator of India in the fifteenth century, Vasco da Gama travelled across the Arabian Sea to the tip of the Indian subcontinent, landing in Cochin in 1498 (Serrão 1978:100; de Oliveira Marques 1998:207).

Initially, the Portuguese had no desire to build settlements in India, but rather intended to establish a trade in spices. As things developed, they realized that an ancient trade network flourished in the area and that in order

Table 3.4. *Oblique case markers in Portuguese- and Spanish-based creoles*

| | Acc | Dat | Ben | Gen | Loc | Goal | Source | Cause | Instr | Comit |
|---|---|---|---|---|---|---|---|---|---|---|
| KV | Ø | Ø | pa | di, -l, jux* | na | Ø, pa | di | pur kauza de (acrol.) | ku | ku |
| KR | Ø | Ø | pa | di | Ø, na | Ø (?), pa, na | di, dedi | – | ku | ku |
| ST | Ø | Ø | da | di | ni | pe | – | punda, nda, da | ku (?) | ku |
| AN | Ø | Ø | ra | jux, ri | ni, pe | pe | fo | punda, nda, da | ku ~ ki | ku ~ ki |
| PR | Ø | Ø | da | jux, de | na | Ø, na | di | poké (+ sentence) | ki (ko) | ki, (ko) |
| DN | pə | pə | pə | də | nə | Ø, nə, pə | də | də, pur kawz də (acrol.?) | ko | junt |
| KO | ku, pV | ku, pV | ku, pV | -su | Ø, nə, də, ku | Ø, nə, də, bɛ, ku | -su, pasun | rhəpəd, -su | ku, -su, Ø | kosid |
| BP | -pə | -pə, -ntu | -pə | -su | -ntu -juntu | Ø, per, -ntu | – | -wi:də | -wɔ:ndə | -ju:ntu |
| PK | ku | ku | padi, pa, pe | di, sa | na | ku, na | di | káuzu di | ku | ku |
| PS | kon | kon | kon, para | de | na | na, para na, para | na, kon, de | na, porkawsa de(l) | kon | kon |

*Note:* See Table 3.2 for abbreviations.

Table 3.5. *Subsequent and antecedent roles in African Portuguese creoles*

| | Subsequent | | Antecedent | | |
|---|---|---|---|---|---|
| | Dat/Rec | Ben | Cause | Instr | Comit |
| KV | Ø | pa | pur kauza de (acrol.) | ku | ku |
| KR | Ø | pa | – | ku | ku |
| ST | Ø | da | punda, nda, da | ku (?) | ku |
| AN | Ø | ra | punda, nda, da | ku ~ ki | ku ~ ki |
| PR | Ø | da | poké (+ sent.) | ki (ko) | ki, (ko) |

*Note:* See Table 3.2 for abbreviations. The grey shading indicates syncretisms.

Table 3.6. *Subsequent and antecedent roles in Asian Portuguese creoles*

| | Subsequent | | Antecedent | | |
|---|---|---|---|---|---|
| | Dat/Rec | Ben | Cause | Instr | Comit |
| DN | pə | pə | də, pur kawz də (acrol.) | ko | junt |
| KO | ku, pV | ku, pV | rhəpəd, -su | ku, -su, Ø | kosid |
| BP | pə, -ntu | -pə | -wi:də | -wɔ:ndə | ju:ntu[a] |
| PK | ku | padi, pa, pe | káuzu di | ku | ku |
| PS | kon | kon, para | na, porkawsa de(l) | kon | kon |

*Note:* See Table 3.2 for abbreviations. The grey shading indicates syncretisms.
[a] Although this is not a syncretism from a synchronic standpoint Battiacaloa Creole Portuguese exhibited a syncretism involving the comitative antecedent role *ju:ntu* and the dative/goal subsequent role *-ntu* (<*juntu*). This may be due to Sri Lankan Tamil, but it needs to be studied further.

to control it they would have to follow a policy of aggressive strategy bent on destruction and ultimately the conquest of the 'enemy' (de Oliveira Marques 1998:213). By 1505, the Portuguese had built trading posts in Cochin and other port towns on the south-western coast. They quickly built settlements further north along the coast, completing one in Chaul in 1523 and in Diu around 1535. The town of Daman offered much more resistance, but surrendered in 1559 after years of the Portuguese destroying and ransacking the area (see Clements and Koontz-Garboden 2002). The Portuguese also travelled further east, establishing settlements in what today are Sri Lanka, Malaysia, Indonesia, and Macau.

For the Indo-Portuguese creoles, the situation in Cochin is relevant. Although today Cochin Creole Portuguese is nearly extinct, the town was the first place to be settled by the Portuguese and very probably the first place in which a Portuguese-based creole language formed in Asia.[5] Following official policy, the Portuguese soldiers were to attempt to marry local women, but as Boxer (1975:68) notes, many men, especially the younger ones, preferred to live with a harem of slave girls rather than marry. Of course, this miscegenation led to mixed offspring, which in turn led to the creation of a creole language. Here I assume that by that time Portuguese soldiers spoke to indigenous people, almost a century after Portugal had begun its colonial expansion, in pidginized Portuguese, Foreign Talk Portuguese, and whatever else worked (Clements 1992a, 1993b). It is well known that pidgin Portuguese was used not only by the Portuguese, but also by the Dutch and the English as well in their colonial expansion (Holm 1989:270–271; Clements 1996:ch. 1). With specific regard to the formation of a creole in Cochin, it would have been substantially influenced by the local language, Malayalam. This language, arguably, would have been instrumental in contributing to some of the lexical and structural features of Cochin Creole Portuguese, which then would conceivably find their way into other Indo-Portuguese creoles. Indeed, we find in all extant Indo-Portuguese creoles today lexical items that are from southern India. One such word is Cochin Creole Portuguese *apa* [apə] 'handbread made of rice flour'. This south Indian lexical item, found in Dravidian languages such as Malayalam and Tamil, is also present in the northern creoles of Korlai (Clements 1996:272), Bassein (Dalgado 1906:217), and Daman (Clements, in preparation). Thus, it is reasonable to assume Cochin Creole Portuguese or a Portuguese creole of that area was taken north to the Korlai and Daman areas, as well as eastwards. For example, the lexical item *apa* is also found in Macau Creole Portuguese, which Batalha (1988:47) attributes to Indo-Portuguese.

Clements (2000) argues for the existence of an Asian pidgin Portuguese that initially formed in Cochin among the soldiers and the indigenous people in that area. Subsequently, Portuguese soldiers, accompanied by natives who spoke pidgin Portuguese or a creole, would have populated the settlements in Goa, Chaul, Bassein, Daman, and Diu in the north. The evidence for a common Asian pidgin Portuguese is the existence in almost all Asian creoles of the question word for 'how' derived from Portuguese *qui laia* 'what manner' (> Daman *kilay*, Norteiro *qui lai*, Korlai *kilε*, Sri Lankan *kilaay*, Kristang *klai*, and Philippine Creole Spanish *kiláya*). The presence of the reflexes of *qui laia* reinforces the hypothesis that an Asian variety of pidgin Portuguese, and very possibly an early variety of Cochin Creole Portuguese was the basis for the Asian Creole Portuguese varieties spoken throughout

---

[5] In its formation, I assume that various varieties of Portuguese (unstable and stable pidgin Portuguese, Portuguese) and Malayalam would have been the bases on which Cochin Creole Portuguese was formed (see Clements 1992b, 1993a, 1993b).

Table 3.7. *Subsequent and antecedent roles in Malayalam*

| | subsequent | | antecedent | | |
|---|---|---|---|---|---|
| | Dat/Rec | Ben | Cause | Instr | Comit |
| Malayalam | -kkə, -ooTə | -kkə, -kkə vendi | -konDə | -konDə | -ooTə (LM), -yuTe kuuTe (SM), -yu mayi (SM) |

*Note:* The grey shading indicates syncretisms.
LM: literary Malayalam.
SM: spoken Malayalam.

India at the very least. It may be, then, that the origins of case marking in these Asian creoles could be found in this original Indo-Portuguese creole. I will present the case for the creoles in India, and afterwards consider it for other Asian creoles.

Given that we find Dravidian influence in the lexicon of the northern Indo-Portuguese as well as in those in Malaysia and Indonesia, etc., we might also expect to find some structural influence from Dravidian in the same creoles. The data suggest that this is also the case, though for the non-Indo-Portuguese creoles in Asia there are also alternative explanations.

I first examine the relevant type of case marking in Malayalam. In this Dravidian language, there are several within-group syncretisms, namely -*kkə* 'dative/recipient, benefactive' and -*konDə* 'Cause, Instrument'. The cross-group syncretism, i.e., the violation to the COH, is -*VTə* (see Table 3.7), which marks both the dative/recipient and the comitative relation. Malayalam possesses three distinct ways of marking the Comitative relation: the affix -*ooTə* is found in literary Malayalam (LM), whereas the compound suffixes -*yuTe kuuTe* and -*yu mayi* are common in spoken Malayalam (SM). There is, however, a semantic difference between -*kkə* and -*ooTə* as markers of the Dative/Recipient role: the semantics of -*kkə* does not imply that what the recipient receives will in turn be delivered to another, whereas the semantics of -*ooTə* does contain this implication.

There are contexts in which one but not the other morpheme is acceptable. For example, a favour or an act of assistance cannot usually be delivered by an intermediary. For this reason, (3.11a) is acceptable, but (3.11b) is not.

(3.11a)  Manushayan  kuTTikkə    oru  sahaayam  cheithu koduthu.
         man         child-DAT   one  favour    did    gave
         'The man did the child a favour.'
(3.11b)  *Manushayan kuTTiooTə   oru  sahaayam  cheithu koduthu.
         man         child-DAT   one  favour    did    gave
         'The man did the child a favour.'

In a neutral context, however, both are acceptable with the difference that with the suffix *-kkə* the notion of further conveyance is not expressed, whereas with *-ooTə* it is, as illustrated by the examples in (3.12).[6]

(3.12a)  orəl    kuTTikkə    pusthəkəm    koduthu.
         man     child-DAT   book         gave
         'The man gave the book to the child.'
(3.12b)  orəl    kuTTiooTə   pusthəkəm    koduthu.
         man     child-DAT   book         gave
         'The man gave the book to the child (with the understanding that the child
              would deliver it to someone else).'

I assume that this cross-group marking found in Malayalam was present in the 1500s and in the process of learning pidgin Portuguese and in the process of creolization of pidgin Portuguese, the cross-group dative–comitative syncretism *-ooTə* in Malayalam found its way into the structure of Cochin pidgin Portuguese and subsequently Cochin Creole Portuguese. The suffixes most used currently in Malayalam to express instrumental/cause (*-konDə*) and comitative (*-yuTe kuuTə*, *-yu mayi*) are arguably more recent developments in Malayalam. In a linguistic study of the fifteenth-century Kannassa Ramayana in Malayalam, Pillai (1973:281–284) does not list them, but does include *-ooTu* (> *-ooTə*), as well as *-kku* (> *-kkə*). In Pillai (ibid.), it is not surprising that no dative reading is linked with *-ooTə*, given that it is principally a comitative marker. Nevertheless, it is not unreasonable to assume that, around the start of the sixteenth century, *-ooTə* was a comitative marker but in spoken language could also have been used to mark the dative of further conveyance.

As the Malayalam-influenced pidgin/creole Portuguese from Cochin was taken up the coast by the Portuguese soldiers and the native Indian speakers of the language, I suggest that this Portuguese variety would have served as a basis for the case-marking system found in Korlai Creole Portuguese. The

----

[6] In its 'further conveyance' reading, the semantics of *-ooTə* is reminiscent of the semantics of causative suffixes in languages such as Kannada, Hindi, and other Indic languages. However, it seems that the use of *-ooTə* as an indirect object marker is not related to today's causative construction in Malayalam, shown in the examples here.

    (a)  Ram    aahaaram    kazhikkunu.
         Ram    food        eat-is
         'Ram is eating the food.'
    (b)  Ram    Siitaye     aahaaram    kazhippiikkunnu.
         Ram    Siita-ACC   food        eat-CAUS-is
         'Ram is making Siita eat the food.'
    (c)  Ram    Siita-konDə  Gitaye     kazhippiikkunnu.
         Ram    Siita-INST   Gita-ACC   eat-CAUS-is
         'Ram is making Siita make Gita eat the food.'

syncretism could not have come from Marathi, the language in contact with Korlai CP, because Marathi exhibits no violations of the COH (see Pandharipande 1997:305–322).

It is interesting that in the sources available there are no other cross-group syncretisms found in the creoles further north of Korlai, i.e., in Norteiro, Daman, or Diu Creole Portuguese. These creoles also have in common the future marker *a(d)*, instead of *lo* found in the creoles of Cochin, Korlai, Sri Lanka, Kristang, and Macau. Thus, it seems that the creoles of Daman, Diu, and Bassein followed a somewhat different development, with influence from features of a different ecology, one that does not seem to have had as much, or any, influence from the Cochin variety of Indo-Portuguese creole. For the creoles in Daman and Diu, note that Gujarati, the contact language, does not exhibit any cross-group violations of the COH (Masica 1993:242–247).

With respect to case marking in the Portuguese creoles to the east of India and Sri Lanka, there may have been other potentially influential factors other than Malayalam, namely the contact languages of Kristang, East Timor CP, and Philippine Creole Spanish. At that time in Malaysia, the Portuguese had contact with Hokkien and Malaysian Bazaar Malay, a lingua franca developed between the Malay and Hokkien Chinese speakers in that area and spoken during the time the Portuguese began contact with speakers of the Malacca area. Hokkien exhibits no cross-group syncretisms, but Malaysian Bazaar Malay does, and in this respect seems to have been similar (to the best of our current knowledge) to Vehicular Malay, which itself was a lingua franca in what today is Indonesia. For my purposes, I assume that with regard to case-marking syncretisms, Malaysian Bazaar Malay and Vehicular Malay (VM) displayed the same pattern. In any case, VM was also used around Malacca when there was a Portuguese colony there, and in fact had been used in that area a long time before the Portuguese arrival.[7]

The earliest documented examples of VM, a word list and letters from Ternate, a Portuguese colony at that time, date from the early 1500s. Ricklefs (1978) provides written evidence of VM in the Batavia–Tugu area in the 1500s and early 1600s. Baba Malay, a creolized variety of Malaysian Bazaar Malay that developed in Malacca around the same time, was also spoken (see Map 3.1). An expert on these varieties states that the syncretisms found in these languages today were already in place in the 1500s and 1600s (personal communication, Scott Paauw, 7 January 2005). Specifically, in these language contact varieties, the form *sama* is used to mark the antecedent relations of instrument and accompaniment, as well as the subsequent relation of IO.[8]

---

[7] I thank Scott Paauw for his assistance with the information on VM in this section.
[8] Paauw (personal communication, 7 January 2005) reports that written documents in VM from the 1500s are easily intelligible today and that he has not found any significant differences.

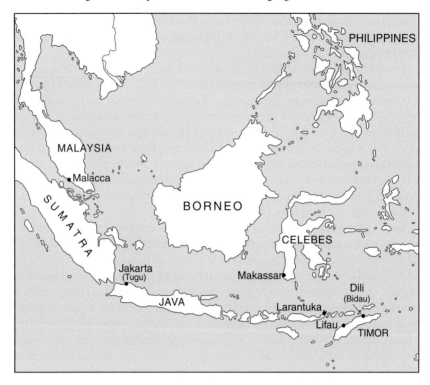

Map 3.1. The Malaysia–Indonesia area (taken from Baxter 1990:1).

The examples in (3.13)–(3.15), provided to me by Paauw, are from colloquial Jakarta Indonesian, a descendant of VM, and closely reflect what can be found in other descendants of VM. In these examples, the standard Malay/Indonesian spelling is used.

(3.13)  Marta   potong kain   **sama**   piso.
       Marta   cut     cloth   sama   knife
       'Marta cut the cloth with a knife.'
(3.14)  John   pi   toko   **sama**   Marta.
       John   go   store   sama   Marta
       'John went to the store with Marta.'
(3.15)  Marta   kasi   buku   **sama**   John.
       Marta   give   book   [sama]   John
       'Marta gave the book to John.'

Moreover, the various varieties of Malay which developed from sixteenth-century VM are remarkably similar today as well – and indeed are easily mutually intelligible (excluding Sri Lankan Malay, which has been geographically removed from the area for centuries).

Thus, the use of *sama* here suggests that at least Kristang (Malacca Creole Portuguese) arguably inherited the marking pattern from an earlier variety of VM, Malaysian Bazaar Malay, or Baba Malay.

Regarding Philippine Creole Spanish (referred to as Zamboangueño or Chavacano in Mindanao), the variety of Creole Portuguese spoken on Ternate (in Indonesia) may have had a pattern like that of Kristang before its speakers were transported to the Philippines in the early seventeenth century (Whinnom 1956). Since that time, it seems that Tagalog in the Manila area and local Philippine languages in the Zamboanga area may have influenced marking patterns in Philippine Creole Spanish. Fernández (2006) addresses the reason for the existence of a high degree of syncretism in Philippine Creole Spanish case marking. He notes that in the Philippine languages, as in Austronesian languages in general, there is an agent-oriented case-marking system in which non-agents, especially the theme/patient arguments that are animate or human, are demoted to obliques. Oblique markers from various relevant Philippine languages are shown in Table 3.8.

As is clear from the form of the markers, Zamboangueño *na* corresponds in its CV syllable structure to the common-noun oblique markers in the other Philippine languages (*sa, pa, ha*). Similarly, Zamboangueño *con* corresponds to the markers from the different languages shown in Table 3.8 not only in its form but also in that it begins with /k/. Moreover, Zamboangueño has borrowed the plural oblique marker *canda* for proper nouns and kinship terms. Fernández argues that the form of the oblique markers in the Philippine languages influenced the selection of *na* and *con* as the oblique markers in Zamboangueño. These facts, along with the fact that the Ternateño Creole Portuguese may have already had a similar marking system, account for the syncretisms in Philippine Creole Spanish, shown in Table 3.9. It also accounts for their deviation from the COH.

To summarize this section, my examination has brought to light an empirical observation regarding the lexical encoding of oblique semantic roles in Spanish- and Portuguese-based creoles: there are syncretisms in the Asian creoles that violate Croft's Causal Order Hypothesis. I have offered an account for the presence of the violation, suggesting that this peculiarity in some Indo-Portuguese varieties is due to influence from Malayalam, whose speakers most likely introduced the violation from Malayalam into the Cochin variety of Portuguese they created. Subsequently, the Cochin variety conceivably influenced Korlai CP, which contains a very similar cross-group syncretism that is not due to influence from Marathi, Korlai's contact language, because Marathi does not contain the syncretism in question.

I have argued that the syncretism in Kristang (Malacca CP) is arguably due to the influence of a variety of Bazaar Malay, which had and has the same cross-group syncretism present in Kristang. Finally, for Philippine Creole

Table 3.8. *Forms used to mark the oblique in various Philippine languages*

|  | Oblique case markers | | |
| --- | --- | --- | --- |
|  | Common noun | Proper nouns and kinship terms | |
| Language |  | Singular | Plural |
| Cebuano | sa | kang | kanila ni |
| Ilonggo | sa | kay | kanday |
| Magindanaon | sa | kaní | kanilá |
| Tagalog | sa | kay | kina (ant. kana) |
| Tausug | pa, ha | kan | kanda |
| Waray-Waray | ha | kan | kanda |
| Zamboangueño | na | con | canda |

*Note:* The grey shading indicates syncretisms.
*Source:* Adapted from Fernández 2006.

Table 3.9. *Subsequent and antecedent roles in Philippine Creole Spanish*

| Subsequent | | Antecedent | | | |
| --- | --- | --- | --- | --- | --- |
| Dat/Rec | Ben | Cause | | Instr | Comit |
| kon | kon, para | na, porkawsa de(l) | | kon | kon |

*Note:* The grey shading indicates syncretisms.

Spanish, I have assumed that Ternate CP had a similar syncretism due to its contact with Vehicular Malay. When the speakers of Ternate CP were taken to the Philippines, the cross-group syncretism was maintained and strengthened due to the influence of the case-marking system of the Philippine languages.

## 3.5    Concluding remarks

In this chapter, I reviewed the situation in southern Portugal in the late fifteenth and early sixteenth centuries. I showed examples of Africans' speech and argued that similar L2 varieties of African Portuguese were one integral part of the Portuguese pidgin that formed along the African west coast during that time. I also observed that key features in the L2 varieties are also found in the Portuguese-based creoles. For me, this suggests a developmental connection between L2 Portuguese, pidgin Portuguese, and certain tense–aspect features of the Portuguese-based creoles.

In section 3.4, I discussed the significance of the Causal Order Hypothesis (Croft 1991, 1998) for the structure of the Portuguese- and Spanish-based creoles. While the predictions made by the COH are adhered to by the African creoles in question, they are shown to be violated by the Asian–Portuguese creoles. I traced these violations back to similar violations in certain of the substrate languages, namely to Malayalam for Korlai CP, to Malaysian Bazaar Malay and Vehicular Malay for Malacca and Ternate CP respectively, and to Vehicular Malay and the case-marking system in the Philippine languages in the case of Philippine Creole Spanish. The influence of the local languages in the restructuring of the case-marking systems in these Asian Portuguese creoles suggests a Founder Principle effect (Mufwene 2001:28–29) in that the case systems that developed in each creole were predetermined by the traits of the vernaculars spoken by the populations present in the founding of the colonies in which the creoles developed. In this respect, then, this chapter has highlighted the importance of processes involved in naturalistic L2 acquisition and substrate influence in the formation and development of certain markers. However, it has also underscored that both language acquisition processes and processes involved in language shift (e.g., the introduction of native language structure into a naturalistically learned second language) must be taken into account to be able to understand the structure of creole languages. This is, in essence, the prediction of the Founder Principle.

# 4    Bozal Spanish of Cuba

## 4.1    Introduction

The debate about whether there was ever a Spanish-lexified creole language spoken in Cuba or elsewhere in the Caribbean is complex and there are arguments for and against its putative existence. Given the overwhelming evidence in the Caribbean of creoles lexified by French, English, Portuguese, and Dutch, there is no a priori reason to exclude the possibility of a Spanish-lexified creole having existed in the Spanish-speaking area of the Caribbean.[1] Specifically in the case of Cuba, Otheguy (1973) argues that references regarding the presence of a black bozal Spanish in Cuba go back more than one hundred years, suggesting that there was once a Spanish creole spoken by the African (and African descendant) population in Cuba. Granda (1978) and Schwegler (1993, 1996a) maintain that a widespread Spanish-based creole was possibly spoken throughout the Spanish Caribbean and Latin America, but that it underwent significant de-creolization, such that today there are only vestiges of it found in the Spanish spoken in Cuba. Perl (1987) discusses texts found in Cabrera (1954) which contain re-structuring like that found in creoles, and more recently Ortiz López (1998) finds evidence of re-structuring reminiscent of creole structure in the speech of older Afro-Cubans currently living in more isolated regions of the island.

Not all scholars, however, share this view. McWhorter (2000), for instance, argues forcefully that no Spanish-based creole ever existed in Cuba or anywhere else in Latin America. He develops an Afro-genesis hypothesis for New World creoles in which he proposes that creole languages developed in West African trade settlements where many of the African slaves were sent before their coerced migration to the New World. However, since such trade settlements were not established by the Spanish and few were ever acquired by them, Spanish did not have the opportunity to become the lexifier language for the

---

[1] Papiamentu is considered today a Spanish-based creole but, as we saw in the previous chapter, it developed from a Portuguese-lexified creole.

creoles spoken in the New World.[2] Mufwene (2001) also maintains that there never was a Spanish creole spoken in Cuba, citing external ecological conditions as the main reason for the lack of development of a creole there.

With respect to the actual language varieties spoken in Cuba during the eighteenth to twentieth centuries, scholars have long discussed the various features that characterize the Spanish of the Cuban *bozales*, that is, the language of the first-generation Africans enslaved or working as freedmen in Cuba during this period. The earliest published reference that I am aware of on the traits of bozal Spanish is found in Pichardo (1953). A late nineteenth-century source on the linguistic characteristics of bozal Spanish can also be found in the work of Bachiller y Morales (1977). With such descriptions of bozal Spanish features, the question arises regarding the extent to which they suggest the existence of a Spanish-based creole language, in either vestigial or full form. The two viewpoints briefly outlined above are at odds: one camp views the presence of the features as evidence suggesting a prior creole (e.g., Otheguy 1973; Granda 1978; Perl 1982, 1987; and Schwegler 1993, 1996a, among others). Opponents of this view argue that the data suggest a case of natural second language acquisition (e.g. Lipski 1985, 1994, 2000; McWhorter 2000; and Mufwene 2001, to name some of the major ones). Ortiz López (1998) and Lipski (1998) propose that a creole or creole-like variety of Spanish may have developed in isolated parts of Cuba, the remnants of which are believed to be captured in texts and accounts such as those published by Cabrera (1954) and Ortiz López (1998). Lipski (1994:102, 111–113; 2005) also mentions the possibility of the influence of Papiamentu on bozal Spanish due to the influx of Papiamentu-speaking workers into Cuba to work on plantations.

To be able to consider the possibility of a Spanish-lexified creole forming in the Caribbean or anywhere in the Spanish-speaking colonies, there are key circumstances that have to have been present. First, the external ecological conditions had to support the formation of a creole language. Second, the attitude of the speakers had to be such that interaction between two or more speech communities would be possible. Concerning this latter point, African captives brought to the Caribbean to be sold into slavery or African slaves brought to Cuba from elsewhere in the Caribbean needed to interact with fellow slaves and the slave bosses if they wanted to survive. Regarding the external ecological conditions, an examination of the black–white ratio in the demographic make-up of the Caribbean in general and of Cuba in particular should shed light on whether the demographic conditions ever supported the formation of a creole language.

---

[2] In 1778, the Spanish came into possession of some slave-trading stations on the west coast of Africa, thereby creating an African base for their slave trade in the Americas (see Aimes 1967:38). These were, nevertheless, the few exceptions referred to by McWhorter.

Table 4.1. *Distribution of the estimated 1,331,000 slaves in the Spanish-speaking Caribbean Islands and in South America (excluding Brazil)*

| Country | Number | Percentage |
|---|---|---|
| Dominican Republic | 30,000 | 2.25 |
| Cuba | 702,000 | 52.74 |
| Puerto Rico | 77,000 | 5.79 |
| Spanish South America | 522,000 | 39.22 |
| Argentina, Uruguay | | |
| Paraguay, Bolivia | 100,000 | 7.51 |
| Chile | 6,000 | 0.45 |
| Peru | 95,000 | 7.14 |
| Colombia, Panama, Ecuador | 200,000 | 15.03 |
| Venezuela | 121,000 | 9.09 |
| Total | 1,331,000 | 100 |

Curtin (1969:88–89) gives a speculative geographical distribution of slave imports during the whole period of the Atlantic slave trade. He estimates that around 5,093,000 slaves were imported to the Caribbean Islands and South America (excluding Brazil). Of these, roughly 1,331,000 slaves were sent to Spanish-speaking countries. Table 4.1 gives the breakdown according to country/region. Note that, according to Curtin's figures, over half of the slaves from West Africa were imported to Cuba alone. Thus, it stands to reason that it would be there where we would expect to find the necessary and sufficient conditions for the formation of a Spanish-lexified creole language.

In this chapter, I first present a survey of Cuba's social history, using available population figures to trace the fluctuations of the black-to-white population from the fifteenth to the twentieth centuries. As a key part of the puzzle, I highlight the instrumental role of the Spanish crown in the slow development of commerce in the Spanish colonies until the second half of the eighteenth century. I then discuss a newly discovered source of evidence on early bozal Spanish of Cuba, taken from Clements and Davis (2004). At face value, it supports the view that there never was a Spanish-based creole spoken on Cuba. The evidence comes from the unusual correspondence in 1835 between two academics, Francis Lieber in the United States and José de la Luz Caballero (henceforth de la Luz) in Cuba, both important figures in the early history of linguistics in their respective countries. In the exchange, Lieber asks de la Luz very direct questions about the nature of what Lieber assumes to be creole Spanish in Cuba. De la Luz, a polyglot philologist familiar with creole languages such as Haitian Creole French in Haiti, responds that a Spanish creole did not exist in Cuba and includes in his correspondence a commentary of the most common features of bozal Spanish, as well as annotations on the *Catequismo acomodado á la capacidad de los negros bozales* 'Catechism adapted to the capacity of the black bozales', initially published in 1796. (He used the reprinted edition from 1818.)

De la Luz's comments, along with the information on Cuba's socio-linguistic ecology from the beginning of colonization to the twentieth century, suggest that conditions in Cuba were not conducive to the development of a stable pidgin or a creole. A comparative examination of the traits of bozal Spanish mentioned by de la Luz in 1835 and those listed by scholars such as Perl (1987) and Lipski (1985, 1994, 2005) also supports the conclusion that, overall, the nature of the traits is more consistent with untutored second language acquisition or with an incipient pidgin than with the presence of a stable pidgin or a bona fide creole.[3] Let us now turn to the discussion of the external ecology of Cuba under colonization.

## 4.2    Cuba's external ecology under Spanish colonization

In my survey of the socio-historical situation in Cuba from the time of the initial European contact until the twentieth century, I cover certain social and labour-related aspects of the history of Cuba, focusing on four general periods (1492–1554, 1555–1696, 1697–1762, and 1763–1808).[4] This will take us into a discussion of the demographic picture of Cuba in the nineteenth century, highlighting the key role played by the Spanish crown in the limited slave trade in the Spanish colonies. Only after the crown loosened its hold on slave trade, which began to take place after 1763, did Cuba develop the necessary conditions for the possible emergence of a pidgin and creole linguistic system.

This survey of Cuban history will also serve as a backdrop for the discussion of the 1835 correspondence between Francis Lieber and José de la Luz, whose letter exchange offers detailed information about whether or not Cuban bozal Spanish is a vestige of a Spanish-based creole language. Before dealing with the later phases of colonial Cuba, I would first like to touch

---

[3] Lipski advances different specific positions on the pidgin or creole nature of bozal Spanish, depending on the population being referred to. Regarding the speech of the slaves on the large Cuban sugar plantations he (1998:317) states: '*bozal* speech [i.e., speech of the first-generation Africans] could have become the native language of the next generation. I agree with Perl that *bozal* speech could have become a creole in very special circumstances [. . .] [I] do not know anything about the history of the most isolated slaves and because of this I cannot exclude the possibility of a creole' (my translation). Lipski (2000) speaks of the 'incipient restructuring' of Spanish among two ethnic groups from Africa in nineteenth-century Cuba. In general, he considers the 'Afro-Hispanic pidgin' Spanish spoken by *bozales* to be a transient phenomenon. I address these questions in more detail later in this chapter.

[4] Unless otherwise indicated, the information in this section is based on that found in Clements and Davis (2004).

briefly upon the reasons why the indigenous population of Cuba played little or no role in the subsequent development of the island.

When in 1492 Columbus landed on the island known today as Cuba, it was inhabited principally by the long-established Ciboneys who lived throughout the island and the more recently arrived Taínos who had settled on its eastern end, the two having different languages and cultures. Originally, the indigenous population on Cuba was thought to hover between 300,000 and 500,000 (ANC 1976:10). When the Spanish colonizers first appeared, they attempted to enslave the Ciboneys and Taínos. This resulted in hundreds of thousands of deaths due to European diseases, slaughter on the part of the Spanish, and suicides, infanticides, and induced abortions on the part of indigenous people. By 1524 (twenty-eight years after the Spanish first arrived), only around 5,000 natives are said to have remained in Cuba (Masó 1976:20).

Given that in Ciboney culture property was passed on through the women, the Spanish soldiers were pushed to marry the heirs of the *caciques* (tribal chiefs) of the different villages and thereby take over possession of the natives' lands. For various reasons, the assimilation of the remaining indigenous people into Spanish culture and into Christianity took place rapidly.

The initial slaughter of the natives by Spanish soldiers was justified by the Spanish crown as a *guerra justa*, a 'just war' against the natives who refused to accept Christianity (Masó 1976:35). About sixty years afterward (around 1550), the indigenous population, still around 5,000 in number, was liberated from slavery by Ferdinand the Catholic (ibid.:38), partially influenced by Queen Isabella, who had always opposed enslaving the indigenous population (ibid.:35). For the most part, however, the natives in the mountains fused with the Caucasian population there (ibid.:93). Apart from an effect on the cultivation methods the plantation-owners would later adopt, the indigenous population did not exercise any influence on the economic and political development in colonial or post-colonial Cuba.

Slaves from Africa were brought, via Spain, to Cuba early on, and in 1524 reports already were circulating of rebellions of the African and indigenous population (Masó 1976:45). At that time, the white population was relatively unstable, as during the first sixty years of the colonization many Spaniards used Cuba as a waystation between Spain and present-day Mexico. In 1544, some 660 Spaniards lived in Cuba, along with around 5,000 indigenous people and 800 Africans. Although Masó (ibid.:45) reports on the considerable number of *mestizos* (European–Indian mixed-race people) at that time, he does not cite any numbers. The overall situation in Cuba between 1492 and 1555 was one of initial economic development (mostly in cattle, hides, and salted meat) followed by a general deterioration, as the Spaniards tended to move on to Mexico or Central America.

During the sixteenth and seventeenth centuries, Aimes (1967:18–19) notes that:

> Spain adhered to her policy of rigidly enforced navigation laws, and her colonies had to depend almost entirely upon their own resources for development . . . Cuba did not fail to protest against the medieval restrictions from which she was suffering. Particularly, the need of labourers for developing the plantation system was repeatedly brought to the attention of the government. Spain did not merely decline to afford relief, but she even shut off completely, in response to the will of the church, the uncertain supply of slaves which had occasionally reached the island. As a result, Cuba sank into the position of a nearly forgotten island. Furthermore, the condition of Cuba was made more hopeless by giving the right to import slaves to *asiento* [contract] companies, an expensive method which placed slaves beyond the reach of poor planters.

Apart from the *asientos*, there were additional factors during these centuries that put the price of slaves out of reach for many land-owners in Cuba. Because of larger crews on Spanish ships, the greater costs connected with ship protection, and Spain's lack of trading establishments on the African west coast, the transportation of slaves by the Spanish also cost more, and this cost was then transferred on to the slave-buyers (Aimes 1967:27).

Although sugarcane had been brought to the island in 1523, authorization by the crown had to be granted before plantations could be set up and slaves imported, and it generally took decades before authorization was given. The first sugar mill in Cuba was installed in 1595; by 1602, seventeen land-owners of sugar mills and sugar refineries each had around twenty-eight African slaves (Masó 1976:61) in their respective homestead-sized operations. Over time, the development of the sugar industry would be one factor in the decrease in the cattle industry, which had been thriving in seventeenth-century Cuba.

Around 1608, the population of Cuba was calculated at about 20,000 inhabitants, including whites, blacks, indigenous people, *mestizos*, and *mulattos*. Despite the diseases affecting the overall population of the island, in 1668 there were reportedly 30,000 people in Cuba, with equal proportions of Africans and Europeans, in addition to roughly 4,000 indigenous Cubans. By the end of the century, the population had reportedly grown to 50,000 inhabitants in approximately the same black-to-white proportion, just under half of which still lived in Havana. The growth of the African population at that time was said to be by natural birth, as well as by further importation of slaves allowed by *asientos*, which, as mentioned, were strictly controlled by the crown and granted only to certain traders.[5] During this period, the Spaniards living in Cuba were largely from Castile and Andalusia, though

---

[5] In each *asiento*, the details regarding numbers of slaves, period of importation, and price of and tariff on each slave were predetermined.

there was also a significant number from the Canary Islands, as well as some Portuguese, but only in Havana (Masó 1976:66).

During the first half of the eighteenth century, Spain was able to retain its monopoly on trade in Cuba. When in 1760 an *asiento* was discussed to import 10,000 slaves over a ten-year period, members of the Cuban company in charge of slave importation argued that introducing so many slaves in such a short period would jeopardize the security of the island, citing revolts in other parts of the Americas as evidence. That is, those in power in Cuba consistently and consciously strove to keep the balance between the black and white population under control. On this topic, Aimes (1967:31) notes that '[t]he argument, which has been present in the Spanish colonies practically from first to last, marks the strong aversion from any policy tending to the too rapid increase of the negro population.'

In the specific period between 1697 and 1762, around 40 per cent of Cuba's population resided in or around Havana. Tobacco cultivation and production predominated during this period because large amounts of land, slave labour, or capital were not needed for tobacco farming, for which European farmers used and improved on the cultivation methods adopted from the island's indigenous population. In economic terms, sugar cultivation and production during this period were second to tobacco. In fact, Aimes (1967:21) remarks that in the eighteenth century 'Cuban tobacco was a monopoly product with a wide, growing market.'

During this time, the number of Africans increased due to *asientos* given to French and English companies, and illegal importation of slaves from Jamaica (Masó 1976:93). The slaves worked in sugarcane and tobacco production, and many were given freedom by their owners or by the king. Other Africans were allowed to work as indentured labourers, paying off their indenture. Moreover, a significant number of blacks, both slaves and freed coloureds, worked as domestics in Cuba's urban centres. But other sectors of the economy were not doing as well. During the latter part of the eighteenth century, for example, the mining sector (copper and silver) in Santiago experienced continued rebellions on the part of the slaves (Masó 1976:96).

In the period between 1763 and 1808, problems with rebellions became more frequent. A wider gap developed between the Spanish rulers and the Cuban-born population, consisting of descendants of blacks, former conquerors, and other white people originally from Spain. Outside Cuba, this period was marked by revolutions in the United States (1776) and France (1789), and the bloody slave rebellions that started around 1791 in Haiti, culminating in a revolution and Haiti's declaration of independence in 1804.

I have already noted that, from the beginning of the Spanish colonization up to 1763, free commerce did not exist in Cuba. Aimes (1967:4) notes that '[t]he strong control which Spain exercised for centuries over the trade of her colonies has been spoken of often as a monopoly.' The pivotal year between the old, monopoly-like system and the new, liberal system of commerce was 1763, the year in which the English occupied the port of Havana for ten months. During the first five months of the occupation, the English brought 10,700 *bozales* (slaves directly from Africa) into Cuba. Instead of contravening the trade policy of this time, it was actually in line with the more liberalized policy put in place just before King Charles III started his reign in Spain. The British occupation helped this trend along considerably. Apart from liberalizing Cuba's economy, the British presence also resulted in the introduction into Cuba of many contraband goods.

During this time, the amount of commercial activity increased around Havana significantly. From the 1774 census we know that there were 1,591 cattle farms and as many as 10,140 butcher shops mostly around Havana supplying the colonial capital with meat. During this period, the number of sugar refineries (*ingenios*) also increased around Havana: from 215 in 1796 (out of a total of 305 on the island) to 480 in 1806 (Masó 1976:109). The 1774 census states that some refineries had as many as 200 slaves (ibid.:112). Also during this time, three coffee plantations were also located near the capital.

In terms of volume of trade based on the number of ships per year, Aimes (1967:35–36) states that before 1762 imports were made in three ships annually from Spain. The trade with Cuba in 1765 required around six ships, and in 1778 two hundred ships. In the period between 1765 and 1770, income from duties collected in Havana increased three-fold and exports from the whole island increased five-fold.

With respect to slave importation, up to 1763, Aimes (1967:36–39) notes that roughly 60,000 slaves had been imported overall. From 1763 to 1789, 41,604 slaves were imported, a large portion of whom came from Jamaica and Grenada. In 1778, subsequent to the Treaty of Pardo (see Middleton 1997 II:51), Spain procured some slave-trading stations on the west coast of Africa, creating thus a base for its slave trade and lowering the price of slave importation. In 1784, Havana became the centre of Spanish–American colonial commerce.

With regard to the black–white population ratio, I mentioned above that the first official census was taken in 1774. Of the 171,620 inhabitants in Cuba at that time, 44 per cent (75,180) were coloured (Spanish *de color* 'of colour') and 56 per cent (96,440) white. Havana was the centre with the densest white population; the rural areas had a majority of the black population; and in the far east of the island there were many *mestizos* (Masó 1976:114). As was the case historically, almost half of the population lived in Havana. Table 4.2 gives the population numbers from Kiple (1976), whose population figures are a result of comparing and contrasting data from various sources.

Table 4.2. *Population of blacks and whites in raw numbers and percentages in Cuba 1774–1899*

| | 1774 | 1792 | 1817 | 1827 | 1841 | 1846 | 1861 | 1877 | 1887 | 1899 |
|---|---|---|---|---|---|---|---|---|---|---|
| *Raw numbers* | | | | | | | | | | |
| Free coloured | 30,847 | 54,152 | 114,058 | 106,314 | 152,838 | 149,226 | 232,493 | | | |
| Male | 16,152 | 25,211 | 58,885 | 51,962 | 75,703 | 72,651 | 113,806 | | | |
| Female | 14,695 | 28,941 | 55,173 | 54,352 | 77,135 | 76,575 | 118,687 | | | |
| Slaves | 44,333 | 84,590 | 199,145 | 286,942 | 436,495 | 323,759 | 370,553 | | | |
| Male | 28,771 | 47,424 | 124,324 | 183,290 | 281,250 | 201,011 | 218,722 | | | |
| Female | 15,562 | 37,166 | 74,821 | 103,652 | 155,245 | 122,748 | 151,831 | | | |
| Coloured | | | | | | | | 480,166[a] | 528,798 | 520,400 |
| Male | | | | | | | | 242,938 | 275,413 | 252,092 |
| Female | | | | | | | | 237,228 | 253,385 | 268,308 |
| White | 96,440 | 133,559 | 239,850 | 311,051 | 418,291 | 425,767 | 793,484 | 1,475,992 | 1,102,889 | 1,052,397 |
| Male | 55,576 | 72,299 | 130,519 | 168,653 | 227,144 | 230,983 | 468,107 | 817,029 | 607,187 | 563,113 |
| Female | 40,864 | 61,260 | 109,331 | 142,398 | 191,147 | 194,784 | 325,377 | 658,963 | 495,702 | 489,284 |
| *Percentages* | | | | | | | | | | |
| Coloured | 44% | 51% | 59% | 56% | 58% | 53% | 43% | 25% | 32% | 33% |
| White | 56% | 49% | 41% | 44% | 42% | 47% | 57% | 75% | 68% | 67% |

*Note:* [a]Starting with this year, this number refers to resident coloureds, making no distinction between free coloureds and slaves.
*Source:* Kiple 1976.

Table 4.3. *Population of Cuba in percentages from 1532 to 1811*

| Year | Whites | Blacks |
|------|--------|--------|
| 1532 | 37.5 | 62.5 |
| 1620 | 93.4 | 6.6 |
| 1775 | 56.2 | 43.8 |
| 1792 | 56.4 | 43.6 |
| 1811 | 45.5 | 54.5 |

*Source:* Masó 1976:115.

During the period from 1774 to 1846, the black population (including coloured people) in Cuba was between 2 and 18 percentage points higher than the white population.[6] After 1846, the black population declined to 14 per cent below the white population (1861), and further to between 50 per cent and 34 per cent of the white population between 1861 and 1899 due to factors such as war and increasing observance of the abolition of slavery. Although there are no official censuses before 1774, Masó (1976:115) offers his approximation of the black–white population ratio in 1532 and 1620, shown in Table 4.3.[7]

Up until the nineteenth century a major part of the population of Cuba lived in the Havana area. Table 4.4 displays the black–white ratio in the colonial capital between 1774 and 1899.[8] In the eighteen years from 1774 to 1792, the percentage of the black population in the city (including slaves and free coloureds) rose 11 percentage points (from 43 per cent to 54 per cent). Although by 1817 the overall population had increased, the black–white proportions remained steady at 54 per cent and 46 per cent respectively. In 1827, the black population in Havana reached 59 per cent, the highest level of the century. By 1846, however, it decreased to slightly less than half, at 49 per cent, due to abolition and related factors, and in the following fifteen years, up to 1861, it decreased further to 32 per cent.

Masó (1976:115) notes that the life of rural slaves in Cuba, especially those on the sugar plantations, was harder than that of the slaves in the urban areas. However, the treatment of slaves overall in Cuba was reportedly better than in the French and English colonies of the area. This was the conclusion, at least,

---

[6] See Lipski 2000 for the breakdown of Africans in Cuba according to ethnic groups.

[7] A comparison of the year 1792 in Tables 4.2 and 4.3 reveals a discrepancy of percentage points. I consider Kiple's data the more reliable as they have been cross-checked with numerous sources.

[8] Kiple (1976) disregards the figures from 1841 and 1877 because of reliability problems in the censuses for those years.

Table 4.4. *Population distribution between whites, free coloureds, and slaves in Havana 1774–1899*

|  | 1774 | 1792 | 1817 | 1827[a] | 1846 | 1861 | 1887 | 1899 |
|---|---|---|---|---|---|---|---|---|
| *Raw numbers* | | | | | | | | |
| Free coloureds | 10,945 | 9,800 | 21,372 | 31,622 | 37,221 | 37,768 | – | – |
| Slaves | 21,281 | 17,970 | 24,341 | 109,535 | 67,219 | 29,013 | – | – |
| Coloureds | – | – | – | – | – | – | 116,146 | 112,214 |
| White | 43,392 | 23,537 | 38,362 | 96,671 | 110,847 | 138,895 | 335,782 | 312,590 |
| *Overall percentages* | | | | | | | | |
| Black | 43% | 54% | 54% | 59% | 49% | 32% | 26% | 26% |
| White | 57% | 46% | 46% | 41% | 51% | 68% | 74% | 74% |

Note: [a] And rural areas.
Source: Kiple 1976.

of Alexander von Humboldt (cited in Masó 1976:115), based on evidence from his journey to Cuba in 1805; he found that there was a significantly higher number of manumissions in Cuba than in other European colonies of the area during the same period. Von Humboldt (cited ibid.:116) attributed this to a number of reasons: the right of slaves in Cuba to buy their freedom, religious sentiment of the slave-owners, and the advantages given to those blacks who performed domestic work or who carried out some form of art or handicraft.

I noted above that the system of *asientos* allowed the Spanish crown to control tightly the importation of slaves to Cuba and elsewhere in their colonial territories. The increase in the black population relative to that of the whites in Cuba was a direct result of the aforementioned English ten-month occupation of Cuba in 1763, and the liberalized policies implemented by Charles III, whereby slave importation increased dramatically. One consequence of this was that the colonial rulers of the island during this period moved to encourage the immigration of whites to Cuba, in order to counterbalance the increasing disparity in the black–white ratio on the island (Masó 1976:116). The rebellions taking place just to the east in Haiti during this time created fear among Cuban rulers that unrest might spread to their island. The *real cédula*, or royal dispatch, of 1817 legally permitted white foreigners to become naturalized citizens as long as they were Catholic and settled on the island indefinitely. They received free passage to Cuba, food for a limited time, and one thirteen-hectare parcel of land. Among those responding to the calls for white immigration in Cuba during this period were many Catalans, who joined the former Canary Islanders, Galicians, Andalusians, and an enclave of French who in the wake of the Haitian rebellions had crossed to settle on the eastern end of Cuba.

Comparing population distributions of different Caribbean islands, we see that the distribution of Cuba's population was more balanced than that of the other islands. For example, at the end of the eighteenth century (1792), Cuba had 54,152 (20 per cent) free coloureds, 84,590 (31 per cent) slaves, and 133,559 (49 per cent) whites.[9] By contrast, around that time Haiti had 452,000 (98 per cent) slaves and 11,000 (2 per cent) whites.

In the period 1808–1837, the sugarcane industry in Cuba expanded, affecting the cultivation of tobacco, which shifted more to the west of the island but maintained its importance for the economy. Coffee cultivation was already experiencing difficulty because it could not compete in the foreign

---

[9] These figures are taken from Kiple 1976. Masó's figures (1976:161) for the end of the eighteenth century are 81,847 (37 per cent) free coloureds, 44,333 (20 per cent) slaves, and 96,440 (43 per cent) whites. Again, I take Kiple's figures to be more accurate because he reports having cross-checked them with various other sources.

market, which produced coffee of a superior quality more efficiently (Masó 1976:154–156). In 1837, Cuba was still a country of small land-owners in which nearly half of its land raised tobacco, cattle, coffee, etc., valued at 41 million pesos, whereas the land dedicated to the production of sugarcane was smaller and yielded only 22 million pesos. The small land-owners, notes Masó (ibid.:171), administered their own lands and lived side by side with the black population. He remarks that cattle raising and tobacco growing on small acreages required less overhead and fewer slaves than did sugarcane cultivation.

In the period around 1837, there was little difference between small business owners and those employed by bosses for a wage. At that time, barbers went house to house and tobacconists often operated alone. Havana had 306 tobacco shops which paid wages to their 2,152 employees, of which 612 were black and 1,540 white (Masó 1976:171). Thus, the black population made up a substantial share of certain parts of the job market and constituted an integral part of Cuban society.

To conclude this section, from the inception of Cuba as a Spanish colony, the Spanish crown sought and succeeded in closely controlling trade with the island until 1763. The result of this strict control on trade was that for two centuries commerce was made to depend more heavily on the production of goods that did not require a large labour force, e.g., tobacco, cattle raising, etc. The other consequence of the crown's control on trade was that the population of African slave labourers was held in check with respect to the white population. With the exception of the situation in 1532 (see Table 4.3), it was only after 1792 that the black population began to outnumber white people on the island. Census records indicate that, between 1774 and 1846, black people outnumbered the white population by between 2 and 18 percentage points (see Table 4.2). That is, the racial imbalance in terms of population favoured black people for around seventy years, a significant percentage of whom were free coloureds, who were better integrated into Cuban society than slaves. Moreover, nearly half of the agricultural activity was carried out on small-scale farms raising tobacco, cattle, and coffee, in which the black-to-white ratio was also maintained in balance. Such conditions, I argue (along with Chaudenson 1992; Lipski 1985, 1994; and Mufwene 2001), were not conducive to the formation or development of a stable pidgin or a creole language in Cuba. While I concede that on some sugarcane plantations the demographic conditions favoured the formation of a pidgin, the time during which this was the case was between 1770 and 1840. If there had been contact varieties of Spanish formed in Cuba during this period, they would have been at most incipient pidgins and at least the result of untutored second language acquisition. Other restructured varieties, such as Papiamentu, may also have played a role in the restructuring of Spanish found documented by researchers (see Cabrera 1954 and Ortiz López 1998). It also stands to reason that, had there been a more widespread pidgin or creole during this time in Cuba, various language experts in Cuba familiar with English- and French-based creole languages would probably have known about it. At this juncture, the recently discovered exchange between the American academic and philologist Francis Lieber and the Cuban educator and philologist José de la Luz takes on an added importance in the debate regarding a purported Spanish pidgin or creole in Cuba.

## 4.3 The letter exchange between Francis Lieber and José de la Luz

The 1835 correspondence on Cuban bozal Spanish between Francis Lieber and José de la Luz is of particular interest because Lieber had written about Caribbean creoles in the first edition of the *Encyclopedia Americana* (13 volumes, 1829–1832) under the entry 'creole dialects' and de la Luz was known to have detailed knowledge about the language situation in Cuba. Both these men were highly educated, multi-lingual, and well versed in the linguistic issues of the period. In examining the range of interests reflected in Lieber's language-related writings, the common theme of language development and change in progress emerges. His entry in the *Encyclopedia Americana* gives some insight into what he knew about the Caribbean creoles and how he viewed them:

Creole dialects are those jargons which have originated from the mixture of different languages in the West Indies. They are spoken by the slaves, who have destroyed the fine grammatical construction of the European languages, and have intermixed with them some original African words. According to the European language which prevails in a Creole dialect, it is called French-Creole, Danish-Creole, &c. In St Thomas, for instance, the latter is spoken; in Hayti, French-Creole. Among the numerous corruptions of European words and constructions, we find very generally, in the Creole dialects, the corruptions of grammar common among children; for instance, *me* is used instead of *I*. Often no distinction is made between the possessive pronoun and the personal; e.g., *me house* for *my house*, or *wi massra* for *our master*. The infinitive is used for the finite tenses, as *moi donner* for *je donne*.

In this passage we see that Lieber is aware of the role of the lexifier language in Caribbean creoles, the possible African influence, a connection with language acquisition, and specific linguistic features of creole languages. It is perhaps of interest that he does not specifically mention Spanish-Creole in the passage. We know that Lieber assumed there was a Spanish-based creole in Cuba because of the nature of his questions sent to de la Luz.

As for José de la Luz (1800–1862), he was born in Havana, Cuba, into a well-known aristocratic family. His great uncle was the Catholic priest Father

José Agustín Caballero (1762–1835) who was considered by some to be the most outstanding cultural figure in Cuba during the first half of the nineteenth century and was one of the first to address the question of an independent Cuba (see Masó 1976:119). An educator, Father José Agustín taught at the renowned San Carlos and San Ambrosio Seminary in Havana and was the teacher of many key Cuban thinkers of the period, one of whom was his great nephew José de la Luz.

The Cuba of the first half of the nineteenth century was one in which there was on the one hand a highly educated aristocracy comprising a small minority of the population, who became the doctors, lawyers, and clergy, and on the other the rest of the people of the island, black as well as white, who were illiterate (Rodriguez 1874:16). De la Luz grew up in a Havana in which more than half of the population during his first twenty-seven years was black. Many of the aristocratic families in Havana had domestic slaves, and José de la Luz grew up with domestic slaves in his house as well.

In his studies, de la Luz excelled in Latin, philosophy, and physics, among other things. In 1817, he graduated as *bachiller en filosofía*, and in 1820 as a *bachiller en leyes* (lit. 'graduate in laws'), after which he decided to dedicate his life and energy to learning and education. Between 1828 and 1832, de la Luz travelled to the United States and Europe, meeting figures such as Henry W. Longfellow, Sir Walter Scott, Alexander von Humboldt, and Francis Lieber. He returned to Cuba and put his time and energy into matters of education.

In a letter dated 4 June 1835 sent by Francis Lieber to William Picard in Cuba, Lieber asks eighteen specific questions on the language situation in Cuba. Picard forwarded the letter to José de la Luz, who not only gives detailed responses to Lieber's queries but also provides his own linguistic commentary on a late eighteenth-century catechism written expressly for chaplains or priests working among Afro-Cubans. De la Luz's letter and commentary provide an important contemporary source on the nature of bozal Spanish in Cuba of the 1830s. I divide this section into two parts. In section 4.3.1, I present in translation from Spanish de la Luz's detailed response to Lieber's questions, and in section 4.3.2, in translation, his detailed linguistic commentary on the catechism. De la Luz's commentary provides particulars on the nature of bozal Spanish with comparison to other varieties of Spanish spoken in Cuba. It supports the view that a Spanish creole in Cuba did not exist.

### 4.3.1    Lieber's eighteen questions

While I have not seen a copy of the original letter from Lieber to Picard requesting information on a Cuban Spanish creole, his eighteen specific queries on the language situation in Cuba are made known in the response he received from José de la Luz (in Spanish) dated 31 July 1835.[10] Below are Lieber's eighteen questions rendered in English with de la Luz's responses (material in square brackets is added for clarity):

[T]he first twelve questions are briefly answered. The clearest ones I will answer categorically one by one, and then I will move on to whatever needs to be said about the others.

1. Does the population of colour of that [island] still speak Creole?
   To the 1st one: No
2. Is there anything published in that dialect?
   To the 2nd one: As a consequence, it cannot exist.
3. or some dictionary?
   To the 3rd one: No
4. or the Bible?
   To the 4th one: No
5. or some songs, or small works?
   To the 5th one: No (although they sing a lot, mixing their languages with ours).
6. Does there still exist in Cuba a Spanish creole?
   To the 6th one: It neither exists nor did it ever.
7. Does it differ much from the Spanish creole that is spoken in other islands?
   To the 7th one: It has already been noted what the variations consist of, that is, of loose words and not phrases.
8. Has there been any book published in creole, like in the territories of the Danish crown?
   To the 8th one: There is nothing printed, except what has been said.

---

[10] In a response to Lieber dated 1 August 1835, William Picard introduces José de la Luz (whom Lieber had previously met). Picard writes the following in his letter:

I write in the utmost haste to avail myself of an immediate first opportunity for New York and send you along with the present some very interesting original notes from our enlightened philologist and philanthropist Don José de la Luz received this moment – these are the replies to your queries on Creole Dialects which I translated into Spanish for his [de la Luz's] more easy understanding and doubt not that they will prove interesting for your investigations as no one in this country is more competent for any sort of local, literary, historical information . . . in this respect Don José de la Luz will prove an invaluable correspondent to you.

From Picard's letter I infer that de la Luz was known among the educated elite in Havana of the 1830s as one of the most (if not the most) competent source on local historical and linguistic information.

The letter written by José de la Luz Caballero, as well as his commentary on the catequismo, can be found amongst Francis Lieber's papers housed at the Hungtington Library in San Marino, CA. The existence of the letter and commentary was brought to my attention by Stuart Davis who had a grant from the Huntington Library to investigate the linguistic related writings of Francis Lieber. I gratefully acknowledge Stuart Davis for sharing these letters with me and we acknowledge the Huntington Library for its support.

9. Has the publishing of books in creole impeded the uniformity of Catholicism, and the fact that the Divine Service is in Latin?

To the 9th one: According to what has been said, this question cannot be posed either. However, by delving into the spirit [of the question], I must say in all fairness that the ecclesiastic class [i.e., the clergy] has done more for the good of the African race than any other class.

10. Has anyone made a collection of African words or phrases in use among the Africans, and have these begun to be generalized among the people of colour?

To the 10th one: Nothing of the kind has been done.

11. Is there much difference between the creole that is spoken in the different points on the Island?

To the 11th one: It has been answered.

12. Does one preach to the slave sometimes in creole, or always in colloquial Spanish?

To the 12th one: It has also been answered.

13. Do other publications exist in Cuba from the first missionaries who were among the Caribs or aborigines?

To the 13th one: None that I know of, and I should know about it, because my uncle, Dr Caballero, was a great researcher of things of this country. What does exist deals with the history of the island, and that has been published by the Patriotic Society, through their history department. The publication of the work by Arrate is the most interesting thing about the Collection, and in it there is nothing about the missionaries who settled among the Caribs or aborigines. In the *Collection of the Travels of Spaniards*, published by Mr Navarrete in Madrid (and which was especially acknowledged by the famous Washington Irving) is where one can find some exact information about the primitive history of the island; also in the works of Herrera (*Décadas*)[11] and Oviedo. I'll see if there is something in Sepúlveda's work, which, translated from Latin by the above-mentioned Dr Caballero, remained among his manuscripts. This is a book that provides some interesting data about the primitive history of America, correcting on many occasions the renowned Las Casas, of whom he was a great antagonist.[12]

14. What are the titles of those works?

To the 14th one: I have already answered in my previous response.

---

[11] De la Luz may be referring here to Antonio de Herrera y Tordesillas' *Décadas de Indias*.

[12] Most likely Bartolomé de las Casas is being referred to here. At this point in the manuscript, we find the following footnote: 'The most comprehensive work about the aborigines is Las Casas' *General History of the Indies*, which has never been published, and which exists only four manuscript volumes in the Archives of the Ministry of Grace and Justice in Madrid. There are also two manuscript copies of the third volume only (which is all about the island of Cuba) at the Biblioteca Real ("Royal Library"), that is, the national library.'

15. Are there manuscripts on the language of the Caribs?
    To the 15th one: Ditto.
16. Do those exist in some convent or in the bishop's library?
    To the 16th one: It has also been answered.
17. Are the archives of that [library] complete?
    To the 17th one: in the Episcopal archives there is more statistical than historical information, in large part due to the zeal and intelligence of our true, universal Father, and always grieved for, Bishop Espada.
18. Or have many of the papers belonging to them [the archives] been lost?
    To the 18th one: In the other public offices there have been losses of papers in earlier times, but not in the bishop's archives. Perhaps moths (which in this climate are a formidable foe) have gnawed away at an important document or two, although in the ecclesiastical Curia great pains have been taken to safeguard the material in good condition and copy whatever has been moth-eaten, at least under Espada's watchful eye.

Finally, with regard to the conclusion, I must say that since no foreigner has come to visit our archives, I have not had the opportunity to know if that would help him/her with his/her inquiries. But much can be achieved through a venerable person. Havana, 31 July 1835

[As a postscript]: I [de la Luz] reiterate to Dr [Lieber] that I am always at his service, and that I have read with great pleasure his latest papers. I hope that he will send others in the same vein, because I too am a friend of humanity, and precisely in and through the path of education.

Questions such as 6, 7, 9, 11, and 12 suggest that, as previously mentioned, Lieber assumed there were Spanish creoles in the Caribbean and that a Spanish creole was or had been spoken in Cuba. It is also clear from question 12 that Lieber distinguished creole Spanish from colloquial Spanish and, further, that he wondered about variation within the Spanish creole (questions 7 and 11). We also see his interest in African words or phrases that are in use (question 10). Finally, in questions 13–18 Lieber sought information on the aboriginal languages of Cuba, expressing interest in personally examining the government archives there.

De la Luz's responses to Lieber's eighteen questions are of interest because they constitute what I believe to be the earliest recorded discussion on the issue of a Spanish creole in Cuba. In his responses, as well as in the body of the letter that accompanied the responses, de la Luz is unequivocal in his denial that there ever existed a Spanish creole in Cuba. The text and its translation are found in Appendix A.

De la Luz corrected Lieber's false assumption of such a creole by pointing out that while there were corruptions in the pronunciation of Spanish by Africans it could not be called a creole; rather, it was a variety of Spanish. He also remarked that there had never existed a Spanish creole in Cuba in his answer to Lieber's sixth question about whether one was still in existence at that time in Cuba. He did point out that people recently arrived from Africa would have certain expressions, but that these were mainly of English origin and probably were learned in the slave huts (*barracones*) and used to communicate during the sea journey. This could be seen as a type of incipient pidgin English.

In his letter, de la Luz mentioned an eighteenth-century catechism published for the clergy who administer to the slaves' religious needs. He sent Lieber a commentary on the document, which contains additional information on the nature of bozal Spanish and again asserts that the Afro-Cubans did not speak a Spanish creole.

## 4.3.2   *De la Luz's commentary on the catechism*

In 1796, as mentioned, a catechism was published in Cuba aimed at priests preaching to the *bozales*. Regarding the bozal speech contained in the catechism, Lipski (1998:312) states that the examples in the text are far from what would be considered a coherent creole. McWhorter (2000:27) specifically mentions this catechism, citing Castellanos and Castellanos (1992:349) who note that the priests were instructed to 'talk to them [i.e. the *bozales*] in the kind of language they use, without cases, tenses, conjunctions, agreement, order.' This, I argue, would imply a close relation between bozal and the Foreigner Talk of the priests rather than the existence of a Spanish creole, especially in comparison with early accounts of Sranan and Haitian, which are treated as separate languages not obtainable by the restructuring of the European language. McWhorter concludes that such evidence does not support the view that bozal Spanish reflected the existence of a creole. The conclusions of both Lipski and McWhorter are supported by José de la Luz's detailed linguistic commentary on this 1796 catechism. De la Luz wrote his commentary specifically for Lieber in response to this scholar's inquiries about what he thought to be a Spanish creole in Cuba. In his commentary, de la Luz explains that while there are usages and constructions used by Africans, these constitute neither a dialect nor a creole.

Although the entire commentary is found in Appendix B, I include here the quote containing the list of the main traits that de la Luz acknowledges as forming part of bozal Spanish:

> 1st: use of the adjective instead of the noun, e.g., *Dios no habla mentiroso* 'God does not speak lying' (page 46, line 6) instead of *mentira* 'lie'; *no tiene enfermo* 'he doesn't have sick', instead of *no tiene enfermedad* 'he has no sickness';
>
> 2nd: it is very frequent for them to use the plural instead of the singular with verbs, particularly with the verb *ser* 'be'. [There is an]

example in the following line [of the *catequismo*]: **son** *verdad* [lit.
'they are true'] instead of *es* 'is'; and

3rd: right there, one will note another idiom, which is to repeat the
word *verdad* 'true' to indicate that something is genuine, not bogus,
and generally it is repeated for emphasis.

4th: doing away with the article in the accusative: e.g., *Si ustedes
miran huevo* 'if you look at egg' instead of *un huevo* 'an egg' or *el
huevo* '**the** egg'; and sometimes in the nominative, too;

5th: not varying [the form of] the adjective, as in English, which is
quite normal. Thus, *mismo muger* [lit. same-MASC woman] instead
of *misma muger* [lit. same-FEM woman];

6th: putting a verb in the third instead of the first person, e.g., *yo tiene
dinero* 'I has money' instead of *yo tengo* [lit. I have-1SG.PRES.
INDIC] 'I have';

7th: similarly, using this third person (form) in place of the infinitive,
e.g., *yo quiere compra* [lit. I wants buys] instead of *comprar* 'to buy';

8th: sometimes they do not decline the personal pronouns either. Thus,
one often comes across *yo* 'I' in the catechism instead of *me* 'me'
[i.e., accusative/dative clitic] or *mi* 'me' [used after prepositions].

9th: quite frequently they delete the prepositions and thus one will see
*no está barriga de su madre* 's/he is not his/her mother's womb'
instead of *en la barriga* 'in his/her mother's womb';

10th: The blacks almost always repeat the negative. Thus, they say *no
va á juntar no* 's/he is not going to gather (the things)', *no va á salir
no* 's/he is not going to leave';

11th: they also put the adverb in place of the adjective, e.g., *hizo malo*
's/he did bad' instead of *mal* 'badly';[13]

12th: they often use the negative adjective *ninguno* 'no, not any'
instead of *no* 'no', *nada* 'nothing', *nada absolutamente* 'absolutely
nothing'.[14] An example from the catechism itself: *Puede la yegua
ir al cielo?* **Ninguno**. 'Can the mare go to heaven? No'; *El no
entiende **ninguno*** 'he does not understand any/no (one)' instead of
*no entiende nada* 'does not understand anything.[15]

---

[13] In this statement, de la Luz seems to have switched 'adverb' with 'adjective'. It is more likely
that he meant to say that the adjective was often used instead of the corresponding adverb.

[14] De la Luz puts an English translation of *nada absolutamente* ('nothing at all, by no means') in
the text.

[15] As alluded to by de la Luz, *ningun(o)* is used to negate NPs, as in *ningún edificio fue
construido este año* or *no fue construido ningún edificio este año* 'no building was built this
year'. Note that if *ningún(o)* is not in sentence-initial position, there is an obligatory double
negative in Spanish. If *ningun(o)* appears in sentence-initial position, there is no double
negation. This negation pattern is common in all varieties of Spanish.

13th: The blacks, that is, those living in the countryside, hardly or never use the conditional *si* 'if'. In its place they simply state the condition without any particle, e.g., *hombre va á luchar, el no tiene fuerzas, el se cae* 'man goes to fight, he does not have any strength, he falls', and in this way the repetition of the pronoun compensates for the lack of the conditional particle.

It is interesting and revealing that many of the traits mentioned by de la Luz are also found in more recent lists of bozal Spanish and/or of a putative Spanish-based creole. In the next section, I compare de la Luz's list and comments to those cited by other scholars, including two of de la Luz's contemporaries, as well as current researchers of bozal Spanish.

## 4.4    Comparison of Afro-Cuban Spanish features in de la Luz (1835) with those in later studies

Two contemporaries of de la Luz also dedicated a considerable amount of time to questions of language and language variation in Cuba. Esteban Pichardo was born in 1799 in what was then Santo Domingo, which his family abandoned for Cuba in 1801 due to the transfer of the country from Spanish to French rule.[16] Pichardo studied in the same San Carlos seminary as did de la Luz, and it is probable that the two youths knew each other or at least knew of each other from adolescence onwards. Although Pichardo also earned a degree in law, he spent little time practising law, dedicating much of his time and energy to the study of Cuban Spanish and geography, for which he spent a good deal of time travelling throughout the island (Alonso and Fernández 1977:72). In 1836, the first edition of Pichardo's *Diccionario provincial de vozes cubanas* was published, but it was in the second edition of 1849 that Pichardo included in the prologue comments on the Spanish of first- and later-generation Africans in Cuba of that time. He writes (1953:53–54):

Another loose and confusing type of speech is heard daily all over the Island [Cuba] among the *bozal* blacks, born in Africa, as happened to the French creole of Santo Domingo: this speech is common and identical among the blacks, regardless of the nation of their origin, and they always maintain it unless they came [to Cuba] as young children: it is a disfigured Castilian, babbled, without grammatical agreement, number, declension, or conjugation, without strong R, final S or D, with Ll for N, E for I, G for V, etc. In sum, [it is] a jargon more confusing the more recent the date of their immigration; but which can be understood by any Spaniard aside from some words common to all [the black *bozales*] which need translation . . . . The Creole blacks

---

[16] I have been unable to determine whether William Picard is related to Esteban Pichardo. Because Lieber wrote to William Picard in English, he would have anglicized his name as was typical in the academic correspondence of Lieber and others in this time period.

[those blacks born in Cuba] speak the variety of Spanish spoken by whites in their vicinity.

Pichardo wrote this excerpt fourteen years after de la Luz's letter to Lieber, and the traits mentioned coincide to a large extent with those mentioned by de la Luz, although de la Luz's tone in speaking about these varieties is more neutral than Pichardo's. The traits also turn out to be common to second language varieties of Spanish, as Pichardo himself mentions.

The other contemporary of de la Luz, Antonio Bachiller y Morales, was born in 1812, twelve years after de la Luz, and also attended school at San Carlos Seminary. Given that de la Luz taught there and was affiliated with the seminary as an educator, Bachiller y Morales must also have known de la Luz. Like de la Luz and Pichardo, Bachiller y Morales studied law, graduating in 1832 with a degree in law from the Real y Pontificia Universidad, twelve years after de la Luz. Bachiller y Morales specialized in civil law, and held various administrative positions in education and government. In 1862, at the age of fifty, he stepped down as dean of the School of Philosophy and in 1863 took on the directorship of the Institute of Secondary Education, which he was forced to relinquish in 1869 because of his separatist ideas regarding Cuba. He spent the following ten years (1869–1878) in the United States, after which he returned to Cuba as a journalist.

Bachiller y Morales was asked to respond to an 1882 letter from linguist and creolist Hugo Schuchardt, in which Schuchardt expressed interest in knowing about alterations that Spanish had undergone in the mouths of Africans and their descendants in Cuba. In his 1883 response, Bachiller y Morales (1977:107) states that one must distinguish between the modifications to Spanish made by the first-generation Africans, the *bozales*, and their descendants born on the island: 'the *bozal* black spoke Spanish in a way so distinct from that of his children that there is not a Cuban ear that would confuse the two'.[17] He cites two differences: *bozal* speakers, he says, tend to confuse the vowels *u* and *o*; *criollos*, the descendants of the *bozales*, he says, replace *l* with *i* in articles and at the end of words. He further notes that some of the traits found in the mouths of black characters in older plays are present in the speech of *bozales*, such as the word *enapué* (< *y después* 'and afterwards'), the use of *f-* for *h-*, the loss of *-s*, and the confusion of *l* and *r*. Bachiller y Morales includes an excerpt of a *criollo* text and one of an *africano* text, which I reproduce here, with a rendering in standard Spanish along with the English translation.

---

[17] The original is: 'El negro bozal hablaba el castellano de un modo tan distinto al que sus hijos usaban, que no hay oido cubano que pudiese confundirlos.'

(4.1)  *Criollo* (**Cuban Spanish as spoken by descendants of African parents**)
Venga uté      á tomar seivesa, y búquese un compañero
Venga Usted    a tomar cerveza, y búsquese un compañero
Que hoy se me sobra ei dinero, en medio de la grandesa.
Que hoy se me sobra el dinero, en medio de la grandeza.
Dió mirando mi probesa, me ha dado una lotería
Dios, mirando mi pobreza, me ha dado un premio en la lotería.
Y en mi radiante alegría, me ha convertido en poeta;
Y en mi radiante alegría, me he convertido en poeta;
Y aquí está mi papeleta, que no he cobrao entuavía.
Y aquí está mi billete/boleto, que no he cobrado todavía.

'Come have some beer and find yourself a companion, because today I have more than enough money in the midst of grandeur. God, looking upon my poverty, gave me a prize in the lottery and in my radiant joy He has made me a poet. And here is my ticket that I have yet to cash in.'

(4.2)  **Cuban Spanish as spoken by** *bozales*
Ah! Si oté      no lo cubrá, si oté      tovía      no fué
Ah! Si Usted   no lo cobra, si Usted   todavía   no ha ido (a cobrarlo)
¿Pa      que buca que bebe?    ¿Con qué oté lo va pagá?
¿Para   qué busca qué beber?   ¿Con qué Usted lo va a pagar?
Cuando oté lo cubra, anjá, antonsi ma qui ti muere
Cuando Usted lo cobre, bueno, entonces mas que te mueres
Bebé oté      como   dan  gana y durmí oté una semana
Beba Usted   como le dé la gana y duerma Usted una semana
Ma que lan tempo si piere.
Más que el tiempo se pierde.

'Ah! If you don't cash it in, if you haven't yet gone, why are you looking for something to drink? How are you going to pay for it? When you cash it in, well then more than dying you can drink as you like and sleep a week, more than time gets lost.'

With the exception of the sound changes Bachiller y Morales mentioned, the language sample of the *criollo* in (4.1) is the same as standard Spanish. The sample of the *bozales* in (4.2) also contains the same phonological characteristics alluded to by the author, and morphosyntactically exhibits three clear cases of restructuring: the lack of the required subjunctive form in the imperative (in [4.3a] and [4.5a]) and the use of a non-standard form in an idiomatic expression (in [4.4a]). The corresponding native Spanish equivalents for each are shown in (4.3b), (4.4b), and (4.5b). In all cases, a less frequently used form (the formal imperative and the subjunctive form) is replaced by a more commonly used one (the infinitival form or the 3PL form).[18]

---

[18] In the case of the forms of 'sleep', the imperative and subjunctive tokens in CREA are: *duerma* 'sleep-1MPER.SG.FORMAL; sleep-PRES.SUBJ.3SG' 248, *duermas* 'sleep-PRES.

(4.3a)  bebé             oté (< *beber Usted*)
        drink- INF       2SG.FORMAL
        'Drink you!'

(4.3b)  Beba             Usted
        drink-IMP        2SG.FORMAL

(4.4a)  como    dan              gana
        as      give-3PL         desire

(4.4b)  como le                  dé               la    gana
        as    2SG.FORMAL.DAT     give.PRES.SUB    the   desire

(4.5a)  y       durmí    oté                una   semana
        and     sleep-INF  2SG.FORMAL       a     week
        'and sleep a week'

(4.5b)  y       duerma                   Usted            una semana
        and     sleep-IMP.FORMAL.SG      2SG.FORMAL       a   week

Towards the end of this article, Bachiller y Morales adds an important comment regarding the nature of these passages: 'However, it must be confessed that a big part of their alterations [those of the *criollos* and *bozales*] are initiated by the majority of the people of the country, especially those from the countryside. The Andalusians were the most numerous of the settlers, followed by the [Canary] Islanders, the Catalans, and other poorly spoken people who left traces that are in the process of disappearing, although not as quickly as one would hope in the more neglected classes' (1977:109) (my translation). He finishes the article by giving other examples of modified Spanish, a literary example of the speech of a typical Cuban street vendor and an excerpt of Papiamentu.

There are several commonalities in the respective descriptions given by Pichardo and Bachiller y Morales about the speech of the Africans and their descendants in Cuba. First, both mention the difference in speech between *bozales* and *criollos*. Second, either by giving examples or making explicit statements, both authors identify similar pronunciation traits, as well as the deletion or levelling of conjugation and agreement affixation. Third, both scholars imply or explicitly state that the varieties spoken by *bozales* and

---

SUBJ.2SG' 99, *duerman* 'sleep-PRES.SUBJ.3PL' 74, *durmamos* 'sleep-PRES.SUBJ.1PL' 12, *durmáis* 'sleep-PRES.SUBJ.2PL' 3. The form *duerme*, 3SG present tense as well as 2SG imperative, has 1,579 tokens. By contrast, the infinitival form *dormir* has 8,343 tokens. The corresponding forms of *beber* are largely analogous in that the infinitival form has many more tokens than all subjunctive and imperative ones taken together. In CREA we find: *beba* 'drink-IMPER.SG.FORMAL; drink-PRES.SUBJ.3SG' 221, *bebas* 'drink-PRES.SUBJ.2SG' 46, *beban* 'drink-PRES.SUBJ.3PL' 46, *bebamos* 'drink-PRES.SUBJ.1PL' 28, *bebáis* 'drink-PRES.SUBJ.2PL' 4, *bebe* 'drink-PRES.IND.3SG; drink-IMPER.SG.FORMAL' 1,385, *beber* 'drink'-INF' 4,216 tokens. As for the forms *dé* and *dan*, in CREA, their respective token frequency is 5,310 and 14,683, the latter almost three times more frequent than the former.

*criollos* were intelligible to anyone who was familiar with Cuban Spanish. Furthermore, it is said that all Africans and Afro-Cubans shared many of their traits with the less-educated white population of the island. Finally, both Pichardo and Bachiller y Morales were familiar with creole languages. Pichardo knew of the French-based creole in Saint Domingue (today's Haiti), and Bachiller y Morales was well aware of Papiamentu, including numerous examples of the language which he mentions in his correspondence with Schuchardt: 'However, if he [Schuchardt] wishes to know to what point the lovely language transplanted in America [Spanish] can be disfigured, he should direct his attention to the dialect that has developed in Curaçao, with the name of *Papiamentu*' (my translation). Thus, these scholars were in a position to compare Afro-Cuban Spanish to Papiamentu or to Haitian French Creole. The conclusion of such a comparison was that Afro-Cuban Spanish varieties were less 'disfigured' than, for example, Papiamentu. It is also interesting to note than some of the traits mentioned by Bachiller y Morales, i.e., the confusion of *u* and *o* and the vocalization of lateral *l* to *i*, could be traits influenced by Papiamentu, which has Portuguese-based lexical items (e.g., Papiamentu *mustra* 'to show' vs Portuguese [muš-trar] vs Spanish [mos-trar]).

In the twentieth and twenty first centuries, the traits discussed by these nineteenth-century scholars have been understood in two opposing ways: one group takes the traits to represent vestiges of a previously spoken Spanish-based creole – possibly a very old one – while the other takes them to be instances of untutored second language acquisition. There are, however, other positions between these two sides. Perl (1987:4) asserts that 'stabilization of *bozal* speech (i.e., *habla bozal*) took place, in my opinion, in the nineteenth century and no further development of an earlier language variety is to be assumed' (my translation). Perl is joined by Lipski (1998:317) who, quoting Pérez de la Riva (1978), states that we do not know anything about the reality of plantation slavery in Cuba. He continues: 'I agree then with Perl that the *bozal* language could have become a creole in very special circumstances. As Pérez de la Riva points out to us, we are completely unknowledgeable about the history of the most isolated slaves, because of which we cannot rule out the option of a creole' (my translation).

For my part, I agree that there were varieties of African Spanish in nineteenth-century Cuba. The question is whether there was a creole language that formed in Cuba itself, not directly derivable from Papiamentu. I acknowledge that this possibility cannot be ruled out *a priori*. We know from the 1774 census, for example, that some sugar refineries had as many as 200 slaves (Masó 1976:112). Thus, there were conditions, albeit for at most sixty to seventy years, for a pidgin to have formed and creolized. However, the probability of that is small. On the other hand, we have the observations from de la Luz, which I take to be the most definitive statement so far on the linguistic situation in Cuba in the first half of the nineteenth century. Based on his comments to Lieber and on the *catequismo*, I assume that de la Luz had detailed knowledge of plantation life, for instance, regarding modes of punishment on plantations (see the discussion above of *tabla* and *boca abajo* in de la Luz's commentary of the *catequismo*). From his commentary, it can also be assumed that a creole most likely did not exist. We must recall that de la Luz was familiar with creole languages, although I do acknowledge that it is impossible to assume that de la Luz had detailed knowledge of even the most isolated plantations.

Certain of de la Luz's comments speak directly to the differences in the Spanish of the *bozales* themselves, depending where they originally were from. He remarks that 'we whites understand some blacks more easily than we do other blacks, [just as we understand] people coming from a certain country better than we do people from another [country]. The Congos, for example, make themselves understood and pronounce with more clarity than do the Carabalíes.' De la Luz addresses, as well, differences in speech between urban and rural *bozales*: 'However, there are some uniform ways of corrupting it [Spanish], and this is natural, among all of them, particularly in the countryside, not only by altering the pronunciation of certain words uniformly, but also by giving them sometimes a different meaning, and other times [by giving them] a meaning analogous to the genuine one. For example, it is rather common for them to say *dos viages* "two trips" instead of *dos veces* "two times".' As alluded to above, such particularities would have been passed on from one generation to another, especially in rural areas, thus becoming part of the linguistic repertoire of Cuban-born blacks.

In this quote by de la Luz, he notes that, despite the individual differences between speakers of African descent, depending on where they work, their origin in Africa, and so on, there were some ways of restructuring the Spanish language that were generally used by all *bozales*, i.e., the items recorded in the *catequismo*. These, I suggest, would constitute part of the Afro-Cuban variety of Spanish spoken in Cuba. The items listed by de la Luz can be classified according to the type of restructuring, involving agreement, non-distinction of word classes, re-analysis of words, non-use of function words, and repetition, given in (4.6)–(4.10).

(4.6) *Agreement* (noun–adjective, noun–determiner, or subject–verb)
    a. Lack of subject–verb agreement: *yo tiene dinero* [lit. I has-3SG. PRES.INDIC money] instead of *yo tengo dinero* [lit. I have-1SG. PRES.INDIC money] 'I have money'.
    b. Preference of 3SG form over other forms: *yo quiere compra* [lit. I want-3SG.PRES.INDIC buy-3SG.PRES.INDIC] instead of *yo quiero comprar* [lit. I want-1SG.PRES.INDIC buy-INF] 'I want to buy'.

    c. Lack of noun–adjective agreement: *mismo muger* [lit. same-MASC woman] instead of *misma muger* [lit. same-FEM woman] 'same woman'.

    d. Use of *son* 'they are' as a singular: ***son** verdad* instead of *es verdad* 'it is true'.

(4.7) *Non-distinction of case or word category*

    a. Non-distinction of adjectives and nouns: *no tiene enfermo* [lit. s/he NEG has sick] instead of *no tiene enfermedad* [lit. s/he NEG has sickness] 's/he has no sickness'.

    b. Non-distinction of adjectives and adverbs *hizo malo* 's/he did bad' instead of *hizo mal* 's/he did badly'.

    c. Non-distinction of subject and object pronouns: *yo* 'I' is found in accusative instead of *me* 'me' or *mi* 'my, me [after prepositions]'.

(4.8) *Re-analysis of certain words*

    a. Use of *verdad* to refer to something genuine, not bogus.

    b. Use of NP negator/negative pronoun *ninguno* 'no, no one' instead of the simple negator *no* 'no' or *nada* 'nothing', as in *puede la yegua ir al cielo? Ninguno* instead of *puede la yegua ir al cielo? No* 'Can the mare go to heaven? No' or *él no entiende **ninguno*** instead or *él no entiende nada* [lit. he NEG understands nothing] 'he does not understand anything'.

(4.9) *Non-use of function words*

    a. Prepositions: *no está barriga de su madre* instead of *no está **en** la barriga de su madre* s/he is not in his/her mother's womb';

    b. Determiners: *si ustedes miran huevo* instead of *si ustedes miran el/ un huevo* 'if you look at the/an egg';

    c. Conjunctions: *hombre va a luchar, él no tiene fuerzas, él se cae* instead of *si un hombre no tiene fuerza y va a luchar, se cae* 'if a man has no strength and goes to fight, he falls'.

(4.10) *Repetition/redundancy*

    a. Repetition of the negative marker sentence-finally: ***no** va á juntar **no*** [lit. NEG go-3SG.PRES.INDIC COMP gather-INF NEG] instead of ***no** va á juntar* 's/he is not going to gather'.

The categories in (4.6)–(4.8) involve the notions of salience or defaults or both. We know from Bybee (1985:71), as well as from the discussion regarding Table 1.4 in chapter 1, that in spoken Spanish the most frequently used verbal forms are 3SG, 1SG, and 3PL in that order. This applies to the Spanish of the nineteenth century, as well. Thus, it is not surprising to find that the 3SG form is the preferred form in (4.6a) and (4.6b), as the 3SG form is used roughly twice as frequently as either of the other forms. Regarding the preference in (4.6c) of the masculine over the feminine grammatical gender, in Spanish the former is uncontroversially accepted as the default form. As for the use of *son* 'are.3PL' instead of *es* 'is' or *soy* 'I am' in (4.6d), one would expect that *es* would be the default based on the frequency argument. However, if we assume, uncontroversially, that *es* was realized largely as [eh] or [e] by Spanish-speaking settlers in Cuba (i.e., largely Andalusians and Canary Islanders), then we are dealing with a shorter, less perceptible form ([eh] or [e]) arguably in competition in the feature pool with the perceptually more salient form *son*. In this case frequency was overridden by perceptual salience.[19] Thus, even though *es* ([eh] or [e]) may have been used much more frequently than *son*, *son* would be more easily perceived.

Regarding the examples in (4.7), the fact that case or lexical category becomes confused in bozal Spanish is not surprising if we appeal to language processing and production. For example, the preference of *enfermo* 'sick' in (4.7a) as the default form for 'sick' as well as 'sickness' may be as simple as this: given that *enfermo* is shorter than *enfermedad* 'sickness', it is easier to produce and conveys essentially the same information. Apart from being longer, the form *enfermedad* ends in a CVC structure, which is not as easy to produce as the CV ending of *enfermo*. This argument would also account for why *malo* would be preferred to *mal* in (4.7b). Neither of these arguments, however, is applicable to the preference of *me* 'me' or *mí* 'me' over *yo* 'I' to express 1SG of any case in (4.7c) since the syllable structure of all of these forms is CV. In this case, I would argue that it is a matter of frequency. In Alameda and Cuetos (1995), we find that the relative frequency of the pronouns *me* (8,648 tokens, 28 per cent) and *mí* (940 tokens, 7 per cent) combined is far greater than that of *yo* (3,697 tokens, 28 per cent).[20] Thus, on

---

[19] In the Portuguese-based creoles, the 3SG present copula *é* is not often found (e.g., notably in Palenquero (Schwegler 1998:263) and Daman Creole Portuguese, due to de-creolization [Clements and Koontz-Garboden 2002]). However, *son* is found in Makanese Creole Portuguese, and reflexes of Portuguese *tem* 's/he has' or *ter* 'have-INF' are found in Indo-Portuguese creoles other than Daman CP.

[20] For the frequency count, Alameda and Cuetos (1995) took text from 164 novels (50 per cent), press stories (25 per cent), essays (15 per cent) and science/technology articles (10 per cent). Note that the data from CREA reveal that, of all the first-person singular pronouns, *me* is the most frequently found, followed by *yo* and then *mi*. Combined, *me* and *mi* count for 77 per cent of the occurrences:

Table. Frequency of *yo, me, mi* in twentieth-century oral and written texts

|         | *yo*          | *me*          | *mi*          | Total  |
|---------|---------------|---------------|---------------|--------|
| Oral    | 43215 (41%)   | 45791 (43%)   | 17572 (16%)   | 106578 |
| Written | 109221(20%)   | 288876 (52%)  | 156882 (28%)  | 554979 |
| Total   | 152436 (23%)  | 334667 (51%)  | 174454 (26%)  | 661557 |

Chi-square = 7879.57, df 2, p < 0.001.

grounds of frequency, if both forms are present in the speech of this type (i.e. speech reflecting untutored second language learning), we would expect *me* to be selected over *yo*. However, we would not *predict* that both forms would be found in such speech given that *me* is a clitic and, as an unstressed particle, would be less likely to be perceived than *yo*.[21]

With respect to the re-analysis of certain words in (4.8), this is common in naturalistic second language acquisition and not at all surprising to find.[22] The omission of function words in (4.9) is also not surprising to find in bozal Spanish if we consider the notion of logical bootstrapping discussed in section 1.3 of chapter 1. First, before first or second language learners can relate lexical items with functional markers, they have first to have learned such items to be able to relate them to one another in a grammatical construction such as a sentence (see Bates and Goodman 1999:52; Zobl 1982). Second, such functional markers are often not necessary as the information is recoverable from the context.

Finally, the repetition of the negative particle mentioned in (4.10), also found in the Portuguese-based creoles formed in Africa (see Parkvall 2000:60–62), is a trait in bozal Spanish undoubtedly attributable to African language substrate influence. Thus, all the traits commented on by de la Luz can be accounted for by appealing to the notions of production, processing, and frequency of occurrence of the forms in question, or of substrate influence in the case of double negation.

If we compare the traits commented on by de la Luz to those traits found and discussed by scholars dealing with bozal Spanish, we find that the former largely overlap with the latter as compiled by Lipski (1994:113–117) from the various scholars who have written on the issue and which I list below in (4.11)–(4.15), following the above classification as a guideline.[23]

(4.11) *Agreement* (noun–adjective, noun–determiner, or subject–verb)
    a. Lack of gender and number agreement in nouns and adjectives
    b. Infinitives where conjugated verb forms would be expected (*para tú hacer eso* 'for you to do that')

---

[21] This is apparent in other varieties of naturalistic second language acquisition. For example, Clements (2003a) documents an immigrant learner of Spanish who does not incorporate any of the clitic pronouns in her variety of Spanish, but does have the stressed pronouns such as *yo* 'I', *tú* 'you-SG', *él* 'he', *ella* 'she', etc. See chapter 6 for a discussion of this.
[22] I would expect, in a competition between *nada* (realized as [ná-ɗa] or [na:]) and *ninguno*, that the former would be preferred based on frequency of occurrence (2,097 and 125 respectively, according to Alameda and Cuetos 1995). However, based on perceptual salience, [niŋ-gu-no] could be considered more salient than [na:].
[23] Ortiz López (1998:71–117) discusses an extensive list of traits, the most important of which are included in Lipski's (1994) list as well.

(4.12)  *Re-analysis of certain words*
   a. Use of *tener* 'have' as a presentational verb instead of *haber*
   b. Use of the all-purpose preposition *na*
   c. Use of *vos* 'you'
(4.13)  *Non-use of function words*
   a. Loss of common prepositions
   b. Occasional elimination of the copula
   c. Loss of articles
   d. Lack of syntactic complementizers such as *que* 'that'
(4.14)  Restructuring involving word order
   a. Non-inverted questions *¿qué tú quieres?* [lit. what you.SG want-2SG
      'what do you want?'
   b. Post-posed demonstratives
   c. Pre-posing *más* 'more', as in *más nada* [lit. more nothing] for
      'nothing more'
(4.15)  *Redundancy*
   a. Redundant use of subject pronouns (Standard Spanish is a pro-drop
      language)

We find that Lipski's (1994) list lacks two crucial bozal Spanish traits: the tense–aspect-like particles, shown in (4.16) and discussed by Perl (1982:428), Ortiz López (1998:83–88), and Lipski (2000), and the repetition, sentence-finally, of the negative particle, noted by Schwegler (1998:235) and Ortiz López (1998:113–115) among others, and shown in (4.17).

(4.16)  TMA-like tense–aspect markers *ya* 'past', *tá* 'present', and *vá* 'future'
(4.17)  Double negation with a sentence-final negator: *yo no* hablo ingles *no* [lit. I
        NEG talk-1SG.PRES English NEG] 'I don't speak English.'

Since the discussion of the traits presented in (4.6)–(4.10) covers those included in (4.11)–(4.15), I will not discuss them in detail here. (For a discussion of the individual traits, see Lipski 1994:113–117 and Ortiz López 1998:71–117.) I would, however, like to add a general comment. It turns out that such traits are found to be very common in naturalistically learned second language acquisition. As mentioned in chapter 1, Klein and Perdue (1992:315) find a basic variety in naturally learned second language acqui-sition in which the development for all of their learners from various lan-guage backgrounds, though not identical, is remarkably similar. These general traits correspond largely to those just identified here for bozal Spanish. Moreover, in a detailed study of the Spanish variety of a Chinese immigrant residing in Spain, Clements (2003a, 2003b, 2005, and chapter 6 of this volume) finds evidence that suggests the presence of incipient tense–aspect markers. Thus, we see that in large part these second language varieties possess the same features as those found in bozal Spanish. We find this near overlap between the traits in naturalistic L2 acquisition and in bozal Spanish expected given the similarities in the socio-historical backgrounds of the nineteenth-century *bozales* and some immigrant communities in Europe today.[24]

However, the particle *ta* warrants particular attention. Perl (1987) gives examples taken from Cabrera (1954) which cannot be reductions of *está*. Ortiz López (1998:83–88, 140) and Lipski (2000) also provide numerous examples, two of which I show in (4.18) and (4.19), from Ortiz López (1998:85) and Lipski (2000) respectively, with additional glosses.

(4.18)  En     ese     tiempo        yo      bailaba                  mucho...
        in     that    time          I       dance-PAST.IMPER    a lot
        **Ta**    bailando    tre(s)    día(s)    seguido.
        TMA    dancing     three     days      in.a.row
        'At that time, I used to dance a lot. I danced three days in a row.'

(4.19)  Horita     ta         bení      pa      cá.
        now        TMA    come    DIR    here
        'Now she's coming here.'

It is unlikely that Spanish *estaba bailando* [eh-ta̱-βa-βaj-la̱ŋ-do] or *está viniendo* [eh-ta̱-βa-βi-nie̱ŋ-do]) would reduce to *ta bailando* or *ta bení*. In the first case, the maximally reduced form of *estaba* would arguably be [ta-βa], although it could also be argued that the intervocalic [β] could have disappeared, yielding [ta:] and then [ta]. In the second case, the vowels of the verb roots are different but, more importantly, the stress assignment of the two forms is different.

According to Lipski (2000), *ta* in bozal Spanish has two possible sources. Before discussing these, I provide some external ecology to contextualize the situation. In his correspondence to Lieber, de la Luz mentions that slaves coming to Cuba often knew expressions from English, which, he said, they must have learned on their way to Cuba. Lipski (2000:438) notes that in the nineteenth century '[s]laves in colonial Cuba were drawn from all parts of Africa as well as from other Caribbean territories.' Many of those coming from Africa, he adds, came from well-defined geographical areas and ethnic groups (e.g., those of the Lucumí, Carabalí, Congo, Gangá, Mina, Bibí, etc.). Lipski also (ibid.:442) notes that of the thousands of sugarcane cutters brought from other Caribbean islands to Cuba in the nineteenth century, there were well-documented pockets of Papiamentu speakers coming from Curaçao, Bonaire, and/or Aruba. One of the sources, then, for bozal Spanish *ta* is arguably Papiamentu. Indeed, the present marker in Papiamentu is *ta*, as shown in the examples in (4.20), taken from Maurer (1998:162).

---

[24] See the discussion of *va* and *ya* in Lipski 2000.

| (4.20a) | Awor | mi | **ta** | lesa. | | |
|---|---|---|---|---|---|---|
| | now | I | PRES | read | | |

'I am reading now.'

| (4.20b) | Mi | **ta** | lesa | tur | dia. |
|---|---|---|---|---|---|
| | I | PRES | read | all | day |

'I read every day.'

The other, Lipski argues, is from slaves with Yoruba or another related language as their native language. The particle *(eh)ta*, then, in the speech of these untutored Spanish learners, was re-analysed as *ta* to mark the present, based on the pattern in Yoruba shown in (4.21), taken from Lipski (2000:443).

| (4.21) | mo | n | jeun. |
|---|---|---|---|
| | I | am | eating. |

'I {am eating/eat}.'

Thus, the particle *ta* in bozal Spanish can be accounted for without appealing to creolization or the existence of a stable pidgin, which the demographic statistics have shown to be unlikely. In a similar way, Lipski accounts for the particles *ya* (< Spanish *ya* 'already') and *va* (< Spanish 's/he is going') in bozal Spanish by appealing to re-analysis during L2 acquisition. Thus, the particles found in bozal Spanish can be reasonably accounted for by phenomena other than the presence of a prior creole language. In his detailed survey of real-time speech sampling from Afro-Cubans, Ortiz López (1998:116) comes to the same conclusion.

Finally, double negation of the type illustrated in (4.17) is a common feature in the relevant African languages represented in Cuba during the nineteenth century, as Schwegler (1996a) has shown, and it is common in various varieties of Portuguese and Spanish that have had significant contact with African language speakers, such as Brazilian Portuguese and Palenquero, a Portuguese- and Spanish-based creole spoken in Colombia. Double negation in Cuban bozal Spanish is most easily and uncontroversially accounted for by the substrate influence of the relevant African languages (e.g., Kikongo, Kimbundu; see Schwegler 1998:234–237). For example, Lorenzino (1998:182–183) notes that Kimbundu exhibits a double negation of the same type as found in Angolar and São Tomé Creole Portuguese, as well as Brazilian Portuguese, and bozal and Dominican Spanish. An example is given in (4.22).

| (4.22) | Eme | (ki) | ngi | mutu | ami |
|---|---|---|---|---|---|
| | I | NEG | a | person | NEG |

Thus, processing and production strategies, frequency, and African and creole language substrate influence together may reasonably account for all the traits found in bozal Spanish without having to posit the existence of a stable pidgin or a creole in Cuba.

## 4.5     Concluding remarks

In this chapter, I have introduced into the discussion of the origins of Cuban bozal Spanish the contribution made by a recently discovered 1835 correspondence exchange between two scholars and linguists, one from Cuba, José de la Luz Caballero, the other from the United States, Francis Lieber. To understand better the context of the letter exchange, I briefly examined the external ecology of Cuba, specifically, the Spanish crown's influence on trade in Cuba, and surveyed some of the social and labour history of the island. I found that the circumstances for the emergence of a Spanish-based pidgin in Cuba started around 1770, thirty years before de la Luz's birth. I maintain that if de la Luz, who knew the linguistic situation of Cuba well – and was well versed on the development and structure of creole languages in neighbouring Haiti and Jamaica – knew of no evidence of a pidgin or creole on the island, then such a linguistic system likely did not develop or exist there.

De la Luz's comments on the Spanish varieties of Cuba are written in two documents. One is a commentary on a catechism first published in 1796 with the goal of aiding chaplains in their effort to impart religious doctrine to recently arrived Africans. This commentary is useful as a linguistic document because in it de la Luz comments on expressions, idioms, structures, and usages we might otherwise have considered to be found only among the black population. De la Luz's commentary reveals to us that this is not the case, that many, perhaps most, of the particularities of black speech were shared by other non-black segments of the Cuban population.

The second document is a response to a query by Francis Lieber as to the existence of a Spanish-based creole on Cuba. From the precise nature of Lieber's questions, as well as the detailed commentary provided by de la Luz, we recognize that both men were sophisticated linguists who were knowledgeable about language structure and language change. Indeed, most of Francis Lieber's linguistic interests involved language contact phenomena. Both Lieber and de la Luz were well travelled polyglots, and knew some of the most impressive minds of that day in the field of European linguistics and letters, such as the von Humboldt brothers and Sir Walter Scott, among others. Their exchange offers us a rare view of an erudite exchange on Cuban Spanish in 1835, fourteen years before de la Luz's contemporary, Esteban Pichardo, published his dictionary on Cuban Spanish in which he also comments on Cuban Spanish varieties. What is most unique about the Lieber–de la Luz exchange is the specific nature of the expert questioning by Lieber regarding the existence of a Cuban Spanish-based creole and the denial of its existence by a Cuban linguist who had access to an extensive variety of information sources, including all his great uncle's writings on the topic. (His great uncle, Father José Agustín Caballero, apart from being an educator at the renowned San Carlos Seminary in Havana, was considered an important figure in the intellectual history of the turn of the nineteenth century (Masó 1976:137–150).)

Given the detail of de la Luz's responses and commentary and his credentials and those of his correspondent Francis Lieber, I believe that these documents constitute the most definitive evidence to date – albeit not conclusive – that there never existed a Spanish-lexified stable pidgin or creole at any time in the colonial history of Cuba or at any point in Cuba as an independent state.

This information on the external ecology of Cuba is supported by the linguistic facts available on bozal Spanish that have been attributed to the existence of a stable pidgin or a creole. I have argued that the sources of the bozal Spanish features are convincingly accounted for by appealing to strategies in language processing and production, and to the influence of African languages (e.g., Yoruba, Kikongo, Kimbundu, etc.), and Papiamentu, the Portuguese- and Spanish-based creole language taken by slaves from Curaçao to Cuba during the first half of the nineteenth century. The discovery of the Lieber–de la Luz exchange on bozal Spanish also opens new avenues for research as the manuscript is studied in more detail by other scholars in the field and more is discovered about these relatively unknown nineteenth-century linguists.

# 5   Chinese Coolie Spanish in nineteenth-century Cuba

## 5.1   Introduction

During the first half of the nineteenth century, the African slave trade in Cuba became illegal and the laws prohibiting it were increasingly enforced, a topic touched upon in chapter 4. Alarmed by the slave revolts of the 1790s in Haiti, movements began in Cuba with the purpose of settling whites on farms and in villages in Cuba not only to infuse the labour force with new manpower, but also in part to counterbalance the large black population and thereby diminish the possibility of revolt. As we saw in chapter 4, the black population in Cuba began to outnumber the whites around 1791 and according to Kiple (1976) this situation lasted up until 1846. Corbitt (1971:2) notes that in 1841 in Cuba there were 589,333 blacks (58 per cent) (436,495 slaves and 152,838 free coloureds) and 418,211 whites (42 per cent).[1] This situation made Cuban plantation-owners uncomfortable and as a consequence incentives were offered to planters to hire workers from Spain, but with little success. The Spanish government then agreed to a plan drawn up by the Junta de Fomento (Promotion Committee) to introduce Chinese coolies (indentured labourers) into Cuba, following an idea the British had used in their colonies. From 3 June 1847 – the arrival date of the first Chinese coolies from China – onwards, nearly 500,000 of them came to the island (Corbitt 1971:6). In this chapter, I discuss some details of the ecology of the Chinese in Cuba between 1847 and the late twentieth century, focusing on the relations among the Chinese, the Africans, and the Afro-Cubans, and the development of the Chinese variety of Spanish. I then examine the traits found in some of the sources of Chinese Spanish. The data suggest that the Spanish variety spoken by the Chinese in Cuba is similar to varieties of Chinese Immigrant Spanish, to be taken up in chapter 6. That is, it is more akin to a naturalistically learned

---

[1] One of Corbitt's statistics differs minimally from Kiple's: the former cites the number of whites at 418,211, whereas the latter uses an adjusted figure of 418,291. I take Kiple's figure to be the more accurate one.

L2 Spanish variety, highly comparable to the 'basic variety' mentioned in sections 1.2, 1.3, 3.2, and 4.4, than to a pidgin proper.[2]

## 5.2     External ecology of the Chinese in Cuba

### 5.2.1     The period of Chinese coolie indentured labour (1847–1877)

Until 1762, when the English occupied Havana for ten months, the Spanish crown had a vise-like grip on trade with its colonies, including slave trade in Cuba. In the 1760s, trade barriers began to break down and this allowed an influx of slave labour, followed by rapid development in Cuban agriculture, which in turn led to the need for additional slave labour (see chapter 4 for more details). But, just at the moment that slave labour became more accessible to Cuban land-owners, between the 1760s and 1791, the slave revolts began in Haiti (then Saint Domingue). Caught between the need for labour and the fear of their African slaves revolting, Cuban plantation-owners turned to the idea of trying to attract white labour. Corbitt (1971:1–4) reports on the less than successful attempts by the Junta de Población Blanca (Committee of the White Population) to lure white labour to Cuba while slave labour continued to be exploited.

In 1821, the African slave trade was curtailed by a treaty signed by Spain and Britain to outlaw it by 1820. However, enforcement of the treaty was weak to non-existent and Cuban plantation-owners were still able to import illegal slave labour, though they were ever wary of the possibility of uprisings. In 1835, Britain obtained another treaty to enforce the first one, which obliged the Cuban plantation-owners to look elsewhere for their labour needs.

In 1842, some high-profile Cuban businessmen and planters founded the Junta de Fomento which took over some of the duties and budget of the Junta de Población Blanca. This committee hatched the idea of offering prizes to the planters who attracted the most white settlers from among the Catalans, Canary Islanders, and Galicians in Spain (Corbitt 1971:3), but the experiment attracted only around 1,000 settlers in two years. The Junta de Fomento became increasingly desperate to find labour, and they gathered the idea of importing labourers from China using an English firm, Zulueta and Company, which had been shipping in Chinese indentured labour for England.

The members of the Junta de Fomento saw several apparent advantages to this proposal. First, the Chinese would be considered white so that the stipulation that white labour be sought would be fulfilled. Second, from the

---

[2] By 'pidgin proper', I mean a language variety spoken by members of two or more language communities that has developed conventionalized structures and has to be learnt (see Bakker 1995: 26).

experience of the Spaniards in the Philippines, the Chinese were viewed as docile and hard-working, and would thus be ideal labourers.[3] Third, it was thought that the supply of Chinese labourers, referred to as *culíes* or coolies, would be plentiful.[4] The reaction of the Spanish government to the plan, recorded in a royal order of 3 July 1847, was favourable. Interestingly, according to Corbitt (1971:5–6), it was roughly one month earlier (3 and 12 June 1847) that two ships carrying the first Chinese immigrants arrived in Havana. Of the 612 men who had begun the journey, 515 were able to work upon arrival; some had died during the voyage or just after arrival in Cuba, while others were rejected for being too old, sickly, or thin. Thus began the exploitation of Chinese coolie labour in Cuba, which would last until 1877.

After the first two shipments of coolies to Cuba, problems arose between China and Britain regarding the trafficking of coolies to the Caribbean, and so the importation into Cuba was temporarily suspended (Jiménez Pastrana 1963:37–38). On 5 August 1851, the Junta de Fomento agreed to a plan to import more Chinese (Corbitt 1971:14–15), and permission was granted to two firms to import 3,000 coolies over a period of two years. Around 1855, the practice of using Chinese labourers on the plantations was evaluated by the planters. Although the experiment received mixed reviews, overall it was considered a success; the importation of coolies continued, and by the end of 1860 around 49,077 coolies had been taken to Cuba (ibid.:18).

During this time, problems of abuse of the coolies (who were treated little differently from slaves) and other problems with the importation of Chinese indentured labour to Cuba prompted riots and protests in Hong Kong and in Chinese cities such as Amoy (Xiamen, in Fujian province), one of the major ports used to ship the labourers to Cuba. As a consequence, Britain closed the port in Hong Kong to the coolie trade and the Chinese imperial authorities adopted the policy of beheading the recruiting agents. As a result, by 1859 only the Portuguese colony of Macau was used to ship Chinese labourers to Cuba (Corbitt 1971:19). Virtually all the people taken to Cuba were men from Canton province who spoke Cantonese.

In 1859–1860, regulations were established to safeguard the Chinese labourers being shipped to Spanish colonies, and the Spanish government, which had called a temporary halt to such shipments to the New World, bestowed its blessing on the resumption of the trade, after which coolie importations rose sharply (between 1 January and 21 July 1861, for example,

---

[3] The expression *manila chino* was used by the Spanish colonizers to refer to Chinese indentured labourers, also in Cuba. See (5.28) for an example of the expression being spoken by a Chinese soldier fighting for Cuba against the Spanish.

[4] According to the OED, the term 'coolie' probably derived from Gujarati *kulī*, initially the name of a tribe in Gujarat that migrated to South India. There, the term apparently mixed with Tamil *kūli* 'hire' and eventually came to denote hired labourers or burden carriers.

Table 5.1. *Number of coolies arriving in Cuba from 1847 to 1859*

| Year | No. of ships | Coolies embarked | Coolies landed | Deaths | Death rate |
|------|------|------|------|------|------|
| 1847 | 2 | 612 | 571 | 41 | 6.7 |
| 1853 | 15 | 5150 | 4307 | 843 | 16.37 |
| 1854 | 4 | 1750 | 1711 | 39 | 2.23 |
| 1855 | 6 | 3130 | 2985 | 145 | 4.63 |
| 1856 | 15 | 6152 | 4968 | 1184 | 19.25 |
| 1857 | 28 | 10,116 | 8547 | 1569 | 15.51 |
| 1858 | 33 | 16,414 | 13,385 | 3029 | 18.45 |
| 1859 | 13 | 6799 | 6027 | 772 | 11.36 |
| Total | 116 | 50,123 | 42,501 | 7748 | 15.2 |

6,223 coolies were taken to Cuba). As mentioned, this practice continued until 1877. Although the Cuban planters favoured the further importation of coolies, the Spanish government entered into a treaty with Peking that shut down the trade and closed a painful chapter in Chinese–Spanish relations (Corbitt 1971:23).

The year-by-year arrival of coolies in Cuba between 1847 and 1859 is shown in Table 5.1. Corbitt (1971:52) notes that these figures, while not complete or necessarily entirely accurate, are the most reliable ones available. After 1859, he adds, there is no complete information about the number of coolies taken to Cuba. He states (ibid.:24) that the tabulation of the arrivals reported in the daily shipping column of the newspaper *Diario de la Marina* from 1847 to 1874 gives a total of 114,232. Thus, between 1859 and 1877, roughly 71,731 coolies were transported to Cuba.

After the importation of coolies was halted in 1877, Chinese immigrants continued to arrive in Cuba, but under substantially different circumstances (Corbitt 1971:92). Of those who were in Cuba as coolies, if the available estimates are reliable, less that 40 per cent lived to complete their eight-year term of 'service' (ibid.:88). Corbitt (ibid.:90) also notes that, for every Chinese man who achieved success in Cuba, there were dozens who either eked out a bare existence against innumerable odds, or scraped together sufficient means to buy a return passage to China.

In 1899, when the Spanish were finally defeated and the Cuban flag was raised over the island, Corbitt (1971:92) estimates that around 15,000 Chinese remained. According to the census of 1899, the Chinese men were mainly day labourers (54 per cent), servants (19 per cent), merchants (13 per cent), and peddlers (3 per cent), with other professions making up the remaining 11 per cent. In the same census, only twenty Chinese women were listed as having professions.

Chinese immigration to Cuba during the republic is hard to ascertain because of what Corbitt (1971:95) calls the 'hopelessly conflicting statistics on the subject'. The figures maintained by the Chinese consulate in Havana reveal that, between 1903 and 1916, 6,258 Chinese arrived in Cuba, and that between 1917 and 1924 some 16,005 came to the island. Around 1930, the reports on the number of Chinese in Cuba continue to display a wide range of estimates, from 30,000 (Chinese consulate) to 150,000, a number reported by the Cuban newspaper *El Mundo*. Corbitt (ibid.:105) maintains that even the estimate of 150,000 was probably too low.

At the beginning of the Second World War, estimates of Chinese in Cuba range from 18,000 (those registered at the Chinese consulate) to 30,000. During this time, the Chinese kept to themselves with respect to Cuban politics, although they were deeply interested in the politics of their homeland and maintained in Cuba off-shoots of the different Chinese political parties (see Ramos Hernández, Pedroso Alés, and Cassola Triamma 2000). Corbitt (1971:113–15) reports that while some Chinese took Cuban nationality to meet legal requirements, overall they adjusted to citizenship requirements for Cuban work permits by other means and maintained a strong relationship with their homeland. Given that most Chinese men had wives back in their native land, there continued to be few Chinese women in Cuba. For example, of the 18,484 Chinese registered at the Chinese consulate in 1942, a large majority was from Canton and only 56 were women.

Chinese continued to come to Cuba throughout the twentieth century, well after the cessation of the importation of Chinese indentured labour. Today there are still roughly 400 'pure Chinese' people that speak Cantonese, and courses in Mandarin are even offered by an organization called Grupo Promotor Chino (Chinese Promotion Group), which is in charge of developing activities on Chinese culture in Cuba. A bilingual newspaper is also maintained. Havana still has a Chinatown – where many Chinese originally lived – which was built towards the end of the 1890s. Thus, the ties to China still remain relatively strong.

### 5.2.2    Relations between the Chinese and Africans in Cuba

The documents consulted by Corbitt (1971) indicate that the relations between the Chinese and Africans/Afro-Cubans were difficult at best. In 1848, the coffee bean grower Urbano Feijóo de Sotomayor (cited in Corbitt 1971:10) wrote to the Spanish crown, stating: 'they [the Chinese] are not inclined to associate with the Negroes, and if all the planters thought as I do and maintained on their farms a line of separation between the races, I believe it would be possible to make one race a defence against the other'.

Corbitt (1971:63) notes that:

The treatment accorded the coolies in Cuba was as varied as the characters of the persons who supervised their work and the conditions under which they lived. Bitter was the lot of Chinamen supervised for absentee masters by overseers who were often their intellectual inferiors (scarcely a coolie but could read and write, and as much could not be said for the overseers) and forced to work alongside Negroes for whom they had, and have, a supreme contempt. And when through ignorance of the haughty Chinese character, Negroes were placed in charge of the coolies, the results were tragic.

Corbitt goes on to mention that the policies, laws, regulations, official reports, and private accounts of the time serve as testimony that there was a 'mutual ignorance' of language, customs, religion, manners, food, methods of work, and tools. What is not clear is whether 'mutual' refers to the relation between the planters, owners, and policy-makers on the one hand and the slaves on the other, or between Africans and Chinese, or both. Needless to say, the policies, laws, regulations, and official reports were generated by people with direct input from the plantation-owners, who either were ignorant of or did not care about the significant differences between the Africans and Chinese. That the Africans and Chinese did not know anything about each other is not surprising. However, there is also evidence that members of the two groups co-existed harmoniously. In the Ten Years' War and later on in the war for independence, there are clear examples of Chinese and Afro-Cubans fighting alongside one another for Cuba (Jiménez Pastrana 1963). These cases notwithstanding, Corbitt (1971:113) notes that as recently as the Second World War, the Chinese still maintained contempt for Afro-Cubans.

### 5.2.3    Chinese and the Spanish language

With regard to the acquisition of Spanish on the part of the Chinese coolies, Corbitt (1971:11, after Erenchun 1856:778–779) quotes the well-known scholar Antonio Bachiller y Morales, who wrote in 1856 that:

[h]omicides, rebellions and uprisings were repeated on some plantations, while more tactful masters obtained better results. A large part of the problems arose from lack of competent interpreters. At present, although there are still some that doubt the advantage of this type of immigrant, the early difficulties occur less frequently, a fact that is due in great part to the coolies' being directed by men who speak their language.

Nine years after the first Chinese had arrived in Cuba, there was no indication that they had learned Spanish, nor would it be expected of them, since these labourers lived and worked together with fellow Cantonese speakers and likely used their native language almost exclusively.

In 1874, a recruiting agent named Francisco Abella, who had transported more than 100,000 Chinese to various countries, including Cuba, wrote about the recruiting process that, '[b]efore loading the transports the Portuguese authorities would address a group of coolies through an interpreter, who often knew only one of the eleven dialects spoken in China, asking them if they were willing to embark' (cited in Corbitt 1971:41). This system changed, according to Abella, in that five or six interpreters came to be used by the recruiters, each speaking a different dialect of Chinese. Although these statements suggest that a great majority of those Chinese going to Cuba were speakers of one or more varieties of Chinese, they were largely varieties of Cantonese.

The varieties of Spanish found in Jiménez Pastrana (1963), taken from documents that attempted to capture the manner in which the Chinese spoke Spanish, exhibit characteristics consistent with naturalistic second language acquisition, with two notable exceptions. One is the use a sentence-final negator, as in (5.1). Assuming the data accurately reflect the Spanish of Chinese Cuban soldiers, this feature is most likely due to the influence of Afro-Cuban Spanish (see Ortiz López 1998; Schwegler 1998; sections 4.2.2 and 4.4 from this book, and examples (4.10) and (4.17) and the accompanying discussion).

| (5.1) | ¡No | es | un | chino | manila, | *no*! |
|-------|-----|-----|-----|--------|---------|-------|
|       | NEG | is | a | Chinese | Manila | NEG |
|       | 'I'm not a Chinaman!' | | | | | |

The other feature involves case marking. In the example in (5.2), the logical subject of a stative predicate is marked as the grammatical object. The interesting point about these examples is that the only other Iberian language-based creoles that mark stative-predicate subjects in this manner, though not all stative predicates, are found in India (the Indo-Portuguese creoles of Korlai and Daman).[5]

| (5.2a) | Pa | mi | no | sentí | gente | pasá. |
|--------|-----|-----|-----|-------|-------|-------|
|        | for | me | NEG | heard-1SG.PRET | people | pass.by |
|        | 'I didn't hear the people pass by.' | | | | | |
| (5.2b) | Pa | mi | no | sabe. | | |
|        | for | me | neg | know-3SG.PRES | | |
|        | 'I don't know.' | | | | | |

[5] Although this type of case marking is found in IP creoles, in neither Korlai nor Daman Creole Portuguese is the subject of *sab* 'know' or *sabe* 'know' marked as the grammatical object. In KCP, *sití* (< Ptg. *sentir* 'feel') in its original Portuguese meaning of 'feel' takes a dative subject, as in *pari sitin friw* [lit. me feeling cold] 'I'm feeling cold'.

In general, then, it seems that the Chinese learned enough Spanish to fulfil their needs in the jobs they had. For example, one story tells of a cook who learns how to speak Spanish, arguably because of his position (Corbitt 1971:77). However, it is also clear from the documents and statistics in Corbitt (ibid.) that the Chinese, although some fought alongside whites and Afro-Cubans in two wars in the nineteenth century, generally were not integrated in Cuban society.

## 5.3    Structure of Chinese Coolie Spanish in Cuba

In this section, I consider who constituted the probable speakers of Chinese Coolie Spanish and what their TMA system in Spanish looked like, and discuss other salient characteristics of their speech. I draw on data found in Jiménez Pastrana (1963), a small corpus containing approximately 300 words.

### 5.3.1    The speakers of Chinese Coolie Spanish in Cuba

In section 5.2.1 above, we saw that from 1847 to 1859 the Chinese coolies who arrived in Cuba embarked from various ports, two of the most prominent being Amoy (Xiamen) in Fujian province where Min dialects were and are spoken, and Macau, where Cantonese dialects were and still are found. After 1859, ships carrying coolies to Cuba embarked only from Macau. Records from that time indicate that coolies speaking various Chinese dialects, tantamount to different languages in some cases, were recruited for Cuba. Initially, then, I assume that the Chinese arriving in Cuba were speakers representing various Min and Cantonese dialects, but that over time the proportion of Cantonese dialect speakers among those recruited to work in Cuba increased. This assumption is supported by the fact that most people of Chinese origin in Cuba today are of Cantonese background.

Almost all of the Chinese arriving in Cuba in the nineteenth century were literate and used the same writing system (Corbitt 1971:63). Moreover, they all shared a similar culture, especially as compared to the culture predominant in Cuba in the middle of the nineteenth century. I assume that speakers of each of the Min or Cantonese varieties could and would cluster into same-dialect groups, such that they could maintain their variety of Chinese in Cuba. Thus, when they were thrown into a quasi-slave situation in Cuba, the bonds between the different dialect speakers among themselves, and even speakers across dialects, were beneficial for survival, and I assume that such bonds were cultivated and maintained to the extent that they improved the chances of survival.

As already mentioned, reports indicated that the Chinese and Africans seldom mixed (Corbitt 1971:63, 78, 113). And although this may have been generally true, Lipski (1999:217) reports the existence of Chinese–African intermarriages and Jiménez Pastrana (1963:69–70) describes African–Chinese co-operation in the time leading up to the Ten Years' War. In the war for Cuban independence, the Chinese also fought alongside Cubans of African and European descent. In fact, the only example of an Afro-Cuban linguistic trait in my corpus comes from a Chinese soldier.

To my knowledge, there are two main sources of evidence for Cuban coolie speech. I have already commented on the sources found in Jiménez Pastrana's (1963) history of the Chinese between 1847 and 1930. The other general source is literary texts in which Chinese speech is portrayed. I prefer to draw primarily from Jiménez Pastrana (ibid.) because the portrayal of Chinese speech in the sources he uses seems to me to constitute a serious attempt to approximate, as closely as possible, the Chinese Spanish of that time.

Although Lipski (1999) calls the variety of Spanish spoken by the Chinese coolies a pidgin, this depends on the definition of the term *pidgin*. Lipski's definition seems to be closer to that advanced by Hall (1966), according to which even a highly unstable incipient pidgin constitutes a pidgin proper. If we define pidgin according to Bakker (1995), as a linguistic system with its own set conventions and rules which can be spoken to different degrees of proficiency, there is little socio-historical evidence to support the existence of a Chinese pidgin Spanish in this sense, especially given that the Chinese had no apparent motivation to speak anything other than Chinese among themselves. The variety found in Jiménez Pastrana (1963), I argue, is closer to a naturalistically learned L2 variety. This view is also suggested by quotes of dialogues found in Jiménez Pastrana (1963) between Cuban superiors and Chinese soldiers in which the Cubans speak colloquial Spanish and the Chinese their own variety of Spanish. An illustrative exchange is given in (5.3), a dialogue between a Spanish-speaking captain and an official originally from Canton, in which the captain speaks standard Spanish and the official talks in what I consider to be an L2 Spanish variety (ibid.:100). In this conversation between the captain and Achón, I have added the standard colloquial Spanish version of Achón's speech so the reader can appreciate the difference between the two varieties.

(5.3)  Captain:  Mira, Achón; a los oficiales les está prohibido usar armas largas.
'Look, Achon; the officers are prohibited from using long rifles.'
Achón:  ¿Qui cosa usa Ficiá? (Standard Sp.: ¿Qué usan los oficiales?)
'What do officers use?
Captain:  Machete y revólver. Es una orden superior . . . .
'Machete and revolver. It's an order from above.'
Achón:  Londi ta Ginilá Maceo, que yo va pleguntá si son vel esi cosa?
(Standard Sp.: ¿Dónde está General Maceo?, que (yo) voy a preguntar si {es verdad esa cosa/si son verdad esas cosas})
'Where is General Maceo? I'm going to ask him if that thing is true.'

Of note in this exchange is that there is no attempt on the part of the captain to accommodate his interlocutor linguistically.[6] Achon uses 3sG verb forms (except for *son* 'they are') and no plural marking of the nouns, both of which are traits also found in Chinese Immigrant Spanish.[7] The choice of 3PL *son* is interesting because it is also found in Luis' speech (see chapter 6) as the default *ser* copula. Moreover, its Portuguese counterpart *sã* (Ptg. *são* 'they are') is the default copula form in Macau Creole Portuguese.

Having discussed the background of the Chinese coolies in Cuba and considered some of the salient traits of Chinese Coolie Spanish (CCS), let us now turn to a more systematic examination of its features.

### 5.3.2    TMA system in Chinese Coolie Spanish

To analyse the verb forms gleaned from Jiménez Pastrana (1963), I categorize them as types and tokens according to verb-predicate class and verb form, as well as whether or not the forms were used in a context appropriate to their tense. Forms were judged to be appropriately used according to the context in which they appear. That is, present forms were judged to be correct in those situations in which present events, activities, or states in the text are being referred to by those being quoted. Present-tense forms were judged to be incorrect in discourse situations involving past events, activities, or states. Only tense and grammatical aspect were taken into account for classifying a verb as correctly or incorrectly used. In other words, correctness of person and number marking was not considered. The results, shown in Table 5.2, indicate that the speakers do not exhibit a preponderance of correctly used verbal forms.

The distribution of the correctly used finite forms is comparable to that found in CIS: CIS displays 64 per cent correct finite forms, compared to 70 per cent (40/57) of correct finite forms in CCS. However, the distribution of the non-finite forms in CCS, at 55 per cent (6/11), is significantly higher than in CIS (16.5 per cent), but the raw numbers are low. Important in this comparison is that, in terms of the distribution of finite and non-finite forms correctly and incorrectly used, nineteenth-century CCS is largely comparable

---

[6] In one short story collection (Bueno 1959:66), I have found evidence of Foreigner Talk: '"¿Capitán, tú estar triste, tú pensar en Cantón . . ." le decía Acacio, poniendo los verbos en infinitivo para que lo entendiera mejor.' '"Captain, you be sad, you think about Canton . . ." Acacio was saying to him, putting the verbs in the infinitive so that he would understand better.' In this story, the Spanish of the Chinese captain is stereotypically portrayed in that all verbs are in the infinitive, all instances of *r* are rendered as *l*, all copulas are deleted, etc.

[7] Here, Chinese Immigrant Spanish (CIS) refers to the speech of two native Chinese informants who are immigrants in Spain. The traits of their speech are the topic of chapter 6.

Table 5.2. *Distribution of correctly and incorrectly used verb tokens in Chinese Coolie Speech*

| Form | Correct | Incorrect | Total |
|------|---------|-----------|-------|
| Present | 38 *[70%]* (83%) | 16 *[30%]* (73%) | 54 [100%] (79%) |
| Past | 2 *[67%]* (4%) | 1 *[33%]* (5%) | 3 *[100%]* (4%) |
| Infinitive | 6 *[55%]* (13%) | 5 *[45%]* (23%) | 11 *[100%]* (16%) |
| Total | 46 [100%] (68%) | 22 [100%] (32%) | 68 [100%] (100%) |

*Note:* $\chi^2 = 1.04$ (*df* = 2); $p < 0.05$ if critical value = 5.99. The distribution is not significant. However this is not because of the distribution *per se*, but rather because of the dearth of data. For example, if the numbers are multiplied by ten while maintaining the same proportions, the distribution becomes significant. Totals may not reach 100 because of rounding.
*Source:* Jiménez Pastrana 1963.

to CIS in the twenty-first century, which is not surprising given the proposed 'basic variety' of Klein and Perdue (1992).

If we compare the distribution of states, durative atelic events, durative telic events, and punctual events in CCS with those found in CIS, we find similarities and differences that I think are attributable to the different range of topics found in the different samplings. The data of the three varieties are shown in Table 5.4.

The proportion of stative tokens in CCS is comparable to that in CIS. One CIS informant's speech, however, that of Luis, is closer to CCS. This may reflect the nature of the narratives in each case. The speech samples of CCS, compiled by Jiménez Pastrana (1963) from various sources, are short statements with one or two dialogues. The topic is war: the speakers discuss moving from one place to another and fighting. Because of this, the narratives have fewer stative tokens and a relatively high number of durative telic tokens, due mainly to the presence of many predicates with a goal or an implied count noun. For instance, *viene Oliente* [lit. s/he comes Oriente] 'we came from Oriente' has an implied goal ('here') and is therefore counted as durative telic. Luis' narrative is shorter than that of the other CIS informant, Jenny, and he discusses mainly how he got to Spain, what his family members do in Spain, who they associate with, and so forth. Jenny's narrative is longer, and she talks about a wider range of topics, including various direct speech segments. It appears, then, that the distribution of predicate classes shown in Table 5.4 reflects more about the type of narrative and the range of topics covered than about the nature of these L2 varieties.

Regarding the presence or absence of individual forms in CCS, the heavy preponderance of present-tense forms, and particularly 3SG.PRES forms, as

Table 5.3. *Predicate forms in Chinese Coolie Spanish*

| Verb Form | Static situations | | | | Dynamic situations | | | |
| | States | | Atelic situations | | Telic situations | | Punctual | |
| | Stative | | Durative | | Durative | | | |
| | Type | Token | Type | Token | Type | Token | Type | Token |
|---|---|---|---|---|---|---|---|---|
| 1SG.PRES | 1 (8%) | 1 (5%) | | | 1 (5%) | 1 (4%) | | |
| 2SG.PRES | | | | | 4 (21%) | 4 (14%) | 1 (25%) | 1 (25%) |
| 3SG.PRES | 7 (58%) | 13 (68%) | 5 (42%) | 7 (41%) | 9 (47%) | 18 (64%) | 1 (25%) | 1 (25%) |
| 1PL.PRET | | | | | | | 1 (25%) | 1 (25%) |
| 1SG.PRET | 1 (8%) | 2 (11%) | | | | | | |
| 3SG.PAST (preterit or imperfect) | | | | | | | | |
| Infinitive | | | 4 (33%) | 7 (41%) | 4 (21%) | 4 (14%) | | |
| Gerund | | | | | | | | |
| Past participle | | | | | | | | |
| Other | 3 (25%) | 3 (16%) | 3 (25%) | 3 (18%) | 1 (5%) | 1 (4%) | 1 (25%) | 1 (25%) |
| Total | 12 (100%) | 19 (100%) | 12 (100%) | 17 (100%) | 19 (100%) | 28 (100%) | 4 (100%) | 4 (100%) |

*Note:* Totals may not equal 100 because of rounding.

Table 5.4. *Distribution of stative, durative atelic, durative telic, and punctual predicates in Chinese Coolie Spanish and Chinese Immigrant Spanish*

| Group | Stative | | Atelic durative | | Telic durative | | Punctual | |
|---|---|---|---|---|---|---|---|---|
| | Type | Token | Type | Token | Type | Token | Type | Token |
| Chinese Immigrant Spanish | 62 (29%) | 359 (44%) | 63 (30%) | 189 (23%) | 40 (19%) | 122 (15%) | 47 (22%) | 155 (19%) |
| Chinese Coolie Spanish | 12 (26%) | 19 (28%) | 12 (26%) | 17 (25%) | 19 (40%) | 28 (41%) | 4 (9%) | 4 (6%) |

*Note:* Totals may not equal 100 because of rounding.

well as the dearth of other finite forms, is just what one would expect, and is comparable to what we find in CIS. As for the non-finite forms, the presence of some infinitive form tokens in CCS is expected, and the absence of gerund form tokens is not surprising: in Luis' speech we find only one gerund form in a sampling of 223 verb-form tokens. However, in CIS samples, past participle forms are present for the non-stative verbs (forty-nine tokens), but we find none in CCS. This is the only area in which modern-day Chinese Immigrant Spanish and nineteenth-century CCS are not roughly comparable; it is not clear why there are no past participle forms in CCS.

Lastly, in CCS we find one example of a possible TMA marker. It appears in an exchange between a Spanish army commander and the Chinese Cuban insurgent, Andrés Chiong, who the commander did not realize was part of the Cuban army. The exchange is reproduced in (5.4). The element *ta* appears in the last line.

(5.4)  Spanish
       commander:    Tú chino, ¿no ha pasado alguien anoche por aquí?
                     'You, Chinaman, did anyone pass by here last night?'
       Chiong:       No  señó Capitán, pa mi no    sentí       gente pasá.'
                     NEG sir  Captain  for me NEG hear-INF   people pass-INF
                     'No sir, Captain, I didn't hear people go by.'
       Spanish
       commander:    ¿Tú viste un grupo de insurrectos armados esta mañana que
                     venían de Varadero?
                     'Did you see a group of armed insurgents this morning that
                     were coming from Varadero?'
       Chiong:       Yo no    mila          gente    suleto    tiene arma por la
                     I   NEG look.at-3SG people insurgent has  arm  in  the
                     mañana.
                     morning
                     No señó, pa mi no sabe, *ta* trabaja, quema carbón.

NEG sir for me NEG knows *ta* works, burns coal
'I didn't see armed insurgent people in the morning.
No sir, I don't know, I was working, burning coal.'[8]

The element *ta* with the verb *trabaja* 's/he works' is reminiscent of the present-tense marker found in the Spanish-based creole Papiamentu and the imperfective found in Palenquero, also a Spanish-based creole (5.5–5.6). (See Maurer 1998:162; Schwegler 1998:254–256.)

(5.5)  Mi     *ta*     traha   na    pòstkantor.
       I      PRES     work    in    post office
       'I work in the post office.'                     (Maurer 1998:162)
(5.6)  Ele    *ta*     ablá.
       s/he   IMPER    speak
       'S/he is speaking.'                              (Schwegler 1998:255)

The form *ta*, derived from *está* and/or *estar*, is also found in CCS as a copula (5.7), corresponding to the use of *estar* in Spanish. In Papiamentu, *ta* is also a copulative verb, with the key difference that in this language *ta* corresponds to both *ser* and *estar* in Spanish (5.8).

(5.7)  Tó   la   gente   *ta*   qui    jabla   bonito   na        má.
       all  the  people  is     here   talks   pretty   nothing   more
       'All the people who are here talk pretty and nothing else.'
                                                        (Jiménez Pastrana 1963:75)
(5.8a) E      *ta*      dòkter.
       'He    is a      doctor.'                        (Maurer 1998:169)
(5.8b) E      ta        kansá.
       'He    is        tired.'                         (ibid.:170)

I take the presence of *ta* in these three varieties to be related only indirectly. In CCS, it is clearly a reduction of *está* and/or *estar*, and used as is *estar* in Spanish, with the exception of the possible case of the re-analysed TMA marker shown in (5.4) above. Were it such a marker in CCS, it would have to be marking imperfectivity, as in Palenquero. The indirect link between Papiamentu and Palenquero on the one hand, and CCS on the other, is that reflexes of *está* and/or *estar* lend themselves to re-analysis as aspectual or tense markers because, being forms that have their own stress and precede a main verb, they are easily perceived.

So far, I have compared the verb system of CCS to those of CIS. I have found that, in terms of distribution of forms and of verb classes the three varieties are comparable, though there are not enough data for CCS to

---

[8] 'Burning coal' most likely refers to the process of making charcoal from wood by slowly burning it in an earthen oven until the wood becomes charcoal.

Table 5.5. *Phonological traits of Chinese Coolie Spanish*

| Trait | Source |
|---|---|
| a. r → l, l → r | Chinese |
| b. b, d, g devoicing (g → k) | Chinese |
| c. š → s and s → š | Chinese |
| d. voicing of stops | Chinese |
| e. three types of syllable simplification strategies | |
|    i. vowel epenthesis | Chinese |
|    ii. cluster simplification | Chinese |
|    iii. deletion of syllable coda | Chinese |
| f. preference of CV structure | Chinese, other |
| g. retention of closed syllables in -s | Spanish |

make any definitive claims. I noted that one possible case of re-analysis of *ta* as a TMA marker is present in CCS. If it is authentic, then it could be an indication that re-analysis was taking place.[9] We now turn to the discussion of other aspects of CCS.

### 5.3.3    *Other characteristics of Chinese Coolie Spanish*

The phonological traits in CCS cited in Jiménez Pastrana (1963) are largely those found in CIS. I use here the adapted list of traits for Chinese Pidgin English found in Shi (1991). Table 5.5 contains the traits in the left-hand column and their sources in the right-hand column. In contrast to CIS, not all traits in Table 5.5 are found in CCS. The confusion of liquids is attested in Jiménez Pastrana (1963), but only as the replacement of [r] by [l] as in (5.9), but not as [l] by [r], as we encounter in CIS.

(5.9)    nosotlo (< Sp. nosotros 'we, us'; ibid.:75)
       dinelo (< Sp. dinero 'money'; ibid.:80)
       quiele (< Sp. quiere 's/he wants'; ibid.:99)
       tiloteo (< Sp. tiroteo 'shootout'; ibid.:100)
       lifle (< Sp. rifle 'rifle'; ibid.:100)

No cases of voiced stop devoicing are found in Jiménez Pastrana or in the literary sources consulted (Bueno 1959; Feijóo 1960, 1965; and various stories found in Los Archivos del Folklore Cubano). There is one possible case of voicing of a voiceless stop in the form *pasa*, shown in (5.10).

---

[9] As will be discussed in chapter 6, one speaker of CIS, Jenny, displays uses of Spanish *ya* 'already' in environments in which it could be seen as an incipient perfective marker. Thus, such particles can already begin to develop in L2 varieties.

In Jenny's speech (chapter 6), I found she had conflated the form *pasa* 'pass by, move on' and the phrase *vas a* 'you go to', with the interpretation 'go'. It is possible, then, that *pasa* in (5.10) could represent a voiceless *vas a* with the meaning 'go, went'.

(5.10)  Nosotlo     principia       peleá       Lemelio,    Cienfuego,
        we          at.the.beginning  fight      Remedios,   Cienfuego
        nosotlo **pasa**       la  Trocha, nosotlo  vinimo      Camagüey.
        we      went/moved  the  Trocha  we       came-1.PL   Camagüey
        'At the beginning, we fought in Remedios and Cienfuego; we went to
            Trocha, then to Camagüey.'

                                                        (Jiménez Pastrana 1963:76)

Syllable simplification is found in CCS, examples of which contain cluster simplification or coda consonant deletion, but not epenthetic vowel insertion. Examples of the first two phenomena are given in (5.11) and (5.12) respectively.

(5.11)  gobieno (< Sp. gobierno 'government'; ibid.:76)
        life (< Sp. rifles 'rifles'; ibid.:75, 76)
        libe (< Sp. libre 'free'; ibid.:76)
(5.12)  españó (< Sp. español 'Spanish'; ibid.:73)
        pañól (< Sp. español 'Spanish'; ibid.:99)
        señó (< Sp. señor 'sir'; ibid.:91)
        ficiá (< Sp. oficial 'officer'; ibid.:100)
        tilá (< Sp. tirar 'shoot'; ibid.:100)

Note that in (5.11) there are examples of apheresis, the elision of the word-initial syllable, attested in Jiménez Pastrana but not in CIS. The effects of cluster simplification in the speech reported on by Jiménez Pastrana suggest a notable preference for CV syllable structure, also apparent in CIS. Interestingly, in the literary sources, as well as in Jiménez Pastrana, there is only one instance of a plural noun (*no tenel amigos* (< Sp. *no tener amigos* 'not have friends')), although in Jiménez Pastrana nouns such as *life* 'rifles' and *cásula* 'shells' are used in a plural context but not pluralized. This suggests that the latter source is closer to CIS.

As far as morphosyntactic phenomena are concerned, we find that CCS and CIS, to be examined in chapter 6, are highly comparable. The traits to be considered are listed in Table 5.6. The predominant order found in CCS is SVO order (Table 5.6a), examples of which are given in (5.13). There are no examples of transitive clauses with overt objects in which the object is not post-verbal.

(5.13a)  ¿Tú       **quiele      pollo?**   Mata   **capitán    pañol.**
         2SG.FAM  want-3SG    chicken   kill    captain    Spanish
         'If you want to eat chicken, kill a Spanish captain.'

Table 5.6. *Morphosyntactic traits of Chinese Coolie Spanish*

| Trait | Source |
|---|---|
| a. SVO word order | Spanish, Chinese |
| b. S adjunct V word order | Chinese |
| c. No passive voice | Other |
| d. Classifier equivalent to English *piece* | Not present |
| e. N + N (with genitive or modifier relation) | Chinese |
| f. No prepositions as such | There are prepositions |
| g. Adv + Adj | Spanish, Chinese |
| h. V + IO + DO order with no marking for IO or DO | Chinese |
| i. Adv + V + NP | Chinese |
| j. V + N + Adv | Spanish, Chinese |
| k. *ya* completive | Chinese |
| l. Evidence of other TMA markers | Other |
| m. Copula with Ns, absent with Adjs. | Chinese |
| n. In-situ and fronted *wh*-words | Spanish, Chinese[a] |
| o. Bimorphemic *wh*-words | Other |
| p. No equivalents of *yes* and *no* to questions | Spanish[b] |
| q. Negation: *no* before the predicate | Spanish, Chinese |
| r. Double negation: *antes nunca no pensado* 'I had never thought [about it] before.' | Not present |
| s. Headless relative clauses | Chinese |

*Notes:*
[a]fronted
[b]there are

(5.13b)  Tú     no     da     pa     nosotlo     **cásula**.
         2sg    NEG    give   for    us          shell
         'You don't give us any ammunition.'

Adjuncts (Table 5.6b) usually appear after the verb, as in the examples in (5.14).

(5.14a)  Luego     nosotlo     **viene Oliente**.
         then      we          comes Oriente
         'Then we came to Oriente.'
(5.14b)  Tó    la    gente **camina**    **pa**    **la**    **Camagüey.**
         all   the   people walks        for       the      Camagüey
         'All the people walked to Camagüey.'

However, there is an interesting example, shown in (5.15), in which an instrument adjunct phrase appears pre-verbally, as in Cantonese, the native language the vast majority of the Chinese coolies spoke.

(5.15)  Yo    mimito   **con    lifle**   tilá     pañole    tlentacinco   tilo.
        1SG   EMPH     with    rifle    shoot    Spanish   thirty-five   shots.
        'I myself shot 35 rounds at the Spaniards.'

Cantonese has a similar construction with a comitative or instrumental phrase with an equivalent of 'with', as in (5.16).

(5.16)  Jeui       hóu       tùhng     ngàhnhòhng    je        chin.
        most       good      with      bank          borrow    money
        'It's best to borrow money {with/from} the bank.'
                                                (Matthews and Yip 1994:143)

In the CCS corpus, there is no evidence of a passive voice, a classifier element, or the N + N construction in the corpus (Table 5.6c–e). There is, however, a clear example of a N *de* N construction, shown in (5.17), also found in CIS (see (6.9a–c)).

(5.17)  Generá     de        nosotlo       muere     aquí.
        general    of        we/us         dies      here
        'Some of our generals died here.'

Regarding prepositions (Table 5.6f), verbs of motion in CCS carry either no directional marker (5.18), or appear with the element *pa* (< Spanish *para* 'for') as a marker of direction (5.19). The lack of prepositions is the norm in Jenny's speech (see (6.13)), though not in Luis' (see examples in (6.14)).

(5.18a) Baja Ø      la        plasa      españó,       y         pelea.
        go.down     the       square     Spanish       and       fight.
        'Go down to Spanish Square and fight.'
(5.18b) nosotlo vinimo Ø Camagüey . . . luego nosotlo viene Ø Oriente.
        1PL        came-1PL Camagüey     then we     comes     Oriente
        'We came to Camagüey . . . then we went to Oriente.'
(5.18c) Nosotlo    pasa          Ø         la        Trocha.
        we         goes                    the       Trocha
        'We went to Trocha.'
(5.19a) Tó     la     gente    camina     ***pa***    la        Camagüey.
        all    the    people   walks      for         the       Camagüey.
        'All the people walked to Camagüey.'
(5.19b) Tú         dise   nosotlo   va       ***pa***    la        Camagüey.
        2SG.FAM    says   we        goes     for         the       Camagüey.
        'You tell us to go to Camagüey.'

With locative adjuncts, we find a lack of marking, as illustrated by the examples in (5.20).

(5.20a) Nosotlo    principia           peleá Ø     Lemelio.
        we         at.the.beginning    fight        Remedios
        'At the beginning, we fought in Remedios.'
(5.20b) Nosotlo    peleá         Ø         Camagüey.
        we         fight                   Camagüey
        'We fought in Camagüey.'

| (5.20c) | Nosotlo | tá | Ø | Oliente. |
|---|---|---|---|---|
| | we | is | | Oriente |

'We were in Oriente.'

| (5.20d) | Nosotlo | peleá | Ø | Oliente. |
|---|---|---|---|---|
| | we | fight | | Oriente |

'We fought in Oriente.'

There are no data in the CCS sample related to adverb–adjective order (5.6g). However, there are important data in the sample relating to object marking (5.6h): We find one example, an IO marked by its immediately post-verbal position, shown in (5.21).

| (5.21) | Tú | dise | nosotlo | va | pa | la | Camagüey. |
|---|---|---|---|---|---|---|---|
| | 2SG-FAM | says | we/us | goes | for | the | Camagüey |

'You tell us to go to Camagüey.'

Although we have one example of V-IO-DO order, there is no established pattern in CCS of V-IO-DO order with no marking on the IO or DO. However, we do find a fairly consistent pattern of V-IO-DO order, in which the IO is marked with the element *pa* (< Spanish *para* 'for'). The examples are given in (5.22). Whereas in Spanish the default order is V-DO-IO, in these examples the order is V-IO-DO, following the Chinese (i.e., Cantonese) order. Nevertheless, in (5.22c), we have an example attributed to a Chinese doctor, who uses the default order found in Spanish.

| (5.22a) | Tú | no | **da** | **pa** | **nosotlo** | **life**. |
|---|---|---|---|---|---|---|
| | 2SG-FAM | NEG | gives | for | we/us | rifle |

'You don't give us rifles.'

| (5.22b) | Tú | no | **da** | **pa** | **nosotlo** | **cásula**. |
|---|---|---|---|---|---|---|
| | 2SG-FAM | NEG | gives | for | we/us | shell |

'You don't give us shells.'

| (5.22c) | Yo | le | **da** | **medicina** | **pa la gente poble**. |
|---|---|---|---|---|---|
| | 1SG | CL.3SG.IO | gives | medicine | for the people poor |

'I give medicine to the poor people.'

In Jenny's speech, we find ample use of *para* as an IO marker (see 6.22), while in Luis' speech we find the Chinese pattern (see 6.15).

In our corpus, there are no clear examples of Adv-V-NP order (5.6i), but we do find one example of V-NP-Adv (5.6j), shown in (5.23).

| (5.23) | Suleto | tiene | arma | por | la | mañana. |
|---|---|---|---|---|---|---|
| | insurgent | has | arm | at | the | morning |

'The insurgents (who) had guns in the morning.'

Although the CCS sample contains no instances of *ya* 'already' used as a tense–aspect marker (5.6k), we do encounter a particle reminiscent of progressive aspect marker, the use of *ta*, mentioned in (5.4) above and shown again in (5.24), that is reminiscent of a present or an imperfective marker.

(5.24)  No  señó, pa mí no  sabe,  **ta**    trabaja, quema carbón.
        NEG sir   for me NEG knows AUX  works,  burns coal
        'No sir, I don't know, I was working, burning coal.'

Regarding the use of the copulas *ser* and *estar* (5.6m), there are various examples of *ta* (< Spanish *estar* 'be [resultative or locative]'), shown in (5.25), and of *soy* 'I am' and *son* 'they are' in (5.26).

(5.25a)  Tó   la   gente  **ta**   qui   jabla  bonito  na       má.
         all  the  people is      here  talk   pretty  nothing  more
         toda la   gente que está aquí  habla  bonito  nada     más
         'All the people who are here talk pretty, nothing else.'

(5.25b)  'Nosotlo  **tá**    Oliente,          nosotlo peleá  Oliente.
         we        is       Oriente           we             fight.INF Oriente
         nosotros  estuvimos en Oriente,  nostros        peleamos en Oriente
         'We were in Oriente, we fought in Oriente.'

(5.25c)  Londi   **ta**   Ginil        Maceo?
         where   is       General      Maceo?
         dónde   está     General      Maceo
         'Where is General Maceo?'

(5.26a)  Cuidado,       yo      **soy**     cabo      José.
         careful        1SG     am          private   José
         'Watch out, I'm Private José.'

(5.26b)  que       yo va       pleguntá    si **son** vel esi  cosa?
         COMP      1SG goes     ask         if are   true that thing
         que yo voy a preguntar si son verdad esas cosas
         'I'm going to ask him whether these things are true.'

The presence of *soy* is probably due to a fixed phrase. In the text, the context clarifies that the soldier in question would routinely utter (5.26) when others addressed him. It is interesting to note that in the small corpus, there are no instances in the corpus of zero copula.

With regard to fronted and in-situ *wh*-words (5.6n), there are two instances of a fronted *wh*-word: one shown above in (5.25c) and the other below in (5.27). The latter is of note because it is bimorphemic: *qui cosa* 'what thing' (with mid-vowel *e* raised to *i* instead of the standard *qué* 'what'). Such bimorphemic *wh*-words are considered to be more transparent and consequently not uncommon in certain restructured language varieties (see Muysken and Smith 1990; Clements and Mahboob 2000). These were also found in Chinese pidgin English (see Shi 1991).

(5.27)  **Qui   cosa**   usa    Ficiá?
        what   thing    uses   officer

¿Qué          usan  los  oficiales?
'What do the officers use?'

Regarding the use of *si* 'yes' or *no* 'no' to yes–no questions (5.6p), we have one example of a negation of a question, given in (5.28).

(5.28)  ¡No        es      un    chino     manila,    **no**!
        NEG       is      a     Chinese   Manila     NEG
        'I'm not a Chinaman!'

The use of the sentence-final negator *no* in this sentence suggests African influence, as argued by Schwegler (1998:235), Ortiz López (1998:113–115), and in this book sections 4.2.2 and 4.4, examples (4.10), (4.17), and the accompanying discussion.

Finally, in the small corpus used here we find one example of headless relative clause (5.6s), shown in (5.29). As is evident from the comparison between the CCS sentence and its Spanish equivalent, the relative pronoun *que* (whose place is marked with the symbol Ø) is absent.

(5.29)  Tó    la  gente    Ø    ta   qui   jabla   bonito   na       má.
        all   the people   is   here talk   pretty   nothing  more
        toda  la  gente [que] está aquí  habla   bonito   nada     más.
        'All the people who are here talk pretty, nothing else.'

With regard to discourse properties of CCS, note that one, object deletion, occurs when the information is recoverable from the discourse context. There are several examples of this phenomenon, shown in (5.30).

(5.30a) Si tiene dinelo  paga         pala mí. Si no   tiene, no   paga Ø
        if has   money pay-3SG.PRES for me. if NEG has  NEG pay-3SG.PRES
        Si tienes  dinero, me pagas.  Si  no   tienes,    no me pagas.
        'If you have money, you pay me. If you don't, you don't pay.'[10]
(5.30b) No      señó,    pa    mí        no    sabe.
        no      sir     for   me        NEG   know-3SG.PRES
        No      señor,   no    sabía.
        'No sir, I didn't know.'
(5.30c) Si   tú    pue     cogé Ø Ø coge;      y   si    no, Ø  leja.
        if   you   can     catch-INF catch-IMP and if   NEG   leave-IMP
        Si tú puedes cogerme, cógeme, y si no, me dejas [en paz].
        'If you can catch me, catch me; otherwise leave me alone.'

Of these three examples, it is possible to find null objects in Spanish as well for (5.30a) and (5.30b). However, in standard Spanish it is impossible to delete the animate direct objects, as in (5.30c).

---

[10] Spanish can delete an object in discourse if it is a mass term (noncount noun or bare plural). In this example, *dinero* 'money' is a mass term and can be unexpressed in Spanish.

## 5.4    Concluding remarks

In this chapter, we have seen that both the socio-historical and the linguistic evidence suggest that the variety of Spanish spoken by the Chinese coolies in the nineteenth century was in all likelihood not a pidgin, with its own conventionalized vocabulary and grammar, but constituted rather individual instances of naturalistic second language acquisition. As indentured labourers, the Chinese coolies would have spoken Chinese among themselves, even though several dialects of Cantonese were surely represented. While there is anecdotal evidence, found in a short story (Bueno 1959:66), that Foreigner Talk was used in addressing Chinese coolies, there is no historical evidence that any re-structured variety of Spanish emerged in the communication between Cubans and Chinese. The practice of shipping labourers to Cuba from China continued for around thirty years (1847–1877). Thus, the short period of time was not conducive to the creation of a Chinese pidgin Spanish variety either.

The linguistic evidence, based on a comparison between CCS and CIS, suggests that the CCS and CIS are highly similar and that both are good examples of what I have been referring to as the 'basic variety' of naturalistically learned L2 Spanish (Klein and Perdue 1992). And although the socio-historical evidence suggests that the Chinese and Africans did not interact, there is some evidence that at least some of the Chinese had enough contact with Afro-Cubans to be influenced by their speech, apparent in the African language trait of the sentence-final negation particle (i.e., ¡No es un chino manila, **no**!).

The external ecology of the Chinese in Cuba and the linguistic data coincide to give a picture of a people who learned enough Spanish to fulfil their needs and desires, but whose children (the second generation, most of whom had Cuban mothers) spoke Cuban Spanish, with few or no features of their first-generation ancestors.

# 6    Chinese Immigrant Spanish

## 6.1    Introduction

There is a substantial body of work that focuses on the linguistic systems immigrant workers construct in the naturalistic acquisition process of the host country language (Heidelberger Forschungsprojekt 1975; Blackshire-Belay 1991; Klein and Perdue 1992, and bibliography therein). One key observation expressed by Klein and Perdue (1992:315) in their comparative study of immigrant speech in Europe is that many of the L2 learners' speech, independently of the source or target languages involved, shared a basic variety of naturalistically learned L2 in which the development, though not identical, was remarkably similar.

I consider naturalistic L2 acquisition by immigrants as interesting for various reasons, two of which are: it can show us in some cases the processes through which speakers of one language acquire another that is typologically different, and it can give us insights into the initial stages of pidginization, as I suggested in chapter 3.

When one thinks of pidginization and pidgins, what often comes to mind is the image of plantation pidgins involving several languages in contact and people under the yoke of slavery. However, manuals on contact languages (e.g. Bakker 1995; Holm 1988, 1989; Mühlhäusler 1986; Sebba 1997; Winford 2003) remind us that pidgins also form in other language contact situations, such as those involving inter-ethnic and/or immigrant communities, trade, or tourist situations. In the latter two cases, we also encounter instances of naturalistically learned L2 varieties instead of pidgins (e.g., Hinnenkamp 1984), and it is at times difficult to distinguish between pidgins on the one hand and untutored L2 varieties on the other (cf. Blackshire-Belay 1991; Heidelberger Forschungsprojekt 1975).[1] As we shall see, whether a particular variety is labelled a pidgin or an L2 variety depends on the definitions employed. Using Hall's (1966) definition, for example, the linguistic system resulting from a day-long interaction between a tourist and a tourist

---

[1] I use the terms 'untutored Spanish' and 'naturalistically learned Spanish' synonymously.

guide can be a pidgin. However, by Bakker's (1995) definition (and by that proposed by Winford (2003) to a certain extent), a pidgin must be a stable linguistic system, with its own rules, which one can speak to varying degrees of proficiency.

Inter-ethnic situations can often be bi- or multi-lingual settings in which a variety of one of the languages emerges as the lingua franca. In this type of situation, the L2 variety or pidgin can develop alongside its lexifier, as is the case with the pidgin Hiri Motu, spoken in Papua New Guinea (Dutton 1997). Hiri Motu developed among speakers of different languages in the same general geographic area. In such inter-ethnic contact situations, short-distance displacement may be implicit, whereas long-distance displacement of one or more groups (e.g. displacement of a population hundreds or even thousands of kilometres for purposes of labour) may, but need not, be part of the definition of the situation type.

By contrast, immigrant situations involving workers (with or without their families) are defined by, among other things, long-distance displacement of one or more groups of people who need or want to live and work in another place. The language manuals speak almost exclusively of trade, rather than tourist, situations – that is, situations in which travelling traders develop a communication system with peoples living in the areas they visit. Short- or long-distance displacement of one or more groups is also implicit in the definition of this situation type.

Given that language contact situations concerning immigrants also involve semi-permanent to permanent long-distance displacements, the isolating mechanisms that inhibit immigrants from integration play a large role in the development of immigrant varieties of a given language. Taking isolation mechanisms in biology as a basis, Croft (2000:199) distinguishes three types of isolation mechanisms for language as well: geographical, ecological, and reproductive. Geographical isolation is self-explanatory, referring to the spatial separation of speakers in two populations 'to a distance beyond the normal geographical mobility of the speakers'. Ecological isolation refers to social separation, whereby Croft equates ecological differences in biology with social differences in language. In the same geographical area, certain individuals may not talk to each other because they belong to different social, ethnic, and/or caste groups. For language, biological reproductive isolation translates into isolation in conversational intercourse. As an example, Croft mentions the deaf, who communicate with a language based on the use of hands, body, and eyes instead of voice and ears. In the case of immigrants in a host country, both ecological isolation and reproductive isolation are relevant. The native Chinese-speaking informants whose varieties of Spanish are the focus of this chapter are ethnically distinct from the Spanish, and they also have a different linguistic background from the Spanish-language speakers of their host country. Thus, social and conversational isolation have played a role in their acquisition of Spanish.

The two Chinese immigrants in question went to Spain for different reasons. In the case of Jenny, it was to seek a better life economically, to achieve economic stability. Luis' motivation for moving to Spain was to find a better academic and social environment for his children. He was already married and economically secure when he arrived in Spain, whereas Jenny was single and not economically secure. The different varieties of Spanish the informants speak reflect, to a certain extent, this difference in their respective social and economic status upon arriving in Spain.

Both informants learned Spanish naturalistically. Recall from chapter 1 that naturalistic L2 acquisition can be the first stage in the process of a shift to a target language, potentially culminating in the total abandonment of one's native language for the target language. If we view some cases of naturalistic L2 acquisition as part of an eventual process of language shift, it is possible to understand as two points on a continuum the differences between individual solutions to the problem of communication (variably stable L2 varieties, exhibiting a significant degree of innovation on the part of the immigrants) and social solutions to the same problem (variably stable shared varieties, involving varying degrees of propagation or adoption). The former are considered L2 varieties, the latter pidgin varieties.

The extent to which immigrants learn the host-country language depends on various factors, such as the age of individuals when they reach the host country, their status there, attitudes of the immigrant and of host-country communities, the extent of conventionalization of the immigrant variety within the community, and the typological differences between the immigrant and host-country languages. By *conventionalization*, I mean the emergence of a pattern in language, for example, the pattern of subject-verb-object order in a sentence or the increasing use of an adverb to mark past tense (see Goldberg 1998:205–208).

An immigrant's age influences how well s/he learns a language and can also influence the extent to which s/he interacts with host-language speakers. Adult learners typically find it more difficult to achieve native-like performance in an L2 than children between approximately four and twelve years of age. Moreover, the younger one is, the easier it is for one, given the opportunity, to interact with peer host-language speakers in school and on the playground.

The asymmetrical social status between different communities in contact, in our case the Chinese immigrants and the host-country Spanish speakers, lessens the access to Spanish by these speakers. As discussed in detail below, the conditions in which Jenny worked limited her access to Spanish almost exclusively for the first several years of her residence in Spain. In Luis' case, he interacts with Spanish speakers only professionally, and only within the domain of his expertise (he is a barber).

In naturalistic L2 acquisition of the type to be discussed here, each speaker of the non-dominant community has developed individual mappings from their native Chinese to the target language, Spanish. The lexical features of their speech correspond in large measure to the generally accepted mappings, but others are clearly innovations, such as cases of re-analysis. As far as I could ascertain, the members of the Chinese community do not use Spanish among themselves. Thus, the various innovations in a community for a given mapping from Chinese to Spanish have not had a chance to spread through the L2 variety of their Spanish and no compromise solutions between different innovations in the L2 varieties in question have been found (i.e., levelling). If there were evidence of such processes, this would be an indication of a further development in the pidginization process. In the cases in question, however, the varieties of Spanish are instances of the incipient stage (the jargon stage) of a potential case of pidginization, but also the first stage of a potential language shift.

If the target language of an immigrant is typologically very different from his or her L1, it is conceivably more difficult to find L1–L2 correspondences, due to the differences in the respective feature pools. Chinese speakers who learn Spanish, for instance, struggle more with inflectionally marked distinctions of tense, person, and number than do Italian speakers learning Spanish because Italian and Spanish mark these distinctions more similarly. As the first stage of a potential language-shift situation, one would also expect significant substratum interference, i.e., interference from Chinese as the Chinese immigrants acquire Spanish. In the shift process, speakers learn the target-language lexicon (i.e., the lexical or substance features) but carry their native-language structural features into the target language as far as it allows for successful communication. By creating a variety of Spanish for their specific communicative needs, these speakers may overcome the isolation in conversational intercourse, but ecological isolation remains.

To the extent that adult speakers of two or more communities – in a situation of relative isolation due to attitudinal factors and social asymmetry – are obliged to create a common language to communicate with one another, these communities over time will produce a linguistic system that will range from a naturally learned L2 to a pidgin, depending on the circumstances. In this chapter, I focus on the incipient stage of the creation process, that is, on the manner in which our Chinese speakers have constructed their variety of Spanish given their different backgrounds and, to the extent recoverable, from their different inputs.

## 6.2    The ecology of the Chinese immigrant community in Spain and two of its members

Before discussing some details of the two informants, I provide a view of the general ecology in which our informants live by briefly describing the Chinese community in Spain.

### 6.2.1    The ecology of Chinese Immigrant Spanish in Spain

The Chinese ethnic community in Spain is heterogeneous, breaking down along dialectal and extended familial lines. What they share, as Beltrán and García (2001) point out, is being Chinese in a foreign country. Spain has a history with the Chinese that spreads over several centuries. The Spanish encountered Chinese in their colonization of the Philippines in the sixteenth century. In the nineteenth century, Spain had Chinese workers in the mines and plantations of their territories in Peru and Cuba. In the twentieth century, Spain was home to itinerant Chinese peddlers who sold small items on the streets of the country's major cities in the 1920s and 1930s. In the 1950s, Madrid had resident Chinese circuses, and in the second half of the century there was a substantial increase of the Chinese presence in Spain's service industry. As the Chinese restaurant industry has grown in Spain, services dependent on this industry have emerged, such as import companies, shops, travel agencies, Chinese vegetable farming, transport companies, skilled and unskilled construction labour for restaurant renovation, etc. Given that their work involves predominantly restaurants and restaurant-dependent services, the largest concentrations of Chinese are in urban areas, with Madrid and Barcelona having the two largest communities. Ninety-eight per cent of this community works in the service industry. As of 2000, there were unofficially around 60,000 Chinese in Spain, though the official number is 10,816. The families established in Spain are related to each other through multiple connections of kinship, economics, and place of origin (Beltrán and García 2001:284–285).

Chinese communities abroad come from a society in which the superiority of their own values is an accepted assumption, though it is said to be more pronounced in the People's Republic than in Taiwan (Beltrán and García 2001:291–293). This, along with other factors, has an impact on the degree to which Chinese assimilate in their host countries. The Chinese in Spain emigrated from their homeland generally to seek a better life in terms of their economic or social status. Had they been able to attain these goals in their own country, they would not have emigrated to Spain or other countries. But this was not the case for Taiwan-born Luis, who settled in Spain for the sake of his children.

As the Chinese language is the pillar of education, and education is highly prized in Chinese culture, the learning and maintenance of the native language in Chinese immigrant communities are important. According to Beltrán and García, the Chinese set up their communities to isolate and protect their language and culture from the culture in which they live, and thus tend not to learn Spanish. Literacy data discussed in Beltrán and García (2001:289–290) reflect this tendency. Of the 264 Chinese immigrants who applied for legalization in 1991, only 27 per cent (72 people) could read and write Spanish. Indeed, Beltrán and García (ibid.:291) note that 'wherever the Chinese immigrate, they build their own communities in isolation from mainstream society, with their own culture, values, and language'. One result of this is that they do not take advantage of the assistance the government offers immigrants, preferring to be self-sufficient and unattached to the host country. Integration, generally speaking, is neither needed nor desired. One of several strategies the Chinese use to preserve their culture is to send their children to study in China and then have them return as adolescents or young adults. These children end up learning little Spanish because they are not educated in the Spanish education system (ibid.:292). As noted, however, there are exceptions to this marked tendency, one of which I will be discussing in the next sub-section.

## 6.2.2    The informants

Of the Chinese immigrants currently residing legally in Spain, 86 per cent have arrived since 1986. One of the two informants of this study, Jenny, came to Madrid in 1985, in her late twenties.[2] Born in Nanking, Jenny is a speaker of Mandarin Chinese. She knew she wanted to emigrate and thus learned Chinese massage and acupuncture before leaving her homeland. Upon arriving in Madrid, she knew no Spanish and had studied Russian and English for no more than one year. During her first nine years in the Spanish capital, she worked in a Chinese restaurant, in which she carried on most of her communication in Mandarin Chinese. For the first years of her residence in Madrid, Jenny lived with other Chinese women but since then has lived alone. Her main goal in Madrid has been to become financially stable, and she has learned Spanish to the extent that the language helped her to do so. Currently, she works with Spaniards as a professional manicurist, masseuse, and acupuncturist. She maintains little contact with the Chinese community in Madrid, preferring instead to spend her time with Spaniards, although she has

---

[2] The information on the informants' varieties of Spanish is taken from data collected by the author. Some of the statistical analysis of Jenny and Luis' speech was first published in Clements 2003a, 2003b, and 2005.

a sister and some Chinese-speaking friends in Madrid. Thus, for the first nine years the minimal Spanish input Jenny received resulted in the Chinese features in her environment outweighing the Spanish ones. During this formative stage of language development, she acquired neither articles nor clitics, nor features such as gender and number agreement. Since 1994, she has increasingly become integrated into Spanish society, and as a consequence her vocabulary is substantial. Even though the feature pool she has access to contains largely Spanish lexical material and structure, her language development is constrained by the system she created during the first nine years of her residence in Madrid.

Before settling in Spain, Luis, the other informant, had already worked as a barber for a number of years in Taiwan. He also had made a trip to Spain to determine in which Spanish city he wanted to settle with his family. He decided on Madrid, having a sister there; while in Spain she had married a man of Chinese descent who himself had grown up in the country. Luis brought his wife and child to Madrid in 1989. For the first several years, they leased a hair-cutting and -styling business. From the beginning, then, he has had contact with Spanish-speaking clients six days a week, forty-eight weeks a year.

In his interview, Luis reported that he learned a lot of his Spanish from his clients. Initially, he used textbooks brought from Taiwan to master the Spanish alphabet and language, and he has been able to practise his Spanish with his clients. In 2000, he and his wife, who is also a hair stylist, were able to buy their own hair salon. Professionally, Luis seems well established in his neighbourhood in Madrid.

Contrary to the general reasons for Chinese immigration to Spain, and to Europe in general, Luis wanted to live in Spain because of his children. As a hairdresser, he and his wife made a comparable living in Taiwan, so the incentive for settling in Spain was not financial or to raise their social status, but rather to allow his children to study in the Spanish school system. In Taiwan, as well as in Japan and Korea, Luis reported that the high level of competitiveness among children at the primary and secondary level is highly stressful. Luis and his wife wanted to avoid this type of stressful situation in the education of their children and felt that in Spain this was possible.

Luis and his wife have contact with Spanish speakers only in their work place. Outside their working environment, Luis reported that he and his family have virtually no contact with Spanish speakers, socializing exclusively with relatives and close friends from their home town in Taiwan who also now live in Madrid. Thus, on the one hand, Luis' acquisition of Spanish has been supported since his arrival in the sense that he maintains regular contact with the Spanish-speaking clientele in his business. However, the lack of diversity of interaction with Spanish speakers in a wide variety of situations outside his profession has limited the richness of Spanish input he has received. As a result, the feature pool to which Luis has had access has been substantially richer in Chinese-language than Spanish-language features.

The data used for the comparison of our informants' Spanish varieties were collected in interviews that took place at the informants' residence (Jenny) or place of business (Luis). The author was the interlocutor. The topics covered were: birth place, education and professional life in China, family, reasons for emigrating, likes and dislikes of Spanish society, food, professional life in Spain, and their future in Spain. A loose phonetic transcription of the interview was used for the analysis.

An examination of the data reveals that both Jenny's and Luis' varieties of Spanish share key traits, such as the devoicing of voiced stops, the preference of CV structure, the confusion of /r/ and /l/ (and /n/ in Luis' case), the lack of noun and verb morphology, verb-final word order in certain constructions (more pronounced in Jenny's speech), the lack or non-standard use of articles and clitic pronouns, and the re-analysis of certain forms or phrases, among other things. I also found numerous differences in their respective varieties. For example, while Jenny's speech contains virtually no articles, Luis' speech reveals consistent use of the article *la* 'the.FEM.SG'. Moreover, Luis' speech exhibits more consistent use of verb forms than does Jenny's speech (see Tables 6.3 and 6.4). Jenny's speech, in contrast, shows the development of a stable pronominal system distinct from that of standard Spanish; moreover, her variety of Spanish displays signs of developing a perfective particle. Neither of these is as evident in Luis' speech. Finally, in Jenny's speech we find far fewer disfluencies than in that of Luis. These differences follow directly, I suggest, from the respective ecologies of the informants. Jenny has fewer verb forms and no articles because her early Spanish feature pool was significantly restricted, whereas Luis' feature pool, though limited with respect to diversity and depth, has always been constant. By contrast, the greater fluency, richer vocabulary, and more developed pronominal and aspectual system in the Spanish displayed by Jenny is a direct reflection of her situation between 1994 and 2004, during which she has increasingly spent time with Spanish speakers rather than Chinese speakers. She not only interacts with Spanish speakers verbally, but regularly reads popular *revistas de corazón* 'magazines of the heart' and keeps up on various aspects of current events. Thus, Jenny's Spanish feature pool has continually increased while Luis' has remained constant, though limited, over time. This suggests that the differences in their speech are attributable to this difference in ecology, but also to ease-of-processing considerations as will be discussed below.

Even though Jenny and Luis speak non-standard varieties of Spanish, they both can express themselves, though (as mentioned) Jenny displays greater fluency. Their respective Spanish varieties represent two independent cases of natural L2 acquisition with a different degree and type of restricted input. And although each variety constitutes an individual solution to the speaker's communicative needs in Spain, their respective structure not only suggests substantial L1 transfer, but also reveals certain tendencies in form–function mapping not traceable to their L1 that make these varieties especially interesting when compared to certain pidgins and creoles. In chapters 3 and 5, I touched upon the similarities between immigrant varieties, Chinese Coolie Spanish, and pidgins/creoles. I note here a revealing similarity: Luis has selected the 3PL present-tense form of the copula *son* 'they are' (infinitive *ser*) as his copulative verb. As argued in chapter 1, this has to do with the preference of CV(C) (*son*) syllable structure over VC syllable structure (*es* 's/he/it is'), even though *es* is many times more frequently used than *son*. Interestingly, we encounter this same preference among those Cantonese speakers who chose the analogous Portuguese form *são* [sãw] 'they are' instead of *é* [e] 's/he/it is' as their copula in Makanese Creole Portuguese. I will return to this and other features of Chinese Immigrant Spanish, but before doing so, I need to examine in some detail the tense–aspect systems that Jenny and Luis have developed in their respective Spanish varieties.

### 6.3    The tense–aspect system in Jenny's and Luis' speech

#### 6.3.1    Distribution of verb forms

To analyse the verb forms produced by the two informants, I categorized them as types and tokens as in chapter 5, that is, according to predicate class (stative, atelic durative, telic durative, punctual) and verb form (first-/second-/third-person-singular present, first-/third-person-plural present, first-/second-/third-person-singular past (preterit and imperfect), infinitive, gerund, past participle, other), and whether or not the forms were used in a context appropriate to their aspect and tense. Forms were judged to be appropriately used according to the context in which they were uttered. Present-tense forms were judged correct in discourse contexts involving present states of affairs being referred to by the informants at the time of speech.[3] They were judged incorrect, however, in discourse situations involving past events, activities, or states referred to at the time of speech. As in chapter 5, only tense and grammatical aspect were taken into account for classifying a verb form as

---

[3] A verb type is considered a member of one verb class or another on the basis of how it is used. For example, *pasa Australia* 'went (to) Australia' is telic and durative, but *no pasa nada* 'there is no problem' is stative. Some predicate types were difficult to categorize. For example, *vivir* 'to live' can be argued to be a stative or atelic durative. The verb–token ratio is calculated per category. For instance, *sabe* 'know' in the cell of third-person-singular present correct forms and *sabe* in the corresponding incorrect forms are counted as two types.

Table 6.1. *Distribution of correctly and incorrectly used finite and non-finite verb tokens in Jenny's speech*

| Form | Finite | Non-finite | Total |
|------|--------|------------|-------|
| Correct | 230 (61%) | 48 (21%) | 278 (46%) |
| Incorrect | 146 (39%) | 178 (79%) | 324 (54%) |
| Total | 376 (100%) | 226 (100%) | 602 (100%) |

*Note: p < .001, $\chi^2 = 90.6$ (df = 1).*

Table 6.2. *Distribution of correctly and incorrectly used finite and non-finite verb tokens in Luis' speech*

| Form | Finite | Non-finite | Total |
|------|--------|------------|-------|
| Correct | 96 (67%) | 12 (15%) | 108 (48%) |
| Incorrect | 47 (33%) | 68 (85%) | 115 (52%) |
| Total | 143 (100%) | 80 (100%) | 223 (100%) |

*Note: p < .001, $\chi^2 = 55.8$ (df = 1).*

correctly or incorrectly used. Correctness of person and number marking were not considered. The results, shown in Tables 6.1 and 6.2, clearly indicate that neither Jenny nor Luis exhibits a preponderance of correctly used verbal forms.

Although a substantially greater percentage of the situations referred to by both informants was in the past, Jenny's speech contains only 4 preterit forms (*nació* 's/he was born', *murió* 's/he died', *fue (a(l))* 's/he went (to (the))', *sacabó* 'it finished') and 20 tokens out of a total of 602 tokens and 141 types. Luis's speech has only 2 preterits (*ví* 'I saw' and *fue* 's/he went') and 2 imperfect forms (*sabía* 's/he knew' and *era* 's/he/it was') out of a total of 223 tokens and 71 types. Given that the forms Jenny and Luis used were almost exclusively present-tense or non-finite forms, any past context referred to by a present-tense verb form was considered incorrect, as was any context referred to by using solely non-finite forms (i.e., infinitive, gerund, or past participial form). Tables 6.1 and 6.2 display, in raw numbers and percentages, the distribution of correctly and incorrectly used present-tense finite and nonfinite verb forms.

Based on this overview of the informants' verb-form use in Spanish, it is safe to say that neither speaker exhibits a tendency towards approximating the target verbal system, but, as the chi-square values suggest, the distribution is not random. For referring to the present, they used present-tense finite forms correctly only 61 per cent and 67 per cent of the time respectively, and they used non-finite forms inappropriately (infinitive, gerund, past participle, or re-analysed forms) 79 per cent and 85 per cent of the time.[4]

Tables 6.3 and 6.4 summarize the distribution of Jenny's and Luis' verb forms, as types and tokens. Their respective verbal systems reveal substantial sensitivity to lexical aspectual distinctions: (a) stative predicates occur with high frequency in present-tense forms (84 per cent for both Jenny (218/258) and Luis (85/101)), predominantly the 3SG-present-tense form (Jenny 81 per cent and Luis 52 per cent);[5] (b) atelic durative predicates occur almost exclusively in present-tense, infinitival, and gerund forms; (c) telic durative predicates, although occurring in all categories except for gerund, are most frequently found in 3SG-present and infinitival forms;[6] and (d) punctual verbs and predicates are distributed principally over the 3SG-present, infinitival, and past participial forms. Noteworthy for telic durative and punctual predicates is the stronger presence of past participle forms.

Also of note is that, although it is variable, we find a bias towards finite forms in reference to the present tense. The present forms, at 56 per cent (336/602) and 61 per cent (136/223) for Jenny and Luis respectively, are overall the most frequently used forms by far. This is not surprising given that in Spanish usage the present is twice as frequently used as the preterite (Gili Gaya 1960, cited in Bybee 1985:121). Thus, the present-tense forms, and more particularly the 3SG-present forms, are the default forms. This is most apparent, as mentioned, with the stative predicates.[7]

Although past participial forms are infrequently used overall (5 per cent (30/602) and 8.5 per cent (19/223) for Jenny and Luis respectively), they occur more frequently with telic than with atelic predicates (77 per cent (23/30) and 53 per cent (10/19), for Jenny and Luis, respectively) and are more strongly represented by forms in *-ado* (87 per cent (13/15) and 79 per cent (15/19) for

[4] The term *gerund* is used here to refer to the Spanish forms in *-ndo*, as in *cantando* 'singing' and *bebiendo* 'drinking'.

[5] Stative and atelic durative predicates (forms of *vivir* 'to live') are calculated together here.

[6] The category 'other' includes non-verbal or chunked lexical items, such as the use of *alquiler* 'rental', *fuera* 'out(side)', and *conóselo* 'be acquainted with', which have been re-analysed as verbs in Jenny's speech. This last item is most likely a re-analysed form from *conoce lo que* 'is acquainted with that which'.

[7] Luis' speech exhibits a wider variety of present-tense forms than does Jenny's. This may be attributable to a number of factors. First, as a barber Luis was exposed to one-to-one Spanish conversation situations from early on and may have learned some more forms. That said, note that all thirteen instances of 2PRES forms are of one type *¿entiende?* 'do you understand?', which was spoken to the interlocutor. Although it is known from the context that we are dealing with a second-person form, it does not have the corresponding morpheme *-s*. This may be due to one of two reasons. Luis may be accessing the formal form or, more likely, he fails to realize word-final sibilants. Luis' speech rarely displays the word-final *-s*. For example, all ten examples of the 1PL present form are realized as [tenemo] (standard Spanish *tenemos*). Moreover, the 3PL-present forms are all of one verb, the copulative form *son* 'they are'.

Table 6.3. *Verb forms in Jenny's speech*

| Verb Form | Stative | | Atelic Durative | | Telic Durative | | Punctual | |
|---|---|---|---|---|---|---|---|---|
| | Type | Token | Type | Token | Type | Token | Type | Token |
| 1SG-PRES | 5 (13.9%) | 11 (4.3%) | 2 (5.0%) | 8 (7.0%) | 1 (4.0%) | 1 (1.0%) | 1 (2.5%) | 3 (2.3%) |
| 3SG-PRES | 24 (66.7%) | 207 (80.2%) | 14 (35.0%) | 39 (34.2%) | 6 (24.0%) | 22 (22.2%) | 11 (27.5%) | 45 (34.4%) |
| 3SG-PAST (preterit and imperfect) | — | — | — | — | 2 (8.0%) | 7 (7.1%) | 4 (10.0%) | 13 (9.9%) |
| Infinitive | 3 (8.3%) | 7 (2.7%) | 12 (30.0%) | 17 (14.9%) | 11 (44.0%) | 50 (50.5%) | 11 (27.5%) | 24 (18.3%) |
| Gerund | — | — | 7 (17.5%) | 44 (38.6%) | — | — | — | — |
| Past participle | 1 (2.8%) | 2 (0.8%) | 3 (7.5%) | 3 (2.6%) | 2 (8.0%) | 2 (2.0%) | 9 (22.5%) | 23 (17.6%) |
| Other | 3 (8.3%) | 31 (12.0%) | 2 (5.0%) | 3 (2.6%) | 3 (12.0%) | 17 (17.2%) | 4 (10.0%) | 23 (17.6%) |
| Total | 36 (100%) | 258 (100%) | 40 (100%) | 114 (100%) | 25 (100%) | 99 (100%) | 40 (100%) | 131 (100%) |

*Note:* Totals may not equal 100 because of rounding.

Table 6.4. *Verb forms in Luis' speech*

| Verb form | Stative | | Atelic Durative | | Telic Durative | | Punctual | |
|---|---|---|---|---|---|---|---|---|
| | Type | Token | Type | Token | Type | Token | Type | Token |
| 1SG-PRES | 3 (11.5%) | 4 (4.0%) | 3 (13.0%) | 15 (20%) | 1 (6.7%) | 1 (4.3%) | – | – |
| 2SG-PRES | 1 (3.8%) | 13 (12.9%) | 1 (4.3%) | 3 (4%) | – | – | – | – |
| 3SG-PRES | 12 (46.2%) | 53 (52.5%) | 4 (17.4%) | 17 (22.7%) | 7 (46.7%) | 10 (43.5%) | 3 (42.9%) | 5 (20.8%) |
| 1PL-PRES | 1 (3.8%) | 10 (9.9%) | – | – | – | – | – | – |
| 3PL-PRES | 1 (3.8%) | 5 (5.0%) | – | – | – | – | – | – |
| 1SG-PAST (preterit and imperfect) | 2 (7.7%) | 2 (2.0%) | – | – | – | – | – | – |
| 2SG-PAST (preterit and imperfect) | 1 (3.8%) | 3 (2.9%) | – | – | – | – | | |
| 3SG-PAST (preterit and imperfect) | 1 (3.8%) | 1 (1.0%) | – | – | 1 (6.7%) | 1 (4.3%) | – | – |
| Infinitive | 4 (15.4%) | 10 (9.9%) | 11 (47.8%) | 29 (38.7%) | 4 (26.7%) | 8 (34.8%) | 2 (28.6%) | 13 (54.2%) |
| Gerund | – | – | 1 (4.3%) | 1 (1.3%) | – | – | – | – |
| Past participle | – | – | 3 (13.0%) | 10 (13.3%) | 2 (13.3%) | 3 (13.0%) | 2 (28.6%) | 6 (25.0%) |
| Other | – | – | – | – | – | – | – | – |
| Total | 26 (100%) | 101 (100%) | 23 (100%) | 75 (100%) | 15 (100%) | 23 (100%) | 7 (100%) | 24 (100%) |

*Note:* Totals may not equal 100 because of rounding.

Jenny and Luis respectively). As we shall see below, the correlation between telic predicates and the past participle form is what one would expect. We also expect the past participles in *-ado* to be more strongly represented because the *-a* verb class (e.g. *cantar* 'sing' vs *beber* 'drink' or *vivir* 'live') is numerically by far the most strongly represented morphologically defined verb class in Spanish. In those cases where the past participial form does not appear with punctual predicates, it marks anteriority in Jenny's speech (*pensado* 'I had thought'), the past in Luis' speech (*pensaw* 'I thought/was thinking', *mirado* 'I looked around'), or a resultant state (*casado* 'married').[8]

The gerund form in both Jenny's and Luis' speech is found only in atelic durative predicates, but never with punctual, telic durative, or stative predicates. All the gerund forms are from the *-a* verb class (*cantando*), and none is from the *-e* or *-i* verb classes (e.g., *bebiendo* 'drinking' or *viviendo* 'living').

Based on what we have seen so far, the evidence strongly suggests that the Spanish aspect systems of these two speakers display some fairly clear patterns. A significant correspondence obtains, according to the figures in Tables 6.3 and 6.4, between lexical class and verb form: in Jenny's case, $\chi^2 = 467.48$ for tokens, $p < .001$ and $\chi^2 = 55.92$ for types, $p < .001$; for Luis, $\chi^2 = 98.72$ for tokens, $p < .001$ and $\chi^2 = 39.27$ for types, $p < .20$ ($p < .05$ would be 43.77). I take the non-significant $\chi^2$ for Luis' types to be due to an insufficient amount of data rather than an insignificant relation, since Luis' tokens show a highly significant relation between lexical class and verb form. Thus, both Jenny and Luis have mapped the lexical classes on to the aspectually appropriate forms in a highly non-random manner. The reason for this is not only the informants' sensitivity to aspectual distinctions but also the frequency with which Spanish speakers in interacting with them use these forms. This is accounted for by appealing to the Primacy of Aspect (POA) and Distributional Bias (DBH) Hypotheses (Andersen 1993, Andersen and Shirai 1996). As noted in chapter 1, the POA states that L2 learners initially restrict

---

[8] Jenny's example containing a past participle marking anteriority is the following:

(i)  Yo    pensa muchisima, antes    nunca  no    pensado.
     I     think a lot        before   never  NEG   think-PPART
     'I think about it a lot, before I had never thought about it.'

Luis' example is:

(ii)  y       cuando antério,  me  pensaw porə  viene  aquí ...
      and     when    earlier   I   thought COMP come   here
      'When before, when I was thinking about coming here ...'

In Luis' speech, four of the seven instances of *pensaw* refer to past situations, the other three to present situations. Both instances of *mirado* refer to past situations.

past or perfective marking to telic predicates and imperfective and progressive marking to atelic verbs, whereby the progressive marking is not usually over-extended to stative predicates. It accounts for the strong tendencies found in Jenny's and Luis' speech. In their speech, all gerunds (imperfective forms) appear with atelic dynamic predicates, over 80 per cent in Jenny's case (83 per cent (25/30)). Moreover, nearly half of Luis' (47 per cent (9/19)) participial forms are found in telic predicates, and around 80 per cent of states (84 per cent (218/258) for Jenny and 70 per cent (70/101) for Luis) are encoded with the imperfective, present-tense forms. I take the lower number of participial forms in Luis' telic predicates to be a function of his exposure to Spanish from the beginning. As mentioned above, this longer exposure to Spanish also accounts for the higher number of forms found in his speech (see Tables 6.3 and 6.4).

Although the POA predicts that perfective marking will appear first with telic predicates and extend from there, it does not address the exact form–function mapping. That is, it does not predict that precisely the 3SG.PRES form will match up with gerund forms, stative, and atelic predicates, while past participles appear with punctual predicates or stative predicates denoting resultant states. The DBH can predict this, however. Andersen (1983:320) describes the DBH this way: 'Native speakers will tend to use past or perfective inflections more with telic and punctual events than with states or activities, progressive inflections primarily with activities and imperfective inflections more with states and activities than with telic and punctual events.'[9] I assume that learner-directed, as well as foreigner-directed, varieties influenced to some extent the input that Jenny and Luis have received, especially during their first years as residents in Madrid. If this accommodation on the part of the native speakers interacting with our informants indeed took place, which is a reasonable assumption, it would have facilitated their task of mapping the aspectual functions on to the appropriate forms.

In chapter 1, we saw that the 3SG present-tense form is the most frequently occurring form in the oral corpus of Madrid Spanish, the Spanish variety Jenny and Luis have been exposed to. In Jenny's speech, this form is the most frequently used (313/602 tokens or 52 per cent) and in Luis' speech the most frequently used overall (53 tokens of 223 overall tokens, 24 per cent), which according to the DBH would reflect the input they receive. Note that Jenny's

---

[9] Andersen and Shirai (1996:553) also state that, 'It appears that learner-directed speech is more consistent with the DBH than is N[ative] S[peaker]–N[ative] S[peaker] discourse . . . However, it is not clear whether the topic of the conversation or the simplified nature of the learner-directed speech is the key determining factor.'

Table 6.5. *Comparison of the distributions of verb forms (raw numbers and percentages) according to imperfective (present, imperfect) and perfective (preterit) verb forms in spoken language in Spain, Jenny's speech, and Luis' speech*

|  | Stative predicates | Atelic predicates | Punctual predicates |
|---|---|---|---|
| *Spoken language in Spain* | | | |
| Imperfective | 24409 (97.9%) | 951 (91.4%) | 394 (45.4%) |
| Perfective | 525 (2.1%) | 90 (8.6%) | 473 (54.6%) |
| *Jenny* | | | |
| Imperfective | 218 (99.1%) | 83 (96.5%) | 48 (57.8%) |
| Perfective | 2 (0.9%) | 3 (3.5%) | 35 (42.2%) |
| *Luis* | | | |
| Imperfective | 85 (96.6%) | 36 (76.6%) | 5 (45.5%) |
| Perfective | 3 (3.4%) | 11 (23.4%) | 6 (54.5%) |

and Luis' stative predicates appear in the 3sg-present form, an imperfective form, 80 per cent (207/258) and 52 per cent (53/101) of the time.[10]

If we disregard the infinitive forms and telic durative predicates (sometimes difficult to judge) and consider solely the distribution of verbs with imperfective (gerund, 1sg.PRES, and 3sg.PRES) and perfective (3sg.PRET and PPART) morphology, comparing it to the distribution of the same forms in the oral corpus from Madrid, we obtain Table 6.5, taken from Clements 2005. The fact that the distribution of forms in spoken language from Spain is so close to that found in Jenny's and Luis' speech suggests that the DBH is strongly supported.

An additional interesting aspect of the tense–aspect systems discussed here is that their forms correspond in revealing ways to the forms that mark tense–aspect in Spanish- and Portuguese-based creoles. Given this correspondence, shown in Table 6.6, the deduction is that the POA and the DBH can also account for the distribution of forms in contact-induced pidginized or creolized varieties of Spanish and Portuguese. That is, the form–meaning mapping tendencies predicted by the POA and the DBH were present at the pidgin stage and then generalized across the respective tense–aspect systems of the creoles during the process of creolization. It is also not surprising that

[10] In studies on English L1 acquisition by Bloom, Lifter, and Hafitz (1980) and Shirai (1991), on English L2 acquisition by Robison (1995), and on an L1 acquisition connectionist simulation by Li and Shirai (2000), the 3sg.PRES was also found to be the default form.

Table 6.6. *Form–function correspondences between Jenny's and Luis' speech and Spanish- and Portuguese-based creoles*

| Form | Jenny's and Luis' speech | Chabacano | Palenquero | Papiamentu | Many Portuguese-based creoles | Spanish and Portuguese |
|---|---|---|---|---|---|---|
| *ya* (*já*, Portuguese) | possible perfective marker | perfective marker | – | – | perfective marker | 'already' |
| gerund form | atelic predicates | – | dynamic verbs | dynamic verbs (recently adopted) | dynamic verbs | dynamic and some stative verbs |
| past participle | telic durative predicates | – | – | resultative states and passives | perfective | all verbs |
| third-person singular | stative predicates | stative predicates | stative predicates | stative predicates | stative predicates (e.g., *ker, te, sab*) | all verbs |

*Sources:* Chabacano (Forman 1972); Palenquero (Schwegler 1998); Papiamentu (Maurer 1998); and Portuguese-based creoles (Clements 1996; Clements and Koontz-Garboden 2002).

the same distribution found in Chinese Immigrant Spanish is comparable to that in Chinese Coolie Spanish examined in chapter 5.

### 6.3.2   Other characteristics of Jenny's and Luis' Spanish varieties

The phonological traits shared by Jenny and Luis are almost identical. To display these, I have adapted a list of traits for Chinese pidgin English found in Shi (1991). Table 6.7 gives the trait in the left-hand column and the source of the trait in the right-hand column.[11]

All traits except Table 6.8g are pervasive in Luis' speech and common though less frequent in Jenny's speech. Examples of traits (a–f) of Table 6.8 are given in (6.1) and (6.2).

(6.1)   Examples from Jenny
   *mucho año* (< Sp. *muchos años* 'many years')
   *abrá* (< Sp. *hablar* 'speak')
   *fuela* (< Sp. *fuera* 'outside')
   *solisidá* (< Sp. *solicitar* 'apply for')
   *cuatro* (< Sp. *cuadros* 'paintings')
   *iguá* (< Sp. *igual* 'same')
   *detlás* (< Sp. *detrás* 'behind')
   *dosə* (< Sp. *dos* 'two')

(6.2)   Examples from Luis
   *aší* (< Sp. *así* 'thus, this/that way')
   *esprigá* (< Sp. *explicar* 'explain')
   *kirienta* (< Sp. *clienta* 'customer')
   *unisé* (< Sp. *unisex* 'unisex')
   *abra* (< Sp. *habla* 's/he speaks')
   *coleto* (< Sp. *correcto* 'correct')
   *despué* (< Sp. *después* 'afterwards, after')
   *tiporəma* (< Sp. *diploma* 'diploma')
   *seguridá sociá* (< Sp. *seguridad social* 'social security')
   *tepende* (< Sp. *depende* 'it depends')
   *caná* (< Sp. *ganar* 'to earn, win')
   *catose* (< Sp. *catorce* 'fourteen')

In addition, neither Jenny nor Luis has Castilian /θ/ in their speech. They produce Castilian /katorθe/ as [ka-tó-se]), with /rθ/ to /s/ reduction. This may be due to variable input on the part of the Spanish speakers they have been in contact with, as Andalusian Spanish speakers, some of whom live in Madrid, do not have /θ/, but rather /s/ in their speech (e.g., [ka-tór-se]). It could also be

---

[11] For my purposes, the use of the term 'Chinese' to refer to Mandarin and to Taiwanese is uncontroversial as both varieties are nearly identical with regard to the features discussed in this chapter. The information on Chinese is taken from Li and Thompson 1981, Smith 1991, and Li and Shirai 2000.

Table 6.7. *Phonological traits of Chinese Immigrant Spanish*

| Trait | Source |
|---|---|
| a. r → l, l → r | Chinese |
| b. b, d, g devoicing (g → k) | Chinese |
| c. š → s and s → š | Chinese |
| d. voicing of stops | Chinese |
| e. three types of syllable simplification strategies | – |
|    i. vowel epenthesis | Chinese |
|    ii. cluster simplification | Chinese |
|    iii. deletion of syllable coda | Chinese |
| f. preference of CV structure | Chinese, other |
| g. retention of closed syllables in -s | Spanish |

Table 6.8. *Morphosyntactic traits of Chinese Immigrant Spanish*

| Trait | Source |
|---|---|
| a. SVO word order | Spanish, Chinese |
| b. S Adjunct V word order | Chinese |
| c. No passive voice | Other |
| d. Classifier equivalent to English *piece* | Not present |
| e. N + N (with genitive or modifier relation) | Chinese |
| f. No prepositions as such | There are prepositions |
| g. Adv + Adj | Spanish, Chinese |
| h. V + IO + DO order with no marking for IO or DO | Chinese |
| i. Adv + V + NP | Chinese |
| j. V + NP + Adv | Spanish, Chinese |
| k. *ya* completive | Chinese |
| l. Other than *ya* and *-do*, there are no TMA markers | Other |
| m. Copula with Ns, absent with Adjs. | Chinese |
| n. In-situ and fronted *wh*-words | Spanish, Chinese[a] |
| o. Bimorphemic *wh*-words | Not present |
| p. No equivalents of *yes* and *no* to questions | Spanish[b] |
| q. Negation: *no* before the predicate | Spanish, Chinese |
| r. Double negation: *antes nunca no pensado* 'I had never thought [about it] before.' | Spanish[c] |
| s. Headless relative clauses | Chinese |

*Notes:*
[a] Fronted.
[b] There are.
[c] Generalization of a restricted option in Spanish.

due to an ease-of-processing tendency, producing an interdental voiceless fricative as an alveolar voiceless sibilant.

The preference for CV syllable structure is seen in the elision of the word-internal consonant clusters in words like *catose* 'fourteen' (< *catorce* 'fourteen') and word-final -*l*, as in *iguá* 'same, even' (< *igual* 'same, even'), as well as in the epenthetic vowels, as in *kirienta* for *clienta* 'customer'. I suggest that the preference for CV structure is also the reason for the choice of indefinite and definite determiners made by these speakers. The Spanish definite articles are *el* 'the.MASC.SING', *la* 'the.FEM.SING', *los* 'the.MASC.PL', *las* 'the.MASC.FEM'. In Jenny's and Luis' speech, the plural determiners appear only as part of lexicalized chunks, as in the city name (e.g., Las Palmas, the capital city of Gran Canaria in the Canary Islands) or in phrases they repeated after the interlocutor. The singular definite article preferred almost exclusively is *la* over *el* (see examples in (6.7)). One alternative account would be that *la* may occur overall (i.e., the sum of /la/ as a determiner and a pronoun) more often than *el*. Indeed, this argument accounts for the preference, as in Alameda and Cuetos' (1995) frequency corpus *el* appears 54,027 times and *la* 78,700 times, or 1.45 times as often as *el*. The indefinite article *una* 'one.FEM.SING' is preferred to the masculine counterpart *un*, although *una* occurs less frequently in discourse than *un* (19,973 tokens for *una* compared to 25,119 tokens for *un*). I suggest that one reason for the preference of *una* may lie in that it contains a CV structure whereas *un* does not. The CV argument also accounts for the preference shown by Luis in his choice of copula forms: in singular contexts, past and present, he prefers *son* (< Spanish 'they are') to *es* (< Spanish 's/he/it is') four to one. Again, frequency would predict the opposite because *es* occurs five times more frequently than *son* (14,453 to 2,897). The argument based on CV preference accounts, then, for all these cases, whereas the frequency argument makes the correct prediction only once. Assuming that *la*, *una*, and *son* have been selected because they contain a CV structure, this is a case of a L1 structure – a highly unmarked structure – displaying a stronger influence than frequency of forms available in the feature pool of the informants.

There is weak evidence in the informants' speech of sibilant retention in coda position. It is only found in those cases where it does not have an independent morphemic status. That is, the plural morpheme -*s* is never found on plural forms (cf. *mucho año* 'many years' instead of *muchos años*), but invariable words with word-final -*s*, such as *nosotros* [nosotros] are occasionally found alongside [nosotro]. In terms of the phonological systems, Jenny's system appears to be closer to the native system than that of Luis. This follows, I suggest, from the respective ecologies in which each speaker has moved: although Jenny received minimal Spanish input during the first years of her residence in Madrid, she has had constant input in her personal and professional life since 1994 and has therefore been able to adapt her speech accordingly. In Luis' case, even though he has received Spanish input from the beginning, it has only occurred in his place of business, and has been related only to situations involving his profession. It is not surprising, then, that Jenny's speech should exhibit more native-like traits than Luis' speech. As we will see, however, this is not the case for her syntactic traits.

With respect to morphological traits, there is no evidence of consistent person, number, or gender marking (except in pronouns), nor is there any evidence of consistent use of verbal inflection in their speech.

As for syntactic traits, a list of those considered is given in Table 6.8. SVO order and S-Adjunct-V order (Table 6.8a, b) are prevalent in Jenny's speech (6.3–6.4), while in Luis' speech both objects and adjuncts appear postverbally (6.5–6.6).

(6.3a) Él    no      **sabe**    **mio.**
       he    NEG     knows     mine
       Él    no      me        conoce.
       'He doesn't know me.'

(6.3b) yo    no      **sabe**    **el.**
       I     NEG     knows     he
       Yo    no      lo        conozco.
       'I don't know him.'

(6.4a) yo    dise    tio    **conmigo hablando**, puede    fuela   China.
       I     says    uncle  with-me  talking   can-3SG  outside  China
       'I said, "Uncle was telling me I could leave China."'

(6.4b) Casa    puede    **junto**    **vive.**
       house   can-3SG  together   lives
       '[You] can live with us.'

(6.5a) Nosotro,   único    **aprendé**    **españó.**
       we         only     learn-INF    Spanish
       'The only thing we did was learn Spanish [on our own].'

(6.5b) Eso    **tiene**    **dos,**    **dos**    **forma.**
       that   has        two       two      form
       'That [learning Spanish] has two ways.'

(6.6a) Nosotro    **llegá**    **porə**    **español**    casi    doce    año.
       we         arrive-INF  for        Spanish      almost  twelve  year
       'We arrived in Spain almost twelve years ago.'

(6.6b) nosotro    también [. . .]    **aprendé**    españó **con**    **la kirienta.**
       we         also              learn-INF    Spanish with    the.FEM client
       'We also learned Spanish with the clients.'

In the speech of our informants, I found no examples of passive voice (Table 6.8c; neither with *se* nor with *ser*) nor of a noun classifier equivalent to *piece* in Chinese Pidgin English (Table 6.8d). In both Jenny's (6.7) and Luis' (6.8) speech, we find the N + N with a genitive relation (Table 6.8e).

(6.7)   Mi    **papá mamá familia**   diferente. (Jenny)
        my    father mother family   different
        'The families of my father and mother were different.'

(6.8a)  Mi **mujer la**        **padre**   casi    son
        mi wife    the.FEM father    almost are.3PL-PRES
        la        año       noventa y      cuatro,   ya      mueto.
        the.FEM   year      ninety   and    four      already dead
        'My wife's father was almost ninety-four years old [when] he died.'

(6.8b)  para   **la**    **niño**       **fotulo**
        for    the.FEM   child-MASC    future'
        'for the child's future'

(6.8c)  **la**        **campo**        **pərəduto**
        the.FEM    field-MASC   produce
        'produce of/from the field'

In Jenny's speech, we also find N *de* N constructions, examples of which are given in (6.9). In Chinese, the particle *də* is used to link a modified and modifying element and to mark source and genitive semantic roles. Jenny uses Spanish *de* 'of' in this manner as well, but also uses it to mark the locative relation, not found in Chinese. *Də* in Jenny's speech is the nearest element to an all-purpose preposition.

(6.9a)  segundo, escuela   **de**    mayor . . .    hasta   diesiocho año, (modifier)
        second    school   of      older         until   eighteen year
        y       salí        campo trabajando.
        and     left-1SG    field   working
        'Afterwards, I was in secondary school until I was eighteen, and I left to work in the field.'

(6.9b)  masahe   **de**   olientá (modifier)
        massage  of     oriental
        'oriental massage'

(6.9c)  nasioná   **de**   fiesta (modifier)
        national  of     holiday
        'national holiday'

(6.9d)  Hay        tiene   mio   **de**   cliente. (determiner modifier)
        there-is   has     my    of     cliente
        'I have my own clients.'

(6.9e)  Yo    con    Yuen . . . **de**   Taiwan. (source)
        I     with   Yuen      from   Taiwan
        'I [was] with Yuen from Taiwan.'

(6.9f)  Metro     **de**   Barrio            Pilar,       linea nueve (genitive)
        Subway    of     Neighbourhood Pilar,   line nine
        'Pilar neighbourhood underground station, line nine.'

(6.9g)  China nació   **de**   Nanking. (locative)
        China born-3SG of     Nanking
        'In China, I was born in Nanking.'

Luis shows more native-like uses of *de*, using it largely as it is used in Spanish (see examples in (6.10a, b)). There are no instances in his speech of locative *de*, but he does use it, as in Chinese, to link modifiers to modified elements (6.10c, d).

(6.10a)  mi cuñado        **de, de**        chino. No, no, **de** Hangá. (source)
         my brother-in-law  from, from  Chinese. No, no, from Hong Kong
         'My brother-in-law is from China, no, no, he's from Hong Kong.'

(6.10b)  serəkíta  **te** Taipei (< Spanish *cerquita de Taipei* [lit. near-DIM of
                                                                        Taipei])
         near-DIM of Taipei
         'quite near Taipei'

(6.10c)  mucho amigo **de** español (modifier)
         many   friend of Spanish
         'many Spanish friends'

(6.10d)  aprendé   ra   lengua    **de**   españó (modifier)
         learn     the  language  of    Spanish
         'learn the Spanish language'

However, Luis has created an all-purpose preposition in *poro* (which doesn't exist in Spanish) and variants thereof. In (6.11) I give an excerpt in which *poro* and variants are used to mark various different relations.

(6.11a)  Año [. . .]    ochenta nueve,  pero ví      cuando antério,
         year           eighty  nine    but  saw-1SG when   before

(6.11b)  yo pensáw       **poro** viene              aquí, pero que [. . .] mi hemana
         I thought-PPART poro  come-3SG.PRES here  but  that      my sister
         mayó,
         older

(6.11c)  caši  llegá       **por** quí  año, año  ochenta y dos
         almost arrive-INF poro here year year eighty  two

(6.11d)  y    cuando mi hemana llegá       **por** aquí, primer estudio
         and  when   my sister arrive-INF poro here first   study-1SG.PRES

(6.11e)  y despué conoce mi cuñado,        y . . . casá la,   **por** hora casá [. . .]
         and after meets my brother-in-law and   marry-INF poro now  marry-INF

         'In 1989, but I saw [her] before when I came [to visit]. I was thinking to come here but my older sister, she arrived here in 1982; she studied first then met my brother-in-law and then married. Now she's married.'

In (6.11), *por(o)* functions as a complementizer in (6.11b), as a locative in (6.11c) and (6.11d), and as a temporal marker in (6.11e). The first may be modelled on Spanish purpose clauses with *para* 'for', as in *para estudiar* 'in order to study'. The last two are very likely modelled on the Spanish expressions *por aquí* 'around here' and *por ahora* 'for now, for the time being'. It seems that Luis has generalized the use of *por(o)* to use as a complementizer, as well as a spatial and temporal marker. Luis does use the adverbs *ahora* 'now' and *aquí* 'here' without the accompanying *por(o)*, and he uses *para* to mark purpose, as well (6.12).

(6.12a)  Y    aquí tambié muy tranquilo,           má    tranquilo cuando fiesta,
         and here also   very relaxed              more relaxed  when    holiday
(6.12b)  Y    **para, para trabajá** tambié má    tranquilo . . . no    como mi
         and for,  for   work-INF also   more relaxed . . .  NEG  like  my
         país.
         country
         'And here it's very relaxed, more so when there are holidays and to work
         here, it's also more relaxed, not like in my country.'

Although it is clear that both Jenny and Luis employ prepositions and linking
elements (Table 6.8f), there are various contexts in which they do not appear
in Jenny's speech (6.13); in Luis' speech, however, location and direction are
almost always overtly marked (6.14), often with the aforementioned *por(o)*.
Note that in Chinese motion verbs are not accompanied by a preposition,
but a lack of preposition with locative predicates is not a feature of Mandarin
(Li and Thompson 1981).

(6.13a)  yo      **llegá Ø Madrid**, . . .   **vive Ø Madrid** casi    cuanto
         I    arrive     Madrid            live    Madrid almost how-many
         año?
         year
         'I arrived in Madrid, I lived in Madrid almost how many years?'
(6.13b)  **Pero Ø    España,** español nada    nada,    no    sabe.
         but        Spain   Spanish nothing nothing  NEG   know-3SG.PRES
         'But in Spain, I knew nothing, nothing of Spanish.'
(6.14a)  Momento   no     pensaw        poro    vuelva **poro**   mi país.
         momento  NEG   thought-PPART poro    return  poro     my country
         'For the moment, I don't plan on returning to my country.'
(6.14b)  Llevá  **poro**  ra     ciudá
         take    poro   the.FEM  city
         'take to the city'
(6.14c)  Me    viene **por**   aquí.
         me   comes poro     here
         'I came here.'
(6.14d)  Trabajá  **en**  la       seguridá    sociá
         work-INF  in    the.FEM   security     social
         'work in the social security [hospital]'
(6.14e)  Iguá       que **en**  mi     país
         same       as  in    my     county
         'the same as in my country'
(6.14e)  La      hija       no     quiere trabajá . . . **poro**  peluquería.
         the.FEM daughter  NEG   wants work              poro    hair salon
         'Her daughter didn't want to work in the hair salon.'

Thus, although Luis uses non-standard elements such as his prepositions, he is
consistent in marking both directional and locative relations, whereas Jenny
tends not to mark either of them.

Degree adverb–adjective order (Table 6.8g), as in *ma tranquilo* 'more
relaxed' or *muy tranquilo* 'very relaxed', is found in both speakers' speech, as
well as in Spanish and Chinese, and is thus not surprising.

In Luis' speech, we also find V-IO-DO order (Table 6.8h, illustrated in (6.15)), which is common in Chinese (Li and Thompson 1981:370–374), but impossible in Spanish.

(6.15a)  Kiriente enseña        [nosotro]$_{IO}$ [cómo habra        españó para
        client    teach-3SG.PRES we        how speak-3SG.PRES Spanish for
        coreto]$_{DO}$
        correct
        'The    clients teach us how to speak Spanish correctly.'
(6.15b)  Ahora  no      puede        enseñá  [mi hija]$_{IO}$
        now   NEG   can-3SG.PRES  teach   my daughter
        [ahora hecho qué,   hecho        qué]$_{DO}$ ¿entiende?
        now    do-PPART  what  do-PPART     what understand
        'Now I cannot teach my daughter, "What have you done, what have you
        done", you understand?'

The question of argument order in a clause is related to argument marking, both of full and pronominal NPs. The pronominal systems created by the informants, as far as they are discernible, are highly innovative. Jenny's is given in (6.16) and Luis' in (6.17).

(6.16)  **Subject pronouns**                **Object pronouns**
      *Singular*   *Plural*              *Singular*   *Plural*
      yo        nosotros              mio[12]     nosotros
      tú        –                     tuyo       –
      él/ella   ellos                 él/ella    ellos[13]
(6.17)  **Subject pronouns**                **Object pronouns**
      *Singular*   *Plural*              *Singular*   *Plural*
      yo/me     nosotros              –          nosotros
      tú        –                     –          –
      –         –                     –          –

For 1SG and 2SG, Jenny has re-analysed the masculine forms of the possessive pronoun (*mio* 'mine', *tuyo* 'yours') as DO pronouns. Moreover, she uses the 3SG subject pronouns *él* 'he, him' and *ella* 'she, her', as well as 1PL *nosotros* 'we', as DO pronouns. Illustrative examples are given in (6.18).

(6.18a)  Él   no    **sabe**    **mio.**
      he   NEG   knows    mine
      'He doesn't know me.'
(6.18b)  yo   no    **sabe**    **el.**
      I    NEG   knows    he
      'I don't know him.'

---

[12] Spanish possessives (singular and 3PL) have proclitic forms (*mi(s)* 'my', *tu(s)* 'your', *su(s)* 'his, her, their'), as well as stressed, post-placed forms (*mío(s)*, *mía(s)* 'my', *tuyo(s)*, *tuya(s)* 'your', *suyo(s)*, *suya(s)* 'his, her, their') (Picallo and Rigau 1999). Jenny interprets the former as possessives and has re-analysed the latter as object pronouns.
[13] In Spanish, *él* 'he, him', *ella* 'she, her', and *nosotros* 'we, us' are used as subject pronouns, but also after prepositions, as in *de él/ella/nosotros* 'from/of him/her/us'.

(6.18c)  ¿Quién  **ayuda tuyo?**
         who      helps  yours
         'Who would help you?'

(6.18d)  Una   amiga    **presenta**      **nosotros.**
         a     friend   introduces       we
         'A friend introduced us.'

The data on Luis' pronominal system are more incomplete. What we glean from his speech sample is that he uses *yo* 'I' and *me* 'me' interchangeably for the 1SG subject pronoun (6.19) and uses *nosotros* 'we, us' as a subject, a DO, and an IO pronoun (6.20).

(6.19a)  **Yo  pensaw**               poro   viene   aquí.
         I    thought-PPART      LINK   comes   here
         'I thought about coming here.'

(6.19b)  cuando anterio,  **me  pensaw**           porə   viene  aquí.
         when  previous   me   thought-PPART LINK  comes here
         'When earlier I thought about coming here.'

(6.20a)  yo    con    mi    mujé    anterio
         I     with   my    wife    previous
         cuando  **losotro**    **llegá**       españó . . .
         when    we             arrive-INF   Spanish
         'When my wife and I, when we arrived in Spain . . .'

(6.20b)  Mi cuñado              **ayuda nosotro** mucho.
         my brother-in-law     helps  we         much
         'My brother-in-law helped us a lot.'

(6.20b)  Kiriente **enseña nosotro** cómo habra  españó    para   coleto.
         clients  teaches we          how  speaks Spanish   for    correct
         'The clients teach us how to speak correctly.'

Note that these pronominal systems, as far as they are explicit, show some similarity with their Chinese counterpart (6.21), but diverge from it in significant ways.

(6.21)  **Chinese subject and object pronouns** (Li and Thompson 1981:134)
        *Singular*     *Plural*
        wǒ             wǒmen
        nǐ             nǐmen
        tā             tāmen

The similarities are that Luis uses both *yo* and *me* as 'I', and *nosotros* as a subject, a DO, and an IO pronoun. Similarly, Jenny uses *él* as 'he, him', *ella* as 'she, her' and *nosotros* as 'we, us'. As for the differences, Jenny has developed a new set of non-nominative pronouns, *mio* 'me.OBJ' (< Spanish *mio* 'mine-MASC.SING') and *tuyo* 'you.OBJ' (< Spanish *tuyo* 'you-MASC.SING), which is more similar to the Spanish system than her native Chinese one.

In addition to the pronominal system, Jenny has developed an innovative manner of marking IOs, not like that found in Luis' speech in (6.15). She marks IOs with either *para* 'for' or with *con* 'with'. Examples are given in (6.22).

(6.22a)  Un    gente presenta    una    presona  **para  mi.**
         a     people introduce   a      person   for   me
         'A person introduced me to a person.'

(6.22b)  yo    siempre sale            levista,   pasa        allí,  coge,
         I     always  comes.out       magazine  goes-by     there picks-up
         sube  casa,    milando, luego bajo,                 volvé  **para ella.**
         goes.up house looking  then  descend-1SG.PRES return-INF for her
         'I always, when the magazines hit the stand, go by there, pick them up, go
         up to my place, look at them, then take them down and return them to her.'

(6.22c)  Ya    **conmigo** dise, 'tú    no    pasa      Austalia,
         already with-me  says  2SG  NEG  goes-to[14] Australia
         con    nosotros        fue    para Malaga, o   Almería."
         with   us              went   for  Malaga or  Almería
         'She said to me, "If you don't go to Australia, you can come with us
         to Málaga or Almería."'

With regard to the construction Adv + V + NP (Table 6.8i), it is rare in my data, but V + NP + Adv order (Table 6.8j) is common in the speech of both speakers, and is also the one common to both Chinese and Spanish.

With respect to verbal markers, Jenny's speech shows what I believe to be an incipient completive marker in her use of *ya* (< Spanish 'already') and the past participle ending *-do* (Table 6.8k). Some examples are given in (6.23), in which *ya* is not used with its adverbial meaning of 'already'. This use does not correspond to any usage in Spanish.[15]

(6.23a)  Yo    luego a    la cuatro, cuatro año   **ya**   volvé      Sanghay.
         I     after at   the four   four  year  already return-INF Shanghai
         'I returned to Shanghai after four years.'

(6.23b)  Mil novesiento ochenta cuatro, de junio o julio **ya**   coge            pasaporte.
         1984                           of June or July  already get-3SG-PRES passport
         'I got my passport in June or July of 1984.'

(6.23c)  Primero estudio, ahora **ya**      casado          con una    señor.
         first   study    now   already  married-PPART  with a-FEM man
         'She studied first; now she's married to a man.'

(6.23d)  **Ya**    selado         y   selado        lɔgo yo pensando, mehó negocio.
         already close-PPART  and close-PPART  then I  thinking  better business
         'It closed, and after it closed, I thought, better [to launch] another business.'

---

[14] In Jenny's speech, *pasa* seems to be an amalgam of *pasa* 'goes by' and *vas a* 'you.SG go to'. In Spanish, the letter *v* stands for /b/ as there is no labio-dental sound in Castilian. As seen in Table 6.7 above, it is common for Chinese to devoice voiced stops. In this way, Spanish *pasa* and *vas a* come to be realized identically as [pása] by Jenny.

[15] See Clements 2003a for details.

It was mentioned above that the past participial forms in Jenny's speech occur more frequently with telic predicates. One possibility for this preference might be that Jenny has identified the Spanish past participial suffix *-do* as another perfective marker. If we look at Mandarin Chinese translations of some of Jenny's Spanish utterances containing participial forms, the distribution of the Chinese perfective marker *-le* corresponds somewhat regularly to Spanish *-do*. An example from a connected discourse segment is given in (6.25). Of the Spanish verb forms in (6.25) referring to the past (that is, *machado, venido, viene, llegado*) three are past participles. Although I can offer no explanation for why Jenny used the 3SG.PRES *viene* instead of *venido*, the data suggest that she may have made a connection between the notion of perfectivity and the Spanish past participial suffix. However, she has also extended the use of the past participial suffix to punctual verbs that do not refer to perfective contexts.

(6.25)  Jenny:
Mi tio    macha-**do**    Estados Unido. Tu     sabe  Yuen Taiwan
my uncle leave-PPART   United States   you.SG know Yuen Taiwan
veni-**do**?
come-PPART
Chinese:
wǒ yizhang likai-**le**    Meiguo. Nǐ   renshi Yuen Taiwan lai-**le**. . .
my uncle   leave-PERF America you know  Yuen Taiwan come-PERF
Jenny:
Yuen más  detlás viene.          Yo  más  temprano llega-**do**.
Yuen more behind come-3SG-PRES 1SG more early      arrive-PPART
Chinese:
Yuen yihou      lai-**le**     wǒ zao     lai-**le**.
Yuen afterwards come-PERF ISG early   come-PERF
'My uncle came to the United States. You know Yuen, who came from Taiwan?
Yuen came afterwards. I came before her.'

One example occurred in a phone conversation with Jenny in which she gave directions about how to reach her neighbourhood by subway. In spite of being a generic statement, her explanation in (6.26) contains the past participial form of *llegar* 'arrive'.

(6.26)  Aquí llegado      línea uno o  dos.
here arrive-PPART line  one or two
'One can get here by line one or two.'

In Luis' speech, we also find two examples ((6.8a) and (6.27)) that suggest there may be an incipient completive marker developing, but there are also other examples of *ya* use that are similar to standard Spanish (6.28).

(6.8a)  Mi mujer la      padre casi  son        la      año noventa y cuatro, **ya**    mueto.
mi wife  the.FEM father almost are.3SG-PRES the.FEM year ninety and four already dead
'My wife's father was almost ninety-four years old [when] he died.'

(6.27)  Caši    son              la            cuando niño
        almost are.3SG.PRES  the.FEM.SG  when   child
        cinco año, **ya**          llegá          porə      españo.
        five year already      arrive-INF    locative   Spanish
        'He [the brother-in-law] was a child of five years when he arrived in Spain.'

(6.28a) entonse  awra  **ya, ya**        no   tiene  tiporəma.[16]
        then     now   already, already it   has    diploma
        'Then, now he already has a diploma.'

(6.28b) **ya**    lo                       sabía                      trabajá   peluquería.
        already DO.MASC/NEUT.SG  knew-1,3SG.IMPERF  work-INF  hair salon
        'I already knew how to work in a hair salon.'

(6.28c) nosotro en mi país    **ya**    tenemo                  una        peluquelía.
        we    in my country already have.1PL.PRES  a          hair salon
        'In my country we had already owned a hair salon.'

(6.28d) **ya**    lo                       jubilado.
        already DO.MASC/NEUT.SG  retired
        '[My father] is already retired.'

While the use of *ya* and *-do* in Jenny's speech as well as the use of *ya* in Luis'
are suggestive of a developing completive or perfective marker, it cannot be
said that such a marker is fully developed in their varieties. Nor is there any
evidence that other tense or aspect markers are developing in their respective

---

[16] The form *no* here I interpret as a realization of the Spanish DO pronoun *lo*. In Luis' speech,
there is an anomalous use of clitic pronouns, which seem to be re-analysed as part of the verb
itself. For example, the form *sabía* 'know, knew' (< Spanish 'I/she/he knew') always appears
with this pronoun, realized as [lo] or [no], in non-negative contexts. The examples are given
below. Note that the instances of *lo* in (a, b, c) have no reference; we can therefore
hypothesize that [lo] or [no] forms part of the verb for Luis.

(a)  ya    lo                       sabía                      trabajá   peluquería.
     already DO.MASC/NEUT.SG  knew-1,3SG.IMPERF  work-INF  hair salon
     'I already knew how to work in a hair salon.'

(b)  tu    lo                       sabía.
     you   DO.MASC/NEUT.SG    knew-1,3SG.IMPERF
     'You know.'

(c)  Como  tu              no                       sabía,
     as    you.FAM.SG   do.MASC/NEUT.SG   knew-1,3SG.IMPER
     cuando  fuera                   otro país,  hay        paisano.
     when    go-3SG.IMPER.SUB  other country there is/are  country.people
     de      mismo   puebro
     of      same    town
     'As you know, when you go to another country, there are countrymen from your own
     town.'

(d)  Cómo se dise?  Lo                      sabía.
     how is-it-said  DO.MASC/NEUT.SG   knew-1,3SG.IMPER
     'How do you say it? I know it/used to know it.'

systems (Table 6.8l). This is not surprising given that we are dealing with naturalistically learned L2 varieties of Spanish, individual solutions to the problem of communication that exhibit a substantial amount of innovation on the part of the speakers, but that have not gone, and in all likelihood will not go, through the process of propagation (also called adoption or diffusion) or levelling (see Croft 2000:ch. 7 and Siegel 2000:ch. 1).

The copula in the informants' speech is often deleted (Table 6.8m), mostly with adjectival predicates, as is the case in Chinese, but also occasionally with nominal or prepositional predicates, which is not the case in Chinese. Examples from Jenny are given in (6.29) and from Luis in (6.30). Note that the copula deletion affects *ser* as well as *estar*. In the examples, the appropriate copula is included in parentheses.

(6.29a) Por ejemplo, ahola yo Ø (estoy) sola. Todavía no Ø (estoy) casado . . . yo
for example now I (am) alone still NEG married I
siempre Ø (estoy) con Yuen, está también hablando, yo no puede Ø
always (am) with Yuen is also talking I NEG can.3SG.PRES
(estar) sola.
(be) alone
'For example, now I am alone. I'm not yet married. I'm always with Yuen, and am saying [to her that] I cannot be alone.'

(6.29b) Mamá poquito pénsa. Cabesa más ave. Dise, 'tu Ø (eres)
Mamá a.little think head more agile says you.FAM.SG (are)
joven puede fuela para trabajo gána dinero.'
young can-3SG.PRES out for work earn-3SG.PRES money
'Mum thought a little. She has a good head. She said, "You are young, you can leave to work and make money."'

(6.29c) Papá dise tú no, '(eres) una sola mujer,
Father says you.FAM.SG NEG (are) an alone woman,
porque fuera Ø (está) muy lejo.'
because outside (is) very far
'Father said, "You can't [leave China], you're a single woman, because to leave China, that would be going very far away."'

(6.29d) Mi papá mamá familia Ø (es) diferente.
my father mother family (is) different
'The families of my mother and father are different.'

(6.30a) En mi país . . . como iguá a Japón y iguá Korea su, Han Kang,
in my country like same to Japan and same Korea south, Hong Kong
cuando ra niño pəqueño estudio Ø (es) muy pesaw, muy fuelte . . .
when the child small study (is) very heavy, very strong
'In my country, as it is in Japan, South Korea, and Hong Kong, when a small child studies, it is very difficult, very intense.'

(6.30b) Sí, sí, eso Ø (es) muy importante.
yes, yes, that very important
'Yes, yes, that is very important.'

(6.30c) la fase no Ø (eran) coleto.
the phrase NEG correct
'The sentences weren't correct.'

(6.30d)    y    ahora **Ø** (está) solo  mi šuegra      en Taiwán, con  la  hija.
         and now                alone my  mother-in-law in Taiwan, with the daughter
         'And now my mother-in-law's alone in Taiwan, with her daughter.'

(6.30e)    nosotro   puebro en la Taiwan **Ø** (está) en šentro.
         we        town   in the Taiwan        en centre
         no    notre, no es sur,    en la         šientro
         NEG north, NEG is south,   in the-FEM.SG centre
         'Our home town in Taiwan is in the centre of the country, not in the north,
         not in the south, in the centre.'

(6.30f)    Pero cuando     eso pate **Ø**   (es)    casi   más que españó.
         but when        that part    (is)    almost more than Spanish
         'But that part [social security benefits in Taiwan] is almost more than in Spain.'

The data on *wh*-word placement (Table 6.8n) reveal fronting as well as in-situ placement. Examples from Jenny are (6.18c) below, as well as those in (6.31). The sole example from Luis is shown in (6.15b) below.

(6.18c)    ¿Quién    **ayuda tuyo**?
         who        helps  yours
         'Who would help you?'

(6.31a)    Y    enfermo, ¿cómo?    **¿Quiené    cuidado?**[17]
         and  sick     how     who     care/cared-PPART
         'And what if you become sick? Who will care for you?'

(6.31b)    y   selado       lɔgo yo pensando, meho negocio, negocio de qué?
         and closed-PPART then I  thinking  better business business of what
         'After [my restaurant business] closed, I was thinking about a
         better business, what type of business?'

(6.31c)    Yo todo . . ., antes    todo complá, ahola **complá  para qué**?
         I  all    before   all buy-INF now buy-INF for   what
         'Before I used to buy [all the magazines], but now why buy them?'

(6.31d)    Tu          escribe libro  o  **de   qué**?
         you-sg.fam writes book  or  of   what
         'What are you writing a book about?'

(6.15b)    Ahora  no puede            enseñá  mi hija
         now    NEG can-3SG.PRES        teach    my daughter
         ahora  **hecho     qué, hecho**    **qué** ¿entiende?
         now    do-PPART   what do-PPART    what    understand
         'Now I cannot teach my daughter, "What have you done, what have you
         done", you understand?'

In the speech of the informants, I found no bimorphemic *wh*-words (e.g., *qué persona* 'what person' for *quién* 'who') that were not also part of the target language (e.g., *para qué* 'for what') (Table 6.8o). However, the speech of both informants has equivalents of 'yes' and 'no' to questions (Table 6.8p), a Spanish

---

[17] The form *cuidado* corresponds to the past participle of *cuidar* 'care for', and is also a noun, meaning 'care'.

trait, lacking in Chinese (Li and Thompson 1981:557–563). Both Jenny and Luis use the negator *no* before predicates (Table 6.8q), an expected outcome given that it is the default manner of negating a sentence both in Spanish and Chinese. Although there is no double negation found in Luis' speech (Table 6.8r), in Jenny's speech we do find double negation present (6.32) that seems to have been generalized to constructions in which it does not exist in Spanish.[18]

(6.32)  Yo  pensá        muchísima,   antes  **nunca no**    pensado.
        I   think-INF    a lot        before never  NEG   thought-PPART
        'I think a lot now; I had never thought [about it before].'

This last trait, the presence of headless relative clauses (Table 6.8s), is found in both Jenny and Luis' speech (6.33 and 6.34 respectively). I attribute it to Chinese, where it is common, and not to Spanish, where it is impossible.

(6.33)  Pelo  todavía  yo    no . . .  conóselo              una              amigo
        but   yet      I     NEG       acquainted.with  INDEF-FEM-SG  friend
        Ø     le       gusta           mucho mucho.
              3SG-DAT  like-3SG-PRES  a-lot a-lot
        'But I haven't yet met a friend who I really like a lot.'
(6.34)  hay           cosa Ø    no, no me       gusta              perque aquí
        there-is      thing     NEG NEG to.me please-3SG-PRES  because here
        hay      mucho comida,   mucho sa.
        there.is  much food       much salt
        'There's something that I don't like because here in much of the food there's a lot of salt.'

The evidence we have seen from the speech of Jenny and Luis in this section suggests that their language systems follow from their individual ecologies. From the beginning of his residence in Madrid and over the years, Luis has received more constant Spanish input, although this has been restricted to the work place. Consequently, his speech contains a wider variety of verb forms, there is evidence of articles in his speech, and he has some pronominal clitics in his speech though they seem to be part of re-analysed lexical chunks. Given that Luis uses Spanish only in the work place, his speech exhibits more disfluencies than Jenny's and shows less evidence of aspectual

---

[18] The restriction in standard Spanish is that the two negative particles *no* and *nunca* cannot both appear pre-verbally, as in (a). If *no*, which is obligatorily in pre-verbal slot, is used, *nunca* can only appear post-verbally, as shown in (b). If *nunca* appears pre-verbally, it must be the only negative particle, as in (c).

(a) *Yo pienso muchísimo ahora; antes nunca no pensaba en ello.
(b) Yo pienso muchísimo ahora; antes no pensaba nunca en ello.
(c) Yo pienso muchísimo ahora; antes nunca pensaba en ello.

marker development. By contrast, Jenny's speech has in *ya* and *-do* what I consider to be incipient aspectual markers. Moreover, although initially she had minimal exposure to Spanish – for which reason her speech contains fewer verbal forms, little to no sign of articles or pronominal clitics, and head-final order where adjuncts are involved – in recent years her exposure to the language has increased significantly; her fluency in the Spanish variety she has created, therefore, is substantially greater than that of Luis.

With regard to the various traits of their speech, all the phonological processes discussed in Table 6.7 stem from Chinese except the occasional retention of closed syllables in *-s*, which is a Spanish trait. As for the morphosyntactic traits in Table 6.8, seven features are exclusively attributable to Chinese (Table 6.8b, e, h, i, k, m, s) and five to both Chinese and Spanish (Table 6.8a, g, j, n, q), but only two exclusively to Spanish (Table 6.8p, r).

The fact that neither passive voice nor other TMA markers except for the incipient *ya* and *-do* are found is, I believe, attributable either to the nature of the varieties (naturalistic L2 varieties) or to the current developmental stage of each of the varieties. Given the evidence of the development of *ya* and *-do*, I think it is best not to rule out the possibility of innovative aspectual markers, and possibly even innovative tense markers, developing in naturalistic L2 varieties. The same may be said of a type of passive voice. The fact that these features have not developed in these varieties and possibly have not been documented in naturalistic L2 varieties is perhaps accounted for by the observation that the circumstances necessary for the development of such features are very specific and most likely do not often come together.

Finally, in the Spanish varieties spoken by Jenny and Luis there is no noun classifier, such as Chinese Pidgin English *piece*, and no bimorphemic *wh*-words. These might be expected for different reasons: an equivalent of *piece* would be expected due to Chinese having abundant noun classifiers, and the development of bimorphemic *wh*-words would be expected because they are more transparent than monomorphemic *wh*-words (e.g., *what person* and *what thing* are more transparent than *who* and *what* (see Clements and Mahboob 2000 and Muysken and Smith 1990)). That these two traits are not found in these varieties of Spanish may have to do with the nature of the input they received, as well the structure of their own language. Regarding the noun classifier, there may not have been any particular lexical item in their Spanish input that lent itself to re-analysis as a noun classifier; or there may have been one but its use did not further successful communication; or there may be another reason why it did not emerge as a trait. As for the bimorphemic *wh*-words, given that neither Chinese (Li and Thompson 1981:522) nor Spanish has a system of bimorphemic *wh*-words, this would arguably militate against the emergence of these features in their respective varieties, even though bimorphemic *wh*-words are more transparent.

## 6.4     Concluding remarks

In this chapter, I have examined the untutored varieties of Spanish spoken by two native Chinese speakers. I concentrated on two areas: their verb systems and general phonological and morphosyntactic traits. I was able to establish that the Spanish verb forms that Jenny and Luis use are a function of the input they receive. This is shown most conclusively by the data in Table 6.6. I linked this to the forms found in Portuguese- and Spanish-based creoles, suggesting that the input and intake processes used in the formation of L2 varieties, pidgins, and creoles are similar, and constrained by their input, which is accessible through analysis of oral corpora. This finding also lends further support to Klein and Perdue's (1992) notion of 'basic variety' in L2 language varieties.

In my examination of the different traits found in Jenny's and Luis' speech, I found that the individual ecologies of each person accounted for the differences. For example, Luis' speech contains a wider variety of verb forms than Jenny's speech. This was accounted for by the constant Spanish-language input Luis has received from the beginning of his residence in Madrid at his work place, while in the first several years Jenny had considerably less constant contact with Spanish speakers. More recently, Jenny has almost exclusive contact with Spanish-language speakers whereas Luis has maintained his contact with Spanish only in the work place. Consequently, Luis' speech exhibits substantially more disfluencies than Jenny's speech.

Both Jenny and Luis were adults when they came to Spain to work and neither had any formal instruction in the language. The features that their respective Spanish varieties display can almost always be accounted for by similarities to Chinese. However, in Jenny's speech we witness what I consider to be the emergence of aspectual markers in the use of *ya* 'already' and the past participial ending *-do*. While the use of *ya* is reminiscent of the tense markers that emerged in some Portuguese-based creoles (see Table 6.6), that of *-do* seems to correlate fairly consistently with the use of the Chinese perfective marker *-le*. That is, in Jenny's speech two aspect-marking strategies seem to be present: one a re-analysis of an adverb that often occurs preverbally, and the other a mapping between two suffixes that have comparable functions, Chinese *-le* and Spanish *-do*.

In the next two chapters, I discuss varieties that have different ecologies from those examined so far, Andean Spanish and Barraquenho, a variety of Portuguese with notable influence from Extremeño Spanish.

# 7   Andean Spanish

## 7.1   Introduction

The Americas – North, Central, and South America – were initially populated, as far as we know, around or before 11,000 BCE by way of the Bering Strait and Alaska. Although between then and now some contact may have taken place between South America and Polynesia, and the Norse did reach North America prior to 1492, such contacts had no major impact on the societies that developed in the Americas. The 'collision' between the Old World and the New, as Diamond (1999:67) expresses it, began in 1492 with Columbus' 'discovery' of the densely populated Caribbean Islands. Diamond speaks of proximate and immediate causes for the relatively rapid colonization of the New World by Europeans. In essence, it can be said that disease, superior weaponry, and the literate culture of the Europeans played decisive roles in the rapid colonization of South America by the Spanish. Regarding disease, Diamond (ibid.:67–81) notes that the Spaniards had been exposed to many diseases from their centuries-long close proximity to domesticated animals. They had thus developed immunity to diseases which had become endemic among them; the indigenous populations, on the other hand, had had no exposure to these diseases and so were decimated in the first New World–European encounter. As for weaponry, the Incas' clubs, maces, and hand axes (made of stone, bronze, and wood), as well as their slingshots and quilted armour, were no match for the Spanish horses, guns, steel swords, and steel armour. Finally, although Francisco Pizarro, the conqueror of the Inca Empire and founder of Lima, Peru, was illiterate, he had a wealth of information at his disposal from written history, including written accounts of how Cortés defeated Montezuma in what is now Mexico. Diamond remarks that '[f]rom books, the Spaniards knew of many contemporary civilizations remote from Europe, and about several thousand years of European history. Pizarro explicitly modelled his ambush of Atahuallpa [the Inca king] on the successful strategy of Cortés', who defeated the Aztec king Montezuma in Mexico (ibid.:80).

Before the Spanish arrived in the Andean region, the linguistic landscape of the Inca empire was a mosaic of languages spoken by speech communities of different sizes and extensions (Cerrón-Palomino 2003:137–138). However, the Incas had been successfully consolidating power and had managed to unify, socio-economically and politically, a vast area of land that encompassed primarily Ecuador, Bolivia, and Peru, along with the northern-most part of Chile and Argentina; they also reached as far northward as southern Colombia. The Incas had also succeeded in spreading their language, Quechua, throughout their empire by means of teachers and a cadre of linguistic emissaries they called *mitmaq*, 'foreigners' in Quechua. These *mitmaq* (borrowed into Spanish as *mitimaes*) came from different regions of the empire to Cuzco to learn the culture and language of the Incas, then to return to their respective home regions to teach their people Quechua and Incan culture. The Incas also used as *mitmaq* vanquished rebels whom they sent to regions other than their own. Being thus separated from their home and their language, these rebels were unable to create further rebellions. As a consequence, they ended up aiding the spread of Quechua throughout the Andean region (Carranza Romero 1993:25).

At the time of the Spanish arrival in Cajamarca (Peru) – where they first encountered Atahuallpa – the Inca empire was relatively unstable. Atahuallpa and his army had just won decisive battles in a civil war but the empire was divided and vulnerable, a situation that Pizarro and his men realized and were able to exploit. The reason for the civil war in the first place was, as Diamond (1999:77) observes, 'that an epidemic of small pox, spreading overland among South American Indians after its arrival with Spanish settlers in Panama and Colombia, had killed the Inca emperor Huayna Capac and most of his court around 1526, and then immediately killed the designated heir, Ninan Cuyuchi. Those deaths precipitated a contest for the throne between Atahuallpa and his half brother Huascar. If it had not been for the epidemic, the Spaniards would have faced a united empire.'

The collapse of the Inca empire and the subsequent, albeit gradual and modest, introduction of Spanish into the region through colonization created a distinct type of diglossic situation that even now has not reached a balance. To be sure, there was enormous linguistic diversity in the Andean region prior to the presence of Spanish, but as Cerrón-Palomino (2003:138–139) notes, all these languages shared the same general oral tradition and largely the same conceptual world, which was the product of cultural synthesis that had been developing for millennia. By contrast, the introduction of Spanish language and culture into the Andean region created a profoundly asymmetrical linguistic hierarchy: 'not only because the language [Spanish] was the carrier of a highly developed technology, whose adoption rendered the subjugated societies suddenly archaic, but also because [. . .] it was equipped with an instrument that made it even more powerful and efficient: its writing system. With such a system, the indigenous languages were in no condition to hold their own in the situation brought on by the conquest' (Cerrón-Palomino 2003:139; my translation).

Although the attitude of the Spaniards towards the indigenous cultures in the Andean region was one of general contempt, for both their gods and their languages, Quechua did become known as *lengua general* because it was so widespread and knowledge of it was useful to the Spanish for purposes of general communication and evangelization.[1] After the conquest, Quechua was taken to other places by missionaries, explorers, and *yanaconas* 'black slaves', places where it had not reached during the Inca empire, including Santiago de Estero in Argentina and the southern part of Colombia (Carranza Romero 1993:35).

In the next section, I give an idea of how Spanish and Quechua co-existed in two areas in the Andean region, in terms of numbers of inhabitants and maintenance of the two languages.

## 7.2     The external ecology of two areas in the Andean region

There is no consensus regarding the size of the population of the Inca empire (primarily Ecuador, Bolivia, and Peru) just prior to the Spanish invasion and conquest. Difficulties in arriving at an accurate estimate arise from a dearth of data and a lack of knowledge about the effects of disease on the area. Denevan (1992:xxv) states that a recent range of population estimates for the Inca empire in 1520 is from 2.03 million to 14 million, but that by 1620 there remained approximately only 670,000 natives in Peru. This decline was apparently not only due to disease. Sánchez-Albornoz (1974:54) cites reports from González and Mellafe (1965) which state that birth rates among Andean people in the Huánuco region dropped from six per family to two and a half after the arrival of the Spaniards. It is likely that the trend was also present in other regions of the Inca empire as well, since it is known to have been common in other Spanish colonies, such as among the Taínos and Ciboneys in Cuba (see chapter 4, as well as Masó 1976:20).

As is typically the case in colonial situations, the 'rules of the language game', as Cerrón-Palomino (2003:140) describes them, were set: the vanquished were the ones obliged to speak the language of the conquerors. However, in the initial period of the Spanish colonization of the Andean region, there were significant exceptions, accounted for by practical rather

---

[1] The term *lengua general* should not be confused with the Portuguese term *lingua geral* 'common language' which refers to two varieties of Tupi, both of which were re-structured versions of languages spoken by the Tupi people in Brazil. When Portuguese colonizers reached the area in the sixteenth century, they were confronted with an indigenous population that spoke many languages. The two varieties of *lingua geral* were used in the Jesuit missions and by early colonists as a means to speak with the indigenous population.

than policy-driven reasons (ibid.:141). Given the facts that in the beginning of the colonization there was a lack of Quechua–Spanish interpreters and that Quechua was already the *lengua general* of a vast area, the Spanish realized that it was the logical vehicle for evangelization. In 1580, so that priests could be instructed in indigenous languages, Philip II ordered that two university chairs be established, one for Nahuatl in Mexico and another for Quechua in Lima. On 19 September 1580, the king emphasized this in his comment to the Audiencia of Quito (the predecessor to the judiciary) that the Lima chair had been instituted so that no priest would receive ordination without knowing the *lengua general* (Torre Revello 1962:507–508).

But despite this support, as well as earlier efforts discussed in the provincial councils of 1551 and 1567 to use native languages for the evangelization mission, there were also some people who favoured the use of Castilian over the native languages. For example, on 7 June 1550, Charles V issued the first law regarding the teaching of Castilian:

As one of the main things that We wish for the well-being of that land is the salvation and instruction and conversion to our holy Catholic faith of its indigenous population and that they also adopt our policy and good customs; and regarding the means that could be had for this goal it has seemed that one of them and the main one would be to give the order that those people be taught our Castilian language because it is known, they could be indoctrinated with greater ease in the matters of the Holy Gospel and obtain everything else that is right for them for their way of life. (Torre Revello 1962:511; my translation)[2]

In 1586, the Spanish crown ordered the viceroy of Peru to force the indigenous population to learn Castilian, which was followed by a royal decree in 1590. In light of the paltry results of priests learning *lengua general*, additional royal decrees calling for the Castilianization of the natives were issued in 1605, 1634, and 1686 with the justification that the 'holy mysteries of the faith' could not be taught in the indigenous languages. A royal decree issued in 1690 also suggested that natives who knew how to speak and write Castilian could be considered for posts such as governors, mayors, scribes, and so forth.

The eighteenth century is characterized as one of total support for the Castilianization of the native population. After the confrontation with and defeat of Tupac Amaru in 1780–1781, laws were issued against the Quechua language and culture (Carranza Romero 1993:28–30). Even though the

---

[2] The original reads: 'Como una de la principales cosas que Nos deseamos para el bien de esa tierra es la salvación y instrucción y conversión a nuestra santa fe católica de los naturales de ella y que también tomen nuestra policía y buenas costumbres; y así tratando de los medios para este fin se podrían tener, ha parecido que uno de ellos y el más principal sería dar orden como a esas gentes se les enseñase nuestra lengua castellana, porque sabida está, con más facilidad podrían ser doctrinados en las cosas del Santo Evangelio y conseguir todo lo demás que les conviene para su manera de vivir.'

nineteenth century ushered in the independence of the countries in the Andean region, on the whole the indigenous populations did not receive any benefits until around the second half of the twentieth century, when the period known as *indigenismo* 'indigenism' began. During this period, for example, Quechua was made an official national language in Peru (1975), theoretically on equal footing with Spanish, although this was not followed up with the necessary language planning. Peru's General Education Law of 1982 made it clear that language planning involving indigenous languages was just a means of ultimately teaching students Spanish: 'In the communities whose language is not Spanish this education in the native language was to be initiated with a tendency towards Castilianization in order to consolidate in the student the socio-cultural characteristics that correspond to modern society' (ibid.: 33; my translation).[3]

Despite the centuries-long attempt to Castilianize the Andean region, various factors have contributed to its failure. Among them, Rivarola (1989:155, 160) notes the disproportion in numbers between indigenous language speakers and native Spanish speakers and the fact that the manner of colonization itself, oriented exclusively towards the exploitation of indigenous labour (especially for work in the mines), made impossible the inter-ethnic contact necessary for generalized bilingualism. This type of relation with the Spaniards and their language put the learning of Spanish out of reach for the indigenous masses of the Andean region.

From early on, there are examples of approximative systems of Spanish in the region. Cerrón-Palomino (2003:135–170) comments in detail on the case of Francisco Tito Yupanqui, a sculptor known for, among other things, his sculpture of the Virgin of Copacabana. Yupanqui left a document, written in his own hand, about his experiences of being ridiculed by the colonizers because of his artistic work. In this letter, we find systematic confusion of /e/–/i/ and /o/–/u/, devoicing of /d/ and /g/, cases of analogy such as *sabíbamos* (formed by analogy with *íbamos*, instead of *sabíamos* 'we knew'), and systematic occurrences of certain morphosyntactic phenomena, among which Cerrón-Palomino mentions three: the favouring of the masculine (and singular) suffixes in cases of agreement (see (7.1)), the neutralization of the object-pronominal system to the masculine singular *lo* (see (7.2)) and the use of *lo* with copulative and certain intransitive verbs, such as *ser–estar* 'be', *parecer* 'seem', *ir* 'go', *venir* 'come', *salír* 'leave', *entrar* 'enter', *llegar* 'arrive', and *reír* 'laugh', sometimes called false-pronominalization (see

---

[3] The original reads: 'En las comunidades cuya lengua no es el castellano se debe iniciar esta educación en la lengua autóctona con tendencia a la castellanización progresiva a fin de consolidar en el educando sus características socio-culturales con las que son propias de la sociedad moderna.'

(7.3)). Cerrón-Palomino notes that these same phenomena are still found today in the Andean highlands and in north-west Argentina.

(7.1a)  determiner-MASC noun-FEM (ibid.:168)
  *il mañana* 'the morning'
  *el celda* 'the cell'
  *el falta* 'the mistake'
  *el pintadura* 'the painting'
  *un petición* 'a request'
  *el Santa Vergen* 'the Holy Virgin'
  *estes obra* 'these works'
  *todos los gentes* 'all the people'

(7.1b)  noun modifier-MASC~FEM (ibid.)
  *imagen bueno* 'good image'
  hichora [. . .] bueno 'good creation' ~ hichora [. . .] mala 'bad creation'
  imagen acabado, blanqueado 'finished, whitened image'
  ~Vergen pentada 'painted Virgin'

(7.2a)  noun phrase + *lo* + verb (ibid.)

| Al | | Vergen el patre | lo | | estaba aguardando. |
|---|---|---|---|---|---|
| OBJ-the.MASC.DO | Virgin the priest | 3SG.MASC.DO | | was | awaiting |

  'The priest was awaiting the Virgin.'

(7.2b)  *lo* + verb + noun phrase

| Lo | | llevé | un Emagen del | | Vergen pentada. |
|---|---|---|---|---|---|
| 3SG.MASC.DO | took-1SG | an image | of-the.MASC | Virgin | painted |

  'I took a painted image of the Virgin.'

(7.3a)

| para | que | lo | | seays | | pentor |
|---|---|---|---|---|---|---|
| for | that | 3SG.MASC.DO | be.PRES.SUB-2PL | | painter |

  'so that you may be a painter'

(7.3b)

| el | | Imagen [. . .] lo | | parece | como | hombre. |
|---|---|---|---|---|---|---|
| the.MASC | image | 3SG.MASC.DO | | seems | like | man |

  'The image seems like a man.'

(7.3c)

| Lo | | vino | otro | padre. |
|---|---|---|---|---|
| 3SG.MASC.DO | came.3SG | other | father |

  'Another priest came.'

The mismatch in agreement phenomena illustrated in (7.1) is arguably due to the speaker being a native speaker of Quechua and having learned Spanish as a second language. Quechua does not have gender agreement; for its part, the number agreement (not always obligatory in Quechua) follows a different set of rules from those for Spanish. In subject–verb agreement, for example, there is obligatory agreement in first person (7.4), obligatory or optional agreement in second person (7.5), and entirely optional agreement in third person (see (7.6), where-*ku* is optional) (see Cerrón-Palomino 1987:273–274; 2003:156).

(7.4)

| ñuqa-nchik | miku-nchik. |
|---|---|
| 1POSS-PL.POSS | eat-PL.POSS |

  'We eat.'

(7.5)  qam-kuna    miku-nki-chik.
       2POSS-PL     eat-2.PRES-POSS
       'You all eat.'
(7.6)  pay-kuna miku-n-(ku).
       3-PL      eat-3-(PL)
       'They eat.'

With regard to the systematic use of the masculine singular for object pronominalization, Cerrón-Palomino (2003:156) comments on the coherency of pronominal use in the speech of this sculptor: where there was a choice, Francisco Tito Yupanqui chose for the most part nominal and pronominal forms in *-o*, without plural. As for pseudo-pronominalization, Cerrón-Palomino notes that the phenomenon is found only in Andean Spanish, even in those areas where Quechua is no longer spoken. He sees this aspect-marking use of *lo* as possibly a calque of the Quechua aspectual marker *-lʔu* in some dialects and the analogous *-pu* in others (see Nardi 1976 and Middendorf 1970, cited in Cerrón-Palomino 2003:158–159).

All these traits, Cerrón-Palomino (2003:160–161) emphasizes, are not only found in L2 Spanish of Quechua native speakers, but also in areas such as Mantaro Valley and north-west Argentina that are completely 'dequechuizadas', i.e., entirely monolingual Spanish areas. In other words, these phenomena now characterize certain varieties of monolingual Andean Spanish. I address this below in more detail.

Rivarola (1989) states that colonial documentation is replete with almost three centuries of testimony (from the seventeenth to the nineteenth centuries) regarding the lack of Spanish proficiency in the vast majority of the indigenous population. In the nineteenth century, he mentions the first testimony from linguists regarding the nature of Andean Spanish. Responding to a request in 1883 by Hugo Schuchardt, the well-known nineteenth-century linguist considered by some to be the father of creole linguistics, the South American philologist Rufino Cuervo answered questions regarding the variety of Spanish spoken in the Andean region. Rufino Cuervo responded that in places such as Quito, Quechua was almost the only language heard in the markets, that large property-owners had to know Quechua to function in society, and furthermore that he did not think that the Spanish of the region was a dialect but rather the equivalent of an L2 variety, in the sense of an inter-language. However, Rivarola (ibid.:157–158) provides evidence of a distinct, monolingual Andean dialect, found in Spanish-language documents of Spanish aristocrats that exhibit many of the same traits illustrated in the examples in (7.1–7.3). He also mentions the migration from rural areas to the cities that took place during the second half of the twentieth century, with the result that in capitals such as Lima Quechua was ever present in the street markets, full of merchants from the highland, which were Quechua-speaking areas.

With the more recent migration of Quechua speakers to urban areas, new identities have begun to emerge. This is reflected, arguably, in the unique variety of Spanish spoken by these people. The 'informal' Spanish, as Rivarola (1989:158) calls it, is used by a multitude of Andean bilinguals who 'are in an accelerated process of acculturation and in search of a new form of social and cultural identity'. He continues by noting that this process is happening at a pace that over time will have linguistic repercussions difficult to stop by 'the normative dikes of Standard Spanish'.

The above allusions to the enormous majority of indigenous people in the Andean region are borne out by census statistics. I have selected two places from the region to illustrate this, one in Peru (Mantaro Valley), and the other in north-west Argentina (Salta), both mentioned by Cerrón-Palomino.

First, to give a general idea of the population distribution in an Andean country, I have selected Peru, for which I show the data from the 1878 census that distinguish between different ethnic groups in the population (Table 7.1). The total counted population in Peru in 1878, including whites, Indians, blacks, *mestizos*, and Asians, comes out to 2,630,387. The indigenous population at that time made up 58.2 per cent of the Peruvian population; the mixed-race population was next with 25.5 per cent. Whites made up only 14 per cent of the total number of inhabitants in Peru then, and the Asians and blacks each comprised less than 2 per cent of the population. It is clear, then, that the indigenous and the mixed population, those who spoke and/or understood Quechua, made up over 80 per cent of the Peruvian population at that time.

Mantaro Valley is located in the department of Junín. Table 7.2 compares the percentages of the different ethnic groups in the country as a whole, and those in Junín. Noteworthy is that while the relative distributional tendencies of the ethnic groups in Junín and Peru as a country were comparable in 1878, Junín had slightly higher Indian and *mestizo* populations relative to the national averages at that time. From this distribution, we can assume that in 1878 Quechua was most likely the dominant, if not the exclusive, language spoken in Junín, especially in rural areas.

In the twentieth century, the percentage of monolingual Quechua speakers experienced a steady decrease. In Junín, for instance, the percentage of monolingual Quechua speakers went from 42 per cent in 1940 to 12 per cent in 1961 (*Censos nacionales* 1968, III). Table 7.3 shows the distribution of speakers according to their mother language or dialect for Junín as a whole, as well as for the provinces of Huancayo, Concepción, and Jauja, where Mantaro Valley is located. The number of Quechua speakers relative to others is low in Junín as compared to the national average. According to the census figures from Peru (Table 7.4) cited in A.M. Escobar (2000:30), 52 per cent of the

Table 7.1. *Census data from Peru, 1878, by ethnic group*

| Department | Whites | Indigenous population (Indians) | Blacks | European–Indian mixed-race people (*mestizos*) | Asians |
|---|---|---|---|---|---|
| Ancachs | 18706 | 132792 | 2453 | 126904 | 3975 |
| Apurimac | 14427 | 64681 | 96 | 39306 | 15 |
| Arequipa | 19878 | 68056 | 2887 | 35175 | 1050 |
| Ayacucho | 18427 | 102827 | 311 | 20607 | 43 |
| Cajamarca | 59774 | 73806 | 1051 | 78809 | 357 |
| Callao | 13439 | 8228 | 2646 | 8705 | 1474 |
| Cuzco | 22109 | 182904 | 417 | 37555 | 47 |
| Huancavelica | 9682 | 80923 | 161 | 12291 | 12 |
| Huanuco | 8182 | 47241 | 343 | 23143 | 82 |
| Ica | 5529 | 33188 | 5380 | 11236 | 5022 |
| Junín | 8728 | 129475 | 472 | 70910 | 174 |
| Lambayeque | 8127 | 48599 | 2683 | 23242 | 4087 |
| Libertad | 17071 | 57857 | 2467 | 61125 | 8816 |
| Lima | 50761 | 99764 | 15404 | 35581 | 24290 |
| Loreto | 10479 | 29749 | 110 | 21540 | 27 |
| Moquegua | 5956 | 19041 | 621 | 2581 | 586 |
| Piura | 13930 | 79792 | 3860 | 37965 | 74 |
| Puno | 8278 | 239161 | 224 | 11749 | 37 |
| Tacna | 7469 | 21807 | 1299 | 5210 | 222 |
| Tarapaca | 12918 | 11686 | 564 | 6766 | 791 |
| Totals | 333870 (12.7%) | 1531577 (58.2%) | 43449 (1.7%) | 670400 (25.5%) | 51181 (20%) |

Table 7.2. *Comparison of the population distribution in Peru and Junín in 1878*

| | Peru | Junín |
|---|---|---|
| Indians | 57% | 61.7% |
| *Mestizos* | 25% | 33.8% |
| Whites | 14% | 4.2% |
| Blacks | 2% | 0.2% |
| Asians | 2% | 0.1% |

population were monolingual Quechua speakers throughout Peru in 1961, far higher than the 26 per cent of speakers in Junín with Quechua as their mother tongue. And even though the statistics in Tables 7.3 and 7.4 do not measure exactly the same thing (speakers with Quechua as their mother tongue vs

Table 7.3. *Speakers five years and older in Junín department, and in Huancayo, Concepción, and Jauja provinces (located in Junín department), according to their mother language or dialect*

| 1961 | Junín department Per cent (raw no.) | Huancayo province Per cent (raw no.) | Concepción province Per cent (raw no.) | Jauja province Per cent (raw no.) |
|---|---|---|---|---|
| Aboriginal | 33.5% (145,571) | 57.9% (95,531) | 40.8% (16,173) | 18.1% (14,549) |
| Aymara | 0.1% (723) | 0.2% (330) | 0.1% (32) | 0.1% (104) |
| Quechua | 20% (112,767) | 16.6% (27,393) | 16.6% (6,589) | 21.2% (16,952) |
| Spanish | 39.0% (169,281) | 24.1% (39,852) | 40.9% (16,213) | 59.1% (47,313) |
| Other langs. | 0.5% (1,623) | 0.4% (664) | 0.1% (55) | 0.2% (170) |
| No entry | 0.9% (3,976) | 0.8% (1,308) | 1.5% (587) | 1.3% (1,029) |
| Total | 100% (433,941) | 100% (165,078) | 100% (39,649) | 100% (80,117) |

Table 7.4. *Relative percentages of the Quechua–Spanish-speaking population and the monolingual Quechua-speaking population from 1940 to 1989 in Peru*

|  | 1940 | 1961 | 1972 | 1981 | 1989 |
|---|---|---|---|---|---|
| Quechua– Spanish | 33% (816,967) | 48% (1,293,322) | 57% (1,715,004) | 60% (2,979,347) | 60% (3,602,006) |
| Monolingual Quechua | 67% (1,625,156) | 52% (1,389,195) | 43% (1,311,062) | 40% (2,025,225) | 40% (2,364,507) |

*Source:* A. M. Escobar 2000:30.

monolingual Quechua speakers), it is clear that the Quechua speakers referred to in Table 7.3 could be mono- or bilingual and are far fewer than the national average in 1961.

Table 7.4 also indicates that the percentage of monolingual Quechua speakers is decreasing while that of Quechua–Spanish bilinguals is increasing. That is, in the Peru of 1940, two-thirds of the population were monolingual Quechua speakers. By 1989, however, the percentage of monolingual Quechua speakers had decreased to less than half (40 per cent).

Late in the twentieth century, the decrease of Quechua speakers had a significant impact upon Junin department, affecting both the urban and rural populations. In the 1972 and 1993 censuses, the percentage of people five years and older who claimed Spanish as their mother tongue increased by more than 20 percentage points in urban areas (67.6% to 89%) and more than 30 in rural areas (43.5% to 74.3%). Conversely, people five years and older

Table 7.5. *Distribution of speakers five years and older in urban and rural areas of Junín department in the 1972 and 1993 censuses, according to their mother language or dialect*

| Department<br><br>Language | Junín department,<br>1972 urban<br>Percentage<br>(Raw no.) | Junín department,<br>1972 rural<br>Percentage<br>(Raw no.) | Junín department,<br>1993 urban<br>Percentage<br>(Raw no.) | Junín department,<br>1993 rural<br>Percentage<br>(Raw no.) |
|---|---|---|---|---|
| Quechua | 18.9% (71,609) | 43.5% (101,087) | 9.6% (57,193) | 18.5% (55,996) |
| Spanish | 67.6% (256,035) | 43.4% (100,944) | 89.1% (531,738) | 74.3% (225,217) |
| Aymara | 0.1% (290) | 0.1% (209) | 0.4% (2,287) | 0.3% (934) |
| Aboriginal | 11.5% (43,414) | 11.8% (27,443) | 0.3% (1,813) | 5.9% (17,851) |
| Other langs. | 0.2% (825) | 0.1% (137) | 0.1% (363) | 0.02% (90) |
| No entry | 1.7% (6,360) | 1.1% (2,517) | 0.6% (3,398) | 1.0% (3,004) |
| Total | 100% (378,533) | 100% (232,337) | 100% (596,792) | 100% (303,092) |

*Note:* Totals may not equal 100 because of rounding.

claiming Quechua as their mother tongue declined by around 10 percentage points in urban areas and around 25 percentage points in rural areas. The statistics are shown in Table 7.5.

In Table 7.6, the distribution is shown of speakers in 1993 in the three provinces where Mantaro Valley is located. Quechua native speakers have all but disappeared in Jauja province (4.16 per cent), whereas in Concepción there are just over 10 per cent remaining and in Huancayo the figure is just over 15 per cent. This is the situation to which Cerrón-Palomino (2003) refers: in Mantaro Valley Quechua has been overtaken by Spanish to a great extent. Yet, as Cerrón-Palomino convincingly argues, while Spanish has overtaken Quechua in terms of the lexicon, many key Quechua structures remain in place, incorporated into the Spanish of the area. I will discuss these structures below.

The second monolingual area to be discussed here, also historically Quechua-speaking at the time the Spaniards arrived, is the Salta province in north-western Argentina. Up to the fifteenth century, the Calchakí language constituted a major cultural and linguistic presence in Salta province, especially in the southern valleys of Salta. The Incas conquered Salta starting in 1480, 'establishing their political and economic dominance, as well as a noteworthy communications system with roads and supply centres on the routes that united Peru and Bolivia with the north and west of Argentina and with Chile, protected in strategic locations by forts' (*Censo nacional* 1980:xii; my translation). Just prior to the Spanish conquest of the region, what is now the north-west of Argentina was the most densely populated area of the whole

Table 7.6. *Speakers five years and older in Huancayo, Concepción, and Jauja provinces (in Junín department) in 1993, according to their mother language or dialect*

| Province Language | Junín Dept. Huancayo 1993 Percentage (Raw no.) | Junín Dept. Concepción 1993 Percentage (Raw no.) | Junín Dept. Jauja 1993 Percentage (Raw no.) |
|---|---|---|---|
| Quechua | 16.0% (61,552) | 11.6% (6,448) | 4.2% (3,804) |
| Spanish | 82.6% (318,531) | 87.1% (48,570) | 95.0% (86,848) |
| Aymara | 0.3% (1,322) | 0.3% (151) | 0.1% (63) |
| Aboriginal | 0.4% (1,674) | 0.1% (58) | 0.1% (126) |
| Other langs. | 0.1% (188) | 0.04% (22) | 0.03% (30) |
| No entry | 0.6% (2,231) | 0.9% (529) | 0.6% (542) |
| Total | 100% (385,498) | 100% (55,778) | 100% (91,413) |

*Note:* Totals may not equal 100 because of rounding.

country, with 48 per cent (an estimated 195,000 of 403,000) of the population (*Censo nacional* 1980:xii).[4]

The Spanish colonization of Salta proceeded from Peru, and by 1582 the area was under Spanish rule. The Spanish crown generally followed the process of urban colonization in South America, especially in the Andean region, and Argentina was no exception. That is, the primary linguistic and cultural impact of the Spanish colonization was found in the cities such as Salta. The majority of the population, however, lived in rural areas. For example, in 1778 the city of Salta had 4,305 or 37 per cent of the residents of the province, while the other 7,260 (63 per cent) residents lived in the countryside. By 1801, the urban–rural population distribution, at 5,093 (38 per cent) and 8,435 (62 per cent) respectively, had not changed appreciably (*Censo nacional* 1980:liv).

Regarding the ethnic distribution of the population in Salta province, we have figures only for 1778, given in Table 7.7. The indigenous population at that time made up 27% of the total number of inhabitants in the province, nearly the same percentage as the whites (28%). In contrast, there were 46% Africans, which included Africans proper as well as *mulattos* (African-Europeans), and *zambos* (African-Amerindians).[5]

---

[4] It is not clear what the exact relationship was between Quechua and the language spoken by the Calchakies. Their language was part of the Cacán language group that became extinct between 1650 and 1700.

[5] In censuses subsequent to 1778 in Argentina, the categories of indigenous ethnicity are not included.

Table 7.7. *Population distribution of whites, indigenous people, and blacks in 1778 in Salta province*

| Ethnicity | Percentage (raw numbers) |
|---|---|
| Blacks, *mulattos,* and *zambos* | 46% (5,305) |
| Whites | 28% (3,190) |
| Indigenous people | 27% (3,070) |
| Total | 100% (11,565) |

*Note: Mulattos* are of mixed African and European descent; *zambos* are African-Amerindians. The total does not equal 100 because of rounding.

At that time, the Salta area was connected administratively to the mining centre of Potosí, located north of Salta in what is currently Bolivia. The substantial presence of Africans, *mulattos,* and *zambos* in the Salta region was due to the labour needs of that area. Specifically, members of these communities worked in the mines, as well as on the mule trains which connected the Potosí mines and Tucumán, south of Salta (Fernández Lávaque and del Valle Rodas 1998:18).

Unfortunately, the nineteenth- and twentieth-century Argentinean censuses do not contain information regarding indigenous populations and their languages. This gap was not addressed until 1985, the year in which Salta completed the first indigenous census for its province. Although the study was never published, Fernández Lávaque and del Valle Rodas (1998:28–29) report some of the findings, one of which is that the indigenous population of Salta in 1985 constituted less than 3 per cent of the population of the province. These authors report (ibid.:31) that Quechua has probably not been spoken by original Salta inhabitants since the middle of the twentieth century at the latest. Nevertheless, as in the case of Mantaro Valley, the Spanish spoken in Salta contains numerous key structures from Quechua. In the next section, I examine some of these monolingual Spanish traits found in the speech of the inhabitants of Mantaro Valley (Peru) and Salta (Argentina). What becomes apparent is the considerable similarity in these native varieties of Spanish, although they have developed independently. The link, of course, is the historical presence in both areas of sizeable numbers of Quechua speakers. That is, the Quechua features were strongly represented in terms of number of speakers in the areas in question. What is crucial is that, in each area, the Quechua speakers learning Spanish, independently of one another, often came up with similar to identical solutions in mapping Quechua structures on to the Spanish lexicon.

## 7.3.    Some key linguistic traits of Andean Spanish in rural Mantaro Valley (Peru) and in Salta province (Argentina)

The Andean contact situation involves differing degrees of bilingualism in languages that are typological opposites – Spanish is a prepositional, inflectional SVO language while Quechua is a post-positional agglutinative SOV language. Thus, the feature pool created in areas of Spanish–Quechua contact contains a wide range of typologically diverse features, though not equally represented over the centuries, as we can deduce from the demographic information discussed in the previous section. That is, it is to be expected that a substantial number of Quechua-language features would find their way into the Spanish of the area during those centuries in which Quechua was the dominant language in terms of numbers of speakers. We will see that this expectation is borne out: the Spanish of these highland regions where Quechua was dominant exhibits many particularities not found in other varieties of Spanish. This state of affairs is also consistent with interference through shift, whereby features from the native language of the shifting speakers (Quechua) are carried into the target language (Spanish). Importantly, Quechua Spanish also contains unique features not shared with other Spanish varieties. Before discussing the features of monolingual Andean Spanish, I need to point out some key features of Quechua in order to have a better understanding of the nature of the feature pool present in the Quechua–Spanish contact situation.

### 7.3.1    Some key linguistic features of Quechua

Quechua is divided into two main language groups: Quechua I, spoken in central Peru, and Quechua II, found in southern Colombia, Ecuador and the non-central parts of Peru, as well as in Bolivia, northern Argentina, and northern Chile (Cerrón-Palomino 1987:226; Haboud 1998:32). Both Quechua I and Quechua II have a three-vowel system (/a, i, u/), although in both groups [e] and [o] are found as allophones of /i/ and /u/, respectively. In the Quechua proto-vowel system, the same three vowels (but without phonemically long vowels) are also assumed (Cerrón Palomino 1987:128). In Quechua I dialects and some Quechua II dialects, long vs short vowel length is distinctive.

Regarding consonants, the same consonantal system is not shared by all Quechua varieties. Cerrón-Palomino (1987:128) shows the reconstructed proto-consonantal system of Quechua, reproduced in Table 7.8. For his part, Adelaar (1992) posits a distinction between /r/ and /r̄/, whereas Cerrón-Palomino (1987:128) does not acknowledge this distinction. The reason may be due to what Weber (1989:450) observes for Huanco Quechua, namely, that

Table 7.8.  *The reconstructed consonant inventory of proto-Quechua*

|  | Labial | Alveolar | Alveo-palatal | Retroflex | Velar | Uvular | Glottal |
|---|---|---|---|---|---|---|---|
| Stops | p | t | č | ĉ | k | q |  |
| Fricatives |  | s | š | (ẓ) |  |  | h |
| Nasals | m | n | ñ |  |  |  |  |
| Vibrants |  |  |  |  |  |  |  |
| Flap |  | r |  |  |  |  |  |
| Laterals |  |  |  |  |  |  |  |
| Glides | w |  | y |  |  |  |  |

*Source:* Cerrón-Palomino 1987: 128.

Table 7.9.  *The consonant inventory of Cuzco Quechua*

|  | Labial | Alveolar | Alveo-palatal | Velar | Uvular |
|---|---|---|---|---|---|
| Stops |  |  |  |  |  |
| Voiceless |  |  |  |  |  |
| Plain | p | t | č | k | q |
| Aspirated | $p^h$ | $t^h$ | $č^h$ | $k^h$ | $q^h$ |
| Glottalized | p' | t' | č' | k' | q' |
| Voiced | (b) | (d) |  | (g) |  |
| Fricatives | (f) | s | š | h | x |
| Nasals | m | n | ñ |  |  |
| Vibrants |  |  |  |  |  |
| Flap |  | r | rr |  |  |
| Laterals |  | l |  |  |  |
| Glides | w |  | y |  |  |

the grapheme *rr* actually represents the retroflex fricative [ẓ], which is an allophone in this variety for /ř/. This information is incorporated into Table 7.8. The consonant inventory in Cuzco Quechua, shown in Table 7.9, has been influenced by Aymara in the three-way distinction among the voiceless stops and by Spanish in /f/, /l/, and voiced stops. Stress assignment is on the penult in almost all words in both Quechua groups, and reduction of unstressed vowels is common. The general syllable structure of Quechua is V, VC, CV, CVC, whereby V and VC are found only word-initially, though in some dialects word-initial V and VC are preceded by a glottal stop. Syllables of the type CCV or VCC are not allowed (see also Zúñiga 1974:97–99 and Feke 2004:176). Examples from Junín Quechua are given in (7.7).

(7.7)   V:      [a-ma] 'no'
        VC:     [ut-ka] 'cotton'
        CV:     [ča-ki] 'dry'
        CVC:    [pam-pa] 'plain'

Quechua's morphology is agglutinative, suffixal, and highly complex, but extremely regular (Adelaar 1992:306). Three suffix types are distinguished, derivational, flexional, and independent: the first type appears closest to the root, followed by the flexional and the independent types, in that order. The sentence in (7.8) illustrates the order of derivational and inflectional suffixes.

(7.8)   wasi    -nna?    -kuna
        house   without  PL
        'the ones without (a) home'        (Cerrón-Palomino 1987:264)

In Quechua, *nna?* 'without' is a derivational suffix and it appears closer to the noun than -*kuna*, the plural marker.[6] In (7.9), we see that independent suffixes in Quechua appear outside inflectional suffixes. Quechua overtly marks the perspective of the speaker as to whether an event is directly witnessed or not. Thus, an event can be overtly marked in Quechua as being first-hand knowledge, received through an intermediary as second-hand knowledge, or as conjecture. For example, with regard to the speaker's perspective of the situation, the proposition 'it will die' can be expressed three different ways (from Weber 1989:421; see also Cerrón-Palomino 1987:266–267). In a situation in which a diviner is commenting on possible death of something in a given situation, (7.9a) expresses that the diviner himself asserts the proposition, (7.9b) expresses that someone is reporting on the diviner's prediction, and (7.9c) expresses that perhaps the entity referred to in the proposition may die. Note that the suffixes -*mi*, -*shi*, and -*chi* appear outside the person and tense markers.

(7.9a)   Wanu-nqa-paq-mi.
         die-3FUT-FUT-EVID.1ST.HAND
(7.9b)   Wanu-nqa-paq-shi.
         die-3FUT-FUT-EVID.2ND.HAND
(7.9c)   Wanu-nqa-paq-chi.
         die-3FUT-FUT-EVID.CONJ

As expected, there are derivational and flexional suffixes for both nominal and verbal roots (ibid.:261–262). Case marking has the nominative–accusative pattern and is marked with suffixes (see 7.10), and number on nouns is marked with -*kuna* 'plural', as seen above.

---

[6] The symbol /?/ represents a glottal stop.

With regard to syntax, Quechua exhibits SOV (7.10) and modifier-head order (7.11).

(7.10)  Hwan    Tumas-ta      maqa-n.
        Hwan    Tumas-OBJ     hit-3
        'Hwan hits Tumas.'              (adapted from Weber 1989:14, ex. 13)
(7.11a) hatun   runa (ADJ-N)
        big     man
        'big man'         (ibid.:17, ex. 16)
(7.11b) Hwan-pa       wasi-n (possessor-possessed)
        Hwan-GEN      house-3SG.POSS
        'Hwan's house'        (adapted from ibid.:254, ex. 1028)
(7.11c) chay    ishkay    hatun    wasi-kuna (Det/Numeral-N)
        that    two       big      house-PL
        'those two big houses'        (adapted from ibid.:17, ex. 17)
(7.11d) sumaq   wira    waaka (Deg-Adj)
        very    fat     cow
        'a/the very fat cow'        (ibid.:17, ex. 19)
(7.11e) Weqruyllapa    purin (Adv-VP)
        limpingly      he.walks
        'He walks with a limp.'        (ibid.:17, ex. 20)

The word orders displayed in (7.10) and (7.11a, c, e) are default rather than rigid orders in Quechua. That is, other orders are not uncommon, dictated by pragmatic factors, such as topicality, emphasis, etc. Note that there is no number (7.11c) or gender agreement between modifier and head. However, there is person agreement, which involves possessive suffixes, an example of which is given in (7.12): we find agreement between *qam-kuna* '2-PL' and *-yki* '2'.

(7.12)  qam-kuna      -p      wasi   -yki   -kuna (Quechua I)
        2-PL          GEN     house  2      PL
        'your houses'

Quechua possesses some interesting complex-verb constructions, some of which seem like serial verb constructions. One such construction involves the suffix *-shpa (-spa)*, called by some a gerund suffix (Grajeda Challco and Vela Flores 1976:145; Catta Quelen 1987:170), by others a same-actor subordinator (SA.SUB) (Carpenter 1982:253), and by still others an adverbial clause marker (Weber 1989:298). Examples are given in (7.13)–(7.15).

(7.13)  Quechua II B (Carpenter 1982:253)
        pay-ta        saki-**shpa**       sham-rka-ni
        3PL-ACC       leave-SA.SUB   come-personal.knowledge.PAST-IS
        'I came, leaving them (at the house).'

(7.14)   Quechua II C from north-west Argentina
         Imata  ruwa-**spa**      kiča-rqu-n         wasi-y-ta?
         what  do-SA.SUB      open-PAST-3s    house-POSS-ACC
         [lit. what $x_i$ doing, $x_i$ has opened my house]
         'How has he opened my house?'
                             (adapted from Fernández Lávaque and del Valle Rodas
                             1998:105)
(7.15)   'integrated' Quechua
         taki-**spa**          hamu-rqa-ni.
         sing-SA.SUB     come-PAST-IS
         'I came singing.' ('come' pertains during the whole event, 'sing' doesn't)
                             (Grajeda Challco and Vela Flores 1976:145; cf. *-rqa* in
                             Weber 1989:99)

As Carpenter notes, with the suffix *-shpa* (or *-spa*) the subject remains the same for the two verbs in the complex construction and the actions denoted by the verbs in each sentence are sequential.

With this brief overview of some of the salient features of Quechua, I will now turn to a characterization of some Andean Spanish features in the Spanish of Mantaro Valley (Peru) and Salta (Argentina).

### 7.3.2   Some salient linguistic features of monolingual Andean Spanish

Various scholars who work specifically on Andean Spanish distinguish, among others, between the Spanish variety spoken by those Quechua native speakers who are L2 transitional speakers, on the one hand, and the Spanish variety spoken by Spanish monolinguals and some Quechua–Spanish bilinguals, on the other (A. Escobar 1978; A. M. Escobar 2000; Cerrón-Palomino 2003).[7] Cerrón-Palomino (2003:26–28) goes so far as to consider certain varieties of monolingual Andean Spanish, such as the one spoken by rural inhabitants of Mantaro Valley, a *quasi*-creole in the sense that it exhibits a lexicon from Spanish but takes many of its grammatical features from Quechua. Because I will return to this point below, suffice it to say for now that the use of the term *creole* by Cerrón-Palomino here is non-canonical given that creole languages are by definition also substantially reduced varieties of their respective lexifier languages, especially in terms of morphology. For the present study, I assume the proposed distinction between L2 transitional Andean Spanish and Andean Spanish as spoken natively by monolinguals and bilinguals. As will become evident, natively spoken Andean Spanish of different areas may exhibit variable restructuring, having

---

[7] A. Escobar (1978, cited in A.M. Escobar 2000:42) distinguishes among three varieties of Spanish in Peru: coastal Spanish, Andean Spanish, and interlect Spanish, an L2 Spanish variety considered a social dialect and spoken by asymmetrical bilinguals in the area, specifically, L1 Aymara and Quechua speakers who are in the process of learning Spanish as a second language.

traits in common (independently of one another), but also displaying differences from one another as well, from one speech community to another.

In chapter 1, I cited Givón's distinction between pre-grammatical and grammatical codes. The Andean Spanish varieties to be discussed here are examples of grammatical codes because they are spoken natively and in the absence of Quechua as a contact language. By contrast, I consider transitional L2 Spanish spoken by some native Quechua-speaking learners of Spanish a type of pre-grammatical code in the sense that morphology is less abundant and less systematic, that it is spoken less fluently, more slowly, with more effort, and with a higher error rate, and that it is a less conventionalized variety (cf. grammatical vs pre-grammatical codes in Table 1.1).

Mantaro Valley Spanish of Peru has been described by Cerrón-Palomino, who points out a number of characteristics, many of which are also found in historical texts such as the one commented on above by Francisco Tito Yupanqui. At the phonological level, Cerrón-Palomino (2003:203) notes that rural Mantaro Valley Spanish speakers use traits of *castellano motoso*, or typical Andean Spanish, which he characterizes schematically in another part of the book (ibid.:94–95). Some of the traits he cites on the phonological level are the confusion of *o/u* and *e/i* and monophthongization of diphthongs, shown in (7.16), and the deletion of articles and prepositions, illustrated in (7.17), which, he notes, have been written in standard Spanish orthography that does not reflect the phonological properties of the examples.

(7.16a)   piluta    (< pelota)
          kurnita (< corneta)
          pulpitu   (< pulpito)
          rásuŋ    (< razón)
          sigoro   (< seguro)
(7.16b)   tinta    (< tienda)
          surti   (< suerte)
(7.17a)   Está en __ calle.
          '(S/he) is in (the) street.'
(7.17b)   ¿Dónde está __ caballo?
          'Where is (the) horse?'

Elsewhere in the volume, Cerrón-Palomino (2003:27) speaks directly about morphosyntactic features of rural Mantaro Valley speakers, which I have reproduced in an adapted format in (7.18)–(7.22). The first example in each triplet (a) is Mantaro Valley Andean Spanish, with the corresponding Quechua counterparts in the second (b) example, and the standard Spanish equivalents in the third (c) examples.

(7.18a)   De mi mama en su          casa   estoy yendo.
          of my mum   in 3sɢ.ᴘᴏss house I-am  going

(7.18b)  Mamaa-pa      wasi-n-tam                    liyaa.
         mum-of        house-3SG.POSS-LOC    go
(7.18c)  Voy    a  (la)        casa   de mi mama.
         go-ISG to (the.FEM) house of my mum
         'I'm going to my mum's house.'
(7.19a)  Mañana      a Huancayo    voy          ir
         tomorrow    to Huancayo  go.ISG    go-INF
(7.19b)  Walaman        wankayyu-ta         lisra.
         tomorrow       Huancayo-GOAL    go-CONT
(7.19c)  Mañana      voy    a       ir     a    Huancayo.
         tomorrow    go-1SG COMP   go-INF to   Huancayo
         'Tomorrow I'm going to go to Huancayo.'
(7.20a)  ¿Qué diciendo no más      te       has        venido?
         what saying    no-more   2SG.REFL have-you  come-PPART?
(7.20b)  ¿Ima   nil-kul-llam       shakamulanki?
         what   say-SUBORD-just  come-PAST-2SG
(7.20c)  ¿A qué/por qué viniste?
         to what/why came-you.SG
         'Why did you come?'
(7.21a)  A mi tía voy        visitar    diciendo no más  me       he        venido.
         to my aunt go-ISG visit-INF saying   no-more 1SG.REFL have-1SG come-PART
(7.21b)  Tiyaa-ta        bisitaasha       nil-kul-llam        shakamula.
         aunt-ACC      visit-INF          say-SUBORD-just  come-PAST-1SG
(7.21c)  Vine        pensando    visitar    a   mi   tía.
         Came-1sg  thinking      visit-INF to   my   aunt
         'I came just thinking to visit my aunt.'
(7.22a)  A tu            chiquito            oveja       véndeme.
         to your.SG.FAM small-DIM-MASC sheep.FEM sell.IMP-me
(722b)   Ychuk uwishlla-yki-ta         lantikama-y.
         little   sheep-2POSS-ACC      sell-2IMP
(7.22c)  Véndeme tu ovejita.
         sell.IMP-me your.SG.FAM small-DIM sheep
         'Sell me your sheep.'

These speech examples constitute a clear result of a feature pool that contains an overwhelming presence of Quechua-language structures relative to Spanish-language structures. This outcome is predictable independently by appealing to the demographic information spanning over two centuries shown in Tables 7.1–7.4. That is, we see that, relative to the non-native population in the area, the indigenous population has been highly dominant in terms of numbers and native language spoken; it is only in the past sixty years that the situation has changed, especially in Junín, as evidenced by the demographic information from 1972 and 1993 in Tables 7.5 and 7.6.

All the Andean Spanish examples in (7.18a)–(7.22a) contain at least one and sometimes more than one Quechua feature. For instance, in (7.18a) the possessive element is overtly realized on the possessor (**de mi** *mama* 'of my mum'), as well as on the item possessed (*en **su** casa* 'in her house'). Although Quechua morpheme order relative to the head is not the same in Andean Spanish, almost all the relevant morphemes have a corresponding Quechua counterpart: Sp. *de* 'of' corresponds to Q -*pa*, Sp. *en* to Q -*tam*, and Sp. *su* to Q -*n*; Sp. *mi* does not have a Quechua counterpart in the example (see also example (7.11b)). Another feature attributable to Spanish contact with Quechua is the use of *en* with a directional verb, arguably a loan translation of the locative suffix -*tam* that we see in (7.18b). Related to this is the use of the locative *en* together with adverbs, a trait also present in rural monolingual Spanish of Mantaro Valley. Two examples are shown in (7.23) (Cerrón-Palomino 2003:195).

(7.23a)    En allí está la soga.
           in there is the rope
           'There is the rope.'
(7.23b)    En el lunes ha llegado mi hermano.
           in the Monday has arrived my brother
           'On Monday my brother arrived.'

Yet another trait attributable to Quechua in (7.18a), as well as in (7.19a), is the clause-final verb order, which in standard Spanish in seldom found. Again, this conforms to Quechua word order, as illustrated by the corresponding examples in (7.18b) and (7.19b).

Example (7.20a) contains a subordinate clause preceding its main clause. In terms of word order, this again corresponds to its Quechua counterpart in (7.20b). As is apparent by the examples in (7.13)–(7.15), the subordinate-clause (SC)–main-clause (MC) order is the norm in Quechua; and according to Cerrón-Palomino, this is also the case for Mantaro Valley Spanish. Even with a subordinate clause, as in (7.20) and (7.21), Mantaro Valley Spanish and Quechua maintain the same SC–MC order, while in standard Spanish we find MC–SC order in the corresponding examples. In these last two examples, we also find another idiomatically typical feature, namely, the use of a verb + subordinator-like *diciendo* 'saying' immediately followed by *no más*, which is a loan translation of the limitative morpheme -*llam*. In this variety of Spanish, as in Quechua, it has the pragmatic function of a softener, not found in the same way in standard Spanish. In Cerrón-Palomino's commentary, it is not clear whether there is a pragmatic or semantic distinction between (7.20a) and the more standard (7.20c). As we will see below, this construction is also found in the Spanish of Salta, Argentina, but with somewhat different pragmatic information.

Finally, in (7.22a), apart from the expected OV word order, we find overt marking of the direct object where in standard Spanish it would most likely remain unmarked. Use of what is called in Spanish 'personal *a*' in this case directly corresponds to the use of the Quechua accusative marker *-ta*. In addition, the use of the diminutive *-it* is more prevalent in Mantaro Valley Spanish, and in Andean Spanish in general, than in Standard Spanish. The use of personal *a* and the diminutive *-it* are perhaps less clear-cut instances of Quechua influence on Spanish because in Spanish they are both used. However, the extent to which these morphemes are found in Mantaro Valley Spanish is said to be greater than in non-Andean varieties of Spanish.[8] Finally, we find a lack of gender agreement in the noun phrase *a tu chiquito oveja* [lit. ACC your.FAM.SG small-DIM-MASC sheep-FEM] 'your little sheep', which according to Cerrón-Palomino is typical of monolingual Mantaro Valley Spanish.

One final trait to mention here, found in Mantaro Valley monolingual Spanish, is what Cerrón-Palomino (2003:158) has called 'false pronominalization'. Examples of the phenomenon are shown in (7.24).

(7.24a)  Ya       lo              llegó.
         already  3MASC.OBJ       arrived-3SG.PRET
         'S/he arrived already.'
(7.24b)  Ya       lo              murió.
         already  3MASC.OBJ       died-3SG.PRET
         'S/he already died.'
(7.24c)  Lo               durmió              rapido.
         3MASC.OBJ        went.to.sleep-3SG.PRET  fast
         'S/he went to sleep quickly.'

In each case, the pronoun form *lo* appears with an intransitive verb. It is worth noting that they are all punctual verbs. Apart from the verbs *llegar* 'arrive', *morir* 'die', and *dormir(se)* 'fall asleep', Cerrón-Palomino states that this type of *lo* is also to be found in the writings of the aforementioned Francisco Tito Yupanqui in the seventeenth century, with *parecer* 'seem' (a stative verb), the movement verbs *ir* 'go', *venir* 'come', *salir* 'leave, go out', *entrar* 'enter, go in' (the last three are punctual verbs), and *reír* 'laugh' (a durative, atelic verb). He considers *lo* in these cases a re-analysis of the masculine pronoun as a marker of immediacy and definitiveness, corresponding to Huanca Quechua *-lʔu*, which has the same function. As to why *lo* was selected for re-analysis by the Mantaro Valley speakers, Cerrón-Palomino points to the sound similarity between Spanish *lo* (lateral + mid back vowel) and Huanca Quechua *-lʔu* (lateral + glottal stop + high back vowel). However, I believe that it also may be related to the frequency of *lo*. I carried out a data base search in

---

[8] In non-Andean varieties of Spanish, personal *a* marks animate direct objects (*ellos ven* **a** *Juanita* 'they see Juanita') and disambiguates subjects from direct objects in cases of possible ambiguity, as it *el amor vence* **al** *odio* 'love overcomes hate'.

Table 7.10. *The frequency of present-tense forms of the transitive verbs* hacer *'do, make', ver 'see', and* querer *'want, love' from the CREA data base (spoken language only)*

| Object Clitic Pronoun | hacer | ver | querer | Total |
|---|---|---|---|---|
| Lo | 1010 (58%) | 563 (51%) | 221 (40%) | 1794 (53%) |
| Los | 79 (5%) | 135 (12%) | 50 (9%) | 264 (8%) |
| La | 153 (9%) | 183 (17%) | 90 (16%) | 426 (12%) |
| Las | 80 (5%) | 46 (4%) | 24 (4%) | 150 (4%) |
| Le | 323 (18%) | 156 (14%) | 117 (21%) | 596 (18%) |
| Les | 101 (6%) | 19 (2%) | 47 (9%) | 167 (5%) |
| Total | 1746 (100%) | 1102 (100%) | 549 (100%) | 3397 (100%) |

*Note:* Totals may not equal 100 because of rounding.

CREA of the most frequently appearing object pronouns with the transitive verbs *hacer* 'do', *ver* 'see', and *querer* 'want, love' in spoken language. The results are displayed in Table 7.10. Here, I assume that the oral Spanish accessible to the Quechua speakers in Mantaro Valley was in general comparable to what we find today in oral Spanish. Note that the frequency of *lo* is far higher than that of any of the other object pronouns, averaging over 50 per cent of all the tokens.[9] Given this situation, it is understandable that *lo* would become the default pronoun in the Andean varieties in question. Similarly, frequency would be an additional argument for *lo*'s being selected for false pronominalization in both varieties.

In sum, rural monolingual Mantaro Valley Spanish is characterized by a series of features. On the phonological level, confusion between *e/i* and *o/u* and monophthongization of diphthongs are found. At the morphosyntactic level, articles and prepositions are commonly deleted; in addition, we encounter default head-final order in VPs, genitive and direct object marking as in Quechua, and the use of *en* with movement verbs and adverbs. Moreover, subordinate clause–main clause order seems to be the preferred order; the Quechua limitative morpheme-*llam* is calqued as *no más*; there is lack of gender agreement; the diminutive -*it* is used extensively; and we find *lo*, corresponding to Huanca Quechua -*l?u*, as a marker of immediacy and definitiveness. It is apparent that the constellation of features present in these

---

[9] It must be noted that the overall frequency of the forms *lo, los, la*, and *las* in oral texts is different because *la, las*, and *los* have homophonous counterparts that are definite articles. The overall form frequencies found in CREA are: *lo* 77,050, *los* 110,900, *la* 282,973, *las* 69,788.

examples, taken together, is the result of the overwhelming presence of Quechua features in the history of the area, even though Quechua is no longer spoken in the part of Mantaro Valley from where Cerrón-Palomino collected his data. I consider this evidence as an indication that the strong presence of Quechua-speaking people in the history of the area, along with the corresponding weak presence of Spanish, led to a linguistic situation in which the feature pool of the region continued to be strongly Quechua-dominant, even though it is now a monolingual Spanish-speaking area and Spanish is the prestige language. It is not surprising that, in this area where Quechua has had such a strong presence until recently, Quechua structures have been favoured.

In the monolingual Spanish-speaking province of Salta in Argentina, we find a situation comparable to the one in the Mantaro Valley. Studies in Fernández Lávaque and del Valle Rodas (1998) address the various traits that characterize the monolingual variety of Spanish of the area, one in which Quechua has not been spoken for seventy years or more. Regarding vowel production, their corpus reveals that vowel realization in nouns, adjectives, and verbs is similar and that *e/i* confusion is more frequently found than *o/u* confusion (ibid.:136). Interestingly, although he does not comment on Mantaro Valley Spanish in this regard, Cerrón-Palomino (2003:152–153) notes this same tendency in the speech of Tito Yupanqui: 'This confusion [*e/i* alternation] is found in larger measure between the front vowels . . . The same occurs, although to a lesser extent, between the back vowels' (my translation). Examples cited by Fernández Lávaque and del Valle Rodas (1998:136–137) are shown in (7.25)–(7.26).

(7.25a)    El tigri si ha henchado. (Cf. El tigre se ha hinchado.)
           'The tiger swelled up.'
(7.25b)    Valgamí Dios. (Cf. Válgame Dios.)
           'Oh, good God.'
(7.25c)    Ricogía la cosicha. (Cf. recogía la cosecha.)
           'S/he harvested the crop.'
(7.26a)    segón decía (cf. según decía)
           'according to what s/he was saying'
(7.26b)    y li dejau tudu esu (cf. y le he dejado todo eso)
           'and I have left him all that'
(7.26c)    onoh anemales (cf. unos animales)
           'some animals'

Another tendency that affects vowels in the Salta data is the monophthongization of diphthongs, present as well in Mantaro Valley Spanish as illustrated in (7.27).

(7.27a)    Lempo lo ha traído. (Cf. Lo ha traido limpio.)
           'S/he brought it over clean.'

(7.27b)  Venían por las fistas de Navidad. (Cf. Venían por las fiestas de Navidad.)
         'They came for the Christmas holidays.'
(7.27c)  Ha pusto de vuelta. (Cf. Ha puesto de vuelta.)
         'S/he returned [it].'

In their corpus, Fernández Lávaque and del Valle Rodas (1998) also find what they call the neutralization of object clitics, referring to the lack of person and gender agreement between antecedent and clitic and the generalization of *lo* as the default. The examples in (7.28) are taken from Fernández Lávaque (1998a:79–80).

(7.28a)  La plantita tiene una flor y hay que apretar*lo*.
         (cf. apretar*la*) [la => lo]
         'The little plant has a flower and one must squeeze it.'
(7.28b)  Che, ha parío otra doh yegua, andá ve*lu* voh.
         (cf. ver*las* vos) [las => lo [lu]]
         'Hey, [the mare] gave birth to another two mares. Go see them.'
(7.28c)  pa loh potroh. Despuéh *lo* hacíh castrar, *lo* hacíh domesticar.
         (cf. los hacís castrar, los hacís domesticar) [los => lo]
         'for the foals. Afterwards they had them castrated and domesticated.'
(7.28d)  Bueno, *lo* dice el zorro al cordero.
         (cf. *le* dice . . . al cordero) [le => lo]
         'Well, the fox says it to the lamb.'
(7.28e)  Entonceh *lo* dijo el chancho a la cabra
         (cf. le dijo) [le => lo]
         'Then the ___ said it to the goat.'
(7.28f)  *Lo* ha dicho a los viejitoh que . . .
         (cf. Les ha dicho . . .) [les => lo]
         '[S/he] said to the old folk that . . .'

Noteworthy is that the default *lo* replaces not only direct object clitics (i.e., feminine singular *la* in (7.28a), feminine plural *las* in (7.28b), and masculine plural *los* in (7.28c), but also indirect object clitics, as shown in (7.28d–f). In these examples, the author also acknowledges -s aspiration (e.g., *hacíh* [< *hacís*]), and vowel raising (e.g., *lu* [< *lo*]), the former a trait of Argentinean Spanish, the latter of Andean Spanish. The neutralization of number, gender, and case distinctions represented in the multi-functional object clitic pronoun *lo* is also found in Peru, and as early as the sixteenth century in the speech of Tito Yupanqui (see Cerrón-Palomino 2003:35–70). In Mantaro Valley Spanish, there are examples of this phenomenon, such as that given in (7.22). As to why *lo* was selected, I argue that it is again a case of high frequency of *lo* relative to the other pronouns (see Table 7.10).

Another phenomenon found in monolingual Spanish of the Salta region, although it is disappearing (Fernández Lávaque 1998b:59), is the use of the locative preposition *en* 'in' together with locative adverbs, as in *en acá* [in here] 'here', *en cerca* [in near] 'near', *en lejos* [in far] 'far', *en allí* [in there] 'there', etc. Fernández Lávaque (ibid.) notes that it seems to be an old trait of the Salta area and agrees with the general consensus among scholars of Andean Spanish that *en* is a calque of the locative Quechua II post-position *-pi*, which appears with locative adverbs, as in *kay-pi* [here-LOC] 'here'. Again, this is found in the rural monolingual speech in Mantaro Valley, illustrated by the example given in (7.23).

In Salta, false pronominalization of the type illustrated in (7.24) is also present. The examples from Salta are given in (7.29), taken from Nardi (1976, cited in Cerrón-Palomino 2003:158).

(7.29a)  Te     **lo**     vamos a      cortar     la       soga.
         you.IO it.MASC go-3S.PRES COMP cut-INF the.FEM rope-FEM
         'We're going to cut the rope for you.'
(7.29b)  Tócamelo                      la        chacarera.
         play.IMP-meIO-it.MASC.DO    the.FEM chacarera-dance-FEM
         'Play me the chacarera dance.'

Nardi (1976) notes that the function of *lo* in these examples is a calque of Argentinean Quechua *-pu*, which expresses a malefactive sense. However, Cerrón-Palomino (2003:158–159) notes that *-pu* has three other readings, the first benefactive, the second iterative, and the third, related to iterativity, to express unexpectedness or suddenness of an action, as in *wañu-pu-* 'die quickly, definitively'. He relates this last reading of *-pu* to that of Huanca Quechua *-lʔu*, which marks immediacy or definitiveness of an action. Thus, even where phonological form does not necessarily favour the re-analysis of *lo* as an aspectual marker, the frequency argument can be made.

As an aside, note that false pronominal *lo* is also found in the writing of Francisco Tito Yupanqui, illustrated in (7.30) (from Cerrón-Palomino 2003:170).

(7.30a)  Se     **lo**         qureys       ser       pentor . . .
         if     MASC.DO    want-2PL    be-INF painter
         (si queréis ser pintor)
         'If you want to be a painter . . .'
(7.30b)  Así    **lo**     intró        [el Vergen]         in la         Eclesia.
         this way MASC.DO entered-3SG [the-MASC Virgin] in the-FEM   church
         (Así entró la Virgen en la iglesia.)
         'In this way, the Virgin entered the church.'
(7.30c)  **Lo**        vino         otro      padre.
         MASC.DO    come-3s    other    father
         (Vino otro padre.)
         'Another priest came.'

With respect to constituent order in the sentence, in rural Salta Spanish Vargas Orellana (1998) found OV and SOV orders in the speech of older people and people with less education. Among the examples she cites from the oral corpora she used were ones that in standard Spanish would represent a type of topicalization, such as in (7.31). The constituent order in these sentences, including the post-nominal determiners *esa* and *ese* respectively, represents standard colloquial usage in Spanish.

(7.31a)  A      la      persona esa      la      invitan de    comer ahí.
         OBJ  the-FEM  person that-FEM  DO-FEM  invite COMP  eat-INF there
         'That person there, they invited her to eat there.'

(7.31b)  La        cabeza no    lo        tenía el              toro   ese.
         the-FEM  head   NEG  DO-MASC   had   the-MASC        bull   that
         'His head, that bull didn't have it on.'

However, what is not clear is whether this topicalization is used as such in this variety of Spanish. Other examples cited by Vargas Ortellana suggest that the constituent order in the sentences in (7.31) may be regular, having nothing to do with direct object topicalization. Consider the examples in (7.32), also cited by Vargas Ortellana.

(7.32a)  Más    miedo ella    ha    tenido.
         more   fear  she    has   had
         'She has been more afraid.'

(7.32b)  Una    media   res   por la  mañana ponía           a      asar.
         A      half    cow   in  the morning put.on-IMPER COMP  roast-INF
         'He put a half cow to roast in the morning.'

(7.32c)  La           vaca  echan         al              corral.
         the-FEM     cow   throw-3PL    to-the-MASC      corral
         'They throw the cow into the corral.'

(7.32d)  Agua bendita hi            traído                de     l' iglesia.
         water holy    have-1SG     brought-PPART        from   the church
         'I have brought holy water from the church.'

Note that in these examples, we find OV order and no resumptive pronoun where in standard colloquial Spanish OV order would trigger the obligatory presence of a resumptive pronoun. That is, in standard colloquial Spanish these sentences would be odd or unacceptable. Moreover, the utterances in (7.31) and (7.32) were produced by third-generation monolingual Spanish speakers, an indication that OV constituent order without a resumptive pronoun is part of their grammar. In Mantaro Valley monolingual Spanish, not only is OV order common (see (7.21)), but verb-final order is the default, as evidenced by the adjunct–verb order in the sentences (7.18)–(7.20).

One last observation regarding this constituent order is that verb-final order in Salta Spanish is found, as mentioned, mostly among the rural and less educated speakers. As such, I assume that it is a socio-linguistic marker. However, not all traits in this variety traceable to Quechua are socio-linguistic markers. One such case is the non-standard use of the gerunds *diciendo* 'saying' and *haciendo* 'doing'. Del Valle Rodas (1998:99) notes that the particular construction in which these gerunds appear in Salta Spanish are used colloquially by members of all social classes.[10]

The forms *diciendo* 'saying' and *haciendo* 'doing' are used in a subordination construction, as well as in question formation, as in (7.33).

(7.33a) ¿**Qué haciendo** te        ensuciaste    así?
       what doing   you.FAM.OBJ  became.dirty-2SG  that.way
       'How did you get dirty like that?'

(7.33b) ¿**Qué haciendo** se    ha    lastimado el    perrito?
       what doing   3S.REFL has  hurt    the.MASC dog-MASC
       'How did the little dog hurt himself?'

(7.33c) ¿Sabías    que    no    vino    nadie?
       know-IMPER COMP  NEG  came-3SG  no one
       'Did you know that no one came?'
       No  sé    **qué diciendo** les    anuncié    que
       NEG know-1SG what saying  them  announced-1SG  comp
       'I don't know why I told them that
       hoy    tenían    control de  lectura.
       today  had-3PL  control of  reading
       today they had control over the reading.'

(7.33d) ¡**Qué diciendo** te    ponés el    saco!
       what saying  you.OBJ put.on the-MASC  jacket
       Te    queda    chico, ¿no    ves?
       you.OBJ  fits    small NEG  see-2SG
       'Why are you putting on that jacket? It's too small, don't you see?'

(7.33e) No sabría    decir  **cómo haciendo** lo   convenció.
       NEG know-1SG.COND  say-INF how doing   him  convinced-3SG
       'I wouldn't know how to say how he convinced him.'

These three constructions have in common that they constitute subordinate gerund clauses that contain a subject co-referential with the main-clause subject. In the case of *qué haciendo* 'what doing', del Valle Rodas (1998:101) states that there is a slight temporal simultaneity or anteriority expressed: in (7.33a) an activity was on-going at the time of getting dirty, and in (7.33b) there was an event that led up to getting hurt. Also of note is that this construction connotes a perspective on the part of the speaker, namely that the event is inexplicable. For example, in (7.33a) in addition to asking why the interlocutor got dirty, the speaker also expresses that s/he finds it inexplicable. Finally, this construction is still considered semantically a subordinate clause. It has not been grammaticalized as in the case of the other two constructions, to which I now turn.

[10] See del Valle Rodas' discussion of the instrument design used to collect the information for the study of these constructions (1998:100–107).

The construction with *qué diciendo* 'what saying' is used with the meaning of interrogative 'why', but it carries the additional information that the speaker thinks the event should not have been carried out. Thus, in (7.33c) the speaker expresses that s/he should have told the people they had control over the readings. Similarly, in (7.33d) the speaker asks the question, expressing that the interlocutor should not put the jacket on.

The construction *cómo haciendo* has a similar interpretation to *qué diciendo* in that in addition to the question asked there is also a concomitant expression of incredulity. Thus, in (7.33e) the speaker expresses that s/he does not know how a third party convinced a certain person and, in addition, that it is hard to believe that it took place. In English, it might be rendered by 'I have no idea how the hell he convinced her', or something to that effect. As with *qué diciendo*, this construction is grammaticalized to the point where it functions semantically like a question word (see del Valle Rodas 1998). Del Valle Rodas also explains why these constructions have permeated the speech of monolingual Spanish speakers: they are not in any way stigmatized but rather are found in the speech of speakers belonging to all strata of Salta society. In short, they are not marked socio-linguistically.

As a final point, we also find the same type of *qué diciendo* construction as those in (7.33) in monolingual Mantaro Valley Spanish (see (7.20)), also with the function of a question word. Although I cannot say whether the two constructions have exactly the same semantic and pragmatic interpretations, what is clear is that the Spanish suffix *-ndo* in both varieties has been iden- tified as a morpheme that can be used as a subordinating conjunction while maintaining the subordinate- and main-clause subjects as co-referential. This mapping, I argue, occurred independently, and I find it interesting from a cognitive perspective that the same mapping solution was found in both cases.

The last trait to be discussed here is the extensive use of the diminutive. Fernández Lávaque (1998c:124) notes that the use of the diminutive (e.g., *-ito, -illo*, etc.) can be distinguished from diminutive use in non-Andean varieties of Spanish in three ways. Fernández Lávaque argues that it attaches to more word classes than in Standard Spanish, it is used more frequently, and it can be used more than once in a given sentence. It is worth examining these claims, which I will do in the order given.

In Salta Spanish, diminutives attach to deictic determiners, quantifier terms, subject pronouns, and even certain interjections (e.g., *aíta* derived from *ay* 'oh'). To see whether this is also true of other varieties of monolingual Spanish, I carried out a search, in spoken language in CREA, of diminutive forms of the deictic determiners *est-e/-o/-a* 'this', *es-e/-o/-a* 'that', *aquel/-lo/-la* 'that over there' (and their corresponding plural forms); the quantifier terms *cualquiera* 'whatever', *nada* 'nothing', and *algo* 'something'; the pronouns *yo* 'I', *tú* 'you.SG.FAM', *él* 'he', *ella* 'she', *nosotros* 'we', and *ell-os/-as* 'they';

the possessive determiners/pronouns *mi-o/-a* 'my/mine', *tuy-o/-a*, 'your(s)', *suy-o/-a* 'his, her(s), their(s)', and their corresponding plural forms; and the interjection *ay* 'oh'. In the search, only three of these items were found in their diminutive form: *nadita* (six times), *alguito* (four times), and *suy-o/-a* (twice). It is safe to say, then, that the diminutivization of these elements is extremely rare and Fernández Lávaque's claim holds for these items.

Second, the author states that diminutives are used with more frequency in Salta Spanish than in non-Andean Spanish, due again to contact with Quechua. In a corpus of non-Andean Colombian Spanish (Catherine Travis, personal communication, 1 May 2006), the ratio of diminutives to words in the corpus is 577 diminutives/70,000 words or around 8/1000. If, however, the 97 tokens of lexicalized *ahorita* 'right now' are discounted, the result is 480/70,000 words or just under 7/1000, significantly lower than the 20/1000 Fernández Lávaque reports for her corpus. Thus, on this measure, the claim by Fernández Lávaque is also upheld.

With regard to the accumulation of diminutives within a sentence or a couple of sentences, we find in Fernández Lávaque (1998c:126) the sentence given in (7.34), in which we have two diminutive forms: *poquito* 'little-DIM' and *aíta* 'oh-DIM', the second of which is repeated. Fernández Lávaque cites a Quechua example, shown in (7.35), taken from Ayacucho (Peru), which also shows the accumulation of affective markers. I include a glossed example in (7.36) which illustrates the same phenomenon.[11] The suffix *-cha* is an affective marker and *-lla* a limitative/affective marker. The first one is often rendered in Spanish as *-ito*, the second as *no más* 'no more' or with the diminutive.

(7.34)  Ha        metío la      manu 'n      **poquito** . . .
        has       put.in the    hand a       little-DIM
        **Aíta,    aíta,**       por favor    señor m'    agarrau
        oh-DIM    oh-DIM        please       sir    me   grab-PPART
        la manu                 -dice-       Ay!
        the hand                says         Oh
        '(He) put his hand on her a little. "Oh, Oh, please sir", she says, "you've just grabbed my hand, oh!"'

(7.35)  Warma**cha**lla**q**a        chakintam       haytakuru**lla**sqa.
        'The poor little boy had hurt himself in the foot.'

(7.36)  Wawa  -**cha**-yki-    ta     llulla-yku-**lla**-y
        baby   DIM 2POSS   ACC   console-INTENS-LIM-INF
        'Do calm your little baby down.'

---

[11] Thanks to Marilyn Feke for directing me to this example, taken from Aráoz and Salas (1993:69).

Thus, the argument advanced by Fernández Lávaque that the diminutive in Salta Spanish appears with a wide range of lexical/functional words, is used more frequently than in non-Andean monolingual Spanish varieties, and is often used accumulatively in the speech chain is supported by solid evidence.

## 7.4     Concluding remarks

Due to its widespread use along the west coast of South America from southern Colombia to northern Argentina and Chile, Spanish *conquistadores* chose Quechua as the language of choice for the purposes of communication and evangelization at the outset of the colonization. Although from the eighteenth century onwards there has been a move towards the Castilianization of the Andean region, the great disproportion in numbers between native Quechua and native Spanish speakers, as well as a colonization geared exclusively towards the exploitation of indigenous labour, made it impossible for the widespread inter-ethnic contact necessary for generalized bilingualism to occur (Rivarola 1989:155, 160). Given these circumstances, we find approximative systems of Spanish in the region from very early on (Cerrón-Palomino 2003:135–170), and the type of bilingualism that has emerged reveals an extremely strong presence of Quechua-language features. Today, we still find pervasive evidence of approximative L2 Spanish systems, as well as evidence of monolingual varieties of Andean Spanish that contain a high number of Quechua features. In the comparison of the monolingual varieties spoken in Mantaro Valley, Peru, and Salta, Argentina, my goal was to examine whether in such monolingual Spanish-speaking communities common traits are present. The comparison suggests that these monolingual Spanish varieties, independently of one another, developed many of the same or similar linguistic traits. A list of the common traits discussed is given in (7.37).

(7.37a)   confusion of *o–u* and *e–i*
(7.37b)   monophthongization *ie* ==> *i*, *ue* ==> *u*
(7.37c)   use of the locative *en* 'in' with motion verbs and adverbs
(7.37d)   lack of gender and number agreement
(7.37e)   generalization of the clitic *lo* as the object pronoun
(7.37f)   use of the clitic *lo* to mark aspect (false pronominalization)
(7.37g)   pervasive use of *diciendo* 'saying' and *haciendo* 'doing' in subordinate
          clause constructions with similar interpretations in both situations
(7.37h)   strong presence of verb-final (as opposed to verb-initial) VPs
(7.37i)   frequent use of diminutives and of *no más*

As I have argued throughout this chapter, this could only have happened if the socio-cultural conditions in Mantaro Valley and Salta were similar, that is, if in each case there was a demographically strong presence of indigenous,

Quechua-speaking people who provided the high frequency of Quechua features during the period of acquisition of Spanish. Moreover, in monolingual Mantaro Valley and Salta, the mappings could not have taken place without also assuming an extended period of bilingualism in which Quechua was the heavily dominant language in terms of numbers of speakers, if not in terms of relative prestige.

Although Cerrón-Palomino (2003) addresses in detail issues of language instruction, language planning, and the choice of which variety of Spanish should be used in education, the relation Andean Spanish speakers have to their variety of Spanish is not addressed directly. In a personal communication (4 March 2007), Cerrón-Palomino states that there are as yet no studies that treat the issue systematically. However, commenting on the situation in Peru, he observes that in the cities certain traits of Andean Spanish (e.g., vowel raising and lowering, non-standard use of the subjunctive) are perceived negatively, while others, such as non-standard person and number agreement, are hardly noticed and are accepted as normal. The point, though, is that as a community it seems that Andean Spanish speakers have not developed a positive link between their cultural identity and the particular variety of Andean Spanish they speak. In the next chapter, I discuss a variety of Portuguese which has come to represent the unique culture of those who speak it.

# 8    Barranquenho

## 8.1    Introduction

Some attention has been paid to the contact situation on the Uruguay–Brazil border where a swathe of border land once belonging to Brazil became part of Uruguay in the nineteenth century. Although a 50- to 100-km strip in Uruguay on the Uruguay–Brazil border has been part of that country for more than 120 years, a variety of Portuguese is still maintained in the area which has been referred to as Portuñol or Fronterizo. (See Waltermire 2006 and references therein.)

The border area between Portugal and Spain, locally known as *A Raia* or *La Raya* 'the border, boundary', has received less attention although there are several Portuguese–Spanish contact situations in that area. For example, in the Spanish city of Valencia-de-Alcántara there is a sizable enclave of Portuguese-speaking citizens and to my knowledge this situation has yet to be studied systematically. In the case of Barranquenho, the variety of Spanish-influenced Portuguese spoken in Barrancos, Portugal, the monograph by Leite de Vasconcelos (1955) and the more recent work by Navas Sánchez-Élez (1992, 1994, 1996, 1997, 2001) are seminal, though this contact situation is also largely unknown among the wider audience in contact linguistics. The Barrancos situation is interesting because, over the centuries, the area has been claimed by both Portugal and Spain. In order to illustrate this, I first give a brief historical overview of the area from the Middle Ages onwards. I then discuss the various features that define Barranquenho, using material found in Leite de Vasconcelos (1955) and a corpus comprising speech of twenty-two Barranquenho speakers. I then address the question of whether the details of the history of Barrancos lead to predictions about the presence of the features we find.[1]

---

[1] When using the terms *Portuguese* and *Spanish* here, I am referring exclusively to European Portuguese and Andalusian Spanish. However, with regard to clitic form and placement in Spanish, my generalizations apply to Spanish in general.

Map 8.1. The area of *A Raia* on the southern Portugal–Spain border.

## 8.2    Historical background of the Barrancos area

The recorded history of Barrancos and nearby Noudar castle goes back to
the Middle Ages. For centuries the area of *A Raia* was under the rule of
the Moors who had conquered the Iberian peninsula in the beginning of the
eighth century. As the Christians began to organize themselves across the
northern part of the peninsula, they confronted the Moors in battle as
expected, but they also faced battles among the different emerging political
entities of Christians. The polities that concern us here are Portugal, Galicia,
and Castile-Leon. From the ninth century to the twelfth, the borders
between what would become these three kingdoms were fluid (Leguay, de
Oliveira Marques, and Beirante 1993:59–60). Portugal defined itself first as
a county in 1094 and later in 1179 as a kingdom (Leguay, de Oliveira Marques,
and Beirante 1993:263 and de Oliveira Marques 1998:35–37). After a series

of border disputes that continued into the thirteenth century, Portugal and Castile signed two important border-related agreements: that of Badajoz and that of Alcañices. In the Badajoz agreement, the two kingdoms reached a decision to use the Guadiana River as the border between the two kingdoms. As is apparent from Map 8.1, this puts Barrancos and Moura in Castile. Da Azevedo Maia (2001:3) states that borders, especially in the Middle Ages, are best understood as *zonas-frontera* or 'border zones' rather than border lines, and that these zones were defined by a long string of castles along the border zone from north to south. The castle closest to Barrancos is Noudar castle, approximately 8 km away, and Noudar castle and the Barrancos area have always been part of the same administrative unit.

De Matos Coelho (1999) offers a synoptic history of Noudar castle, in which it becomes apparent how often the border zones shifted from one kingdom to the other. The account starts in 1167, the year the area was conquered by the Portuguese (ibid.:65–74). In 1184, the area was lost again to the Moors, but was re-conquered in the same year. The next major change occurred in 1253, when Portugal and Castile reached an agreement that Noudar castle would become Castilian, but just thirty years later, on 4 March 1283, Alfonse the Wise of Castile gifted the Barrancos area, along with Moura and Serpa, to his daughter Beatriz. In 1303, the area was again gifted away, this time to the Order of Avis (a Portuguese noble order) and the new owners made renovations to the castle that were completed in 1308. Thirty-one years later, in 1339, the Castilian Order of Santiago laid siege to Noudar castle and took it from the Portuguese within days, holding it until 1372, when as part of a wedding gift it was returned to Portugal. However, as soon as King Dom Fernando, the king who gifted it to the Order of Avis, died in 1383, the Castilians again took over the castle and the adjacent area. Their possession was, however, cut short: in 1399 King João of Portugal, who was also the master of the Order of Avis, retook the castle, keeping it for the next seventy-six years. In 1475, Castile briefly held Noudar castle and the surrounding area for three years, after which it was returned to Portugal in 1478. Between 1478 and 1516, there were disagreements and resolutions between the two kingdoms regarding what municipalities belonged to each kingdom and what rights each kingdom had to the use of the arable fields.

During this period (i.e., in 1493), there is mention of Castilians living in Barrancos. Leite de Vasconcelos (1955:6–7) states that in a 1527 text Barrancos shows up as a village within the area of Noudar castle and is said to have had seventy-three inhabitants, the majority of whom were Castilians. Thus, we can assume that there was a strong Spanish-language presence there, at least from that point onwards. On 3 June, 1516, the Portuguese came into possession of Noudar castle. This lasted until 1580, the year in which Castile-Spain, under Philip II (1556–98), took possession of the whole of Portugal, a period which marked the beginning of the decline of Portugal as a colonial power. In 1640, Noudar castle was re-fortified, and the Portuguese took Barrancos and Noudar castle by force the next year. This occupation of the area lasted until 1662, the year in which the territory in the Noudar area, except Noudar castle itself, was taken back by Spain; by 1707 the castle had also been taken by Spain. Eight years later (in 1715), Spain agreed to return the castle to Portugal.

From 1715 onwards, the Noudar castle–Barrancos area has been part of Portugal, albeit not without complications of status. Throughout the nineteenth century, Portugal and Spain continued to struggle over their respective claims on the territory. The matter languished until 1886, when Portugal and Spain named delegations to negotiate the issue of possession. The diplomatic effort culminated in 1894 with the ratification of a convention whereby Barrancos and Noudar castle became a definitive part of Portugal; in 1910 the castle was made a national monument, ending once and for all the 800-year-old territorial dispute.

Regarding the socio-linguistic relation between Portuguese, Castilian/Spanish, and the other dialects of the area (Galician, Asturian, Leonese), as far back as the twelfth century Castilian was considered a language of prestige. Da Azevedo Maia (2001:2) reports that 'with the definitive union of the kingdoms of Castile and Leon and with the subsequent expansion of the Castilian language, which for a long time had been the prestige language in the Leonese kingdom, the gradual Castilianization [of Leon] took place' (my translation).[2] During his reign as king of Castile (1252–84), Alfonso el Sabio 'the Wise' was a patron of the arts and of learning and was responsible for a number of important publications, including translations of scholarly works. Among the artistic productions were the Cantigas de Santa Maria, a varied collection of songs written in Galician and dedicated to the Blessed Virgin. Thus, Galician, a variety of Portuguese, enjoyed early on some prestige. However, many of the other works produced by the scholars affiliated with the king's court were in Castilian, such as the Castilian versions of the astrology text *Lapidario*, the first history of Spain entitled *Primera Crónica General* 'First General Chronicle', a history of the world *Estoria General* 'General History', the *Saber de Astronomia* 'Knowledge of Astronomy', the *Libro de Ajedrez* 'Book of Chess', and many other texts (Lapesa 1981:237–239).

[2] The original reads, 'Con la unión definitiva de los reinos de Castilla y León y con la expansión del castellano que, desde hacía mucho tiempo, era lengua de prestigio en el reino leonés, se asiste a su paulatina castellanización.'

As the kingdom of Castile expanded, Castilian became the language used in the royal chancellery for the practical reason that it was the lingua franca of the re-conquest effort (Lapesa 1981:172–173, 189–192, 245–247). This is one key reason why Alfonso el Sabio most likely chose to have texts in Arabic and Hebrew translated into Castilian. In turn, the scholarly production in Alfonso el Sabio's court was crucial in establishing Castilian as a more prestigious language than Galician/Portuguese, Leonese, and Asturian. Finally, Castilian was the first Romance language to have a written grammar – Nebrija's (1492) *Gramática de la lengua castellana*.

In the specific relation between Portugal and Portuguese on the one hand and Castile and Castilian on the other, it is important to note that Portugal belonged to Castile for sixty years (1580–1640), a period which coincided with the sharp decline of Portugal as a colonial power. Although Castile's own decline would follow shortly thereafter, it progressed more slowly than that of Portugal. Moreover, Castile was the larger and more powerful kingdom. Thus, as the prestige of a language usually follows social, economic, and military power, Castilian was the more prestigious of the two. Over time it came to be the most prestigious language of the peninsula and a national language.

Since the eighteenth century, Castilian has dominated in many of its colonies. It is the national language of Mexico and almost all Central and South American countries. In addition, it is still spoken in the Spanish territories of Alhucemas, Ceuta, the Chafarinas Islands, Melilla, and Peñón de Vélez de la Gomera in North Africa as well as the Philippines. For its part, apart from Brazil, Portuguese is still spoken in the Cape Verde Islands, some Gulf of Guinea islands, Angola, and Mozambique in Africa, as well as in some localities in Asia. However, it does not have the global presence currently enjoyed by Spanish.

The Portuguese linguist Leite de Vasconcelos (1955:7–8) writes that during his data collection in Barrancos he made the acquaintance of a Senhor Vázquez, from Spain but of Portuguese nationality, who showed him documentation that the Vázquez family was living there in 1790. Senhor Vázquez spoke to the linguist of his paternal grandfather who was born in Spain, but moved to Barrancos because of war and established a respectable business there. More generally, Leite de Vasconcelos learned that during the nineteenth century the professions of medical doctor, veterinarian, school teacher, and grave digger in the Barrancos area were held exclusively by Spaniards, and many others were barbers, shoemakers, carpenters, and merchants. The fact that the professionals spoke Spanish gave the language a certain amount of prestige as compared to Portuguese.

In the past 100 years, Spanish has also remained the more prestigious language on the Iberian peninsula. Again, the reasons have to do, in general, with social and economic strength. With regard to the Barrancos area, its inhabitants have travelled regularly to Spain in the past century for many reasons, chiefly to purchase consumer goods and seek better health care, apart from visiting friends and relatives. Even during the Franco dictatorship in Spain (1939–75), there remained a steady stream of contraband trade across the border, mostly from Spain to Portugal. Since the Barranquenho women carried out most of the cross-border commerce, they maintained their variety of Spanish. Even after the Spanish dictatorship fell and the dictatorship in Portugal dissolved in 1975 through a peaceful revolution, Barranquenho women still sought goods and services routinely on the Spanish side of the border.

Today the situation is largely the same in many ways. For example, Barrancos inhabitants reported in 2003 that there is a greater diversity of merchandise at less expensive prices in Spain than in Portugal. Thus, Barranquenho women still shop on a regular basis in Spain and of course are able to cross the border freely. Moreover, Barrancos has no hospital, so its inhabitants go to Spain for emergency medical treatment; a Spanish doctor travels to Barrancos once a week to attend to the sick.

Leite de Vasconcelos (1955:7–8) reports that, when he visited Barrancos in 1938, almost all the families claimed to be of Spanish heritage and that all inhabitants, whether literate or illiterate, spoke Portuguese and Spanish equally well. He also mentions cases of children who spoke Spanish to their mothers and Portuguese to their fathers, although he also notes that Portuguese was favoured among the younger generation because of the influence of the schools.

The general pattern that emerges from this brief overview is that, from very early on, Spanish has been more prestigious than Portuguese on the Iberian peninsula. Leite de Vasconcelos (1955:29–30) states that there was even a document dated 1245 from which one can infer that in Noudar castle both Portuguese and Castilian were in use at that time. He also reminds us that in 1527 the majority of the Barrancos population was Castilian and that it was only after the passage of much time and through political influence at the local level that linguistic supremacy was transferred to Portuguese. This supports the view that although Barranquenhos were aligned with Portugal in more recent history, they maintain deep ties with Spain. Of course, as polities became better defined in the nineteenth century, Portuguese became the default language of instruction and of the church in Barrancos. And, because more people attended school, more learned Portuguese. However, Barranquenhos have also created a separate, unique identity. Consequently, they maintain, as Leite de Vasconcelos (1955:30) notes, three linguistic varieties: Barranquenho, their local variety; Spanish, the variety that historically they have ties with; and Portuguese, the language of the nation in which they live. In the same monograph (ibid.:10), the linguist comments:

From Barrancos' geographical situation, the mixing of the village's inhabitants and the language they speak, they have acquired a certain character of traditional moral independence. When a villager from another [Portuguese] town such as Moura, Beja, etc. arrives [in Barrancos], the Barranquenhos say: 'He's Portuguese, there comes a Portuguese', as if they were not Portuguese! But they also say about someone coming from Spain, 'There comes a Spaniard!' (my translation).

This independent character among the Barranquenhos is reflected not only in the variety of language they speak, but also in certain defining aspects of their village culture. One of these involves bull fighting. In Barrancos' annual village festival, there are a number of bull-fights and in these the bulls are still killed, as is the custom in Spain, although in Portugal – of which Barrancos is a part – the killing of bulls in bull-fights is strictly prohibited. However, the resistance to the law in Barrancos was intense. Several of the town's key citizens even travelled to Lisbon, presented their case before the national parliament for keeping their bull-fighting tradition in Barrancos, and ultimately were successful in protecting a tradition that is deeply Spanish and no longer Portuguese in character.

The question arises about when Barranquenho became its own linguistic variety. We know that Barrancos had both Portuguese and Castilian speakers (and a majority of the latter) in 1527. A general answer to the question would, then, be that sometime between 1527 and the beginning of the twentieth century Barranquenho was formed, assuming (as I do) that when Leite de Vasconcelos visited the village in 1938 Barranquenho was a fully formed variety that could be spoken with different degrees of accuracy.

The presence of certain lexical items in Barranquenho may give a clue to when it formed. One potential candidate seemed to be the adverb *ansina* 'like this/that', which is an older Spanish form corresponding to present-day *así*. In the speech of the twenty-two informants I collected, there are thirty-three tokens of *assim* (thirty-two of which are from one speaker), none of *así*, and one token of *ansina*, shown in (8.1), from a 64-year-old speaker.

(8.1)  ... purque  a    mãi   não   era capá e   ansina    eu  o
       because the  mother NEG  was able and like.this I  him
       tiré          dali.
       pulled.out    from-there
       'because mum was not able and so I pulled him out of there like this.'

Although today *ancina* or *asina* in Spanish is rarely if ever heard, it was still present in literary texts up until the twentieth century; analysis of this trait, thus, cannot give us an accurate indication of when Barranquenho may have formed.[3]

However, given the history of Barrancos, a reasonable assumption is that Barranquenhos have been bilingual in Portuguese and Spanish at least since the beginning of the seventeenth century, and possibly earlier. (Recall that in 1527 the majority of the Barrancos inhabitants were Spanish speakers.) I suggest that Barranquenho is the result of the Barrancos inhabitants introducing Spanish-language traits into their variety of Portuguese, and that over time these traits came to form part of an emerging linguistic variety that conventionalized as Barranquenho. I will discuss evidence for this in the next section. A major factor in the formation of this variety, I argue, is the rise of consciousness among the speakers of the village that they are unique. That is, they came to see themselves as neither Portuguese nor Spanish, or both Portuguese and Spanish, as evidenced by the quotation above provided by Leite de Vasconcelos. And, although their identity of being culturally and linguistically unique has definitely been in place since around the 1880s, Barranquenhos still preferred Spanish to Portuguese and Barranquenho until recently. An eleven-year-old informant reported in 2003 that, 'the most aged people in Barrancos, the oldest, they almost all speak Spanish, they don't speak Barranquenho. It's now that they are beginning to speak Barranquenho.'[4] I assume that this was the case both for practical reasons and for reasons involving the prestige of Spanish. At present Barranquenho has become a cultural badge of the Barranquenhos. They maintain it because it marks them as culturally unique. It also serves to promote their community

---

[3] The information in the table below indicates that that *ancina* and *asina* were used up until the twentieth century in written Spanish (data taken from the CREA data base maintained by the Real Academia Española). Based on these data, Barranquenho could have formed as early as the sixteenth century and as late as the end of the nineteenth century.

| Form | *ancina* | | *asina* | | *así* | |
|------|--------|-------|--------|-------|--------|-------|
| | Tokens | Docs. | Tokens | Docs. | Tokens | Docs. |
| Year | | | | | | |
| 1400–99 | 5 | | 0 | | 16,568 | 687 |
| 1500–99 | 23 | 15 | 59 | 37 | 54,281 | 1214 |
| 1600–99 | 6 | 6 | 15 | 10 | 37,486 | 1097 |
| 1700–99 | 3 | 3 | 21 | 4 | 11,068 | 1380 |
| 1800–99 | 29 | 11 | 29 | 9 | 35,568 | 1622 |
| 1900–99 | 213 | 25 | 93 | 20 | 50,485 | 2379 |

---

[4] The original reads: 'I ah pesóah mái idoza de Barrancu, a mái belha falom quazi todah a ehpanhola, nãu falom barranquenhu. Agora é que já bãu falandu barranquenhu.'

cohesion. That Barranquenhos are aware of this is suggested by the same eleven-year-old informant. Responding to the question about with whom he speaks Barranquenho and where, he says:

[I speak Barranquenho] with friends, in school no, with friends, with older people sometimes . . . With my family I speak Barranquenho and with my friends, and all. It's only in school that I don't speak Barrenquenho, I speak it sometimes.[5]

The next section looks at a list of features that define Barrenquenho as a contact variety.

## 8.3     Some defining features of Barranquenho

Some of the key features of Barranquenho discussed in this section are found in the Portuguese dialect of the area, called Alentejano. Others, by contrast, are clear cases of influence from Spanish. I discuss phonological as well as morphological, morphosyntactic, and lexical features, comparing them, where relevant, to the features of regional Portuguese and Spanish.

Whereas the Spanish vowel system consists of only the five oral phonemes /i, e, a, o, u/ and no nasal phonemes, and all five vowels can appear in pre-tonic, tonic, and post-tonic positions, in Portuguese there are eight oral phonemes /i, e, ɛ, ə, a, ɔ, o, u/, of which [i, ɨ, ə, u] are found in pre-tonic and post-tonic non-final position and [ɨ, ə, u] in post-tonic final position.[6] In addition, Portuguese also has the five nasal phonemes /ĩ, ẽ, ə, õ, ũ/ (Cunha and Lindley Cintra 1994:36–40). Thus, the Portuguese vowel system has not only three more oral vowel phonemes than Spanish but also a series of nasal phonemes for which Spanish has no nasal counterparts. And, given the different distribution of Portuguese vowels in stressed and unstressed positions, it is apparent that in unstressed positions there is reduction and/or raising whereas this is not the case in Spanish.

Given these considerable differences in the vowel inventories between the two languages, and the sensitivity to stressed and unstressed position in Portuguese, a reasonable expectation would be that if there originally were predominantly Castilian speakers in Barrancos, some Spanish traits would be introduced into the emerging variety that would later become Barranquenho. That is, we might expect to find a reduced vowel inventory in Barranquenho relative to Portuguese and/or a lack of vowel reduction and/or raising in unstressed position and/or a possible lack of nasal vowels. However, neither Leite de Vasconcelos (1955:19)

---

[5] Com uz amigu, na ehcola nãu, com uz amigu, com otra pesóa asim máih belha àh bêzi . . . Com a minha família fálu barranquênhu i com u mez amiguh, içu tudu. So na ehcola é que nãu fálu barranquênhu, fálu à bêzih.

[6] The sound [ɨ] is defined as a high central vowel.

nor I found such features in Barranquenho. That is, the speakers of Barranquenho whose speech I have studied have no apparent lack of reduction or lack of nasal vowels, nor is their oral vowel inventory reduced in any transparent way. What we do find, however, is vowel raising to [i] of /e/ in post-tonic final position, as in the sentence in (8.2), where the standard Portuguese version is given under the sentence in Barranquenho.

| (8.2) | Alguma | bezi | tibi | e? | São Marcu | da | Ataboêra. |
|---|---|---|---|---|---|---|---|
| | Algumas | vezes | estive | em | São Marcos | da | Ataboêra. |
| | Some | times | I was | in | Saint Mark | of | Ataboêra. |

'Sometimes I was in Saint Mark of Ataboêra.' (female, 86 years old:4)

Note that the post-tonic final vowel in *bezi* [bé-zi] and *tibi* [tí-bi] have been raised to [i]. This phenomenon is a regional one, also found in the Portuguese dialect of the area.[7]

With regard to the consonants, Barrancos possesses various traits that are clearly not Portuguese but found in Extremeño Spanish. Before discussing these, I compare the consonant inventories of Portuguese and Spanish, given in (8.3) and (8.4) respectively.

(8.3)   / p, b, t, d, k, g, w /
       / f, (v), s, z, j, š, ž /
       / l, r, r̄, λ, (ɹ)/
       / m, n, ñ/
(8.4)   / p, b, t, d, k, g, w/
       / f, s, y, (λ), x /
       / č /
       / l, r, r̄/
       / m, n, ñ/

Comparing the two consonant inventories, we see that Spanish has a reduced set of fricatives in that it lacks /v/, /z/, /ž/, and /š/. Although Portuguese has three types of rhotics /r, r̄, ɹ /, /ɹ/ is found in urban speech and, as we shall see, in the speech of the younger speakers, whereas /r̄/ is found in rural areas, which includes the region where Barrancos is located (see Cunha and Lindley Cintra 1994:32). And although Standard Portuguese and dialectal Portuguese of the Barrancos area distinguish between /b/ and /v/, this distinction is not found in Barranquenho; instead both orthographic *v* and *b* are realized as [b] or [β]. This cannot be traced to dialectal Portuguese given that the lack of /b/–/v/ is found only north of a line from Coimbra to Bragança (Cunha and

---

[7] To obtain an idea of the linguistic traits in the Alentejano speech, samples taken from Serpa were consulted, a town approximately 60 km west-south-west of Barrancos. The sound files are made available by the Instituto Camões and are available at their website (www.instituto-camoes.pt/cvc/hlp/geografia/mapa06.html). Thanks to Ana Luis for informing me of the audio files of the different Portuguese dialects.

Lindley Cintra 1994:11–13; Teyssier 1984:48–49). Thus, the fact that many Barranquenho speakers have /r̄/ instead of /ʁ/ is a trait of Barrancos-area Portuguese, whereas the non-distinction between /b/ and /v/ is arguably due to Spanish influence.

In Barranquenho, we find three other phonology-related phenomena that are clearly due to contact with Extremeño Spanish. In Extremeño Spanish, as in Andalusian Spanish, the aspiration or deletion of syllable-final -s and the deletion of word-final -r and -l are commonplace (Hualde, Olarrea, and Escobar 2001:337).[8] Similarly, we find that this phenomenon is also widespread in Barranquenho (see also Leite de Vasconcelos 1955:43–44). Some illustrative examples are given in (8.5). For Barranquenho, the aspiration and deletion of syllable-final -s has attracted most attention, as is evident from the studies by Navas Sánchez-Élez (1992, 1994, 1996, 1997, 2001), while the deletion of -r and -l have not been studied in detail. I have found abundant examples of -r deletion, but no examples of -l deletion.

(8.5a)   Purque antiØ . . .          nóØ não tinhamuØ         possi para
         porque antes . . .         nós não tinhamos         posse para
         pagáØ esa coiza i aquela mulhéØ com                 qualquéØ
         pagar essa coisa e aquela mulher com               qualquer
         coizinha que a genti le daba ela ficaba contenti (F86:10–11)
         coisinha que a gente lhe daba ela ficava contente.
         'Because before we didn't have the means to pay for that type of thing
         and that woman, she was content with whatever the people gave her.'

(8.5b)   Eu trabalhu na ehcola, trabalhu com u primêru ciclu, sô auxiliá. (F33:9)
         Eu trabalho na escola, trabalho com o primeiro ciclo, sou auxiliar.
         'I work in the school, I work with the first cycle [primary
         school], I'm an assistant.'

(8.5c)   No, uh da nosa  sala queremuØ fazéØ isu. (male, 11 years old:191)
         Nós, os da nossa sala queremos  fazer  isso.
         'We, the ones from our school year, we want to do that.'

In Barranquenho, word-final /s/ as [z] is retained where the following word begins with a vowel and re-syllabication takes place. An illustrative example of this common phenomenon in Barranquenho is given in (8.6). Leite de Vasconcelos (1955:13–14) also mentions this as a trait of Barranquenho.[9]

(8.6)   a   já   **doj   z**anuh (F19:96)
        há  já   dois  anos
        'two years ago'

---

[8] It is noteworthy that texts such as Lapesa (1981) and Penny (1991) do not mention the deletion of word-final liquids, but refer only to their neutralization.

[9] This scholar also notes (1955:48) that there is retention of -r when it appears intervocalically across word boundaries, as in senhó rAntónio [se- ñó-ran-tó-njo] (< senhor António).

As mentioned above, Barranquenho speakers generally display no distinction between /b/ and /v/ and have /r̄/ instead of /ʀ/. However, some younger speakers, an 11-year-old boy and a 19-year-old girl, both have /ʀ/, but both a 14-year-old boy and a 24-year-old young man exhibit /r̄/. Thus, the possibility exists that the choice between /r̄/ and /ʀ/ is sensitive to sociolinguistic considerations and still needs to be studied.

Finally, we saw above that Portuguese distinguishes between /s/ and /z/, whereas Spanish possesses only /s/. In Barranquenho, the speakers whose speech we examined maintained the distinction between /s/ and /z/ consistently.[10]

With regard to morphology, one might expect Barranquenho speakers' speech to contain irregular Spanish verb forms with frequently used verbs. That is, if Barranquenho speakers favoured Spanish and were dominant in it until recently, we would expect to find forms such as Spanish *estuve* 'I was' instead of Portuguese *estive*. However, this does not seem to be the case. In the speech of a 63-year-old man who regularly uses Spanish in his daily life, we do find evidence of irregular Spanish verbs in his Barranquenho (e.g., *i ehtube trêzanu lá* [Portuguese *e estive trêze anos lá*] 'and I was there for thirteen years'). For his part, Leite de Vasconcelos (1955) does not comment on any morphological phenomena other than Spanish forms of the same verb (*(s)tobe* from *estuvo* 's/he was') and the use of the diminutive *-ito*, not found in speech samples that make up our corpus.

It is in Barranquenho morphosyntax that we find the most revealing influence from Spanish. Between Portuguese and Spanish there is a clear contrast regarding how the progressive aspect is expressed. While Portuguese employs the construction *estar a* + verb-INF, as in *nós estamos a fazer o trabalho* 'we are doing the work', Spanish uses the construction *estar* + verb-GER, as in *nosotros estamos haciendo el trabajo* 'we are doing the work'. In Barranquenho, the more commonly used construction to express the progressive aspect is clearly the Spanish construction. Illustrative examples are given in (8.7).

(8.7a)  Me casei tarde, **ehtaba** já **trabalhando**. (F52:133–134)
        'I married late, I was already working.'
(8.7b)  Nu se si sabi, ondi **ehtãu fazendu** u cini teatru. (M11:126)
        'I don't know whether you know, [the place] where they're making the theatre.'
(8.7c)  . . . i minha irmã **ehtaba bailandu**. (F31:124)
        '. . . and my sister was dancing.'

---

[10] Only one speaker, who had a Spanish-speaking boyfriend, occasionally devoiced /z/, as in [ká-sə] 'house' instead of [ká-zə].

Another phenomenon common in Spanish, but unknown in Portuguese, is indirect object doubling, shown in (8.8).

(8.8)   **Le**      cuento una historia   **a Marta**.
        IO.3s    tell-1s a   story       to Marta
        'I tell/am telling a story to Marta.'

This construction is exceedingly common in Barranquenho. In (8.9), examples from three of the informants are shown.

(8.9a)  **Le**      conté    **a meu pai . . .**   (M11:61)
        IO.3s    told-1s  to my father
        'I told my father . . .'

(8.9b)  i    u     **le**     disse   asi   **au otru . . .**   (M11:215)
        and  one   IO.3s   said-3s so   to-the other
        'and one said to another . . .'

(8.9c)  i    eu    **lhe**    disse   **à rapariga**      (M64:64)
        and  I     IO.3s   said-3sG  to the girl
        'and I said to the girl . . .'

(8.9d)  i    **lhe**      pedi     **a uma colega minha** . .   (F26:176)
        and  IO.3s    requested-1sG   to a colleague mine
        'and I asked a colleague of mine . . .'

Another phenomenon apparent in the examples in (8.9) is the placement of the clitics *le* and *lhe*. To be able to understand the significance of clitic placement in Barranquenho, it will help to explain briefly here how the phenomenon works in both Portuguese and Spanish.[11] In Portuguese, proclisis is found after certain operators, such as negation markers (8.10), quantifiers (8.11), and indefinite pronouns such as 'someone' (8.12), as well as certain adverbs (8.13).

(8.10)  O João **não a**      viu no       cinema      ontem.
        the João NEG her   saw in-the   cinema      yesterday
        'João didn't see her at the cinema yesterday.'

(8.11)  **Tudo a**      chateia.
        all   her     bothers
        'Everything bothers her.'

(8.12)  **Alguém me**  telefonou  ontem.
        Someone me  telephoned yesterday
        'Someone phoned me yesterday.'

(8.13)  **Apenas/até**  o João **te**          reconheceu na televisão.
        Only/even    the João you.OBJ   recognized in-the television.
        'Only/even João recognized you on television.'

---

[11] Unless otherwise indicated, the information regarding clitic placement in Portuguese, Barranquenho, and Spanish is taken from Mira Mateus *et al.* (1989) and Clements and Lorenzino (2006).

Proclisis in Portuguese is also obligatory if there is a non-canonical topicalized element in sentence-initial position, such as an object or an adjunct. An example is shown in (8.14).

(8.14)  **Dele se**          sabe pouca coisa.
        of-him PASSIVE      knows little thing
        'Of him little is known.'

In addition, proclisis is required in subordinate clauses, illustrated by the example in (8.15).

(8.15)  Disseram-me    **que** o João **a**    viu no    cinema ontem.
        told-3PL-me     that the João her    saw in-the cinema yesterday
        'They told me that João saw her at the cinema yesterday.'

Thus, in Portuguese certain operators and certain pragmatically driven word orders call for proclisis. This also holds for compound verbs (i.e., AUX + verb) and modal constructions. Finally, proclisis is required in subordinate clauses, which is true of simple as well as compound tenses.

In contrast to the environments in which proclisis is the norm, enclisis is required in Portuguese finite matrix clauses in which there is no pragmatically driven non-canonical word order and no presence of the aforementioned operators. Examples are given in (8.16–8.18).

(8.16)  O João viu-**a** no          cinema      ontem.
        the João saw-her in-the     cinema      yesterday
        'João saw her at the cinema yesterday.'
(8.17)  O João    tem-**a** visto    últimamente.
        the João  has-her seen     lately
        'João has seen her lately.'
(8.18)  O João deve-**te** reconhecer              /deve reconhecer-**te**
        only the João you.OBJ should recognize   /should recognize-you.OBJ
        'Only João should recognize you.'

According to Luis (2004), enclisis in Portuguese appears to be expanding its domains, independently of age group, socio-economic class, or education level, such that it is becoming the default order in Portuguese, independently of what type of clause it appears in and what type of auxiliary or adverbial it appears with.

In Spanish, clitic placement obeys a different set of rules from those found in Portuguese. Proclisis is obligatory with finite indicative verb forms, with or without an auxiliary (see (8.19)) and negative imperative verb forms (see (8.20)).

(8.19a) Juanita **lo** compró
        Juanita it bought
        'Juanita bought it.'

(8.19b)    Juanita **lo** ha  comprado.
        Juanita it  has bought
        'Juanita has bought it.'

(8.20)    ¡No  **lo** hagas!
        NEG  it  do-IMP-2SG
        'Don't do it!'

Enclisis in Spanish is obligatory in finite imperative verb forms (see (8.21)), and all non-finite forms (see (8.22)).

(8.21)    ¡Haz**lo**!
        do-IMP-it
        'Do it!'

(8.22a)    Después de hacer**lo**. . .
        after      of do-INF-it
        'After doing it . . .'

(8.22b)    Después de haber**lo**      hecho . . .
        after      of have-INF-it done
        'After having done it . . .'

(8.22c)    Buscándo**lo**    por      toda la casa . . .
        looking.for-it through all   the house
        'Looking for it throughout the house . . .'

(8.22d)    Habiendo**lo** buscado por      toda la casa . . .
        having-it looked.for through all   the house
        'Having looked for it throughout the house . . .'

With many modals, proclisis or enclisis is found, as illustrated by the examples in (8.23).

(8.23a)    Juan **te**      debe  ayudar.
        Juan you.OBJ  should help-INF
        'Juan should help you.'

(8.23b)    Juan debe      ayudar**te**.
        Juan should   help-INF-you.OBJ
        'Juan should help you.'

The one environment in which Portuguese and Spanish object pronoun clitic placement does not coincide is in finite matrix clauses with no pragmatically driven non-canonical word order and no presence of a proclisis-triggering element in Portuguese. In these cases, Portuguese exhibits enclisis and Spanish proclisis. I focus here on these particular environments in Barranquenho.

Based on the data from the twenty-two speakers whose transcribed speech made up my Barranquenho corpus, the general trend is for the Barranquenho speakers to follow Spanish clitic placement. Specifically, all Barranquenho speakers represented in our corpus who used third-person indirect object clitics in matrix clauses exhibited proclisis, as in Spanish (even when there were no discourse markers to trigger this morphosyntactic behaviour), and not

Table 8.1. *The instances of enclisis and proclisis in the speech of four male Barranquenho speakers*

| Speaker | Proclisis | Enclisis | No. of words in text |
|---------|-----------|----------|----------------------|
| #1 (age 11) | 25 | – | 5582 |
| #2 (age 14) | 34 | – | 3504 |
| #3 (age 64) | 52 | – | 4927 |
| #4 (age 83) | 16 | 12 | 5394 |

enclisis, as in Portuguese. Some examples are shown in (8.9) above. This aspect of Barranquenho was noted by Navas Sánchez-Élez (1992:239), who writes that clitic placement in Barranquenho is unlike that in Portuguese and more like that found in Andalusian Spanish, citing the example *a furmiga le disse que sim* [lit. the ant him/her told that yes] 'the ant told him/her "yes"' which in standard colloquial Portuguese would be commonly rendered as *a furmiga disse-lhe que sim.*[12]

For my purposes here, I focus on third-person indirect object clitics because they allow comparability: both the Portuguese and the Spanish form possess a CV structure (Portuguese *lhe(s)* /λə(s)/ and Spanish *le* /le/).[13] The study carried out by Clements and Lorenzino (2006) examined general clitic placement, including direct object and indirect object clitics, in four male speakers of Barranquenho. Two age groups were distinguished: the younger group was made up of two individuals of eleven and fourteen years old; the older group comprised two speakers, sixty-four and eighty-three years old. As described in the study, the relation of these individuals to Spanish varies. The two boys do not deal with Spanish on a daily basis, although it can be assumed that they have had exposure to it and understand it. The 64-year-old speaker uses Spanish in his daily life and at home with his family, while the 83-year-old does not use it on a day-to-day basis, but knows it. Of course, the study focuses only on clitic placement in those contexts in which Portuguese requires enclisis and Spanish proclisis. Table 8.1 displays the

---

[12] Navas Sánchez-Élez also mentions another non-standard order variation in Barranquenho, as in *me se saem as canas* [lit. me REFL come.out the grey-hairs] 'I'm getting grey hair', where the pronominal clitic order is 'REFL + me' in Andalusian Spanish. In this particular case, it seems that clitic ordering relative to one another is due to influence of a non-standard variety of Andalusian Spanish, as in Portuguese it does not occur in any variety (Ana Luís, personal communication, 27 March 2006).

[13] The phonological shape of the third-person direct object clitic pronouns in Portuguese and Spanish is quite different (Portuguese *o* [u], *a* [ə], *os* [uš], *as* [əš] vs Spanish *lo* [lo], *la* [la], *los* [los], *las* [las]). This makes a comparison more complex. It remains a project for the future.

results of the study. The results indicate that clitic placement in the relevant environment in the speech of three of the speakers is similar or identical to the system found in Spanish. The oldest speaker exhibited both proclisis and enclisis, though there was a preference for the former.

Not only do Barranquenho speakers display proclisis where Portuguese has enclisis, but in many cases they also have adopted the form of the clitic. For example, five of the twenty-two informants use the Spanish form *le* almost exclusively, another five use both *lhe* and *le* in their conversation. Six speakers chose *lhe* almost exclusively and six others did not use the forms in the controlled conditions.

Another phenomenon involving clitics where Portuguese and Spanish differ substantially is the case of double pronominalization, as in *John gave her it* or *John gave it to her*. Double pronominalization in Portuguese involves a coalescence of the indirect object pronoun *lhe* and the direct object pronoun (*o, a, os, as*) to *lho, lhos, lha*, or *lhas*. In Spanish, the indirect object pronoun in double pronominalization has evolved from *le* via *že* to *se* and the direct object pronouns are *lo, los, la*, and *las*. Thus, the corresponding combinations are *se lo, se los, se la, se las*. As is apparent, these combinations do not undergo any type of coalescence and thus are relatively more transparent than their Portuguese counterparts. While we find examples of both in our corpus, the more frequently occurring construction is the Spanish one. Illustrative examples are given in (8.24).

(8.24a)  **Se        lu** tenhu        que     dizé. (F28:364)
         IO.3s it have-1SG     COMP tell
         'I have to tell it to her.'

(8.24b)  Arranjou        uma cordiom que **se lhu benderom**. (F86:196–197)
         arranged.3SG  an accordion that IO.3SG DO.3SG-it sold-3PL
         'He arranged an accordion that they sold to him.'

Yet another Spanish trait is the non-anaphoric use of *se* in an impersonal or passive construction or as an aspectual or emphatic marker, whereby *se* appears in pre-verbal position. This is commonly found in Barranquenho and illustrated by the example in (8.25). In the corresponding Portuguese construction, *se* would follow the verb.[14]

(8.25)  **Se    comia**    ali,  **se    tocaba**       zambomba. (F86:196)
        SE    eat-IMPER there SE    play-IMPER drum
        'They ate there, and they played drums.'

(8.26)  I     **se lhe       daba**        uma gorjeta para eli. (F57:142–143)
        and   SE IO.3s give-IMPER a     tip     for   him
        'And he was given a tip.'

---

[14] Regarding the different functions of non-anaphoric *se* in Spanish, see Clements 2006.

Leite de Vasconcelos (1955:39) mentions that this trait also appears in the Barranquenho texts he collected.

Another trait found in Barranquenho that is clearly Spanish is the argument structure of the *gustar*-type experience verbs. While in Portuguese the experiencer of *gostar* 'like' is coded as the subject of the sentence, in Spanish the experiencer is coded as the indirect object. Relevant examples are shown in (8.27), taken from the same Barranquenho speaker.

(8.27a)  **Eu gostaria** também    **de    falá**       um bocadinho milhó. (F52:291)
I would.like also     COMP speak-INF a little      better
'I would also like to speak a little bit better.'

(8.27b)  para eu fazé   uma coisa que    a mim tanto      **me gohtaba** (F52:76–78)
for  I  do-INFa    thing COMP to me  so.much me like-IMPER
'for me to do a thing that I like so much'

(8.27c)  A  primera beh  nãu le       guhtó muitu. (F19:113)
the first     time NEG IO.3SG liked  much
'The first time, he didn't like it much.'

We find both argument structures in Barranquenho, sometimes produced by one and the same speaker, such as in the examples in (8.27a, b). However, it is not necessarily the case that Spanish *gustar* has the experiencer IO and Portuguese *gostar* is found with an experiencer subject. Rather, it is more often the case that the form *gostar* (or *gohtar*) is found in both constructions.

One last phenomenon deserves mention as a distinctive trait of Barranquenho. The word *bueno* 'good' ([bueno] or [buenu] in Barranquenho) is a discourse filler, much like *well* is used in English. In (8.28), I give a set of examples taken from speakers of different sexes and ages. It is one of the only single Spanish words found in Barranquenho.

(8.28a)  I depoih disi,      buenu ehta mulhé  i    salta  ela asim. (M24:442)
and then said-1SG good   this woman and jumps she like.this
'And then I said, well, this woman here, and then she jumps like this.'

(8.28b)  Quandu eu ehtaba na      França dizia:        mete-te
when     I was     in-the  France say-IMPER    put-yourself
na       ehcola, buenu   que    não aprendeu    nem    o nomi.
(M64:101–102)
in-the school   good    COMP NEG learned-3SG not.even the name
'When I was in France, she said 'Get in school!' Well, she didn't even learn the name [of the school].'

(8.28c)  Um     assuntu meu    da     minha bida, não?
a       matter my     of-the my     life,  NEG
Buenu poi eu anti   moraba        nu    campu, purque  me pai
well     then I before live-IMPER   in-the country, because my parents
morabom         nu    campu e    fui    criada         nu campu.
(F33:71–72)
live-IMPER-PL in-the country and was-1SG raised-PPART in-the country
'An episode of mine from my life, right? Well then, before I used to live

in the country because my parents lived in the country and I was raised in
the country.'

(8.28d)  Já      não    me    lembru        comu é  esa  cantiga,
         anymore NEG  REFL  remember      how   is  that song
         tã bunita          que    é.      Buenu ali    tocabom
         so beautiful       COMP  is       good  there  play-IMPER-PL
         a       zambomba   se     bailaba.  (F86:205–206)
         the     drum       SE     dance-IMPER-SG
         'I don't remember anymore how that song goes, as beautiful as
         it is. Well, they played the drum there and there was dancing.'

To sum up this section, I have reviewed some of Barrenquenho's distinctive traits that make it different, especially from Portuguese. Naturally,
those traits represent Spanish influence, facilitated by the fact that this variety
is spoken on the border with Spain. The traits I have described and illustrated
are: the non-distinction of /b/ and /v/; the aspiration or deletion of syllable-
final -s; deletion of word-final -r, the 'estar verb + -ndu' construction for the
progressive instead of 'estar a + verb-INF'; indirect object doubling, as in le
conté a meu pai [lit. IO.3SG told-1SG to my father] 'I told my father'; pre-
placement instead of post-placement of indirect object clitics in main clauses;
double pronominalization following the Spanish model, as in i se lhe daba
uma gorjeta para eli [lit. and SE IO.3s give-IMPERF a tip for him] 'and he
was given a tip'; pre-placement of non-anaphoric se; the existence of the
dative experiencer construction gustar le a uno [lit. like-INF IO.3SG to one]
instead of the nominative experiencer construction gostar de [lit. like-INF
of]; and the existence of bueno 'good' as a discourse connector. All these
traits are traceable to Spanish.

## 8.4    Concluding remarks

From the historical overview, it is clear that Portuguese and Spanish in the
Barrancos area have been in contact for centuries. This means that although
Spanish has been the prestige variety and seems to still hold this role, there
has been a strong presence of stable bilingualism in Barrancos for some time,
well before Barrancos definitively and undisputedly became part of Portugal
at the beginning of the twentieth century, and quite possibly before it was first
made part of Portugal at the beginning of the nineteenth century.

The traits that define Barranquenho are notably the Spanish traits discussed
in section 8.3. The non-distinction of /b/ and /v/, the aspiration or deletion of
syllable-final -s, and deletion of word-final -r are clear indications that
Extremeño Spanish has had a major influence on Barranquenho. How would
such traits make their way into this variety of Portuguese? It seems likely that
they were carried into Portuguese by a population that was predominantly
Spanish-speaking who applied the same rules to Portuguese -s and -r that

apply in Extremeño Spanish. I submit that reducing the Portuguese vowel system from eight to five or doing away with Portuguese nasal phonemes could conceivably have impeded intelligibility. This may be a reason why the Spanish speakers of Barrancos who targeted Portuguese did not reduce the Portuguese vowel system or de-nasalize any vowels.

All other Barranquenho traits discussed in the previous section are those that do not undermine intelligibility: the '*estar* verb + -ndu' construction for the progressive, indirect object doubling, proclisis of indirect object clitics and non-anaphoric *se* in main clauses, double pronominalization, and the use of *gustar le a uno* are arguably traits that are close enough to their Portuguese counterpart construction not to cause any problems of intelligibility. In the case of a clear adoption of Spanish function words, the indirect object pronouns *le* and *les* are sufficiently close to their Portuguese counterparts not to create comprehension difficulties. Thus, not only do many Barranquenho speakers maintain the Spanish position of the indirect object pronouns but they also maintain the Spanish form *le* and *les*. Note, however, that – with the exception of *buenu* – Spanish-language vocabulary is rarely used in our corpus, and the occasions in which Spanish is used are not easily classified. They could be cases of code-switching (the more likely option) or cases of lexical transfer. The Spanish lexical items found in Barranquenho are discourse connectors. Apart from *buenu*, we find one example of Spanish *pueš* (< *pues*) 'well, then', but in the vast majority of cases Portuguese-derived *poi* (< *pois*) was used.

The creation of Barranquenho was in my view driven initially by predominantly Spanish-speaking people learning Portuguese because of socio-political circumstances. The maintenance and cultivation of Barranquenho are, I argue, cases of the development of a cultural identity sparked by these political circumstances. The Barranquenhos found that their cultural identity was neither entirely Spanish nor entirely Portuguese, but a hybrid of the two cultures. I hypothesize that, as consciousness of this fact began to grow, a linguistic identity began to take form among them. What we have today in Barrancos, I suggest, is a linguistic variety that solidified out of a cultural identity that was shaped by local and socio-political developments.

# 9 Contact, cognition, and speech community

In this volume, I have appealed to a usage-based model of grammar based on Emergent Grammar and the evolutionary model of language change (Croft 2000; Mufwene 2001) to help us understand the make-up of an array of contact language varieties involving Portuguese and/or Spanish. I started with the assumption that in an incipient pidgin, as well as in a full-fledged language, grammar develops in discourse. I have assumed, and in some cases demonstrated, that the frequency of use of linguistic features, both lexical and structural, is crucial to the development of a linguistic system. I have also assumed that the notion of speech community is key for understanding how language varieties become defined.

From an evolutionary perspective, the analogy of a language as a species allows us to view it as consisting of lexical and structural features (the analogues of genes in biology) and sets of such features (called a feature pool) that are used to encode human communication (communicative intercourse) within speech communities (a group routinely engaged in communicative intercourse in a given language). In these terms, the definition of what a language is becomes one based on the behaviour of individual human beings in a group rather than on any set of abstract linguistic traits. Thus, although the varieties spoken in Portugal and Brazil are quite different on various levels of grammar, both are considered varieties of Portuguese due to the close socio-political and cultural connections on many levels between the two countries.

Given that the emergence of contact language varieties involves language acquisition, both first and second, it is constrained by different types of bootstrapping (Bates and Goodman 1999) as well as by hypotheses such as the Primacy of Aspect Hypothesis and the Distribution Bias Hypothesis (Andersen 1983; Andersen and Shirai 1996). Thus, an immigrant learning a second language naturalistically would first learn lexical items before functional elements and would learn verbal forms as they are used with certain verbs (e.g., acquiring imperfect forms of stative verbs first).

Regarding the actual formation and development of linguistic structure, I have aligned myself with Goldberg's (1999) view that grammar formation is

affected by a combination of linguistic input, functional demands of communication, and general cognitive abilities and constraints. In acquiring or
building a grammar, both in L1 or L2 acquisition, I have followed Bates and
Goodman (1999) in assuming that we use several different types of bootstrapping, building more complex structures upon simpler, more basic
structures. This happens, I argue, not only in parent-to-offspring language
transmission, but – importantly – in adult-to-adult communication, as well.

Finally, in order to understand well the make-up of a contact variety, I have
noted that other factors must be taken into consideration, namely, (1) the
content and structural features of the languages involved in the contact
situation; (2) the number of languages and the number of speakers of each
language; (3) the relative markedness of the competing features in the feature
pool; (4) dominance relations among speakers of the different languages or
groups thereof; and (5) the parts of the feature pool that different speakers had
access to. A majority of these factors were operative in the formation of
central and western Iberian Romance.

While the Romanization of the Tartesian and Iberian populations on the
coasts of the peninsula took place relatively swiftly and completely, central
and western Iberia (inhabited by the Basques, Celtiberians, Lusitanians, and
Galicians) were colonized by Rome only after centuries of fighting. The
Roman population was small compared to the indigenous population in this
region, and the population resisted Romanization for a long period. In such a
demographic situation and taking into account the strong attitudes of the
indigenous population against assimilation, one would expect key substrate
features from the Celtic languages to find their way into the Romance variety
that was eventually adopted. This is indeed the case. We find good evidence
of the Celtic substrate in the phonology, morphology, and lexicon of both
Spanish and Portuguese (chapter 2). At the same time, a key development in
the history of the peninsula allows us to understand the relative uniformity of
the Latin variety that developed into Portuguese and Castilian. The Arabic
invasion in 711 altered the cultural reference points of the peninsula: the
once-influential southern centres (Mérida, Seville, Cartagena, and Lisbon)
and central/eastern centres (Toledo, Tarragona, and Zaragoza) were replaced
by the north-central and northern centres of Oviedo, León, Burgos,
Compostela, Braga, and Barcelona. This gave the area predominance in the
creation of the Iberian Romance varieties that spread southward (Tovar
1977:95).

The notion of speech community, understood here in a political sense,
accounts for the emergence of Portuguese and Castilian as languages. Speciation of these languages was aided greatly, I argue, by the formation of the
kingdoms of Portugal and Castile, which I believe led to the development of
self-awareness on the part of the people. In turn, this led the people to

recognize that what they spoke was different from the variety spoken by people in another kingdom, principality, or county. The speciation of Portuguese and Castilian as separate languages, then, was a function not primarily of linguistic differentiation, but rather of socio-political differentiation, a process that led to relative isolation in communicative intercourse (analogous to reproductive isolation in biology), which in turn led to greater linguistic differentiation among the two communities of speakers. As Castile incorporated Leon and Asturias, the corresponding dialects came to be of little consequence socio-politically. As Portugal and Castile re-conquered ever more territory and were poised to expel the Moors from the Iberian peninsula, they became two of the main power brokers there (along with Catalonia). At the same time, both powers were looking to expand to new regions. This rush to empire by Portugal and Spain set the stage for the introduction of their respective languages into Africa, Asia, and the Americas.

One of the consequences of the Portuguese and Castilian colonial expansion was the formation of Portuguese- and Spanish-based creoles. In southern Portugal in the second half of the fifteenth and early sixteenth centuries there was around a 10–15 per cent sub-Saharan black labourer population who spoke, arguably, immigrant Portuguese. In chapter 3, I noted the similarity between examples of immigrant speech today and Africans' speech portrayed in fifteenth- and sixteenth-century Portugal. Assuming a uniformitarian principle operating in naturalistic second language acquisition, I argued that such L2 varieties of African Portuguese were one integral part of the pidgin Portuguese that formed along the West African coast during that time, key features of which are also found in the Portuguese-based creoles. In my view, this suggests a developmental connection between L2 Portuguese, pidgin Portuguese, and certain tense–aspect features of the Portuguese-based creoles. To highlight this, I compared affixal tense–aspect markers in the Portuguese- and Spanish-based creoles. The presence of rare affixal morphology in Portuguese- and Spanish-based creoles is shown to be a function of the degree of homogeneity in each contact situation, as well as of the extent of subsequent contact between each creole and its corresponding lexifier language. The extent both of contact and of typological kinship among the languages in contact affected the nature of the linguistic feature pool available in the formation and development of the creoles in question and, consequently, affected the number and functions of affixes that found their way into the creoles.

To illustrate individual development in these creoles, I also examined the case-marking systems in the various creoles, noting that the African creoles tend to conform to Croft's (1991) Causal Order Hypothesis, whereas the Asian creoles violate it. I showed that these violations can be traced back to case-marking patterns in the substrate languages of the respective creoles.

In the study of non-creole contact varieties, I looked at immigrant varieties, namely, nineteenth-century bozal Spanish, nineteenth-century Chinese Coolie Spanish, and contemporary Chinese Immigrant Spanish, as well as two varieties that have developed in long-term language contact, Andean Spanish and Barranquenho.

I discussed bozal Spanish in nineteenth-century Cuba in light of a new set of documents: the correspondence between two philologists, Francis Lieber from the United States and José de la Luz Caballero from Cuba, which took place in 1835. From the correspondence, we obtain new insights into the linguistic nature of bozal Spanish. De la Luz's documentation and commentary suggest that in Cuba a Spanish-based creole never existed. This is supported by extensive demographic data I provide on the make-up of Cuban society from the 1770s to the 1840s. Nevertheless, questions still remain because it is unclear how familiar de la Luz was with all the plantations in Cuba at that time.

The linguistic evidence we have of nineteenth-century Chinese Coolie Spanish in Cuba, along with the demographic evidence, suggests that this is also a case of immigrant speech, though it has been called a pidgin. As indentured labourers, the Chinese 'coolies' would have spoken Chinese among themselves, most probably several dialects of Cantonese. While there is anecdotal evidence that Foreigner Talk was used in addressing Chinese coolies, there is no historical evidence that any re-structured variety of Spanish emerged from the communication between Cubans and Chinese. Given the facts that the practice of shipping labourers to Cuba from China lasted only around thirty years, that the interaction of the Chinese with other labourers was minimal, and that there is documentation that Chinese–English interpreters were used, the conditions were not conducive to the creation of a Chinese Pidgin Spanish variety. A comparison between Chinese Immigrant Spanish and Chinese Coolie Spanish revealed that the two varieties are highly similar and, at the same time, good examples of the 'basic variety' of naturalistically learned L2 Spanish (Klein and Perdue 1992).

Based on data collected from two Chinese native speakers living in Madrid, I analysed their naturalistically learned L2 Spanish, employing the lists of features developed by Shi (1991) for Chinese Pidgin English. The informants were chosen because they had learned Spanish naturalistically. Naturalistic L2 acquisition can be viewed as a first stage in the process of a shift to a target language, potentially culminating in the total abandonment of one's native language for the target language. Viewing cases of naturalistic L2 acquisition as a stage in the process of a potential language shift, individual solutions on the one hand, and group solutions on the other, can be seen as two points on a shift continuum. The individual solutions are best characterized as L2 varieties with differing degrees of stability. The group solutions are considered to be variably stable varieties among members of a group, i.e., pidgins or creoles.

Each of the two informants whose speech I studied has developed individual mappings from their native Chinese to the target language, Spanish. The lexical features of their speech correspond in large measure to the generally accepted mappings, but others are clearly innovations, such as cases of re-analysis. The verbal systems of our two informants turned out to be almost a direct reflection of the input they received, calculated using a corpus of oral Spanish from Spain. Moreover, there was evidence of the emergence of aspectual markers in the use of *ya* 'already' and the past participial ending *-do*. While the use of *ya* is reminiscent of the tense markers that emerged in some Portuguese-based creoles, that of *-do* seems to correlate fairly consistently with the use of the Chinese perfective marker *-le*. I also found that the copula *son* was selected due to its perceptual salience relative to the much more frequently used *es*. These varieties of Spanish are especially interesting because they reflect the processes through which speakers of one language acquire another that is typologically different and give us insights into the initial stages of pidginization, which allow us a window into the formation for Chinese Coolie Spanish, bozal Spanish, and African pidgin Portuguese.

In chapters 7 and 8, I discussed two contact language varieties with ecologies that were different from the ones studied so far: Andean Spanish and a Portuguese variety known as Barranquenho. Although from the eighteenth century onwards there was a move towards the Castilianization of the Andean region, the great disproportion in numbers between native Quechua and native Spanish speakers, as well as a colonization geared exclusively towards the exploitation of indigenous labour, made impossible the widespread inter-ethnic contact necessary for generalized bilingualism (Rivarola 1989:155, 160). Given these circumstances, approximative systems of Spanish in the region are common from very early on (Cerrón-Palomino 2003:135–170) and the type of bilingualism that has emerged reveals an extremely strong presence of Quechua-language features. We still find pervasive evidence of approximative L2 Spanish systems, as well as evidence of monolingual varieties of Andean Spanish that contain a high number of Quechua features. In a comparison of two monolingual varieties spoken in Mantaro Valley, Peru, and Salta, Argentina, my goal was to examine whether such monolingual Spanish-speaking communities exhibit some common traits. The comparison suggests that these monolingual Spanish varieties, independently of one another, developed many of the same or similar linguistic traits. A list of the common traits found is given in (7.37), repeated for convenience in (9.1) below.

(9.1a) confusion of *o–u* and *e–i*
(9.1b) monophthongization *ie* ==> *i*, *ue* ==> *u*
(9.1c) use of the locative *en* 'in' with motion verbs and adverbs
(9.1d) lack of gender and number agreement

(9.1e) generalization of the clitic *lo* as the object pronoun
(9.1f) use of the clitic *lo* to mark aspect (false pronominalization)
(9.1g) pervasive use of *diciendo* 'saying' and *haciendo* 'doing' in subordinate clause constructions with similar interpretations in both situations
(9.1h) strong presence of verb-final (as opposed to verb-initial) VPs
(9.1i) frequent use of diminutives and of *no más*

Such a list of traits common to both monolingual varieties could have emerged only if the demographic and socio-cultural conditions in the two areas were similar, that is, if in each case there was a strong presence of indigenous, Quechua-speaking people who provided an equally strong presence of Quechua features during the period of acquisition of Spanish. Moreover, in monolingual Mantaro Valley and Salta, the mappings could not have taken place without also assuming an extended period of bilingualism in which Quechua was the heavily dominant language in terms of number of speakers, if not in terms of relative prestige. In a personal communication (4 March 2007), Cerrón-Palomino stated that there are as yet no studies that treat the issue systematically. However, commenting on the situation in Peru, he observes that in the cities certain traits of Andean Spanish (e.g., vowel raising and lowering, non-standard use of the subjunctive) are perceived negatively, while others, such as non-standard person and number agreement, are hardly noticed and are accepted as normal. The point to be made here is that, as a community, Andean Spanish speakers have not developed a positive link between their cultural identity and the particular variety they speak.

In contrast, Barranquenho, a Portuguese variety spoken in Barrancos, Portugal, is a relatively unstudied variety, notwithstanding the monograph by Leite de Vasconcelos (1955) and the more recent work by Navas Sánchez-Élez (1992, 1994, 1996, 1997, 2001). The Barrancos situation is interesting because, over the centuries, the area has been claimed by both Portugal and Spain. It is documented that a majority of Barrancos inhabitants spoke Spanish natively in 1527 and Spanish has consistently been the prestige variety, but there had been a strong presence of stable bilingualism in Barrancos for a good while, well before Barrancos definitively and undisputedly became part of Portugal at the beginning of the twentieth century, and quite possibly before it was first made part of Portugal at the beginning of the nineteenth century.

First, there is a lack of Spanish influence evident in the Barranquenho vowel system, except the occasional monophthongization of certain Portuguese diphthongs. One would have expected a possible reduction of the Portuguese eight-vowel oral system by one or more, or the de-nasalization of nasalized vowel phonemes, but neither occurred. One possible reason for this could be intelligibility: doing away with Portuguese nasal phonemes or reducing the number of oral vowels would have impeded intelligibility.

The defining phonological traits of Barranquenho involve consonants and are also found in Extremeño Spanish: the aspiration or deletion of syllable-final -*s* and deletion of word-final -*r* are indications that Extremeño Spanish has had a major influence on the realization of Barranquenho consonants. Such traits would become part of Barranquenho through semi-shift. That is, they would be carried into Portuguese by a population that was predominantly Spanish-speaking who applied the same rules to Portuguese -*s* and -*r* that apply in Extremeño Spanish.

Like the phonological features of Barranquenho, its morphosyntactic traits would also have no effect on intelligibility: the *estar* verb + -*ndu* construction for the progressive, indirect object doubling, proclisis of indirect object clitics and non-anaphoric *se* in main clauses, double pronominalization, and the use of *gustar le a uno*. In the case of a clear adoption of a Spanish function word, the indirect object pronouns *le* and *les* are sufficiently close to their Portuguese counterparts, I argue, so as not to create problems for comprehension. Thus, not only do Barranquenho speakers maintain the Spanish position of the indirect object pronouns but they also maintain the Spanish form *le* and *les*. With regard to Spanish lexical items found in Barranquenho, note that with the exception of *buenu*, Spanish-language vocabulary is rarely used in Barranquenho, and the occasions where Spanish is used are instances of code-switching. The items I did find were discourse connectors. For example, there is one example of Spanish *pueš* (< *pues*) 'well, then', but in the vast majority of cases, Portuguese-derived *poi* (< *pois*) was used.

Above I argued that the emergence of Portuguese and Castilian as languages was furthered by the creation of the kingdoms of Portugal and Spain. The political boundary between the two kingdoms aided in the formation of a political identity on the part of the speakers of each kingdom, as well as creation of cultural expressions such as literature, etc., in the respective languages. In the case of Barranquenho, Leite de Vasconcelos (1955) noted that Barranquenhos saw themselves as neither Spanish nor Portuguese, but had developed a unique identity. In interviews with the informants, some expressed that they are definitely Portuguese, but those same informants also defended the Barranquenhos' right to obtaining an exception from the national parliament so they could continue with the recently outlawed practice in Portugal of killing bulls in bull-fights, a centuries-old tradition still followed in Spain. Thus, it is relatively safe to say that the creation of Barranquenho was driven initially by predominantly Spanish-speaking people learning Portuguese because of socio-political circumstances. However, the maintenance and cultivation of Barranquenho are cases of the development of a cultural identity, that is, the awareness on the part of Barrancos's inhabitants that they are culturally neither entirely Spanish nor entirely Portuguese but a hybrid of the two. As consciousness of this fact began to grow, I suggest that a linguistic identity began to take form. The linguistic community in Barrancos today developed from a cultural identity, which itself was shaped by local and socio-political developments.

The contact varieties of Portuguese and Spanish I have examined in this volume have been shaped by demographics and by prestige, as well as by general cognitive abilities and constraints, and by the dynamics of speech community.

# Appendix A: José de la Luz Caballero's responses to Francis Lieber's eighteen questions (original and translation)

### Original

Con sumo gusto contesto a las preguntas del Dr. *Francisco Lieber*, asi por el asunto sobre que versan, como porque tuve a placer de tratarle en Boston 'at Mrs. Kekam's', en cuyo *boarding-house* vivimos junto en agosto y setiembre de 1828.

   Casi todas las preguntas, y especialmente las 12 primeras, descansan en el supuesto de que existe un dialecto criollo en la isla de Cuba distinto de la lengua española, así como hay criollo francés y otros dialectos de las demás lenguas europeas en las colonias de otras naciones. Pero no es así, y diré sencillamente lo único que hay en el particular. Los africanos corrumpen la lengua cada uno a su modo, y esta corrupción consiste principalmente en el modo de pronunciar, lo que, como bien claro se ve, no constituye un dialecto especial, al que podamos darle el nombre de criollo. Esto es tan cierto, cuanto que a los blancos nos es más fácil entender a unos negros más que otros, y a los pertenecientes a una nación más que a los de otra: los *congos* v.g. se esplican y pronuncian con más claridad que los *carabalíes*; pero siempre es la misma lengua española la que todos hablan, aunque estropeándola casi individualmente diríamos. Sin embargo, hay algunos modos uniformes de corromperla, y esto es natural, entre todos ellos particularmente en el campo, no solo alterando uniformemente la pronunciación de ciertas voces, sino también dándoles una significación diferente a veces y otras análoga a la genuina. Por ejemplo, es muy comun que digan *dos viages* en lugar de *dos veces*. Hay otra causa especial para que los españoles-europeos no los puedan entender con tanta facilidad como nosotros, y es el *tono* o *acento* peculiar con que pronuncian. Los estranjeros que hablan la lengua inglesa podrán graduar el valor de esta observación; pues a ellos les debe constar que si no dan a las palabras la *entonación* que acostumbran los ingleses, aun cuando pronuncien bien cada letra, y hasta cada sílaba, a duras penas son entendidos, si es que lo son. Con este motivo no puedo menos de recordar un criado portugués que conocí en Washington, el cual rara era la palabra inglesa que pronunciaba con exactitud, particularmente en las finales, pero daba tan bien el *énfasis* y los *cortes* del idioma, que de lejos le tomábamos por inglés, y de cerca era muy bien entendido.

Hay además otros signos o palabras que son un lenguaje universal para los negros recien-llegados de Africa (bozales), sea cual fuere la nación a que pertenezcan; y esta circumstancia convence evidentemente que se las enseñan en la *factorías*; y tanto más claro, cuanto que recaen sobre las más urgentes necesidades y objetos más precisos. Es de advertir que las más de ellas son conocidamente de origen inglés, y repitiendo la palabra de la raíz; cosa muy natural, pues todos repetimos cuando no nos entienden. Tales son *lúcu lúcu* (look, look) 'ver, mirar'; *guashi guashi* (wash, wash) 'lavarse', y otras a este tenor. Pero este vocabulario no pasa de unas cuantas palabras indispensables para entenderse con los negros en la navegación y en el barracón hasta que se venden.

En cuanto al idioma *provincial* de los blancos del país, no consiste mas que en algunas espresiones y palabras sueltas, tanto que no podria escribirse, no diré un libro, pero sí una nota de cuatro renglones con palabras y frases todas *criollas* o *provinciales*. Sin embargo, las hay en mucho número, y pueden clasificarse en los términos siguientes:

1. algunas, aunque poquísimas comunes a toda la América española.
2. otras a la isla entera
3. otras peculiares a algunos distritos
4. otras, que siendo voces muy españoles se aplican indebidamente a otros objetos, como sucede en la Habana y aun en general en todos los puertos de mar de la Península, donde es muy comun emplear voces marinas para objetos familiares. Así decimos *botar* en lugar de *arrojar*, aunque conocemos y usamos por supuesto una voz tan comun como es *arrojar*.
5. otras que siendo también españoles, y no marinas, las empleamos en distinta acepción: así aquí entendemos generalmente por *majadero* un hombre molesto ('a troublesome fellow') cuando en rigor es un *zopenco* ('a dunce').
6. otras voces hay enteramente criollas, como que representan objetos peculiares al país, y por lo mismo no tienen equivalente en español. Y otras finalmente que son *sinónimos* de las voces españoles.

Muy a los principios de establecida la sociedad patriótica de la Habana, por los años de 1794 o '95, se empezaron a recoger las palabras y espresiones provinciales, a instancias de un distinguido socio eclesiástico. Pero hasta el año del 1813, no vio la luz pública una pequeña colección de ellas, que como muestra, publicó el Sr Dr José Castillo en uno de los números del periódico titulado el *Patriota Americano* del cual era uno de los redactores. Posteriormente, la sección de educación de la sociedad patriótica se ha ocupado y se ocupa en enriquecer este *diccionario provincial* para publicarlo algún día.

Pero aun cuando se publique, en nada puede servir para el objeto de las investigaciones de nuestro apreciable filantropista el Dr Lieber. Pues siendo ese vocabulario de la lengua de los blancos, en nada puede promover la instrucción religiosa de los negros. Sin embargo, si gusta otro tor[1], como objeto de curiosidad, o para otra especie de trabajos, supuesto que él es también gran filólogo, puedo ocuparme en buscarle alguna copia o ejemplar de lo que haya en el particular.

La única tentativa que se ha hecho de esplicar la doctrina cristiana a los africanos en la misma lengua española corrompida, y con símiles, y en un estilo más a su alcance (sobre todo al de los del campo, naturalmente más atrasados) fue acometida en un cateqismo en forma de diálogo que para el uso de los curas y capellanes del campo, compuso hace más de 30 años un benemérito eclesiástico que también había ejercido el ministerio, y se publicó desde entonces. Pero este libro es tan raro, que la mayor parte, aun de los que debían saberlo, ignoran su existencia, y muy pocos lo poseen. Yo mismo, que soy tan buscador en este género, no lo vine a conocer hasta ahora dos años. Escusaré hablar de su mérito o demérito, porque enviaré un ejemplar al mismo Dr Lieber, tan luego como pueda ir a mi casa, pues actualmente me hallo de temporada en el cerro, a una legua de la ciudad, y este papel, como se echará de ver así en su alma como en su cuerpo, va más que de prisa, por salir mañana un buque para Nueva York, según se me aseguran y no quiero perder la ocasión.

Únicamente advertiré que es costumbre que los curas y capellanes antes de *confesar* y *dar la comunión* a los negros, les espliquen el dogma y la moral de un modo que esté a su alcance, y por consiguiente usando un lenguaje corrompido. En cuanto a predicar, siempre se hace en lengua castiza española, bien que los negros del campo poco o nada oyen predicar, pues el precepto del domingo se limita a oír misa o rezar el rosario. Y respecto a los negros de las ciudades, que sí oyen muchas sermones, esas las entienden muy bien, y aun mejor de lo que algunos blanco pudieran imaginarse.

**Translation**

With great pleasure, I answer the questions of Dr Francisco Lieber, because of the issue they deal with, and also because I had the pleasure to make his acquaintance in Boston, at Mrs Lekam's, in whose *boarding house* we lived together in August and September of 1828.

---

[1] This is an abbreviation, which I have not been able to decipher.

Almost all of the questions, and especially the first twelve, rest on the
assumption that there exists a creole dialect on the island of Cuba different
from the Spanish language, just as [we find a] French creole and other dialects
of the rest of the European languages in the colonies of other nations. But
this is not the case, and I will simply tell about the only thing there is in this
respect. The Africans corrupt the language, each in their own way, and this
corruption primarily consists in pronunciation, which, as can be clearly seen,
does not constitute a special dialect which we can call by the name *creole*.
This is true, given that we whites understand some blacks more easily than we
do other blacks, [just as we understand] people coming from a certain country
better than we do people from another [country]. The Congos, for example,
make themselves understood and pronounce with more clarity than do the
Carabalíes.[2] But it is always the same Spanish language that they speak,
although they mangle it, almost individually, we should say. However, there
are some uniform ways of corrupting it, and this is natural, among all blacks,
particularly in the countryside; not only do they alter the pronunciation of
certain words uniformly, but they also sometimes give [certain words] a
different meaning, and other times [give them] a meaning analogous to the
genuine one. For example, it is rather common for them to say *dos viages*
'two trips' instead of *dos veces* 'two times'. There is another special reason
why the European Spaniards cannot understand them as easily as we [Cubans]
can, which involves the tone or peculiar accent with which they pronounce.
The foreigners that speak the English language will be able to gauge the value
of this observation, since it is clear to them that if they do not give their words
the intonation that the English are used to, even though they may pronounce
each letter and even each syllable correctly, they will hardly be understood, if
they are at all. In light of this issue, I cannot but remember a Portuguese
servant that I met in Washington, who rarely if ever pronounced any English
word accurately, particularly the ends of them, but he would get the emphasis
and pauses of the language so well that at a distance we took him for an
Englishman, and up close he was understood very well.

In addition, there are other signs or words that are a universal language to
the people recently arrived from Africa (*bozales*),[3] regardless of the country

[2] The Carabalíes are originally from the Nigerian delta area.
[3] The parentheses around *bozales* is in the original. This makes evident de la Luz's understanding of the term *bozal* as a recently arrived African. Interestingly, we find among Lieber's
unpublished papers at the Huntington Library, San Marino, CA, a clear explanation of the term.
In 1854–55, Lieber began to compile entries for a "people's dictionary of knowledge" that was
never completed. Therein we find an entry for *bozal* meant for the dictionary, which reads
'*Bozal* is the name given to native Africans in the Spanish West Indies. The term is more used
when lately imported negros are spoken of, and we believe that *bozal* has come to be
understood as signifying fresh Africans, as it were. We have not been able to ascertain the
origin of the word, and were frequently told in the West Indies that it is of African origin.'

they belong to; and this circumstance clearly convinces [us/me] evidently that they are taught them [i.e., words] in the *factorías* [trading posts/slave way-stations]. This is all the clearer when the words refer to the most urgent needs and the most precise objects. It is worth noting that the majority of them are known to be of English origin, and repeating the words of the root, a very natural thing [to do], since all of us repeat when people do not understand us. Such are *lúcu lúcu* (look, look) 'see, look', *guashi guashi* (wash, wash) 'wash (oneself)', and others in a similar vein. But this vocabulary is no larger than a few indispensable words to communicate with the blacks during the sea journey and in the *barracon* [where they are held] until they are sold.

With regard to the local language of the whites of the country [Cuba], it merely consists of some expressions, and scattered words, so few that one could neither write a book [about them] nor a four-line note [entirely] with creole or local words and sentences. However, there are numerous words that can be classified according to the following categories: 1st, some (although very few) common to all of Spanish America; 2nd, others to the whole island; 3rd, others particular to some districts; 4th, others which, despite being Spanish words, are applied improperly to other objects, as happens in Havana, and even generally in all the seaports of the peninsula, where it is very common to use maritime words for familiar objects; thus, we say *botar* 'throw' instead of *arrojar* 'throw', although we know and use, of course, a word as common as *arrojar*; 5th, others which, despite being Spanish as well, and non-maritime, we use in a different sense: thus, here we generally interpret *majadero* as an annoying man ('a troublesome fellow'), when, strictly speaking, he is a *zopenco* 'dunce'; 6th, other words are totally creole, since they represent objects peculiar to the country [Cuba] and thus lack an equivalent [word] in Spanish; and finally others that are synonymous with the Spanish words.

At the very beginning of the establishment of the patriotic society in Havana, in the year of 1794 or '95, words and expressions started being collected at the request of a distinguished member affiliated with the church. But a small collection of them was not made public until the year 1813 [when they were] published as a sample by Dr José del Castillo in one of the issues of the newspaper called *the Patriota Americano* the 'American Patriot', of which he was one of the editors. Later, the education section of the patriotic society undertook and is still undertaking the endeavour of enriching this provincial dictionary to publish it some day.

But even when it is published, it will serve no purpose related to the object of the investigations of our dear philanthropist, Dr Lieber, because, although

---

Corominas (1954) does not have an entry for *bozal*, though Moliner (1984) defines it thus: 'it [*bozal*] is used to denote blacks taken from their country' (my translation). The OED has no entry for *bozal*.

that vocabulary belongs to the language of the whites, it can in no way promote the religious instruction of the blacks. However, if you would like another ? [in the ms. the abbreviation *tor.* is found], as a curiosity, or for another type of work, given that he [Dr Lieber] is also a great philologist, I can set out to look for a copy of something on this particular topic.

The only attempt made to explain the Christian doctrine to the Africans in the same corrupt Spanish language, and with similes and in a style more within their grasp (especially, that of the people in the countryside, who are naturally more backward) was undertaken in a catechism in the form of dialogue, which, for the use of the priests and chaplains in the countryside, was composed more than thirty years ago by a distinguished clergyman who had also practised the ministry. It has since been published, but this book is so rarely found that the majority [of people], even those who should know of it, are unaware of its existence, and very few own it. Even I, who am so fond of ferreting out publications about this discipline, did not happen upon it until two years ago. I will decline to talk about its merit or demerit, because I will send a copy to Dr Lieber himself, as soon as I can go to my house, for currently I am temporarily in the hills, a league away from town, and this piece of [writing] paper, as can be perceived in its body as well as in its soul, is going too fast because a boat is leaving for New York tomorrow, as I have been assured, and I do not want to lose the opportunity [to send this letter on the boat].

I will only mention that it is customary for priests and chaplains, before hearing confession from and giving out communion to blacks, to explain the doctrine and morals to them [the Africans] in a way that is within their reach, that is, by using a corrupt language [variety]. With respect to preaching, it is always done in the authentic Spanish language. Nevertheless, the blacks in the countryside hardly ever hear any preaching if at all, because their obligations on Sunday are restricted to hearing Mass or praying the Rosary. With regard to the blacks in the towns, who do hear lots of sermons, they understand them very well, and even better than some whites can imagine.

# Appendix B: José de la Luz Caballero's commentary on the *Catequismo* (original and translation)

### Original

José de la Luz's Commentary on the Catequismo, sent to Francis Lieber

Como un estrangero por mas instruido que esté en la lengua española puede necesitar alguna clave para inteligencia del *cateqismo acomodado á la capacidad de los negros bozales* (impreso en la Habana desde el año de 1796, como se vé al final de la pagina 13, y reimpreso en 1818), me ha parecido conveniente acompañar el exemplar que envio al D$^r$ Fran$^{co}$ Lieber (de Filadelfia) con las siguientes indicaciones que serviran tambien de parte de respuesta á la que yá di á las preguntas que se sirvió dirijirme el mes ántes pasado.

1$^a$ Este libro se encamina directamente no á los negros, sino á los capellanes ó maestros de los negros en la doctrina cristiana. Asi és que se ponen varias ampliaciones, ejemplos, y similes de una misma idea, para que el maestro las use todas, ó escoja entre ellas, segun las circunstancias. De donde se infiere que son mas bien *ideas* que no *palabras* al alcance de los africanos, como que no existe *dialecto criollo* general, ni particular propiamente tal. Asi és que el capellan ó confesor imitará mas en la pronunciacion aquel modo especial de corromper la lengua que tiene cada casta, segun sea la que tenga que catequizar.

2$^a$ Sin embargo, como ya dije en mi respuesta, hay algunos modos de corromper el idioma empleado generalmente por todos los bozales, pero estos se refieren mas bien á las construcciones que no á la pronunciación; y esos módismos son precisamente los que se usan en el presente libro: he aqui los mas principales. 1° Emplear el adjetivo en lugar de sustantivo: v.g. 'Dios, no habla *mentiroso*' (pag$^a$ 46, linea 6) en lugar de *mentira*; 'no tiene enfermo'; en lugar de 'no tiene *enfermedad*' : 2° Es muy frecuente en ellos emplear el plural por singular en los verbos, particularmente en el verbo *ser*: exemplo en la linea siguiente '*Son verdad*' en lugar de *és-* y 3° ahi mismo se advertirá otro modismo, que és repetir la palabra *verdad*, para indicar que una cosa és de *veras*, que no se *engaña*, y en general se repite para dar mas fuerza. 4° suprimir el articulo en el acusativo: v.g. 'Si ustedes miran huevo', en lugar de *un* huevo ó *el* huevo, y tambien á veces en el nominativo. 5° No variar el adjetivo, como en ingles, cosa que es lo mas natural: asi dice 'mismo muger', v.g., en lugar de '*misma*', 6° poner en el verbo la tercera persona en vez de la primera v.g. '*yo tiene dinero*' en lugar de *yo tengo*. 7° Igualmente esta tercera persona en lugar de infinitivo v.g. 'yo quiere *compra*' en vez de '*comprar*' 8° á veces tampoco declinan los pronombres personales asi es que muy amenudo se hallará en el cateqismo *yo* en lugar de *me* ó *mi*. 9° Con mucha frecuencia suprimen tambien las preposiciones y asi se verá v.g. 'no está barriga de su madre' en lugar de *en la* barriga etc. 10° Repiten los negros casi siempre la negativa asi dicen v.g. 'no va á juntar no' 'no va á salir no' 11°. Ponen tambien el adverbio en lugar del adjetivo, v.g. 'hizo *malo* en lugar de *mal*'.[1] 12° usan el adjetivo negativo *ninguno* muy á menudo en lugar de 'no, nada, nada absolutamente' (nothing at all, by no means). Ejemplo del mismo cateqismo '¿Puede la yegua ir al cielo?' '*Ninguno*'. 'El no entiende *ninguno*', en lugar de 'no entiende *nada*'. 13° Los negros es decir los de campo apenas ó nunca usan la condicional *si*, y en su lugar proponen simplemente la condicion sin particula: v.g. 'hombre va á luchar, el no tiene fuerzas, el se cae' y asi se remedian repitiendo el pronombre.

He aqui clasificadas todas las corrupciones que se emplean en este libro pertenecientes al numero de aquellas que hacen generalmente todos los negros. Mas como esta sola clave no bastaría para la inteligencia del librejo, descendere á formar una especie de catálogo esplicativo de aquellas voces y espresiones usadas en él, y con tanta mas razon cuanto semejantes pormenores no dejan de ofrecer alguna corta luz p[a] entender nuestros usos y costumbres. No seguire un orden alfabetico, por que sobre no sér necesario, pediria mas vagar; y asi me contentare con ir apuntando las palabras en el mismo orden que ocurren en la obrita.

A la pagina 46, al fin se usa *viento* en lugar de *aire*; locucion no solo de los negros, sino de nuestro vulgo aqui y en España; y conversion muy natural pues el viento es para ellos lo que hace sensible el aire.

A pagina 48 muy amenudo se verá usado *mas que* en lugar de *aunque* y aunque es tan castizo el uno como el otro, sin embargo nuestro pueblo de todos colores prefiere siempre el primero.

Pagina 49 y en otros muchos lugares – se emplea la voz *candela* en lugar de *fuego*, y es un *provincialismo* (Entiendase que siempre que digo *provincialismo*, ó voz *provincial* me contraigo á expresiones empleadas por los *criollos*, esto es todos los hijos del pais sean blancos o negros pues hay voces solo comunes entre los negros) contrayendonos á la que nos ocupa la voz *candela* es muy castiza pero no en significacion de *fuego*, sino de *vela*, o *luz*

---

[1] Based on the example given, de la Luz probably meant that the blacks often used the adjectival instead of the adverbial form.

*encendida*; y he aquí según dije en mi primera respuesta al D<sup>r</sup> Lieber, como hay provincialismos que solo consisten en significación y no en la espresion.

A la pagina 50 al fin: *aguacate* nombre de una fruta de las antillas: los franceses la llaman *avocat*.

Pagina 52 linea 5<sup>a</sup> y en varios lugares: se usa la palabra *gente* en lugar de una *persona*, cuando en rigor gente (people) és siempre colectivo, y es modismo no solo de los negros, sino del pueblo muy bajo.

*Ninguna pasa á la otra*, esto es, *escede*, ó és *superior*: es una frase que aunque de negros es castiza y solo mas material.

*Tu hablas derecho* se parece mucho á la de *you are right*, y equivale á *Ud. tiene razon*. No es provincial sino esclusiva de los negros.

Pagina 56 *Cuadrilla*, voz muy española la emplean los negros tambien como sinónima de *casta, especie, clase*, sin que por eso dejen de darle su escepcion verdadera. Sin duda como á ellos para todos los trabajos los distribuyen por *cuadrilla*, han tomado de ahi el tipo para decir *clasificacion*.

Pagina 61 *Chapeador*: voz provincial derivada de *chapear* tambien provincial; y significa segador ó cortador de malas hierbas.

Pagina 63 *Viages* en lugar de *veces*: es modismo muy negrero.

Pagina id: lo mismo lo es el siguiente *pasa* en lugar de *mas de*: v.g. *pasa ocho dias* en vez de 'mas de ocho dias'. Algo anglesado ó mejor dicho, muy natural en semejante modo de hablar: v.g. past two, past healing, etc.

Pagina 68 *Machetazo*: voz provincial, golpe dado con el *machete* que es el instrumento cortante con que los negros *chapean*.

Pagina 73 *Ya hay cuje*: es decir *castigo* pues *cuje* significa una cara delgada cortada de un arbol (ordinariamente de la *yaya* por su flexibilidad) con que son castigados los negros en las haciendas. De aqui se ha hecho provincial la palabra aplicandola á toda especia de *látigo delgado* y aun de una persona muy flaca y desmedrada se dice en el pais *que está como un cuje*.

Pagina 74 in fine *Ahi está la tabla*: quiere decir 'pronto estará el castigo' pues para azotar á los negros se les aseguraba atandolos en una *tabla*; asi dar una tabla valia tanto como asegurar para azotar *mucho*, pues unos pocos azotes se pueden dár á un hombre *suelto* – Ya hoy no se dan *tablas*, pero en su lugar se dan *boca abajos*; es decir, se hace acostar al paciente *boca abajo*, y ó bien sugetandole otros negros, ó bien sin sujetarle, se le aplican los azotes.

Cruel es todabia el *boca abajo*; pero la tabla le escedia, toda vez que se ataba un hombre ex profeso para azotarle largamente. Al cabo tambien con el *boca abajo* es mas fácil cese el castigo tan luego como empieze á ceder la colera del Mayoral.

Ala pagina 81 in fine, *bote* del verbo *botar*: es voz marina, y en rigor significa 'echar un Buque al agua' (to launch); pero se usa muchisimo tanto aqui como en todos los puertos de mar españoles en la acepcion de *tirar, arrojar, echar, lanzar*, y tanto que hay hombres del pueblo que no entienden absolutamente cuando se les dice fué *lanzado* v.g. es necesario decirles fue *botado* de la casa, etc. En general (y és muy natural) en todos los puertos de mar se aplican voces maritimas á objetos terrestres, y las mas voces hasta se ignoran las voces que los representan.

A la pagina 82 *Cujazos* (esto és golpeo dado con el *cuje*, azotes).

Al renglon siguiente, asi como en otros muchos pasages de la obrita en la espresion de *malmandados* y varias de este tenor, se echará de ver la maestria con que el autor imita el estilo de la gente del pais, aun emplean voces muy castizas: tal parece á ocasiones que dimos á una madre ó maestro reconvi- niendo á los chicos.

A la pagina 84 'De balde, de balde' frase muy favorita entre los negros, e indica lo que significa.

A la pagina 94 al fin del 1$^{er}$ parrafo '*Emburujar*': este verbo materialmente significa envolver, y asi como á este último se le da en el pais la acepcion de *embaucar, enredar*, etc. y és sumamente espresivo.

Pagina id = *Estancia*, que en español tiene una acepcion muy lata, en el pais se aplica especialmente á una pequeña hacienda de labranza (a farm).

Pagina id = 'No jaya su vegiga' Cualquier estrangero, y aun algunos peninsulares al leer esta frase 'no halla su vegiga' y particularmente y despues de decir *mete mano á la faldriquera*, creería cualquier cosa, ménos lo que en realidad es – Es costumbre en el pais, y mas especialmente en el campo, guardar el tabaco torcido (cigarros y en el pais tabacos) en grandes vegigas de buey ó vaca ahumadas y preparadas al efecto: nuestros *guagiros* (campesi- nos,) no solo guardan en ella el tabaco sino los chismes de encender lumbre (ó de sacar candela como se dice aqui) para estar fumando á cada rato y á dó quiera; y los negros no solo tabaco y chismes sino el dinero menudo (change) y cuantos cachibaches tienen: de modo que la *vegiga* es su verdadera bolsa y hasta su talega.

Al fin de la misma pagina 'se le espantó la yegua'. La frase es muy propia pues los negros mas tienen *yeguas* que *caballos* y no precisamente por que relinchen poco y otras cualidades que aprecian los arabes, sino por que les paren *potricos* y cuestan muy poco en comparación con los caballos.

Pagina 95 'Cuando se acabó de moler.' *Moler* quiere decir aqui *esprimir el jugo de la caña* de azúcar; y toda la frase indica la terminacion de la *molienda*, que dura ordinariamente de 6 á 7 meses, desde Novre ó Diciembre hasta mayo ó Junio (the crop in the sugar plantations).

En esa misma pagina se notará lo que llevo advertido en órden á suprimir particulas y aun verbos, necesarios para el regimen v.g. '¿tiempo ese de chapear que hice yo?'. En lugar de en ese tiempo, etc.[2]

---

[2] The sentence would, then, be ¿en ese tiempo de chapear, qué hice yo? 'During that time of weed cutting, what did I do?'

Pagina idem – *Manigua*: voz provincial que significa lo mismo que la española *matorral* ó *Bosque de yerbas*, y cuando mas de *arbustos*; que cortados sirven de combustible para *moler*, es decir para cocer el *zumo* de la caña ó *guarapo*.

Pagina 98 = 'Cañamazos.' El genero de que se hace el vestido á los negros (por que sale del *Cañamo*), y por conversion el vestido mismo, tanto que hasta la gente del campo suele decir *mis cañamazos* en lugar de mi ropa.

Pagina id. 'Mi amo' vocativo que usan, y repiten mucho los africanos, para dirijir la palabra, no solo á sus *amos*, sino á todo blanco.

Pagina 99 '*Zambumbía*': bebida fermentada dulzaina que se hace con la miel de purga (molasses) ó con el *guarapo* (jugo de caña), y és muy favorita de los negros, y aun de los blancos del pueblo; en términos de haber tiendas espresamente para su despacho y se llaman por eso *zambumberías*.

Pagina 102: Estar brabo: *provincialismo*, que vale tanto como estar *enfadado*.

Pagina 104, al fin 'Cara *lambido*' – corrupción del participio castellano *relamido*; y aun los blancos del pueblo dicen *relambido*.

Pagina 107 *majadero* está en lugar de *majaderia*. En buen castellano *majadero* quiere decir *zote* (a blochead [sic], a dunce), pero en el país se aplica esclusivamente á una persona molestadora, importuna o travieza (a troublesome fellow).

Pagina 108 *Jugamiento*, palabra inventada por el autor, siguiendo las analogias de las que inventan los negros – y equivale á *juguete*, cosa que *no es de veras* (not in good earnest).

Pagina id. '*Bujío* ó bohio' choza donde vive el negro hecha de *cujes* u cobijada con *guano* (palm-leaves). (In both Carolinas they call it *wigwam*, I think.)

Pagina 109 'Mi carabela' significa *compatriota*, ó por lo menos, y con mas propiedad, los que han venido de africa en el mismo buque- Es muy natural la etimologia, á mi entender, pues este és el nombre de unos buques, como Goletas que usaban antiguamente los españoles y portugueses, y en ellos se traerian los negros al principio ¿Quien no sabe que Cristobal Colon vino en sus tres Carabelas á descubrir el nuevo mundo? Advierto que despues en varios pasages de la obrita está mal escrita la palabra; pues ponen calavera (skull) en lugar de Carabela.

Pagina id in fine = 'Pasa mi cabeza' Aqui el verbo *pasar* significa claramente irse un *licor* á la cabeza

Pagina 113 'al castillo del Rey' No solo los negros sino el pueblo (particularmente entre la gente antigua) cuando hablan de las calles, caminos, plazas y obras públicas en general dicen siempre *del Rey*; y esta frase era muy natural, pues equivalia á *cosas públicas*, que no son de la propiedad de nadie, y son de todos.

Pagina 114 'Hacer misa' Es frase negrera en lugar de *decir misa.*

Pagina 119 'Quiebrahacha' madera de las mas sólidas que tenemos, como bien lo indica la composicion del nombre.

Pagina 131 'Comico' voz criolla ó mejor dicho voz de los *aborigenes,* como puede verlo el D^r Lieber en la obra de su famoso compatriota Adelung; titulada 'Vor Mithridatas, oder In allgemeinen Sprachkunde' y es de las poquisimas que se conservan – Significa un pequeño terreno cultivable (a little farm) y mas particularmente aquel pedacito que se señala á cada negro ordinariamente anexo á su *bujío.*

Pagina id in fine 'Fasajo' significa *carne salada,* y muy particularmente la de vaca que asi preparada se trae de Buenos Aires y Montevideo (donde tanto abundan las reses) para el consumo de los negros de campo: tiene un olor y sabor peculiar, y ellos gustan mucho de él. En el comercio corre con ese nombre.

Pagina 134 'No como mula' Esta es la comparacion de que siempre se valen los negros y gente del campo para designar un hombre de pocos alcances. Entre la gente culta es mas provincial la de *Caballo:* ambas son menos exactas que la española de burro, pues el caballo y la mula son animales de grande instinto.

Pagina 135. Los negros nunca dicen '*fumar tabaco*' (to smoke cigar) son chupar (to suck) y aun nuestra gente del pueblo, por que ellos en realidad no se contentan con *echar el humo,* sino que han de *chupar la hoja:* á bien que los anglo-americanos mascan como un demonte (chewing).

Pagina 136 'Para que compre tabaco' es el nombre que da nuestro pueblo á una *propina:* es ist Ihr Trinkgeld.

Pagina 145 = Contra-mayoral. Es un segundo del *mayoral* ó encargado del gobierno de la hacienda, cuya ocupacion es ordinariamente ir detrás de los negros para hacerlos trabajar. Por lo comun lo son los mismos negros (overseers), aunque hay fincas en que por lo menos hay algun blanco con esta comision.

Pagina 148 = 'Pasmo' corrupcion del nombre *espasmo,* aunque no significa el espasmo, que és solo un síntoma, sino la enfermedad del *tétanos,* por desgracia tan comun como funesta en el pais. Es voz provincial.

Pagina 154 = 'Hablar boca sucia' significa entre los negros, hablar obscenidades ó malas palabras, etc.

Pagina 155 'La cara amarrada' es frase muy expresiva, y no enteramente criolla, pues se usa tambien en algunos puntos de España, vale tanto como fruncido[3] – *he frowns.*

---

[3] The text is unclear here. The word appears to be written as *fronricid,* the nearest semantically is *fruncido* 'wrinkled'.

Pagina 159 'Ya guinea se acabó' Modo de decir muy propio de los negros siempre que muere o termina algo prefieren el verbo acabarse á todos los demas.

Descifradas ya las locuciones y palabras que pueden ofrecer algun estorbo para la inteligencia del cateqismo en cuestion, resta tan solo indicar la clave para la ortografia.

No hay mas diferencia entre la adoptada por el autor y la de la lengua española, que, la de escribir con j todas las voces que llevan h, pues los negros *aspiran* siempre esta letra como lo hace el pueblo aqui y en España, y aun antiguamente se aspiraba hasta por los buenos hablistas, como se evidencia por las obras de Fr Luis de Leon y de Granada y de otros clásicas; pero la aspiracion era mas suave que la de j española, la cual segun la pronuncian los castellanos és mas fuerte que la *ch* alemana, que es cuanto hay que decir. Es una pronunciacion verdaderamente arábiga. Solo los montañeses de Escocia (the highlanders) pronuncian esta letra mas guturalmente: casi podria decirse que no la aspiran solo con la *garganta*, sino desde el vientre.

Otra observacion y concluyo – Tambien se hallara escrito *haiga* en lugar de *haya* (subjuntivo del verbo haber): vicio de pronunciación comun también á los blancos del pais, y aun á los andaluces- como lo es igualmente el pronunciar la *ll* como *y*, cuando en castellano tiene el sonido de gl italiana; por lo se verá en el cateqismo empleada muy á menudo la *y* en lugar de *ll*. Y con esto me despido, por ahora del *Catequismo* y del D$^r$ Lieber; pero no de los vivos deseos de emplearme en su obsequio. Habana Septiembre 25 de 1835 = J de la Luz.

### Translation

However versed he may be in the Spanish language, a foreigner may need a key to understand the *Catechism Adapted to the Abilities of the Black Bozales* (printed in Havana since 1796, as can be seen at the end of page 13, and reprinted in 1818). Therefore, I thought it was convenient for me to attach to the copy I am sending to Dr Fran$^{co}$ Lieber (of Philadelphia) the following annotations, which will also serve as an additional reply to the answers I already provided regarding the questions he posed last month.

1st: This book is not squarely aimed at the blacks, but rather at the *capellanes* 'chaplains' or teachers of the blacks in the Christian doctrine. Thus, there are several elaborations, examples, and similes of the same idea so that the teachers may either use them all or choose among them, given the circumstances. From this it can be inferred that these are ideas, rather than words, within the Africans' range of comprehension, since there is neither dialect nor creole as such (whether general or particular). Therefore, the chaplain or priest confessor will imitate the pronunciation of that special way of corrupting the language that each caste has, depending on which caste he has to catechize.[4]

2nd: However, as I said in my reply, there are some ways of corrupting the language which are generally used by all *bozales*, but these ways deal with constructions, rather than pronunciation. And those idioms are precisely the ones that they use in the book. Here are some of the main ones:

    1st: use of the adjective instead of the noun, e.g., *Dios no habla mentiroso* 'God does not speak lying' (page 46, line 6) instead of *mentira* 'lie'; *no tiene enfermo* 'he doesn't have sick', instead of *no tiene enfermedad* 'he has no sickness';

    2nd: it is very frequent for them to use the plural instead of the singular with verbs, particularly with the verb *ser* 'be'. [There is an] example in the following line [of the *catequismo*]: ***son verdad*** [lit. 'they are true'] instead of *es* 'is'; and

    3rd: right there, one will note another idiom, which is to repeat the word *verdad* 'true' to indicate that something is genuine, not bogus, and generally it is repeated for emphasis.

    4th: doing away with the article in the accusative: e.g., *Si ustedes miran huevo* 'if you look at egg' instead of *un huevo* 'an egg' or *el huevo* 'the egg'; and sometimes in the nominative, too;

    5th: not varying [the form of] the adjective, as in English, which is quite normal. Thus, *mismo muger* [lit. same-MASC woman] instead of *misma muger* [lit. same-FEM woman];

    6th: putting a verb in the third instead of the first person, e.g., *yo tiene dinero* 'I has money' instead of *yo tengo* [lit. I have-1SG.PRES. INDIC] 'I have';

    7th: similarly, using this third person (form) in place of the infinitive, e.g., *yo quiere compra* [lit. I wants buys] instead of *comprar* 'to buy';

    8th: sometimes they do not decline the personal pronouns either. Thus, one often comes across *yo* 'I' in the Catechism instead of *me* 'me' [i.e., accusative/dative clitic] or *mi* 'me' [used after prepositions].

    9th: quite frequently they delete the prepositions and thus one will see *no está barriga de su madre* 's/he is not his/her mother's womb' instead of ***en** la barriga . . .* 'in his/her mother's womb';

---

[4] By caste, de la Luz most likely is referring to groups of Africans from different geographical regions, such as the Congos and the Carabalíes he referred to in his response to Lieber.

10th: the blacks almost always repeat the negative. Thus, they say *no va á juntar no* 's/he is not going to gather [the things]', *no va á salir no* 's/he is not going to leave';

11th: they also put the adverb in place of the adjective, e.g. *hizo malo* 's/he did bad' instead of *mal* 'badly';[5]

12th: they often use the negative adjective *ninguno* 'no, not any' instead of *no* 'no' *nada* 'nothing', *nada absolutamente* 'absolutely nothing'. An example from the Catechism itself: *Puede la yegua ir al cielo? **Ninguno**.* 'Can the mare go to heaven? No'; *El no entiende **ninguno*** 'he does not understand any/no (one)' instead of *no entiende nada* '. . . does not understand anything'.[6]

13th: The blacks, that is, those living in the countryside, hardly or never use the conditional *si* 'if'. In its place they simply state the condition without any particle, e.g., *hombre va á luchar, el no tiene fuerzas, el se cae* 'man goes to fight, he does not have any strength, he falls', and in this way the repetition of the pronoun compensates for the lack of the conditional particle.

Here, then, are classified all the corruptions used in this book, which are among those generally used by blacks. But since this key would not be enough to understand the book, I will set out to make an explanatory catalogue of those words and expressions used in it, and with good reason, since such details shed light in order to understand some uses and customs. I will not follow alphabetical order, because in addition to being unnecessary it would require further digressing. Thus, I will content myself with writing down the words in the same order in which they appear in the small book.

At the end of page 46, they use the word *viento* 'wind' instead of *aire* 'air', a use not only characteristic of the blacks, but also of the common people here and in Spain. It is also a very natural conversion, since to them the wind is what makes air perceptible.

On page 48, you will see very often that *mas que* 'more than' is used instead of *aunque* 'although'. And although one is as authentic as the other, our people, of all colours, always prefer the former.

Page 49, and in many other places, the word *candela* 'fire, candle' is used instead of *fuego* 'fire'. This is a provincialism, and by that I mean expressions

---

[5] In this statement, de la Luz seems to have switched 'adverb' with 'adjective'. It is more likely that he meant to say that the adjective was often used instead of the corresponding adverb.

[6] As alluded by de la Luz, *ningun(o)* is used to negate NPs, as in *ningún edificio fue construido este año* or *no fue construido ningún edificio este año* 'no building was built this year'. Note that if *ningún(o)* is not in sentence-initial position, there is an obligatory double negative in Spanish. If *ningun(o)* appears in sentence-initial position, there is no double negation. This negation pattern is common in all varieties of Spanish.

used by the 'criollos', that is, all the sons of the country, whether white or black, since there are words that are common only among the blacks. Continuing with the topic of our discussion, the word *candela* is very authentic, but not with the meaning of 'fire', but rather when it means 'candle' (*vela*) or 'light lit' (*luz encendida*). That is why, as I pointed out in my reply to Dr Lieber, it is an instance of a provincialism that only consists of meaning, and not of an expression.

At the end of page 50: *aguacate* 'avocado', the name of a fruit of the Antilles. The French call it *avocat*.

Page 52, line 5 and in several places: the word *gente* 'people' is used instead of *persona* 'person', when, strictly speaking, *gente* is always [a] collective [noun], and a idiom not only of blacks, but of the lower class.

*Ninguna pasa a la otra* 'not one passes the other', that is, 'exceeds' or 'is above/superior to'; it is an utterance that, albeit typical of blacks, is authentic, only longer.[7]

*Tu hablas derecho* [lit. '2SG.FAM talk-2SG straight/right'] seems much like the one [in English] *you are right*, and is equivalent to *Ud. tiene razón* [lit. '3SG.FAM. have-3SG reason'] 'you are right'. It is not provincial but, rather, restricted to blacks.

Page 56: *cuadrilla* 'team, gang, party', a very peninsular Spanish word, is used by the blacks as a synonym for *casta* 'caste', *especie* 'type', *clase* 'class, group'. They also use it in its true sense. Undoubtedly, since they [the blacks] are arranged in groups for their work, they have taken the meaning of 'classification' from that context.

Page 61: *chapeador*, a provincial word derived from *chapear*, equally provincial, and which means *segador* 'harvester', *cortador de malas yerbas* 'weed-cutter'.

Page 63: *viages* 'trips' instead of *veces* 'times' is an idiom very typical of blacks.

Same page: the same with regard to *pasa* 'she/he/it passes' in place of *mas de*, e.g., *pasa ocho dias* [lit. 'pass.3SG.PRES.INDIC eight days'] 'more than eight days' instead of *mas de ocho dias* 'more than eight days'. This is somewhat Anglicized, or rather very natural in a similar manner of speaking [in English], e.g., *past two*, *past healing*, and forth.

Page 68: *machetazo*, a provincial word meaning 'blow dealt with a machete', *machete* 'machete' being the cutting instrument with which the blacks harvest or remove weeds (i.e., *chapear* above).

Page 73: *ya hay cuje* [lit. already there is stick] 'there will be a whipping', that is *castigo* 'punishment', since *cuje* means a thin stick cut from a tree

---

[7] The entire sentence is: *es castiza y solo mas material*, literally '[it] is authentic and only more material'.

(normally the *yaya* tree, due its suppleness) with which the blacks in the *haciendas* 'farms' are punished. Given this context, the word has become provincial by referring to all types of thin whips, even with reference to a rather thin and emaciated person it can be said, *que está como un cuje* 's/he is like a thin whipping branch'.

At the end of page 74: *ahi está la tabla* 'there's the board' it means 'the punishment will come soon', since in order to whip the blacks they were tied to a *tabla* 'board'. Thus, *dar una tabla* 'to give a board' meant to whip heavily, since [only] a few strokes can be administered to a man untied. Nowadays boards are no longer used. However, in their place, *boca abajos* 'face downs' are used, in which the *paciente* 'person to be whipped' is laid down face down and given whip lashes while being restrained, or not, by other blacks.

The *boca abajo* 'face down' is still cruel, but the *tabla* 'board' was even crueller, since a man was tied on purpose to be flogged at length. Moreover, by using the 'face down', it is easier for the punishment to stop as soon as the ire of the foreman subsides.

At the end of page 81, *bote* from the verb *botar* 'throw' is a maritime word, which strictly means 'launch a boat into the water', but it is used frequently here [in Cuba] as well as in all the other Spanish maritime posts in the sense of 'throw, cast, launch', and so much that there are town men who do not understand at all when they are told *fué lanzado* 'she/he/it was thrown', i.e., it is necessary to tell them *fue botado de la casa* 'she/he/it was thrown out of the house'. In all the maritime posts, people generally use nautical terms (and this is very natural) when referring to objects on land; and most of the time they do not even know the words that originally represented those objects.

On page 82, *cujazos*, i.e., blows given with *cuje*, whip lashes.

On the next line, as well as in many other passages throughout the book, in the expression *malmandados* 'disobedient, unruly' and others in the same vein, one notices the mastery with which the author imitates the style of the people of the country, even though he uses rather authentic words. Sometimes it seems that we have encountered a mother or teacher reprimanding children.

On page 84, *de balde, de balde* 'free, for nothing', a favourite phrase among blacks, which is used with its usual meaning.

On page 94, at the end of the first paragraph: *emburujar*: This verb literally means 'wrap, envelop', which in this country has the meaning of *embaucar* 'dupe, swindle' or *enredar* 'implicate, confuse', and is highly expressive.

On the same page: *estancia* 'stay' has a very broad meaning in Spanish, but in this country it refers to a small farming estate (a farm).

On the same page: *no jaya su vegiga* 'he can't find his/her bladder': Any foreigner, and even some people from the [Iberian] peninsula, when reading the phrase *no halla su vegiga* 's/he can't find his/her bladder' and particularly after saying *mete mano a la faldriquera* 's/he puts her/his hand in the interior pouch' would be inclined to think anything, except what it really means. It is customary in this country, especially in the countryside, to keep twisted tobacco (cigarettes and, in this country, cigars) in smoked bladders of cows or oxen that are treated to serve such a purpose. Not only do our *guagiros* 'farmers, peasants', keep tobacco in it, but they also keep in it the gadgets for lighting up (or, as people say in this country, gadgets for *sacar candela* 'making fire') to be able to smoke anytime and wherever they want. In these *vegigas*, the blacks keep not only their tobacco and lighters, but also small change and all the knick-knacks they have. Therefore, the *vegiga* is truly their purse, and even their bag.

At the end of the same page: *se le espantó la yegua* 'the mare got scared away'. The phrase is very appropriate because the blacks have more mares than horses [stallions], not because they neigh little and have other qualities that the Arabs appreciate, but rather because they [the mares] bear them little colts, which cost very little in comparison with stallions.

Page 95: *Cuando se acabó de moler. Moler* [lit. 'grind'] means (here) 'press the juice out of the sugarcane'. So, the previous sentence means 'when pressing was finished'. The whole sentence refers to the end of the *molienda* 'cane pressing', normally lasting six or seven months, from November or December until May or June (the crop in the sugar plantations).

On the same page, one will notice what I have been mentioning with respect to the suppression of particles and even verbs necessary for the *regimen* [argument structure, i.e., the preposition required by a verb or the case the preposition licenses]: *tiempo ese de chapear que hice yo* 'that weed-cutting time, what was I doing?', instead of *en ese tiempo . . .* 'during that weed-cutting time . . .'

Same page: *manigua*: a provincial word that means the same as Spanish *matorral* 'bushes' or *bosque de yerbas* [lit. 'grass grove'] and also the shrubs that are cut that serve as fuel in the boiling of sugar cane juice, or *guarapo*.

Page 98: *cañamazos*: the fabric out of which the blacks' clothing is made (derived from *cáñamo* 'hemp'), and by extension, the clothes themselves; so much so that those living in the countryside normally say *mis cañamazos* 'my "hemps"' instead of *mi ropa* 'my clothes'.

Same page: *mi amo* 'my master', vocative that the Africans use and repeat a lot to address not only their masters, but also any white person.

Page 99: *zambumbía*: this is a sweet fermented drink made from molasses (*miel de purga*) or from sugarcane juice (*guarapo*), which is very popular among blacks and even whites from the village in the sense that there are shops expressly devoted to dispensing it. That is why these shops are called *zambumbierías* 'zambumbia shops'.

Page 102: *estar brabo* [modern Spanish *bravo*] 'be courageous, fierce': a provincialism equivalent to *estar enfadado* 'be angry'.

Page 104: at the end: *cara lambido* 'affected face': a corruption of the Castilian [Spanish] participle *relamido* 'affected [referring to behaviour]', 'prim and proper'. Even the white people from the village say *relambido*.[8]

Page 107: *majadero* is used instead of *majadería*. In good Castilian Spanish, *majadero* means means *zote* ('blockhead, dunce'), but in this country it refers exclusively to someone annoying, troublesome, or mischievous ('a troublesome fellow').

Page 108: *jugamiento*, a word made up by the author, following the analogies that the blacks make up. It is equivalent to *juguete* 'toy', a thing that is not true ('not in good earnest').

On the same page: *bujío* or *bohio* 'hut where the black person lives made out of *cujes* 'strips cut off the *yaya* tree' [see explanation above] and covered with *guano* 'palm leaves' ('in both Carolinas they call it *wigwam*, I think').

Page 109: *mi carabela* [lit. 'my caravel'] means 'compatriot', or at least, and more properly, those who have come from Africa on the same ship. In my view, the etymology is a very natural one, because that is the name given to the ships that look like schooners, which were formerly used by the Spanish and the Portuguese, and in which the blacks would be brought at the beginning. Who doesn't know that Christopher Columbus came in his three caravels to discover the New World? I must point out that in subsequent passages in the little book the words are incorrectly spelled, since it says *calavera* 'skull' instead of *carabela*.

Same page, at the end: *pasa mi cabeza* [lit. 'passes my head']. Here the verb *pasar* clearly refers to liquor going to the head.

Page 113: *al castillo de Rey* 'to the king's castle'. Not only the blacks but also the village people (particularly the elderly), when they talk about streets, paths, squares, and public works in general, always use *del Rey* 'of the king'. And this phrase was very natural, since it refers to those public things that are nobody's and everybody's.

Page 114: *hacer misa* 'do mass'. This phrase is used by blacks instead of *decir misa* 'say mass'.

Page 119: *quiebrahacha* 'axe-breaker'. One of the hardest woods we have, as the make-up of noun indicates.

Page 131: *cómico*, creole word or, rather, aboriginal word, as Dr Lieber can see in the work of his famous countryman Adelung entitled 'Vor Mithridatas, oder In allgemeinen Sprachkunde' ['Before Mithridatas, or in general

---

[8] Noteworthy here is that in *cara lambido* there is a mistake in agreement. It should be *cara lambida*. It is not clear whether this error is de la Luz's or that of the author of the Catechism, or whether it is supposed to reflect the speech of the black workers.

language learning']. It is one of the few words that have been preserved. It denotes a small stretch of land ('a little farm'), and more particularly, a small cultivable tract that is assigned to each black person, usually adjacent to his *bujío* 'dwelling place' (see above).

Same page, at the end: *fasajo*, this word means 'salted meat', particularly beef, which thus prepared is shipped from Buenos Aires and Montevideo (where cattle abound) for the consumption of the blacks in the countryside. It has a peculiar smell and taste. They like it. It goes by that name in the market.

Page 134: *No como mula* 'not like a mule'. This is the comparison used by the blacks and the countryside people when referring to a person of low intelligence. Among the educated people, this expression is more provincial than when used with *caballo* 'horse'. Both [expressions] are less accurate than Spanish *burro* 'donkey', since the horse and the mule are animals of great instinct.

Page 135: the blacks never say *fumar tabaco* ('smoke cigar'), but *chupar* 'suck', and even our village people say *chupar* [for 'smoke'] because they are not content with exhaling the smoke, but they must suck the leaf, although the Anglo-Americans chew [tobacco] like the devil ('chewing').

Page 136: *para que compre tabaco*, lit. 'so that s/he can buy tobacco' is the expression that our people give to 'tip' [for clarification, de la Luz adds the German expression *Es ist ihr Trinkgeld* lit. 'it is their drink money'].

Page 145: *contra-mayoral*: The person second to the *mayoral* 'farm manager, foreman', or the person in charge of running the *haciendas* 'farms'. His job is to go after the blacks and make them work. Normally, the *contra-mayorales* are black ('overseers'), but there are farms in which white people carry out this job.

Page 148: *pasmo* 'shock' a corruption of the noun *espasmo* 'spasm'. However, *pasmo* does not have the same meaning as *espasmo* 'spasm', which is just a symptom, but rather it refers to the disease of tetanus, which unfortunately is as terrible as it is rampant in the country.

Page 154: *hablar boca sucia* [lit. speak dirty mouth] means, among the blacks, to utter obscenities or bad words.

Page 155: *la cara amarrada* [lit. the tied face] is an expressive but not entirely creole phrase, since it is also used in some parts of Spain. It means 'frowned' ('he frowns').

Page 159: *ya guinea se acabó* [lit. already guinea finished], an expression very typical of the blacks. Every time something dies or ends, they prefer the verb *acabarse* 'end, finish' to all the others.

Having clarified the words and expressions that might hinder the understanding of the catechism in question, there only remains to indicate the key to the orthography.

There are no differences between [the spelling system] adopted by the author and that of the Spanish language, except for the use of the letter *j* in all those words containing *h*, since all the blacks always aspirate this letter, like the people here and in Spain do. Even in former times, *h* was aspirated even by those who spoke properly, as documented in the works of Fr Luis de León y de Granada, and other classical writers. However, the aspiration [of *h*] was softer than that of Castilian Spanish *j*, which, according to the pronunciation of Castilians, is stronger than German *ch*. That is all that needs to be said. It is a truly Arabic pronunciation. Only Scotland's Highlanders pronounce this letter more gutturally: it could almost be said that they do not pronounce it only in their throat, but from their abdomen.

One other observation and I will conclude: one also reads *haiga* instead of *haya* (subjunctive of the verb *haber*): a pronunciation vice also common among the whites of this country, and the Andalusians, like pronouncing *ll* as *y*, when in Castilian Spanish *ll* has the sound of the *gl* in Italian. Thus, in the Catechism *y* is widely written instead of *ll*. And with that, I bid farewell to the Catechism and to Dr Lieber, but not to my desire to be of service to him. Havana, 25 September 1835 – J. de la Luz

# Bibliography

Adelaar, K. A. and D. J. Prentice. 1996. Malay: its history, role and spread, in *Atlas of languages of intercultural communication in the Pacific, Asia, and the Americas*, vol. II.1, *Texts*, edited by Stephen A. Wurm, Peter Mühlhäusler, and Darrell T. Tryon. Berlin: Mouton de Gruyter.

Adelaar, Willem. 1992. Quechuan languages, in *International Encyclopedia of Linguistics*, edited by William Bright. 4 vols. Oxford: Oxford University Press, vol. III, 303–310.

Aimes, Hubert H. S. 1967. *A history of slavery in Cuba*. New York: Octagon.

Alameda, José and Fernando Cuetos. 1995. *Diccionario de frecuencias de las unidades lingüísticas del castellano*. 2 vols. Oviedo: Universidad de Oviedo Servicio de Publicaciones.

Alonso, Gladys and Ángel Luis Fernández. 1977. *Antología de lingüística cubana*. Havana: Editorial de Ciencias Sociales.

ANC (Art Nouveau Corporation). 1976. *Historia gráfica de Cuba: resumen del acontecer cubano en una introducción y 600 grabados*. Miami: Trade Litho.

Andersen, Roger W. (ed.). 1983. *Pidginization and creolization as language acquisition*. Rowley, MA: Newbury House.

1993. Four operating principles and input distribution as explanation for underdeveloped and mature morphological systems, in *Progression and regression in language*, edited by K. Hyltenstam and A. Viborg. New York: Cambridge University Press, 309–339.

Andersen, R. W. and Yasuhiro Shirai. 1996. 'The primacy of aspect in first- and second-language acquisition: the pidgin–creole connection', in *Handbook of second language acquisition*, edited by William C. Ritchie and Tej K. Bhatia. San Diego, CA: Academic Press, 527–570.

Andresen, Julie Tetel. 1990. *Linguistics in America 1769–1924: a critical history*. London: Routledge.

Aráoz, Dora and Américo Salas. 1993. *Gramática Quechua*. Cuzco: Instituto de Pastoral Andina.

Bachiller y Morales, Antonio. 1977 [1883]. Desfiguración á que está expuesto el idioma castellano al contacto y mezcla de las razas. *Revista de Cuba* 14.97–104 (reedited in Alonso and Fernández 1977: 105–111).

Baker, Philip. 1999. Pidginization. Message posted to CREOLIST mailing list, archived at listserv.linguistlist.org/archives/creolist.html (August 31).

Bakker, Peter. 1995. Pidgins, in *Pidgins and creoles*, edited by Jacques Arends, Pieter Muysken, and Norval Smith. Amsterdam: Benjamins, 25–39.

Baldinger, K. 1972. *La formación de los dominios lingüísticos en la península ibérica.* Madrid: Gredos.

Bartens, Angela. 1995. *Die iberoromanisch-basierten Kreolsprachen.* Frankfurt am Main: Peter Lang.

Batalha, Graciete Nogueira. 1988. *Glosário do dialecto macaense: notas linguísticas, etnográficas e folclóricas.* Macau: Instituto Cultural de Macau.

Bates, Elizabeth and Judith Goodman. 1997. On the inseparability of grammar and the lexicon: evidence from acquisition, aphasia and real-time processing. *Language and Cognitive Processes* 12(5).507–584.

Bates, Elizabeth, I. Bretherton, and L. Snyder. 1988. *From first words to grammar: individual differences and dissociable mechanisms.* New York: Cambridge University Press.

    1999. On the emergence of grammar from the lexicon, in *The emergence of language*, edited by Brian MacWhinney. Mahwah, NJ: Erlbaum, 29–79.

Baxter, Alan N. 1988. *A grammar of Kristang (Malacca Creole Portuguese).* Canberra: Pacific Linguistics Series B-No. 95.

Beltrán, J. and C. García. 2001. The Chinese community, in *Multilingualism in Spain*, edited by María Teresa Turell. Clevedon, UK: Multilingual Matters, 282–300.

Berntsen, Maxine and Jai Nimbkar. 1975. *A Marathi reference grammar.* Philadelphia: University of Pennsylvania Press.

Bickerton, Derek. 1977. Pidginization and creolization: language acquisition and language universals, in *Pidgin and creole linguistics*, edited by Albert Valdman. Bloomington: Indiana University Press, 49–69.

    2000. How protolanguage became language, in *The evolutionary emergence of language*, edited by Chris Knight, Michael Studdert-Kennedy, and James A. Hurford. Cambridge: Cambridge University Press, 264–284.

Blackshire-Belay, Carol. 1991. *Language contact: verb morphology in German of foreign workers.* Tübingen: Gunter Narr Verlag.

Bloom, L., K. Lifter, and J. Hafitz. 1980. Semantics of verbs and the development of verb inflection in child language. *Language* 56.386–412.

Bloomfield, Leonard. 1933. *Language.* New York: Holt, Rinehart, & Winston.

Boxer, Charles. 1975. *Women in Iberian Expansion Overseas, 1415–1815.* Oxford: Oxford University Press.

Bresnan, Joan. 1982. *The mental representation of grammatical relations.* Cambridge, MA: MIT Press.

    2001. *Lexical-functional syntax.* Malden, MA: Blackwell.

Brown, James H. 1995. *Macroecology.* Chicago: University of Chicago Press.

Bueno, Salvador. 1959. *Los mejores cuento cubanos*, vol. I. Havana: Segundo Festival del Libro Cubano.

Bybee, Joan. 1985. *Morphology.* Amsterdam: Benjamins.

Bybee, Joan and Elly Pardo. 1981. On lexical and morphological conditioning of alternations: a nonce-probe experiment with Spanish verbs. *Linguistics* 19.937–968.

Bybee, Joan, Revere Perkins, and William Pagliuca. 1994. *The evolution of grammar.* Chicago: University of Chicago Press.

Cabrera, Lydia. 1954. *El monte.* Havana: Ediciones CR.

Carpenter, Lawrence Kidd. 1982. Ecuadorian Quichua: descriptive sketch and variation. Unpublished University of Florida Ph.D dissertation.

Carranza Romero, Francisco. 1993. *Resultado lingüísticos del contacto quechua y español*. Trujillo, Peru: Editorial Libertad.

Castellanos, Jorge and Isabel Castellanos. 1992. *Cultura Afrocubana*, vol. III Miami: Ediciones Universal.

Catta Quelen, Javier. 1987. *Gramática del quichua ecuatoriano*. Quito: Ediciones Abya Yala.

*Censos nacionales de población, vivienda y agropecuario, 1961*. 1968. Dirección Nacional de Estadística y Censos. 23 vols. Lima. vol. III.

Censo nacional de población y vivienda. 1980. *Serie D, Población: total del país, por provincia, departamento y localidad*. Instituto Nacional de Estadística y Censos. Buenos Aires, Argentina.

Cerrón-Palomino, Rodolfo. 1987. *Lingüística quechua*. Cuzco: CERA Bartolomé de las Casas.

    2003. *Castellano andino: aspectos sociolingüísticos, pedagógicos, y gramaticales*. Lima: Fondo Editorial.

Chambers, J. L. and Peter Trudgill. 1980. *Dialectology*. Cambridge: Cambridge University Press.

Chaudenson, Robert. 1992. *Desîles, des hommes, des langues: essays sur la créolisation linguistique et culturelle*. Paris: L'Harmattan.

Chaunu, P. 1979. *European expansion in the later Middle Ages*. Amsterdam: North-Holland.

Clements, J. Clancy. 1990. Deletion as an indicator of SVO ==> SOV change. *Language Variation and Change* 2.103–133.

    1992a. On the origins of pidgin Portuguese. *Journal of Pidgin and Creole Languages* 7(1).75–92.

    1992b. Elements of resistance in contact-induced language change, in *Explanation in historical linguistics*, edited by G. Davis and G. Iverson. Amsterdam: Benjamins, 41–58.

    1993a. Rejoinder to Naro's 'Arguing about Arguin'. *Journal of Pidgin and Creole Languages* 8(1).119–124.

    1993b. A contribution by an old creole to the origins of Pidgin Portuguese, in *East meets West: selected proceedings of the 1990–91 meetings of the Society of Pidgin and Creole Languages*, edited by F. Byrne and J. Holm. Amsterdam: Benjamins, 321–331.

    1996. *The genesis of a language: the formation and development of Korlai Portuguese*. Amsterdam: Benjamins.

    2000. Evidência para a existência dum pidgin português asiático, in *Actas do Colóquio sobre Crioulos de Base Lexical Portuguesa*, edited by Ernesto D'Andrade, Dulce Pereira, and Maria Antónia Mota. Braga: Associação Portuguesa de Linguística, 185–200.

    2001. Word order shift and natural L2 acquisition in a Portuguese creole, in *Romance syntax, semantics and L2 acquisition*, edited by Caroline Wiltshire and Joaquim Camps. Amsterdam and Philadelphia: Benjamins, 73–87.

    2003a. The tense–aspect system in pidgins and naturalistically learned L2. *Studies in Second Language Acquisition* 25.245–281.

2003b. On classifying language-contact varieties, in *Selected Proceedings of the First Workshop on Spanish Sociolinguistics*, edited by Lotfi Sayahi. Somerville, MA: Cascadilla Press, 1–10.

2005. Immigrant speech, creoles, and the 'basic variety': a usage-based account of some traits in the Portuguese-based creoles. *Journal of Portuguese Linguistics* 4.149–165.

2006. Transitivity and Spanish non-anaphoric se, in *Functional approaches to Spanish syntax: lexical semantics, discourse, and transitivity*, edited by J. Clancy Clements and Jiyoung Yoon. London: Palgrave-Macmillan, 236–264.

In preparation. *The origin and evolution of Daman Creole Portuguese.*

Clements, J. Clancy and Stuart Davis. 2004. *Early documents on bozal Spanish: the correspondence between Francis Lieber and José de la Luz Caballero*. Manuscript. Indiana University, Bloomington.

Clements, J. Clancy and Andrew J. Koontz-Garboden. 2002. Two Indo-Portuguese creoles in contrast. *Journal of Pidgin and Creole Languages* 17(2).191–236.

Clements, J. Clancy and Gerardo Augusto Lorenzino. 2006. The contact situation in Barrancos, Portugal. Paper presented at the annual meeting of the Society for Pidgin and Creole Languages, Albuquerque, NM, 5–8 January.

Clements, J. Clancy and Ahmar Mahboob. 2000. *Wh*-words and question formation in pidgins/creole languages, in *Language change and language contact in pidgins and creoles*, edited by John McWhorter. Amsterdam: Benjamins, 459–497.

Clyne, M. 1968. Zum Pidgin-Deutsch der Gastarbeiter. *Zeitschrift für Mundartforschung* 1.40–55.

Comrie, Bernard. 1976. *Aspect*. Cambridge: Cambridge University Press.

Comrie, Bernard and Norval Smith, 1977. Lingua descriptive studies: questionnaire. *Lingua* 42.1–72.

Corbitt, Duvon Clough. 1971. *A study of the Chinese in Cuba, 1847–1947*. Wilmore, KY: Asbury College

Corominas, Joan. 1954. *Diccionario crítico etimológico de la lengua castellana*. Bern: Francke.

Croft, William. 1991. *Syntactic categories and grammatical relations: the cognitive organization of information*. Chicago: University of Chicago Press.

1998. Event structure in argument linking, in *The projection of arguments: lexical and compositional factors*, edited by Miriam Butt and Wilhelm Geuder. Stanford, CA: CSLI, 21–63.

2000. *Explaining language change: an evolutionary approach*. London: Longman.

Cunha, Celso and Luis F. Lindley Cintra. 1994. *Nova gramática do Português contemporâneo*.Tenth edition. Lisbon: João Sá da Costa.

Curchin, L. A. 1991. *Roman Spain: conquest and assimilation*. London: Routledge.

Curtin, Phillip. 1969. *The Atlantic slave trade: a census*. Madison: University of Wisconsin Press.

Da Azevedo Maia, Clarinda. 2001. Fronteras del español: aspectos históricos y sociolingüísticos del contacto con el portugués en la frontera territorial. Paper presented at the II Congreso Internacional de la Lengua Española: el español en la Sociedad de Información, organized by La Real Academia Española and Instituto Cervantes, Valladolid, 16–19 October.

Dalgado, Sebastião Rodolfo. 1906. Dialecto indo-português do Norte. *Revista Lusitana* 9.142–166, 193–228.

De Matos Coelho, Adelino. 1999. *O castelo de Noudar: fortaleza medieval*. Águeda: Câmara Municipal de Barrancos.

de Oliveira Marques, A. H. 1972. *História de Portugal: das origens às revoluções liberais*, vol. I. Lisbon: Edições Ágora.

1998. *Breve história de Portugal*. Third edition. Lisbon: Editorial Presença.

del Valle Rodas, Juana. 1998. Un uso particular de los gerundios diciendo y haciendo, in *Español y quechua en el noroeste argentino*, edited by Fernández Lávaque and del Valle Rodas, 97–108.

Denevan, William M. (ed.). 1992. *The native population of the Americas in 1492*. Madison: University of Wisconsin Press.

Deutsch, Karl W. 1968. The trend of European nationalism, in *Readings in the sociology of language*, edited by J. Fishman. The Hague: Mouton, 598–606.

Diamond, Jared. 1999. *Guns, germs, and steel: the fates of human societies*. New York: W. W. Norton.

Dozy, Reinhart and W. H. Engelman. 1965. *Glossaire des mots espagnols et portugais derivés de l'arabe*. Amsterdam: Oriental Press.

Dromi, Esther. 1987. *Early lexical development*. Cambridge: Cambridge University Press.

Dutton, T. 1997. Hiri Motu, in *Contact languages: a wider perspective*, edited by Sarah G. Thomason. Amsterdam: Benjamins, 9–43.

Erenchun, Felix. 1856–59. *Anales de la Isla de Cuba*. Havana: Imprenta La Habanera.

Escobar, Alberto. 1978. *Variaciones sociolingüísticas del castellano en el Perú*. Lima: Instituto de Estudios Peruanos.

Escobar, Anna María. 2000. *Contacto social y lingüístico: el español en contacto con el quechua en el Perú*. Lima: Fondo Editorial (Pontificia Universidad Católica del Perú).

Feijóo, Samuel (ed.). 1960. *Cuentos populares cubanos*. Santa Clara, Cuba: Departamento de Investigaciones Folklóricas, Universidad Central de Las Villas.

(ed.). 1965. *Cuentos populares cubanos: selección*. Havana: Bolsilibros Union.

Feke, Marilyn. 2004. Quechua to Spanish cross-linguistic influence among Cuzco Quechua–Spanish bilinguals: the case of epistemology. Unpublished University of Pittsburgh Ph.D dissertation. Pittsburgh, PA.

Ferguson, Charles. 1975. Towards a characterization of English foreigner talk. *Anthropological Linguistics* 17.1–14.

Ferguson, C. A. and C. DeBose. 1977. Simplified registers, broken language, and pidginization, in *Pidgin and creole linguistics*, edited by Albert Valdman. Bloomington: Indiana University Press, 99–125.

Fernández, Mauro. 2006. Sobre el origen de con en chabacano. Manuscript. Universidade da Coruña.

Fernández Lávaque, Ana María. 1998a. Neutralización de clíticos (I), in *Español y quechua en el noroeste argentino*, edited by Fernández Lávaque and del Valle Rodas, 75–82.

1998b. En + locativo: *Lo* aspectual, in *Español y quechua en el noroeste argentino*, edited by Fernández Lávaque and del Valle Rodas, 57–65.

1998c. El diminutivo, in *Español y quechua en el noroeste argentino*, edited by Fernández Lávaque and del Valle Rodas, 121–130.

Fernández Lávaque, Ana María and Juan del Valle Rodas (eds.). 1998. *Español y quechua en el noroeste argentino: contactos y transferencias*. Salta, Argentina: Consejo de Investigación, Universidad Nacional de Salta.

Ferraz, Luiz Ivens. 1979. *The creole of São Tomé*. Johannesburg: Witwatersrand University Press.

Forman, Michael Lawrence. 1972. Zamboangueño texts with grammatical analysis: a study of Philippine Creole Spanish. Unpublished Cornell University Ph.D dissertation. Ithaca, NY.

Freidel, Frank. 1947. *Francis Lieber: nineteenth-century liberal*. Baton Rouge: Louisiana State University Press.

Friederici, A. D. 1990. On the properties of cognitive modules. *Psychological Research* 52.175–80.

Futuyma, D. J. 1986. *Evolutionary biology*. Second edition. Sunderland, MA: Sinauer.

Gili Gaya, Samuel. 1960. *Funciones gramaticales en el habla infantil*. Rio Piedras: University of Puerto Rico Press.

1961. *Curso superior de sintaxis española*. Madrid: Vox.

Givón, T. 1984. *Syntax: a functional-typological introduction*, vol. I. Amsterdam: Benjamins.

1998. The functional approach to grammar, in *The new psychology of language: cognitive and functional approaches to language structure*, edited by Michael Tomasello. Mahwah, NJ: Lawrence Erlbaum, 41–66.

1999. Generativity and variation: the notion of 'rule of grammar' revisited, in *The emergence of language*, edited by Brian MacWhinney. Mahwah, NJ: Lawrence Erlbaum, 81–114.

Godinho, Vitorino Magalhães. 1981–1983. *Os descobrimentos e a economia mundial*. 4 vols. second edition. Lisbon: Editorial Presença.

Goldberg, A. E. 1995. *Constructions: a construction grammar approach to argument structure*. Chicago: University of Chicago Press.

1998. Patterns of experience in patterns of language, in *The new psychology of language: cognitive and functional approaches to language structure*, edited by Michael Tomasello. Mahwah, NJ: Lawrence Erlbaum, 203–219.

1999. The emergence of the semantics of argument structure constructions, in *The emergence of language*, edited by Brian MacWhinney. Mahwah, NJ: Lawrence Erlbaum, 197–212.

González, E. R. and R. Mellafe. 1965. La función de la familia en la historia social hispanoamericana colonial. *Asociación Internacional de Investigación Histórica* 8.57–71.

González, Paz. 2003. *Aspects or aspect: theory and applications of grammatical aspect in Spanish*. Utrecht: Netherlands Graduate School of Linguistics, Utrecht Institute of Linguistics OTS.

Goodman, Judith, H. C. Nusbaum, L. Lee, and K. Broihier. 1990. The effects of syntactic and discourse variables on the segmental intelligibility of speech, in *The proceedings of the 1990 International Conference on Spoken Language Processing*. Kobe: Acoustical Society of Japan, 393–396.

Grajeda Challco, Braulio and Orlando Vela Flores. 1976. *Gramática quechua*. Lima: Ediciones Instituto Superior de Quechua del Perú.

Granda, German. 1978. *Estudios lingüísticos hispánicos, afrohispánicos, y criollos*. Madrid: Gredos.

Günther, Wilfried. 1973. *Das portugiesische Kreolisch der Ilha do Príncipe*. Marburg an der Lahn: Selbstverlag.

Guy, Gregory. 1989. On the nature and origins of popular Brazilian Portuguese, in *Estudios sobre el español de América y lingüística afroamericana: Ponencias Presentadas en el 45 Congreso Internacional de Americanistas*. Bogota, Colombia: Instituto Caro y Cuevo, 227–245.

Haboud, Marleen. 1998. *Quichua y castellano en los Andes Ecuatorianos*. Quito: Ediciones Abya-Yala.

Hall, Robert. 1966. *Pidgin and creole language*. Ithaca, NY: Cornell University Press.

Hawkins, John. 1994. *A performance theory of order and constituency*. New York: Cambridge University Press.

Heath, Shirley Brice. 1982. American English: quest for a model, in *The other tongue: English across cultures*, edited by Braj Kachru. Urbana: University of Illinois Press, 237–249.

Heidelberger Forschungsprojekt, Pidgin-Deutsch. 1975. *Sprache und Kommunikation ausländischer Arbeiter*. Kronberg, Germany: Scriptor Verlag.

Herron, D. and Elizabeth Bates. 1997. Sentential and acoustic factors in the recognition of open- and closed-class categories. *Journal of Memory and Language* 37.217–239.

Hinnenkamp, Volker. 1984. Eye-witnessing pidginization? Structural and sociolinguistic aspects of German and Turkish foreigner talk, in *York papers in linguistics: papers from the York Creole Conference September 24–27, 1983*, edited by Mark Sebba and Loretto Todd. York, Canada: University of York, 153–166.

Holm, John A. 1988. *Pidgins and creoles*, vol. I, *Theory and structure*. New York: Cambridge University Press.

1989. *Pidgins and creoles*, vol. II, *Reference survey*. New York: Cambridge University Press.

Holm, John, *et al.* 1999. Copula patterns in Atlantic and non-Atlantic creoles, in *Creole genesis, attitudes and discourse*, edited by John R. Rickford and Suzanne Romaine. Amsterdam: Benjamins, 97–119.

Hopper, Paul. 1987. Emergent grammar, in *Papers of the 13th Annual Meeting, Berkeley Linguistic Society*. Berkeley: Berkeley Linguistic Society, 139–157.

1988. Emergent grammar and a priori grammar postulate, in *Linguistics in context*, edited by Deborah Tannen. Norwood, NJ: Ablex, 117–34.

1998. Emergent grammar, in *The new psychology of language: cognitive and functional approaches to language structure*, edited by Michael Tomasello. Mahwah, NJ: Lawrence Erlbaum, 155–175.

Hualde, José Ignacio, Antxon Olarrea, and Anna María Escobar. 2001. *Introducción a la lingüística hispánica*. Cambridge: Cambridge University Press.

Hull, David L. 1988. *Science as a process: an evolutionary account of the social and conceptual development of science*. Chicago: University of Chicago Press.

Ihalainen, Ossi. 1976. Periphrastic *do* in affirmative sentences in the dialect of East Somerset. *Neuphilologische Mitteilungen* 82.608–622.

Jespersen, O. 1964[1921]. *Language: its nature, development, and origin*. New York: W. W. Norton and Co.

Jiménez Pastrana, Juan. 1963. *Los chinos en la liberación cubana*. Havana: Instituto de Historia.

Karmiloff-Smith, A. 1992. *Beyond modularity: a developmental perspective on cognitive science*. Cambridge, MA: MIT Press.

Kihm, Alain. 1994. *Kriyol syntax: the Portuguese-based creole language of Guinea-Bissau*. Amsterdam: Benjamins.

Kiple, Kenneth F. 1976. *Blacks in colonial Cuba, 1774–1899*. Gainesville: University Presses of Florida.

Klein, Wolfgang and Clive Perdue. 1992. *Utterance structure: developing grammars again*. Amsterdam: Benjamins.

Koontz-Garboden, Andrew J. and J. Clancy Clements. 2002a. Case-marking in Dravidian languages and Indo-Portuguese creoles: substrate influence or independent development? Paper presented at South Asian Language Analysis Round Table, University of Iowa, Iowa City, IA, 21–23 June.

2002b. Some theoretical implications of adpositions in Spanish- and Portuguese-based creoles. Paper presented at the annual meeting of the Society of Pidgin and Creole Languages, San Francisco, CA, 21–23 June.

Kotsinas, U.-B. 1989. *Come, stay,* and *finish*: On the development of aspect markers in interlanguage and pidgin/creole languages, in *Proceedings of the Second Scandinavian Symposium on Aspectology*, edited by L.-G. Larsson. Uppsala, Sweden: Almqvist and Wiksell, 19.33–48.

1996. Aspect marking and grammaticalization in Russenorsk compared with Immigrant Swedish, in *Language contact in the Arctic: Northern pidgins and contact languages*, edited by E. Håkon Jahr and B. Ingvild. Berlin: Mouton de Gruyter, 123–154.

Langacker, Ronald. 1987. *Foundations of cognitive grammar I*. Stanford, CA: Stanford University Press.

Lapesa, Rafael. 1981. *Historia de la lengua española*. Madrid: Gredos.

Leguay, Jean Pierre, A. H. de Oliveira Marques, and Maria Angela Beirante. 1993. *Portugal das invasões germânicas à 'reconquista'*. Lisbon: Editorial Presença.

Leite de Vasconcelos, José. 1955. *Filologia barranquenha: apontamentos para o seu estudo*. Águeda: Grafinal.

Levin, Beth and Malka Rappaport Hovav. 1995. *Unaccusativity: at the syntax–lexical semantics interface*. Cambridge, MA: MIT Press.

Li, Charles and Sandra Thompson. 1981. *Mandarin Chinese: a functional reference grammar*. Berkeley: University of California Press.

Li, Ping and Yasuhiro Shirai. 2000. *The acquisition of lexical and grammatical aspect*. Berlin: Mouton de Gruyter.

Lieber, Francis (ed.). 1829–1832. *Encyclopedia Americana*, vols. I–XIII. Philadelphia: Carey & Lea.

Lipski, John. 1985. Creole Spanish and vestigial Spanish: evolutionary parallels. *Linguistics* 23.963–984.

1986. Convergence and divergence in bozal Spanish: a comparative study. *Journal of Pidgin and Creole Languages* 1.171–203.

1994. *Latin American Spanish*. London: Longman.

1997. Caribbean Spanish: the African connection. Paper delivered at Indiana University, Bloomington, 7 February.

1998. Perspectivas sobre el español bozal, in *América negra*, edited by Perl and Schwegler. 293–327.

1999. Chinese-Cuban pidgin Spanish: implications for the Afro-Creole debate, in *Creole genesis, attitudes and discourse*, edited by John R. Rickford and Suzanne Romaine. Amsterdam: Benjamins, 215–233.

2000. Bozal Spanish: restructuring or creolization?, in *Degree of restructuring in creole languages*, edited by Ingrid Neumann-Holzschuh and Edgar Schneider. Amsterdam: Benjamins.

2005. *A history of Afro-Hispanic language: five centuries, five continents*. Cambridge: Cambridge University Press.

López Meirama, Belén. 1997. *La posición del sujeto en la cláusula monoactancial en español. Lalia, Series Maior, n° 7*. Santiago de Compostela: Universidad de Santiago de Compostela.

Lorenzino, Gerardo A. 1998. *The Angolar creole Portuguese of São Tomé: its grammar and sociolinguistic history*. Munich: Lincom Europa.

Luis, Ana. 2004. Clitics as morphology. Unpublished University of Essex Ph.D dissertation. Colchester.

Macera, Pablo. 1978. *Fuentes de historia social americana: Bolivia tierra y población 1825–1936*, vol. I. Lima: Biblioteca Andina.

MacKay, A. 1977. *Spain in the Middle Ages: from frontier to empire, 1000–1500*. New York: St Martin's Press.

Maillo Salgado, Felipe. 1983. *Los arabismos del castellano en la baja Edad Media*. Salamanca: Universidad de Salamanca, Instituto Hispano-Arabe de Cultura.

Masica, Colin P. 1993. *The Indo-Aryan languages*. Cambridge: Cambridge University Press.

Masó, Calixto C. 1976. *Historia de Cuba*. Miami, FL: Ediciones Universal.

Matthews, Stephen and Virginia Yip. 1994. *Cantonese: a comprehensive grammar*. London: Routledge.

Maurer, Philippe. 1995. *L'angolar: un creole afro-portugais parlé à São Tomé*. Hamburg: Helmut Buske Verlag.

1998. El papiamentu de Curazao, in *América negra*, edited by Perl and Schwegler. 139–217.

McCune, William. 2005. *Brazilian and Continental Portuguese vowels: a spectrographic study of context and style in vowel duration and quality*. Bloomington, IN: Indiana University typescript.

McWhorter, John. 2000. *The missing Spanish creoles: recovering the birth of plantation contact languages*. Berkeley: University of California Press.

Mello, Heliana R. de, Alan N. Baxter, John Holm, and William Megenny. 1998. O português vernáculo do Brasil, in *América negra*, edited by Perl and Schwegler. 71–137.

Middendorf, Ernst W. 1970 [1890]. *Gramática keshwa*. Madrid: Editorial Aguilar.

Middleton, John (ed.). 1997. *Encyclopedia of Africa south of the Sahara*. 4 vols. New York: C. Scribner's Sons.

Mira Mateus, Maria Helena, Ana Maria Brito, Inês Duarte, and Isabel Hub Faria. 1989. *Gramática da língua portuguesa*. Lisbon: Caminho.

Moliner, María. 1984. *Diccionario de uso del español*. Madrid: Gredos.

Mueller-Vollmer, Kurt. 1998. German–American cultural interaction in the Jacksonian era: six unpublished letters by Francis Lieber and John Pickering to Wilhelm von Humboldt. *Die Unterrichtspraxis* 31.1–11.

Mufwene, Salikoko. 1997. Jargons, pidgins, creoles, and koinés: what are they?, in *The structure and status of pidgins and creoles*, edited by Arthur K. Spears and Donald Winford. Amsterdam: Benjamins, 35–70.

——— 2001. *The ecology of language evolution*. Cambridge: Cambridge University Press.

Mühlhäusler, Peter. 1986. *Pidgins and creole linguistics*. Oxford: Blackwell.

Muysken, Pieter and Norval Smith. 1990. Question words in pidgin and creole languages. *Linguistics* 28.883–903.

——— 1995. The study of pidgin and creole languages, in *Pidgins and creoles: an introduction*, edited by Jacques Arends, Pieter Muysken, and Norval Smith. Amsterdam: Benjamins, 3–14.

Nardi, Ricardo L. 1976. Lenguas en contacto: el substrato quechua en el Noroeste Argentino. *Filología* 16–17:131–150.

Naro, Anthony 1978. A study on the origins of pidginization. *Language* 54(2).347.

Naro, Anthony and Maria Marta Pereira Scherre. 1993. Sobre as origins do português popular do Brasil. *Revista DELTA* 9:437–454.

Navas Sánchez-Élez, María Victoria. 1992. El barranqueño: un modelo de lenguas en contacto. *Revista de Filología Románica* 9.225–246.

——— 1994. Canciones cantadas por los quintos de Barrancos: un caso de contacto de lenguas. Variação lingüística no espaço, no tempo e na sociedade, in *Proceedings of the Asociação Portuguesa de Linguística, Miranda do Douro, September 1992*. APL/Edições Colibri, 147–182.

——— 1996. Importancia de los asentamientos humanos en la configuración de un área geográfica: el caso de la margen izquierda del Guadiana, in *Proceedings of the Congreso Internacional Luso-Español de Lengua y Cultura de la Frontera, Cáceres*, vol. II, edited by Juan M. Carrasco González and Antonio Viudas Camarasa. Cáceres: Universidad de Extremadura, 411–430.

——— 1997. Factores lingüísticos y extralingüísticos que determinan la alternancia de variantes de -/s/ en un dialecto luso-español, el barranqueño. *Revista de Filología Románica* 14.391–410.

——— 2001. Relaciones entre las hablas andaluzas y portuguesas meridionales próximas. *Revista de Filología Románica* 18.171–185.

Ortiz López, Luis A. 1998. *Huellas etno-sociolingüísticas bozales y afrocubanas*. Frankfurt am Main: Vervuert.

Otheguy, Ricardo. 1973. The Spanish Caribbean: a creole perspective, in *New ways of analyzing variation in English*, edited by Charles-James N. Bailey and Roger W. Shuy. Washington, DC: Georgetown University Press, 323–339.

Pandharipande, Rajeshwari. 1997. *Marathi*. London: Routledge.

Pargman, Sheri. 2004. Gullah *duh* and periphrastic *do* in English dialects: another look at the evidence. *American Speech* 79.3–32.

Parkvall, Mikael. 2000. *Out of Africa: African influence in Atlantic creoles*. London: Battlebridge.

Penny, Ralph. 1991. *A history of the Spanish language*. Cambridge: Cambridge University Press.

——— 2000. *Variation and change in Spanish*. Cambridge: Cambridge University Press.

Pérez de la Riva, Juan. 1979. *El monto de la inmigración forzada en el siglo XIX*. Havana: Editorial de Ciencias Sociales.

Perl, Matthias. 1982. Creole morphosyntax in the Cuban "habla bozal." *Studii şi Cercetâri Lingvistice* 5.424–433.

1987. 'Habla bozal' – Eine Spanisch-basierte Kreolesprache? in *Beiträge zur Afrolusitanistik und Kreolistik: linguistische Studien*, edited by Matthias Perl 172.1–17.

Perl, Matthias and Armin Schwegler. 1998. *América negra: panorámica actual del los estudios lingüísticos sobre variedades hispanas, portuguesas, y criollas*. Madrid: Iberoamericana.

Petri, H. L. and M. Mishkin. 1994. Behaviorism, cognitivism and the neuropsychology of memory. *American Scientist* 82.30–37.

Picallo, M. Carme and Gemma Rigau. 1999. El posesivo y las relaciones posesivas (ch. 15, vol. I), in *Gramática descriptiva de la lengua española*, edited by Ignacio Bosque and Violeta Demonte. 3 vols. Madrid: Espasa, 973–1023.

Pichardo, Esteban. 1953 [1849]. *Diccionario provincial casi razonado de voces cubanas*. 2nd edn. Havana: Imprenta de M. Soler.

Pillai, Puthusseri Ramachandran. 1973. *Language of Middle Malayalam*. Trivandrum: Dravidian Linguistics Association of India.

Posner, Rebecca. 1993. La romanité des creoles à base lexical romane, in *Actes du XXe Congrés International de Linguistique et Philologie Romanes*, edited by G. Hilty. Tübingen: Francke, 251–263.

Post, Marike. 1995. Fa d'Ambu, in *Pidgins and creoles: an introduction*, edited by Jacques Arends, Pieter Muysken, and Norval Smith. Amsterdam. Benjamins, 191–204.

Quint, Nicolas. 2000. *Grammaire de la langue cap-verdienne: étude descriptive et comprehensive du créole afro-portugais des Îles du Cap-Vert*. Paris: L'Harmattan.

Ramos Hernández, Reinaldo, Arturo A. Pedroso Alés and Flor Inés Cassola Triamma. 2000. Barrio chino de La Habana. *Catauro* 2(2).

Ramos Tinhorão, José. 1997. *Os negros em Portugal: uma presença silenciosa*. Lisbon: Caminho.

Reichmann, Felix. 1945. Francis Lieber: Pennsylvania German Dialect. *American German Review* February:24–27.

Ricklefs, Merle Calvin. 1978. *Modern Javanese historical tradition: a study of an original Kartasura chronicle and related materials*. London: School of Oriental and African Studies, University of London.

Rivarola, José Luis. 1989. Bilingüísmo histórico y español andino, in *Actas del IX Congreso de la Asociación Internacional de Hispanistas*, edited by S. Neumeister. Frankfurt: Vervuert, 153–163.

Robison, R. E. 1995. The aspect hypothesis revisited: a cross-sectional study of tense and aspect marking in interlanguage. *Applied Linguistics* 16.345–370.

Rodríguez, José Ignacio. 1874. *La vida de Don José de la Luz Caballero*. New York: El Mundo Nuevo–La América Ilustrada.

Sánchez, Liliana. 2003. *Quechua–Spanish bilingualism: interference and convergence in functional categories*. Amsterdam: Benjamins.

Sánchez-Albornoz, Nicolás. 1974. *The population of Latin America: a history*. Berkeley: University of California Press.

Sarton, George. 1927–1931. *Introduction to the history of science*. 3 vols. Baltimore: Williams and Wilkins Co.

Schachter, Paul. 1987. Tagalog, in *The world's major languages*, edited by Bernard Comrie. New York: Oxford, 936–958.

Schuchardt, H. 1909. Lingua franca. *Zeitschrift für romanische Philologie* 33.441–461.

Schumann, J. H. 1978. *The pidginization process: a model for second language acquisition*. Rowley, MA: Newbury House.

Schwegler, Armin. 1993. Rasgos (afro-)portugueses en el criollo del Palenque de San Basilio (Colombia), in *Homenaje a José Vidal*, edited by Carmen Diaz Alayon. La Laguna, Tenerife: Litografía A. Romero, 667–696.

1996a. La doble negación dominicana y la génesis del español caribeño. *Hispanic Linguistics* 8.247–315.

1996b. *'Chi ma nkongo': lengua y rito ancestrales en El Palenque de San Basilio (Colombia)*. Frankfurt am Main and Madrid: Vervuert.

1998. El palenquero, in *América negra*, edited by Perl and Schwegler. 219–291.

Schwenter, Scott A. 2006. Null objects across South America, in *Selected proceedings of the 8th Hispanic Linguistics Symposium*, edited by Timothy Face and Carol Klee. Somerville, MA: Cascadilla Proceedings Project, 23–36.

Schwenter, Scott A. and Gláucia Silva. 2002. Overt vs. null direct objects in spoken Brazilian Portuguese: a semantic/pragmatic account. *Hispania* 85.577–586.

2003. Anaphoric direct objects in spoken Brazilian Portuguese: semantics and pragmatics. *Revista Internacional de Lingüística Iberoamericana* 2.109–133.

Sebba, M. 1997. *Contact languages: pidgins and creoles*. New York: St Martin's Press.

Serrão, Joaquim Veríssimo. 1978. *História de Portugal: o século de ouro (1495–1580)*, vol. III. Cacém: Editorial Verbo.

Shi, D. 1991. Chinese Pidgin English: its origin and linguistic features. *Journal of Chinese Linguistics* 19.1–40.

Shirai, Y. 1991. *Primacy of aspect in language acquisition: simplified input and prototype*. Los Angeles: University of Southern California.

Siegel, Jeff. 2000. *Processes of language contact: studies from Australia and the South Pacific*. Quebec: Fides.

Smith, Carlota. 1991. *The parameter of aspect*. Dordrecht: Kluwer.

Smith, Ian. 1977. Sri Lanka Creole Portuguese phonology. Cornell University Ph.D dissertation. Ithaca, NY.

Squire, L. R. 1987. *Memory and the brain*. Oxford: Oxford University Press.

Squire, L. R. and S. Zola-Morgan. 1991. The medial temporal lobe memory system. *Science* 253:1380–1386.

Tarracha Ferreira, Maria Ema (ed.). 1994. *Antologia do Cancioneiro geral de Garcia de Resende*. Lisbon: Ulisseia.

Teyssier, Paul. 1984. *História da língua portuguesa*. Second edition. Lisbon: Sa da Costa.

Thomason, Sarah G. 2001. *Language contact: an introduction*. Washington, DC: Georgetown University Press.

Thomason, Sarah G. and Terrence Kaufman. 1988. *Language contact, creolization, and genetic linguistics*. Berkeley: University of California Press.

Torre Revello, José. 1962. La enseñanza de las lenguas a los naturales de América. *Thesaurus. Boletín del Instituto Caro y Cuervo*, 17.501–526.

Tovar, A. L. 1954. Linguistics and prehistory. *Word* 10.333–350.

1955. *Cantabria prerromana, o lo que la lingüística nos enseña sobre los antiguos cántabros*, vol. II. Santander: Universidad Internacional Menéndez y Pelayo.

1967. L'inscription du Cabeço das Fráguas et la langue des Lusitaniens. *Études Celtiques* 11.237–268.

1977. *Einführung in die Sprachgeschichte der iberischen Halbinsel*. Tübingen: Verlag Gunter Narr.

Van Minde, Don. 1997. *Malayu Ambong: phonology, morphology, syntax*. Leiden: CNWS.

Van Valin, Robert D. and Randy J. La Polla. 1997. *Syntax: structure, meaning, and function*. New York: Cambridge University Press.

Vargas Orellana, Nelly Elena. 1998. Orden de palabras: (sujeto)–objeto–verbo, in *Español y quechua en el noroeste argentino*, edited by Fernández Lávaque and del Valle Rodas, 91–96.

Vendler, Zeno. 1967. *Linguistics in philosophy*. Ithaca, NY: Cornell University Press.

Waltermire, Mark. 2006. Social and linguistic correlates of Spanish–Portuguese bilingualism on the Uruguayan–Brazilian border. Unpublished University of New Mexico Ph.D dissertation. Albuquerque, NM.

Wardhaugh, Ronald. 2002. *An introduction to sociolinguistics*. Oxford: Blackwell.

Weber, David John. 1989. *A grammar of Huallaga (Huánco) Quechua*. Berkeley: University of California Press.

Whinnom, Keith. 1956. *Spanish contact vernaculars in the Philippine Islands*. Hong Kong: Hong Kong University Press.

Willis, C. 1993. The world chopped in half. *La Vida Hispánica* 8.21–27.

Winford, Donald. 2003. *An introduction to contact linguistics*. Malden, MA: Blackwell.

Zobl, H. 1982. A direction for contrastive analysis: the comparative study of developmental sequences. *TESOL Quarterly* 16.169–183.

Zúñiga, Madeleine. 1974. La educación bilingüe y la enseñanza de pronunciación castellana a niños quechua-hablantes. Universidad Nacional Mayor de San Marcos Centro de Investigación de Lingüística Aplicada. The Pontificia Universidad Católica of Perú Ph.D dissertation. Lima.

# Author index

Adelaar, K. A. 171
Aimes, Hubert 69
Andersen, R. W. 14, 17, 138, 210
Aráoz, Dora 187

Bachiller y Morales, Antonio 32, 69, 89, 90, 91, 92, 107
Bakker, Peter 110, 124, 125
Baldinger, K. 32
Bartens, Angela 54
Bates, Elizabeth 11, 12, 13, 14, 26, 96, 211
Baxter, Alan N. 6, 51
Beltrán, J. 128
Bickerton, Derek 1
Blackshire-Belay, Carol 124
Bloomfield, Leonard 139
Bresnan, Joan 11
Bretherton, I. 14
Broihier, K. 12
Brown, James H. 10
Bybee, Joan 48, 94, 134

Cabrera, Lydia 68, 69, 81, 98
Carranza Romero, Francisco 159, 160, 162
Cerrón-Palomino, Rodolfo 159–189, 214, 215
Chambers, J. L. 8
Chaudenson, Robert 80
Clements, J. Clancy 50, 51, 57, 59, 60, 70, 71, 79, 96, 97, 121, 129, 139, 150, 156, 202, 206, 205
Comrie, Bernard 33, 34
Corominas, Joan 31, 34
Croft 5, 8, 10, 11, 18, 26, 36, 38, 42, 55, 56, 57, 153, 210, 212, 125
Curchin, L. A. 28

Da Azevedo Maia, Clarinda 192, 193
Davis, Stuart 70, 71
Del Valle Rodas, Juana 170, 181, 182, 185, 186
De Matos Coelho, Adelino 192

De Oliveira Marques, A. H. 28, 36, 37, 38, 40, 43, 45, 57, 59, 191
Devevan, William M. 160
Dromi, Esther 3, 13
Dutton, T. 125

Escobar, Alberto 175
Escobar, Anna Maria 175

Feke, Marilyn 172, 187
Fernández Lávaque, Ana María 170, 181, 182, 183, 186, 187, 188
Fernández, Mauro 66
Ferraz, Luiz Ivens 51
Forman, Michael Lawrence 51
Friederici, A. D. 14
Futuyma, D. J. 4

García, C. 128–129
Gili Gaya, Samuel 134
Givón, T. 1, 3, 4
Goldberg, Adele E. 3, 11, 13, 14, 26, 210
González, Paz 18, 160
Goodman, Judith 11, 12, 13, 14, 26, 96, 211
Granda, German 68, 69
Günther, Wilfried 51
Guy, Gregory 6

Hall, Rober 110, 124
Hinnenkamp, Volker 124
Holm, John A. 6, 21, 22, 48, 52, 54, 60, 124
Hopper, Paul 3
Hualde, José Ignacio 200
Hull, David L. 8

Ihalainen, Ossi 21

Jiménez Pastrana, Juan 104, 107, 108, 110, 111, 112, 116, 117

Karmiloff–Smith, A. 14
Kaufman, Terrance 11, 18, 26, 49, 50

Kihm, Alain 51
Klein, Wolfgang 11, 13, 47, 97, 112, 123, 124, 157, 213
Koontz-Garboden, Andrew J. 51, 57, 59, 95

Langacker, Ronald 11
Lapesa, Rafael 34, 193, 194, 200
Lee, L. 12
Leite de Vasconcelos, José 192, 194, 195, 196, 197, 198, 200, 201, 207, 215, 216, 190
Levin, Beth 11, 14
Li, Charles 141, 147, 156
Li, Ping 139, 141
Lieber, Francis 81
Lipski, John 69, 71, 77, 80, 86, 92, 96, 97, 98, 99, 109, 110
López Meirama, Belén 4
Lorenzino, Gerardo Augusto 51, 99, 202, 205
Luis, Ana 203

MacKay, A. 39, 40
Mahboob, Ahmar 53, 121, 156
Maillo Salgado, Felipe 37
Masica, Colin P. 63
Masó, Calixto C. 72–80, 92, 99, 160
Matthews, Stephen 119
Maurer, Philippe 51, 54, 98, 115
McCune, William 6
McWhorter, John 68, 69, 86
Megenny, William 6
Mello, Heliana R. De 6
Middleton, John (ed.) 75
Mira Mateus, Maria Helena 202
Mishkin, M. 14
Mufwene, Salikoko 2, 5, 8, 10, 26, 34, 35, 36, 38, 69, 80, 210
Mühlhäusler, Peter 2, 124
Muysken, Pieter 121, 156

Nardi, Ricardo L. 164, 183
Naro, Anthony 6, 46
Navas Sánchez–Élez, María Victoria 190, 200, 205
Nusbaum, H. C. 12

Olarrea, Antxon 200
Ortheguy, Ricardo 68, 69
Ortiz López, Luis A. 68, 69, 81, 96, 97, 98, 99, 122

Pandharipande, Rajeshwari 63
Pardo, Elly 48

Pargman, Sherri 21, 22
Parkvall, Mikael 96
Perdue, Clive 11, 13, 47, 97, 112, 123, 124, 213
Pérez de la Riva, Juan 92
Perl, Matthias 68, 69, 71, 92, 97, 98
Petri, H. L. 3
Pichardo, Esteban 69, 88, 89, 91, 92
Pillai, Puthusseri Ramachandran 62

Quint, Nicolas 51

Ramos Tinhorão, José 10, 43, 45
Rappaport Hovav 11, 14
Ricklefs, Merle Calvin 63
Rivarola, José Luis 162, 164, 165, 188, 214
Rodríguez, José Ignacio 82

Salas, Américo 187
Sánchez-Albornoz, Nicolás 160
Sarton, George 38
Scherre, Maria Marta Pereira 6
Schuchardt, Hugo 164
Schwegler, Armin 68, 69, 97, 99, 115, 122
Schwenter, Scott 6, 99
Sebba, M. 124
Serrão, Joaquim Veríssimo 40, 57
Shi, D. 213
Shirai, Yasuhiro 14, 17, 20, 139, 138, 141, 210
Siegel, Jeff 153
Silva, Gláucia 6
Smith, Carlota 141, 156
Smith, Ian 33, 34, 51
Smith, Norval 121
Squire, L. R. 3

Tarracha Ferreira, Maria Ema (ed.) 46
Thomason, Sarah G. 11, 18, 26, 49, 50
Thompson, Sandra 11, 141, 147, 156
Tovar Llorente, Antonio 28–33, 35, 211
Trudgill, Peter 8

Vargas Orellana, Nelly Elena 183, 184

Waltermire, Mark 190
Weber, David John 24, 171, 173, 174
Whinnom, Keith 50, 52, 65
Winford, Donald 50, 124, 125

Yip, Virginia 119

Zobl, H. 11, 13, 96
Zola-Morgan, S. 3
Zúñiga, Madeleine 172

# General index

Accomplishment (Vendlerian) 15, 47
Achievement (Vendlerian) 15
Activity (Vendlerian) 15, 111, 132, 138
agglutinative 171, 173
Ahmed-ben-Madjid 57
Andean Spanish 25, 79, 95, 158–189
Angolar 42, 50, 52, 99
Arabic 6, 34, 37, 38
*are* [ar] 21
*asina* (also *ancina*) 196–197
Asturias 37–38
Atahualpa 158, 159
Azores Islands 39, 41

'basic variety' 11, 47, 97, 103, 112, 123, 124,
    157, 213
Bassein 40, 60, 63
Bibí 98
bootstrapping 11–14, 26
borrowing 18–24
bozal Spanish 68–99
*buscar* 15

Calicut 40
Canary Islands 39, 74, 79, 95, 143
Cantonese 6, 132
Cape Verde 40, 41, 42, 43, 50, 194
Capeverdean Creole Portuguese (*see*
    Kabuverdianu)
Carabalí 93, 98
Castilian 30–41, 88, 141, 161–162,
    211–212
Castilianization 193, 214
Catalan 32, 33, 36, 38, 79, 103
Causal Order Hypothesis (Causal Chain
    Hypothesis) 42–43, 54, 57
CETEMPúblico Data Base 22
Charles III 75, 79
Chaul 40, 59, 60
Chinese 1, 6, 11, 106–123, 129, 151
Chinese Coolie Spanish 102–123, 132, 141
    (*see also* Coolies in Cuba)

Chinese Immigrant Spanish 102, 111, 114,
    124–157, 213
Cochin 40
Cochin Creole Portuguese 62
communication 1, 2, 3, 4, 10, 13, 26, 126, 127,
    129, 153, 160, 210, 211
    adult-to-adult 10, 18, 26
    grammatical 1, 2
    pre-grammatical 1, 2–3
communicative/conversational intercourse 8,
    36, 38, 210
communicative/conversational isolation 8, 36,
    125–127, 212
Congo 93, 98
contact intensity 18
*contamos* 20, 21
*contar* 20 (*see also cuenta, contamos, cuentan*)
Coolies in Cuba 102–123 (*see also* Chinese
    Coolie Spanish)
copula 1, 2, 4, 10, 14, 20, 21–23, 24, 26, 69,
    71, 81, 93, 95, 101, 111, 115, 121, 132,
    134, 153, 214
creole 132, 157, 164, 175, 212, 213
    English-based 21, 22, 68
    French-based 68, 81, 88, 92
    Portuguese-based 10, 20, 22, 23, 41, 42–65,
        68, 99, 101, 95, 139, 157, 212, 214
    Spanish-based 42–65, 115, 139, 157,
        212, 213
CREA (Corpus de Referencia del Español
    Actual) 15, 21, 90–95, 180, 186, 197
Croatian 8
CRPC (Corpus Referencial de Português
    Contemporáneo) 22
Cuba 68–84
*cuenta* 20, 21
*cuentan* 21
CV structure 20, 21, 22, 23, 25, 26, 48, 49,
    131, 143

*da* (*na*) in some English-based creoles
    21–22, 48

254

Daman Creole Portuguese 60, 63, 70–71,
    81–100, 101, 108
da Mota, Anrique/Enrique 45, 46
Distributional Bias Hypothesis (DBH) 15, 17,
    137–139
Diu 40, 59, 60, 63
Diu Creole Portuguese 7, 17, 38, 68
Dutch 7

Emergent Grammar 3, 13, 26, 210
evolutionary biology 4

Fa D'Ambu 52, 54–63
feature pool 18–27, 34, 47, 49, 127, 130–131,
    143, 171, 177, 181
first language acquisition (see L1 / first
    language acquisition)
French 33, 38, 68, 70, 79
functionalist 5, 1

Galician 28–36, 79, 103, 211
Gangá 98
German 7
Germanic 35
Goa 40, 60
grammatical relation marker 42, 48
Gullah 21
Guyanese 21

Haitian 70, 79, 86, 92
Hanseatic League 40
Henry the Navigator 40
heterogeneity 49
Hindi 5, 6, 62

Iberian Romance 32, 211
immigrant Spanish 1, 4, 11, 14, 20, 23, 24, 26,
    41, 47–49
immigrant speech 40, 52, 59, 124
Inca(s) 158–159
indigenismo 162
Indonesia 61, 63
Indo-Portuguese creoles 57–65, 108
Irish 31
is [z] 21–22

Jamaican 21

Kabuverdianu 23, 52–55
Kannada 62
Kikongo 52, 54–65, 99, 101
Kimbundu 52, 54–67, 99, 101
Knowledge 1
    communication of represented 1
    representation of 1
Korlai Creole Portuguese 54–67, 108

Krio 21
Kristang 60–65 (see also Malay (Malacca)
    Creole Portuguese, and Papia Kristang)
Kriyol 52–55

L1 / first language acquisition 11–14, 11,
    13, 14, 18, 24, 26, 47, 98, 99, 123,
    132, 139
L2 / second language acquisition 124–127,
    132, 213
    untutored L2 acquisition 15, 71, 92
language as parasitic species 8
Latin 28–38, 34, 211
lengua general 161, 160
lexical aspect 14, 15
lexical connections 21
lexical strength 20, 21, 22
Lieber, Francis 70–86, 88–100, 101, 213
Linguistic Data Consortium American English
    Spoken Lexicon 21
Lisbon 32, 43–46, 211
lo (non-pronominal) 179–180, 183–184
locative 119, 121, 145, 146, 147, 150–152,
    178, 214
logo 46, 47, 49
Lucumí 98
luego 49, 118, 119
Lusitania 28–36, 211

Makista (Macau) Creole Portuguese 23, 59,
    60, 111, 63
Malay 52–57, 63, 64
Malay (Malacca) Creole Portuguese 57
    (see also Papia Kristang)
Malayalam 54–63, 60
Mandarin 6, 106, 129, 151, 141
Mandinka 52
Mantaro Valley (Peru) 170, 171–188
manteca 34
manteiga 34
markedness 18, 19, 23, 24, 26, 27, 49–50, 211
mitmaq 159
Montezuma 158
Moor 191, 192, 212
morcela 31, 34
morcilla 31, 34
morir 17

nacer 17
Norteiro 60, 63

Palenquero 54–55, 95, 99, 115
Papia Kristang 52, 54 (see also Malay
    (Malacca) Creole Portuguese)
Papiamentu 54, 57, 69, 80, 91–92, 98, 101, 115
perceptual salience 22, 25, 54, 94, 95, 96, 214

*perna* 33
*perro* 34
Persian 6
Philippine Creole Spanish 50, 52, 54, 57, 60, 63–66
pidgin 1, 2, 4, 10, 13, 14, 20, 24, 26, 46, 48, 49, 71, 80, 81, 92, 99, 100, 103, 110, 123, 124–126, 127, 132, 141, 157, 210, 213
    English 86, 116, 121, 144, 213
    Portuguese 10, 54, 60–66, 212, 214
    Spanish 71, 100, 213
*pierna* 33
Pizarro 158–159
*poder* 15
polyploidy 10
polytypic language 6, 37
Portugal 7, 10, 22, 36–41, 42–47, 57, 210–212, 215–216
Portuguese 6, 10–11, 21, 27, 30–39, 41, 42–65, 92, 99, 190–209, 210–217
    African 10, 11, 48, 54–65, 212
pre-Roman lexicon 30, 31, 33–34
Primacy of Aspect (POA) Hypothesis 14, 15, 17, 137–139, 210
Principense 52
pronominalization, false 163, 179, 183, 188, 215
protolanguage 1
prototype 4

Quechua 19, 21, 24, 159–189, 214, 215
*querer* 15, 33, 180

Romanian 33
*romper* 17

*saber* 15
Salta (Argentina) 171–188, 214, 215
Sãotomense 52, 54
second language acquisition (*see* L2 / second language acquisition)
semantic relation marker 42, 48
*ser* 22, 47, 86, 111, 115, 121, 132, 144, 153, 162
Serbian 8
shift 18–24
sibling language 5

slave trade 45, 69, 70, 71, 75
social network 8
sociolinguistic(s) 5
sociolinguistic marker 19
SOV (subject-object-verb) 171, 174, 183
species 5–10, 26
    essentialist view of 5
    polytypic 5
    sibling 5
Sranan 86
Sri Lanka 40, 59, 60, 63
Sri Lankan Malay 64
State (Vendlerian) 15, 111, 132, 137, 138
substrate 32, 35, 43, 48, 54, 211, 212
    African 21
syncretism 21, 42, 54

*ta* (TMA marker) 97–99, 115–116, 121
Tamil 60
Tartesians 28–29
tense-aspect-mood marker 2, 14, 42, 47, 48–55, 97, 115, 120, 132–139
Ternate 40, 52, 63
Ternateño Creole Portuguese 65
Timor 40
Timor Creole Portuguese 63
*trabajar* 15–25
transfer (in L2 acquisition) 132
Tupac Amaru 161
typological fit 18, 23, 24, 26

Urdu 5, 6

*vai* 48, 97–99
Vasco da Gama 40, 57
Vicente, Gil 45

Welsh 31
Wolof 52

*ya* 47, 49, 97–99, 156–157, 214
Yoruba 101
Yupanqui, Francisco Tito 162, 164, 176, 179, 181, 182, 183

Zamboangueño (*see* Philippine Creole Spanish)